1,00

Write well, speak well

Key Words to Improve and Expand Your Vocabulary

HOUGHTON MIFFLIN

Boston • New York

Previously published as *100 Words Every High School Freshman Should Know* (© 2004), *100 Words Every High School Graduate Should Know* (© 2003), *100 Words Almost Everyone Confuses and Misuses* (© 2004), *100 Words Every Word Lover Should Know* (© 2005), and *Roget's Pocket Thesaurus* (© 2003, 1987) by Houghton Mifflin Company.

Visit our website: www.houghtonmifflinbooks.com

ISBN-13: 978-0-618-66851-9
ISBN-10: 0-618-66851-9

Library of Congress Cataloging-in-Publication Data available upon request.

Manufactured in the United States of America

QUM 10 9 8 7 6 5 4 3 2 1

Table of Contents

100

words every
high school
freshman
should know

Guide to the Entries

THIS GUIDE EXPLAINS THE CONVENTIONS
USED IN THIS SECTION.

ENTRY WORD The 100 words that constitute this section are listed alphabetically. The entry words, along with inflected and derived forms, are divided into syllables by centered dots. These dots show you where you would break the word at the end of a line. The pronunciation of the word follows the entry word. Please see the key on page 7 for an explanation of the pronunciation system.

PART OF SPEECH At least one part of speech follows each entry word. The part of speech tells you the grammatical category that the word belongs to. Parts of speech include *noun, adjective, adverb, transitive verb,* and *intransitive verb.* (A transitive verb is a verb that needs an object to complete its meaning. *Wash* is a transitive verb in the sentence *I washed the car.* The direct object of *wash* is *the car.* An intransitive verb is one that does not take an object, as *sleep* in the sentence *I slept for seven hours.* Many verbs are both transitive and intransitive.)

INFLECTIONS A word's inflected forms differ from the main entry form by the addition of a suffix or by a

---

100 words every high school freshman should know   3

change in the base form to indicate grammatical features such as number, person, or tense. Inflected forms are set in boldface type, divided into syllables, and given pronunciations as necessary. The past tense, past participle, and the third person singular present tense inflections of all verbs are shown. The plurals of nouns are shown when they are spelled in a way other than by adding *s* to the base form.

ORDER OF SENSES Entries having more than one sense are arranged with the central and often the most commonly sought meanings first. In an entry with more than one part of speech, the senses are numbered in separate sequences after each part of speech, as at **flourish.**

EXAMPLES OF USAGE Examples often follow the definitions and are set in italic type. These examples show the entry words in typical contexts. Sometimes the examples are quotations from authors of books. These quotations are shown within quotation marks, and the quotation's author and source are shown.

RELATED WORDS At the end of many entries, additional boldface words appear without definitions. These words are related in basic meaning to the entry word and are usually formed from the entry word by the addition of a suffix.

NOTES Many entries include additional information about the entry words. Some notes explain a scientific concept in greater detail, as at **hologram** and **ozone**. Other notes provide information about the background or history of a word, as at **quarantine** and **yacht**.

EXERCISES At the end of this section, there are exercises designed to help you further strengthen your vocabulary.

Pronunciation Guide

Pronunciations appear in parentheses after boldface entry words. If a word has more than one pronunciation, the first pronunciation is usually more common than the other, but often they are equally common. Pronunciations are shown after inflections and related words where necessary.

Stress is the relative degree of emphasis that a word's syllables are spoken with. An unmarked syllable has the weakest stress in the word. The strongest, or primary, stress is indicated with a bold mark (ˈ). A lighter mark (ʹ) indicates a secondary level of stress. The stress mark follows the syllable it applies to. Words of one syllable have no stress mark because there is no other stress level that the syllable can be compared to.

The key on page 7 shows the pronunciation symbols used in this book. To the right of the symbols are words that show how the symbols are pronounced. The letters whose sound corresponds to the symbols are shown in boldface.

The symbol (ə) is called *schwa*. It represents a vowel with the weakest level of stress in a word. The schwa sound varies slightly according to the vowel it represents or the sounds around it:

a·bun·dant (ə-bŭnʹdənt)   **mo·ment** (mōʹmənt)

civ·il (sĭvʹəl)   **grate·ful** (grātʹfəl)

PRONUNCIATION KEY

Symbol	Examples	Symbol	Examples
ă	pat	oi	noise
ā	pay	ŏŏ	took
âr	care	ŏŏr	lure
ä	father	ōō	boot
b	bib	ou	out
ch	church	p	pop
d	deed, milled	r	roar
ĕ	pet	s	sauce
ē	bee	sh	ship, dish
f	fife, phase,	t	tight, stopped
	rough	th	thin
g	gag	*th*	this
h	hat	ŭ	cut
hw	which	ûr	urge, term,
ĭ	pit		firm, word,
ī	pie, by		heard
îr	deer, pier	v	valve
j	judge	w	with
k	kick, cat, pique	y	yes
l	lid, needle	z	zebra, xylem
m	mum	zh	vision,
n	no, sudden		pleasure,
ng	thing		garage
ŏ	pot	ə	about, item,
ō	toe		edible,
ô	caught,		gallop,
	paw		circus
ôr	core	ər	butter

"Hello," Danny Saunders said softly. "I'm sorry if I woke you. The nurse told me it was all right to wait here."

I looked at him in amazement. He was the last person in the world I had expected to visit me in the hospital. . . .

He smiled sadly, "Can I sit down? I've been standing here about fifteen minutes waiting for you to wake up."

I sort of nodded or did something with my head, and he took it as a sign of approval and sat down on the edge of the bed to my right. The sun streamed in from the windows behind him, and shadows lay over his face and **accentuated** the lines of his cheeks and jaw.

— Chaim Potok,
The Chosen

1

ac·cen·tu·ate (ăk-sĕnt′chōō-āt′)

transitive verb
> Past participle and past tense: **ac·cen·tu·at·ed**
> Present participle: **ac·cen·tu·at·ing**
> Third person singular present tense: **ac·cen·tu·ates**

1. To give prominence to; emphasize or intensify: "*The sun streamed in from the windows behind him, and shadows lay over his face and accentuated the lines of his cheeks and jaw*" (Chaim Potok, *The Chosen*). **2.** To pronounce with a stress or accent: *accentuate the second syllable in a word.* **3.** To mark with an accent mark: *accentuate a word in a line of poetry.*

RELATED WORD:
> *noun* —**ac·cen′tu·a′tion**

al·lit·er·a·tion (ə-lĭt′ə-rā′shən)

noun

The repetition of the same sounds, usually consonants or consonant clusters, especially at the beginning of words. Poets and writers often employ alliteration in their writing, such as *"I have **stood still** and **stopped** the sound of feet"* in Robert Frost's "Acquainted with the Night."

RELATED WORD:
    adjective — **al·lit′er·a·tive**

a·nal·o·gy (ə-năl′ə-jē)

noun
    Plural: **a·nal·o·gies**

1. Similarity in some respects between things that are otherwise unlike. **2.** An explanation of something by comparing it with something similar: *The author uses the analogy of a beehive when describing the bustling city.*

RELATED WORDS:
    adjective — **a·nal′o·gous** (ə-năl′ə-gəs)
    adverb — **a·nal′o·gous·ly**

4
an·ti·bod·y (ăn′tĭ-bŏd′ē)

noun

Plural: **an·ti·bod·ies**

A protein produced in the blood or tissues in response to the presence of a specific toxin, foreign blood cell, or other antigen. Antibodies provide immunity against certain microorganisms and toxins by binding with them and often by deactivating them.

☙ **NOTE:** Antibodies are complex, Y-shaped protein molecules that guard our bodies against diseases. The immune system's B lymphocytes, or B cells, develop into plasma cells, which can produce a huge variety of antibodies, each one capable of grabbing an invading molecule at the top ends of the Y. The molecules that antibodies recognize can be quite specific — they might exist only on a particular bacterium or virus. When that bacterium or virus enters the body, the antibodies quickly recognize its molecules, as if a sentry recognized an enemy soldier from his uniform. Once the invader is caught, the antibodies may make it inactive or lead it to cells that can destroy it. High numbers of a particular antibody may persist for months after an infection. The numbers may then get quite small, but the experienced B cells can quickly make more of that specific antibody if necessary. Vaccines work by training B cells to do just that.

5

as·pire (ə-spīr′)

transitive verb
> Past participle and past tense: **as·pired**
> Present participle: **as·pir·ing**
> Third person singular present tense: **as·pires**

To have a great ambition; desire strongly: *aspire to become a good soccer player; aspire to great knowledge.*

RELATED WORDS:
> *noun* — **as′pi·ra′tion**
> *noun* — **as·pir′er**

6

bam·boo·zle (băm-boo′zəl)

transitive verb
> Past participle and past tense: **bam·boo·zled**
> Present participle: **bam·boo·zling**
> Third person singular present tense: **bam·boo·zles**

Informal
To deceive by elaborate trickery; hoodwink: *In* The Music Man, *the con man bamboozles the citizens of River City into believing that he can teach their children to play in a marching band.*

7
bi·zarre (bĭ-zär**ʹ**)

adjective

Very strange or odd: *a bizarre hat; a bizarre idea.*

RELATED WORD:
> *adverb* — **bi·zarre***ʹ***ly**

8
bois·ter·ous (boi**ʹ**stər-əs *or* boi**ʹ**strəs)

adjective

1. Rough and stormy; violent: *boisterous winds.* **2.** Noisy and lacking restraint or discipline: *the boisterous cheers of an excited crowd.*

RELATED WORDS:
> *adverb* — **bois***ʹ***ter·ous·ly**
> *noun* — **bois***ʹ***ter·ous·ness**

boy·cott (boi′kŏt′)

transitive verb

    Past participle and past tense: **boy·cott·ed**
    Present participle: **boy·cott·ing**
    Third person singular present tense: **boy·cotts**

To act together in refusing to use, buy from, or deal with, especially as an expression of protest: *boycott a store; boycott foreign-made goods.*

noun

1. A refusal to buy from or deal with a person, business, or nation, especially as a form of protest. **2.** A refusal to buy or use a product or service.

  NOTE: Even though his name is now a word in English as well as many other languages around the world, Charles C. Boycott probably did not enjoy becoming so famous. He was an English rent-collector in 19th-century Ireland who refused to lower the high rents that Irish farmers paid to English landowners, and he evicted families who could not pay. In 1880, as part of the struggle for Irish independence from the British Empire, people decided to ignore Boycott and his family completely. The servants stopped showing up for work, the mailman would not deliver the mail, and no one would sell the Boycotts anything in the stores. After the success of the *boycott* of Mr. Boycott in Ireland, his name quickly became the usual word for this way of raising protest without resorting to violence.

10

cam·ou·flage (kăm′ə-fläzh′ *or* kăm′ə-fläj′)

noun

1. A method of concealing military troops or equipment by making them appear to be part of the natural surroundings. **2.** Protective coloring or a disguise that conceals: *An alligator's camouflage makes it look like a log floating in the water.* **3.** Cloth or other material used for camouflage.

transitive verb
> Past participle and past tense: **cam·ou·flaged**
> Present participle: **cam·ou·flag·ing**
> Third person singular present tense: **cam·ou·flag·es**

To conceal or hide by camouflage.

11

chro·nol·o·gy (krə-nŏl′ə-jē)

noun
> Plural: **chro·nol·o·gies**

1. The order or sequence of events: *The lawyer disputed the chronology of events preceding the murder.* **2.** A list or table of events analyzed in order of time of occurrence: *a detailed chronology of modern history.*

RELATED WORDS:
> *adjective*— **chron′o·log′i·cal**
> (krŏn′ə-lŏj′ĭ-kəl)
> *adverb*— **chron′o·log′i·cal·ly**

com·mem·o·rate (kə-měm′ə-rāt′)

transitive verb

Past participle and past tense: **com·mem·o·rat·ed**
Present participle: **com·mem·o·rat·ing**
Third person singular present tense:
com·mem·o·rates

1. To honor the memory of (someone or something), especially with a ceremony: *The crowd gathered in the park to commemorate the firefighters' sacrifice.* **2.** To be a memorial to, as a holiday, ceremony, or statue: *Independence Day commemorates the adoption of the Declaration of Independence.*

RELATED WORDS:
noun — **com·mem′o·ra′tion**
adjective — **com·mem′o·ra·tive**
adverb — **com·mem′o·ra·tive·ly**

cow·er (kou′ər)

intransitive verb

Past participle and past tense: **cow·ered**
Present participle: **cow·er·ing**
Third person singular present tense: **cow·ers**

To crouch or draw back, as from fear or pain; cringe: *"Then the dwarves forgot their joy and their confident boasts of a moment before and cowered down in fright"* (J.R.R. Tolkien, *The Hobbit*).

The dwarves were still passing the cup from hand to hand and talking delightedly of the recovery of their treasure, when suddenly a vast rumbling woke in the mountain underneath as if it was an old volcano that had made up its mind to start eruptions once again. The door behind them was pulled nearly to, and blocked from closing with a stone, but up the long tunnel came the dreadful echoes, from far down in the depths, of a bellowing and a trampling that made the ground beneath them tremble.

Then the dwarves forgot their joy and their confident boasts of a moment before and **cowered** down in fright. Smaug was still to be reckoned with. It does not do to leave a live dragon out of your calculations.

—J.R.R. Tolkien,
The Hobbit

14

de·cor·um (dĭ-kôr′əm)

noun

Proper behavior or conduct; propriety: *"She had pull with the police department, so the men in their flashy suits and fleshy scars sat with churchlike decorum and waited to ask favors from her"* (Maya Angelou, *I Know Why the Caged Bird Sings*).

15

de·duc·tion (dĭ-dŭk′shən)

noun

1. The act of subtracting; subtraction: *The sales clerk's deduction of the cost of installation persuaded us to buy the dishwasher.* **2.** An amount that is or may be subtracted: *She claimed a deduction from her taxable income for medical expenses.* **3.** The process of reaching a conclusion by reasoning, especially from general principles. **4.** A conclusion reached by this process: *The article discusses the judge's deduction that the law violated the Fourteenth Amendment.*

16
deign (dān)

verb

> Past participle and past tense: **deigned**
> Present participle: **deign·ing**
> Third person singular present tense: **deigns**

intransitive verb

To be willing to do something that one considers beneath one's dignity; condescend: *"'We better hurry or we'll be late for dinner,' I said . . . [H]is right foot flashed into the middle of my fast walk and I went pitching forward into the grass. 'Get those one hundred and fifty pounds off me!' I shouted, because he was sitting on my back. Finny got up, patted my head genially, and moved on across the field, not deigning to glance around for my counterattack . . ."* (John Knowles, *A Separate Peace*).

transitive verb

To condescend to give: *The movie star didn't deign so much as a nod in our direction.*

17

de·spon·dent (dĭ-spŏn′dənt)

adjective

Feeling depression of spirits from loss of hope, confidence, or courage; dejected: *"It rained. The procession of weary soldiers became a bedraggled train, despondent and muttering, marching with churning effort in a trough of liquid brown mud under a low, wretched sky"* (Stephen Crane, *The Red Badge of Courage*).

RELATED WORDS:
> *noun* — **de·spon′dence, de·spon′den·cy**
> *adverb* — **de·spon′dent·ly**

18

di·a·logue (*also spelled* di·a·log) (dī′ə-lôg′)

noun

1. A conversation between two or more people: *a friendly dialogue between neighbors.* **2.** The words spoken by the characters of a play or story: *The dialogue of the comedy was very witty.* **3.** A literary work written in the form of a conversation: *Many students of philosophy have read the dialogues of Plato.* **4.** An exchange of ideas or opinions: *a lively dialogue among members of the committee.*

19

di·vulge (dĭ-vŭlj′)

transitive verb

> Past participle and past tense: **di·vulged**
> Present participle: **di·vulg·ing**
> Third person singular present tense: **di·vulg·es**

To make known; reveal; tell: *divulge a secret.*

RELATED WORD:
> *noun*—**di·vulg′er**

20

e·clec·tic (ĭ-klĕk′tĭk)

adjective

Choosing or taking what appears to be the best from various sources: *an eclectic musician blending elements of classical music, jazz, and punk rock.*

RELATED WORD:
> *adverb*—**e·clec′ti·cal·ly**

el·lipse (ĭ-lĭps′)

noun

A figure that forms a closed curve shaped like an oval with both ends alike. An ellipse can be formed by intersecting a cone with a plane that is not parallel or perpendicular to the cone's base. (See top illustration.) The sum of the distances of any point on an ellipse from two fixed points (called the *foci*) remains constant no matter where the point is on the curve. (See bottom illustration.)

THREE-
DIMENSIONAL
ELLIPSE

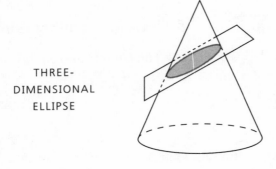

TWO-
DIMENSIONAL
ELLIPSE

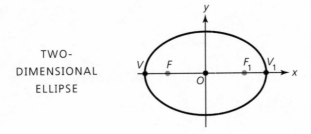

The line running through the foci (F and F_1) of an ellipse
is the major axis. The vertices (V and V_1) mark where
the major axis intersects the ellipse.

22

em·bar·go (ĕm-bär′gō)

noun
> Plural: **em·bar·goes**

1. An order by a government prohibiting merchant ships from entering or leaving its ports. **2.** A prohibition by a government on certain or all trade with a foreign nation.

transitive verb
> Past participle and past tense: **em·bar·goed**
> Present participle: **em·bar·go·ing**
> Third person singular present tense: **em·bar·goes**

To place an embargo on: *The Union government embargoed Confederate ports during the Civil War.*

23

en·thu·si·as·tic (ĕn-thōō′zē-ăs′tĭk)

adjective

Having or showing great interest or excitement: *The principal gave an enthusiastic welcome to the new teachers.*

RELATED WORD:
> *adverb* — **en·thu′si·as′ti·cal·ly**

ex·po·nent (ĭk-spō′nənt *or* ĕk′spō′nənt)

noun

1. A number or symbol, placed to the right of and above the expression to which it applies, that indicates the number of times a mathematical expression is used as a factor. For example, the exponent 3 in 5^3 indicates $5 \times 5 \times 5$; the exponent 2 in $(x + y)^2$ indicates $(x + y) \times (x + y)$. **2.** A person who speaks for, represents, or advocates something: *exponents of mass transit as a way of reducing pollution.*

RELATED WORDS:
    adjective—**ex′po·nen′tial**
    adverb—**ex′po·nen′tial·ly**

ex·ult (ĭg-zŭlt′)

intransitive verb
    Past participle and past tense: **ex·ult·ed**
    Present participle: **ex·ult·ing**
    Third person singular present tense: **ex·ults**

To rejoice greatly; be jubilant or triumphant: *"Laurie threw up his hat, then remembered that it wouldn't do to exult over the defeat of his guests, and stopped in the middle of the cheer to whisper to his friend, 'Good for you, Jo! He did cheat, I saw him'"* (Louisa May Alcott, *Little Women*).

"Yankees have a trick of being generous to their enemies," said Jo, with a look that made the lad redden, "especially when they beat them," she added, as, leaving Kate's ball untouched, she won the game by a clever stroke.

Laurie threw up his hat, then remembered that it wouldn't do to **exult** over the defeat of his guests, and stopped in the middle of the cheer to whisper to his friend, "Good for you, Jo! He did cheat, I saw him. We can't tell him so, but he won't do it again, take my word for it."

— Louisa May Alcott,
Little Women

fal·la·cy (făl′ə-sē)

noun
> Plural: **fal·la·cies**

A false notion or mistaken belief: *It is a fallacy that being popular always means being happy.*

RELATED WORDS:
> *adjective*—**fal·la′cious** (fə-lā′shəs)
> *adverb*—**fal·la′cious·ly**

---

flour·ish (flûr′ĭsh)

verb

> Past participle and past tense: **flour·ished**
> Present participle: **flour·ish·ing**
> Third person singular present tense: **flour·ish·es**

intransitive verb

1. To grow or develop well or luxuriantly; thrive: *Most flowers flourish in full sunlight.* **2.** To do well; prosper: *The lawyer's practice flourished.* **3.** To be actively working, especially in a period of great accomplishment: *a writer who flourished in the later 1600s.*

transitive verb

To wave (something) vigorously or dramatically: *The athletes on the winning team flourished their medals in front of the cameras.*

noun

1. A dramatic action or gesture: *The teacher waved the report with a flourish.* **2.** An added decorative touch; an embellishment: *handwriting with many graceful flourishes.* **3.** In music, a showy passage or a fanfare: *Trumpets played a flourish before the king entered.*

for·mi·da·ble (fôr′mĭ-də-bəl *or* fôr-mĭd′ə-bəl)

adjective

1. Arousing fear, dread, alarm, or great concern: *"The men wish to purchase straw field hats to protect themselves from your formidable Arkansas sun"* (Bette Greene, *The Summer of My German Soldier*). **2.** Admirable; awe-inspiring: *a formidable musical talent.* **3.** Difficult to surmount, defeat, or undertake: *The new assignment was a formidable challenge for the young reporter.*

RELATED WORDS:
>   *noun* — **for′mid·a·bil′i·ty**
>   *adverb* — **for′mi·da·bly**

When the nine prisoners were gathered around the counter the corporal shouted, "Reiker!"

Reiker didn't look quite so tall or strong as the others. His eyes, specked with green, sought communication with my father.

"The men wish to purchase straw field hats to protect themselves from your **formidable** Arkansas sun."

— Bette Greene,
The Summer of My German Soldier

29

gar·goyle (gär′goil′)

noun

A waterspout or ornamental figure in the form of a grotesque animal or person projecting from the gutter of a building.

30

guer·ril·la (*also spelled* **gue·ril·la**) (gə-rĭl′ə)

noun

A member of a military force that is not part of a regular army and operates in small bands in occupied territory to harass the enemy, as by surprise raids.

31

gu·ru (gŏŏr′ōō)

noun

    Plural: **gu·rus**

1. A Hindu spiritual teacher. **2.** A person who is followed as a leader or teacher.

32

her·i·tage (hĕr′ĭ-tĭj)

noun

1. Something other than property passed down from preceding generations; a tradition: *"We will win our freedom because the sacred heritage of our nation and the eternal will of God are embodied in our echoing demands"* (Martin Luther King, Jr., *Letter from Birmingham Jail*). **2.** Property that is or can be inherited.

33

hi·er·o·glyph·ic (hī′ər-ə-glĭf′ĭk *or* hī′rə-glĭf′ĭk)

adjective

Of or related to a system of writing, such as that of ancient Egypt, in which pictures or symbols are used to represent words or sounds: *The ancient tombs of the Pharaohs are marked with hieroglyphic writing.*

noun

1. A picture or symbol used in hieroglyphic writing; a hieroglyph. **2.** *often* **hieroglyphics** Hieroglyphic writing, especially that of the ancient Egyptians.

RELATED WORDS:

> *noun* — **hi′er·o·glyph′**
> *adverb* — **hi′er·o·glyph′i·cal·ly**

☙ **NOTE:** *Hieroglyphic* comes from a Greek word meaning "sacred carvings." *Hieros* meant "sacred" in Greek, and *glyphein* meant "to carve." Although the Egyptians wrote hieroglyphs on papyrus and painted them on walls, the Greeks who visited Egypt must have been more impressed by the stately carvings on the stones of immense temples and tombs. The Egyptians' own word for their writing system was *mdw ntr*, "words of the god." You could pronounce this (mĕd'o͞o nĕch'ĕr). The Egyptians thought the gods themselves used these symbols, which possessed great power. When they wrote hieroglyphs showing dangerous animals, such as snakes, on the walls of their tombs, they would sometimes leave the symbols unfinished—or even damage them intentionally. This would prevent the hieroglyphs from coming alive and harming the person entombed there.

The Egyptians enclosed the names of royalty in an oval shape called a *cartouche*. This oval represented the circular path of the sun around the world, and so indicated that the pharaoh was ruler of "all that the sun encircles."

Below is the full name of one of the greatest pharaohs, Ramses II, written in its original Egyptian form.

hol·o·gram (hŏl′ə-grăm′ *or* hō′lə-grăm′)

noun

The photographic record of a three-dimensional image produced by recording on a photographic plate or film the pattern of interference formed by a split laser beam. The plate or film is then illuminated with a laser or with ordinary light to form the image.

✎ **NOTE:** If you tear an ordinary photograph in two, each piece shows only a part of the original image. If you break a *hologram* in two, each piece shows the entire original scene, although from slightly different points of view. That's because each spot on a hologram contains enough information to show how the entire scene would look if it were viewed from a particular point of view. Imagine looking at a room through a peephole set in a solid door. What you see depends on where in the door the peephole is placed. Each piece of the hologram is a "peephole" view, and that's what makes the image look three-dimensional: as you move the hologram around or look at different parts of it, you see the original object from different angles, just as if you were walking around it. For this reason, holograms are much harder to copy than simple two-dimensional images, because to forge one you'd have to know what the original object looked like from many angles. And that's why credit cards and other important items include stickers bearing holograms as indicators of authenticity.

35

hy·poc·ri·sy (hĭ-pŏk′rĭ-sē)

noun

The practice of showing or expressing feelings, beliefs, or virtues that one does not actually hold or possess.

RELATED WORD:
   noun — **hyp′o·crite′** (hĭp′ə-krĭt′)

36

im·mune (ĭ-myōōn′)

adjective

1. Protected from disease naturally or by vaccination or inoculation: *I'm immune to chickenpox because I had it when I was young.* **2.** Not subject to an obligation imposed on others; exempt: *As a diplomat, he is immune from criminal prosecution.* **3.** Not affected by a given influence; unresponsive: *"I am immune to emotion. I have been ever since I can remember. Which is helpful when people appeal to my sympathy. I don't seem to have any"* (Ellen Wittlinger, *Hard Love*).

RELATED WORD:
   verb — **im′mu·nize′** (ĭm′yə-nīz′)

im·per·ti·nent (ĭm-pûr′tn-ənt)

adjective

1. Offensively bold; rude: *"'I don't like the look of it at all,' said the King: 'however, it may kiss my hand if it likes.' 'I'd rather not,' the Cat remarked. 'Don't be impertinent,' said the King, 'and don't look at me like that!'"* (Lewis Carroll, *Alice's Adventures in Wonderland*). **2.** Not pertinent; irrelevant: *The discussion went on for hours because of the many impertinent questions and remarks.*

RELATED WORD:

    adverb — **im·per′ti·nent·ly**

"Who *are* you talking to?" said the King, coming up to Alice, and looking at the Cat's head with great curiosity.

"It's a friend of mine — a Cheshire Cat," said Alice: "allow me to introduce it."

"I don't like the look of it at all," said the King: "however, it may kiss my hand if it likes."

"I'd rather not," the Cat remarked.

"Don't be **impertinent**," said the King, "and don't look at me like that!" He got behind Alice as he spoke.

"A cat may look at a king," said Alice. "I've read that in some book, but I don't remember where."

— Lewis Carroll,
Alice's Adventures in Wonderland

in·fer·ence (ĭn′fər-əns)

noun

1. The act or process of deciding or concluding by reasoning from evidence: *arrive at a logical conclusion by inference.* **2.** Something that is decided or concluded by reasoning from evidence; a conclusion: *The evidence is too scanty to draw any inferences from it.*

> ✍ **NOTE:** When we say that a speaker or sentence makes an **implication** or **implies** something, we mean that it is indicated or suggested without being stated outright: *Even though you say you like sports, your lack of enthusiasm implies that you don't.* To make an **inference** about something or **infer** something, on the other hand, is to draw conclusions that are not stated openly in what is said: *I infer from your lack of enthusiasm that you don't like sports.*

RELATED WORD:
    verb — **in·fer′**

in·tro·spec·tion (ĭn′trə-spĕk′shən)

noun

The examination of one's own thoughts and feelings.

RELATED WORDS:
    adjective — **in′tro·spec′tive**
    adverb — **in′tro·spec′tive·ly**

jaun·ty (jônt′tē *or* jänt′tē)

adjective
>Comparative: **jaun·ti·er**
>Superlative: **jaun·ti·est**

1. Having or showing a carefree self-confident air: *"A figure was approaching us over the moor, and I saw the dull red glow of a cigar. The moon shone upon him, and I could distinguish the dapper shape and jaunty walk of the naturalist"* (Arthur Conan Doyle, *The Hound of the Baskervilles*). **2.** Stylish or smart in appearance: *a jaunty hat.*

RELATED WORDS:
>*adverb* — **jaun′ti·ly**
>*noun* — **jaun′ti·ness**

jo·vi·al (jō′vē-əl)

adjective

Full of fun and good cheer; jolly: *a jovial host.*

RELATED WORDS:
>*noun* — **jo′vi·al′i·ty** (jō′vē-ăl′ĭ-tē)
>*adverb* — **jo′vi·al·ly**

kil·o·me·ter (kĭ-lŏm′ĭ-tər *or* kĭl′ə-mē′tər)

noun

A unit of length equal to 1,000 meters or 0.62 of a mile.

🖘 **NOTE:** The metric system is a system of measurement that is based on the number 10. Because 12 inches make a foot, and 3 feet make a yard, calculating the number of inches in a given number of yards or miles can often be cumbersome. In the metric system, multiplication is easy. *Kilo-* is a prefix meaning "a thousand," so one kilometer is equal to a thousand meters, and one kilogram is equal to a thousand grams. Likewise, if you know something is 18 kilometers away, you can easily calculate that it's 18,000 meters away.

Some common prefixes in the metric system are:

milli-	"one thousandth"	kilo-	"one thousand"
centi-	"one hundredth"	cento-	"one hundred"
deci-	"one tenth"	deca-	"ten"

The basic units of measurement in the metric system are the *gram*, for weight; the *liter*, for volume; and the *meter*, for distance. The prefixes can be combined with these units to form different measurements: a *centigram* is a hundredth (1/100) of a gram; a *milliliter* is a thousandth (1/1000) of a liter.

But the metric system isn't limited to these units: a *kilowatt* is a thousand watts, and a *millisecond* is a thousandth of second.

There are even more prefixes for larger and smaller units!

micro-	"one millionth"	mega- "one million"
nano-	"one billionth"	giga- "one billion"
pico-	"one trillionth"	tera- "one trillion"

---

kilometer / lichen

43
lab·y·rinth (lăb**′**ə-rĭnth**′**)

noun

1. A complex structure of connected passages through which it is difficult to find one's way; a maze. **2.** **Labyrinth** In Greek mythology, the maze built by Daedalus in Crete to confine the Minotaur. **3.** Something complicated or confusing in design or construction. **4.** The system of tubes and spaces that make up the inner ear of many vertebrate animals.

44
la·con·ic (lə-kŏn**′**ĭk)

adjective

Using few words; terse; concise: *a laconic reply.*

RELATED WORD:
    adverb—**la·con′i·cal·ly**

45
li·chen (lī**′**kən)

noun

An organism that consists of a fungus and an alga growing in close association with each other. Lichens often live on rocks and tree bark and can also be found in extremely cold environments.

46

light-year (līt'yîr')

noun

The distance that light travels in one year, about 5.88 trillion miles (9.47 trillion kilometers).

47

ma·neu·ver (mə-nōō'vər)

noun

1. A planned movement of troops or warships: *By a series of brilliant maneuvers, the general outwitted the enemy.* **2.** *often* **maneuvers** A large-scale military exercise in which battle movements are practiced. **3.** A controlled change in movement or direction of a vehicle or vessel, especially an aircraft. **4.** A movement or procedure that involves skill or cunning: *The gymnast made an acrobatic maneuver and landed squarely on the mat.*

verb
> Past participle and past tense: **ma·neu·vered**
> Present participle: **ma·neu·ver·ing**
> Third person singular present tense: **ma·neu·vers**

intransitive verb
1. To change tactics or approach; plan skillfully: *Our lawyer maneuvered in order to get the trial postponed.* **2.** To carry out a military maneuver. **3.** To make controlled changes in movement or direction: *The ship had to maneuver carefully to avoid the icebergs.*

---

transitive verb

1. To cause (troops or warships) to carry out a military maneuver. **2.** To direct skillfully by changes in course or in position: *"He let me maneuver the skiff through the wreckage of the flood without even peeking over his shoulder to see what I might be about to hit"* (Katherine Paterson, *Jacob Have I Loved*). **3.** To manage or direct, especially by trickery: *She maneuvered her opponent into taking a position that lost him the election.*

RELATED WORDS:

> *noun* — **ma·neu′ver·a·bil′i·ty**
> *adjective* — **ma·neu′ver·a·ble**

48

mar·su·pi·al (mär-soo′pē-əl)

noun

Any of various mammals, such as the kangaroo, opossum, or wombat, whose young continue to develop after birth in a pouch on the outside of the female's body.

met·a·phor (mĕt′ə-fôr′)

noun

A figure of speech in which a word or phrase that is ordinarily associated with one thing is applied to something else, thus making a comparison between the two.
For example, when Shakespeare wrote, "All the world's
a stage," and "Life's but a walking shadow," he was using
metaphors.

mo·sa·ic (mō-zā′ĭk)

noun

1. A picture or design made on a surface by fitting and
cementing together small colored pieces, as of tile, glass,
or stone. **2.** The art or process of making such pictures
or designs. **3.** Something that resembles a mosaic: *I
tried to understand the mosaic of impressions the author
had after visiting Mexico.* **4.** A viral disease of certain
plants, such as tobacco or tomatoes, that causes the
leaves to become spotted or wrinkled.

51

mu·ta·tion (myōo-tā′shən)

noun

1. A change in a gene or chromosome of an organism that can be inherited by its offspring. **2.** The process by which such a change occurs. **3.** An organism or individual that has undergone such a change. **4.** A change, as in form.

RELATED WORD:
verb — **mu′tate**

52

neb·u·la (nĕb′yə-lə)

noun
Plural: **neb·u·lae** (nĕb′yə-lē′) *or* **neb·u·las**

A thinly spread cloud of interstellar gas and dust. It will appear as a bright patch in the night sky if it reflects light from nearby stars, emits its own light, or re-emits ultraviolet radiation from nearby stars as visible light. If it absorbs light, the nebula appears as a dark patch. In dark nebulae, stars form from clumps of hydrogen gas.

RELATED WORD:
adjective — **neb′u·lar**

There were three circumstances in particular which made me think that its [The Morlocks'] rare emergence above ground was the outcome of a long-continued underground look common in most animals that live largely in the dark —the white fish of the Kentucky caves, for instance. Then, those large eyes, with that capacity for reflecting light, are common features of **nocturnal** things—witness the owl and the cat. And last of all, that evident confusion in the sunshine, that hasty yet fumbling awkward flight towards dark shadow, and that peculiar carriage of the head while in the light — all reinforced the theory of an extreme sensitiveness of the retina.

—H.G. Wells,
The Time Machine

53

noc·tur·nal (nŏk-tûr′nəl)

adjective

1. Of, relating to, or occurring at night: *a nocturnal breeze.* **2.** Active at night: *"[T]hose large eyes, with that capacity for reflecting light, are common features of nocturnal things—witness the owl and the cat"* (H.G. Wells, *The Time Machine*).

RELATED WORD:
  adverb—**noc·tur′nal·ly**

54

nui·sance (no͞o′səns)

noun

A source of inconvenience or annoyance; a bother.

55

om·ni·vore (ŏm′nə-vôr′)

noun

An organism that eats both plants and animals.

📖 **NOTE:** Our word *omnivore* comes from Latin *omnivorus,* "eating everything." Like many scientific words that English has borrowed from Latin, *omnivore* is a compound—a single word made by putting two other words together. The first part of the Latin word, *omni-,* means "all" or "every." The second part, *-vorus,* means "eating, swallowing." We can find this same root *-vor-* at the end of several other English words. For example, *carnivore* means literally "meat-eating." Here we see *-vor-* added to the same *carn-* as in *chili con carne,* "chili with meat." *Herbivore,* meaning "plant eater," has the same *herb-* as in *herbal tea.* The English verb *devour* comes from Latin *dēvorāre,* which also contains the root *-vor-.* The same root is found at the beginning of yet another word in this book, *voracious,* from Latin *vorāx,* "ravenous."

56

out·ra·geous (out-rā′jəs)

adjective

Exceeding all bounds of what is right or proper; immoral or offensive: *an outrageous crime; outrageous prices.*

RELATED WORD:
    adverb—**out·ra′geous·ly**
    noun—**out·ra′geous·ness**

o·zone (ō′zōn′)

noun

A poisonous, unstable form of oxygen that has three atoms per molecule rather than the usual two. It is produced by electricity and is present in the air, especially after a thunderstorm. Commercially, it is produced for use in water purification, air conditioning, and as a bleaching agent.

✏ **NOTE:** For the earth's organisms, including people, *ozone* can be a lifesaver or a threat to health, depending on how high it is found in the atmosphere. The ozone that lingers in the lower atmosphere is a pollutant and contributes to respiratory diseases like asthma. But in the upper atmosphere, ozone protects us from the more severe forms of the sun's radiation. The region of the atmosphere in which ozone is most concentrated is known as the *ozone layer,* which lies from about 10 to 20 miles (16 to 32 kilometers) above the earth. Because ozone absorbs certain wavelengths of harmful ultraviolet radiation, this layer acts as an important protection for life on the earth. In recent years the ozone has thinned or disappeared in parts of the ozone layer, especially over the polar regions, creating ozone "holes" that let in dangerous amounts of ultraviolet radiation. Ozone holes are created in part by the presence of certain industrial or commercial chemicals released into the atmosphere.

58

par·a·site (păr′ə-sīt′)

noun

1. An organism that lives in or on a different kind of organism from which it gets nourishment and to which it is sometimes harmful. Lice and tapeworms are parasites. **2.** A person who takes advantage of the generosity of others without making any useful return.

59

par·ti·ci·ple (păr′tĭ-sĭp′əl)

noun

A verb form that is used with auxiliary verbs to indicate certain tenses and that can also function as an adjective. The present participle is indicated by *–ing*, as in *running* and *sleeping*. The past participle is usually indicated by *–ed*, as in *walked* and *nailed*, but many English verbs have irregular past participles, such as *fought, sung,* and *known*. Past participles are also used to make the passive voice: *The board was nailed to the wall.*

> 🖋 **NOTE:** You should always avoid the "dangling" participle, as in the sentence *Turning the corner, the view was quite different.* This sentence is constructed so that it seems that the present participle *turning* modifies the noun *view*. As you read the sentence, you might at first think that the view is turning the corner. You should rewrite such sentences: *The view was quite different when we turned the corner,* or *Turning the corner, we saw a different view.*

60

phlo·em (flō′ĕm′)

noun

A plant tissue that conducts food from the leaves to the other plant parts. Phloem consists primarily of tube-like cells that have porous openings. In mature woody plants it forms a sheathlike layer of tissue in the stem, just inside the bark.

61

pla·teau (plă-tō′)

noun
   Plural: **pla·teaus** *or* **pla·teaux** (plă-tōz′)

1. An elevated, comparatively level expanse of land. **2.** A relatively stable level or stage of growth or development: *The economy has reached a new plateau.*

pol·y·gon (pŏl′ē-gŏn′)

noun

A flat, closed geometric figure bounded by three or more line segments. Triangles, rectangles, and octagons are all examples of polygons.

RELATED WORD:

adjective— **po·lyg′o·nal** (pə-lĭg′ə-nəl)

EXAMPLES OF POLYGONS

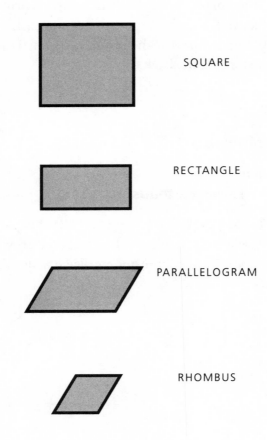

SQUARE

RECTANGLE

PARALLELOGRAM

RHOMBUS

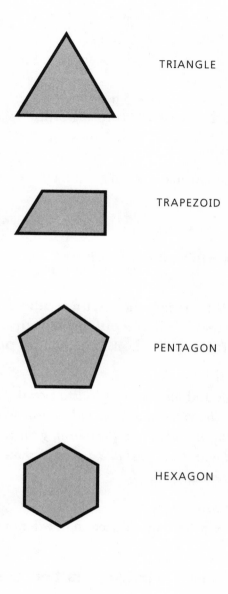

TRIANGLE

TRAPEZOID

PENTAGON

HEXAGON

OCTAGON

63
pro·tag·o·nist (prō-tăg′ə-nĭst)

noun

The main character in a drama or literary work.

64
pul·ver·ize (pŭl′və-rīz′)

verb
Past participle and past tense: **pul·ver·ized**
Present participle: **pul·ver·iz·ing**
Third person singular present tense: **pul·ver·iz·es**

transitive verb
To pound, crush, or grind to powder or dust: *"He felt that the stars had been pulverized by the sound of the black jets and that in the morning the earth would be covered with their dust like a strange snow"* (Ray Bradbury, *Fahrenheit 451*).

intransitive verb
To be ground or reduced to powder or dust.

RELATED WORD:
noun—**pul′ver·i·za′tion** (pŭl′vər-ĭ-zā′shən)

He felt that the stars had been **pulverized** by the sound of the black jets and that in the morning the earth would be covered with their dust like a strange snow. That was his idiot thought as he stood shivering in the dark, and let his lips go on moving and moving.

— Ray Bradbury,
Fahrenheit 451

65

quan·da·ry (kwŏn′də-rē or kwŏn′drē)

noun
> Plural: **quan·da·ries**

A condition of uncertainty or doubt; a dilemma: *I'm in a quandary over what to do next.*

66

quar·an·tine (kwŏr′ən-tēn′)

noun

A condition, period of time, or place in which a person or animal is confined or kept in isolation in an effort to prevent a disease from spreading.

transitive verb
> Past participle and past tense: **quar·an·tined**
> Present participle: **quar·an·tin·ing**
> Third person singular present tense: **quar·an·tines**

To keep (someone or something) confined or isolated, especially as a way to keep a disease from spreading; place (someone or something) in quarantine.

🔖 **NOTE:** The word *quarantine* comes from Italian *quarantina,* "a group of forty"—in this case, a group of forty days. The word originally described the number of days in which a newly arrived ship was kept in isolation, a practice begun in Venice and other port cities as a defense against the plague. The Italian word for "forty," *quaranta,* may remind you of words in other languages you may know, such as French *quarante* or Spanish *cuarenta.* They all descend from Latin *quadrāgintā,* "forty." The first part of this word, *quadr-,* means "four," and we can find it in many other English words. A *quadrangle* has four angles. A *squadron* was originally a group of soldiers in *square* (that is, four-sided) formation. A *quarry* was a place where stone was cut into blocks with square sides.

quo·ta (kwō′tə)

noun

1. An amount of something assigned, as to be done, made, or sold: *a machine shop's production quota.* **2.** A number or percentage, especially of people, that represents an upper limit: *strict immigration quotas.* **3.** A number or percentage, especially of people, that represents a required or targeted minimum: *a system of quotas for hiring minority applicants.*

68

rain·for·est (*also spelled* **rain forest**) (rān′fôr′ĭst)

noun

A dense evergreen forest with an annual rainfall of at least 160 inches (406 centimeters).

🐾 **NOTE:** Rainforests are, not surprisingly, forests where it rains a lot—between 160 and 400 inches (406 and 1,016 centimeters) a year. Most of the world's rainforests lie near the equator and have tropical climates. However, there are also cooler rainforests, such as the one in the northwest United States and southwestern Canada along the Pacific Ocean. The largest rainforest, covering as much territory as the rest of the world's rainforests combined, is in the Amazon River basin in South America. Rainforests are extremely important because they help regulate the world's climate and because they contain a wider variety of plants and animals than any other environment on the earth. Among the many benefits of this biodiversity is its support of important biological research. For example, many of the natural chemicals used in prescription drugs are found in plants that grow only in rainforests.

ran·dom (răn′dəm)

adjective

Having no specific pattern, purpose, or objective: *the random movements of leaves falling from the trees.*

idiom
at random
Without a method or purpose; unsystematically: *Choose a card at random from the deck.*

RELATED WORDS:
    adverb — **ran′dom·ly**
    noun — **ran′dom·ness**

re·cede (rĭ-sēd′)

intransitive verb
    Past participle and past tense: **re·ced·ed**
    Present participle: **re·ced·ing**
    Third person singular present tense: **re·cedes**

1. To move back or away from a limit, degree, point, or mark: *The floodwaters receded from the streets.* **2.** To grow less or diminish, as in intensity: *"[H]e stood and held his abdomen until the hunger cramps receded"* (Gary Paulsen, *Hatchet*). **3.** To slope backward: *a man with a chin that recedes.* **4.** To become fainter or more distant: *Over the years his memory of that summer receded.*

He stood, went back to the water, and took small drinks. As soon as the cold water hit his stomach, he felt the hunger sharpen, as it had before, and he stood and held his abdomen until the hunger cramps **receded**.

He had to eat. He was weak with it again, down with the hunger, and he had to eat.

—Gary Paulsen,
Hatchet

ren·ais·sance (rĕn′ĭ-säns′ *or* rĕn′ĭ-säns′)

noun

1. A rebirth or revival: *a renaissance of downtown business.* **2. Renaissance** The revival of classical art, literature, architecture, and learning in Europe that occurred from the 14th through the 16th century.

adjective

Renaissance Of or relating to the Renaissance or its artistic works or styles.

NOTE: When the Roman Empire crumbled in the middle of the fifth century, literate people in western Europe took refuge in monasteries, where they contemplated the nature of God and prepared for the next world. The art and literature of the ancient Greeks and Romans, and the values that they expressed, were largely forgotten or ignored because of their pagan origins. During the centuries just after the collapse of the empire, it was difficult to pass on knowledge from the past because of the great decline in living conditions. Then in the fourteenth and fifteenth centuries, a new interest was kindled in the achievements of Greece and Rome—first in Italy and then spreading to the rest of western Europe. A thousand years after the fall of Rome, the fall of another empire helped bring about a revival of classical civilization in the West. The Greeks of the Byzantine Empire had preserved manuscripts of classical literature and the knowledge of how to read them. As the Byzantine Empire crumbled and finally fell to the Turks in 1453, Greek scholars fled as refugees to Italy, and manuscripts were brought to western Europe for preservation. When Western scholars and artists examined the great achievements of Greece and Rome, they found new inspiration to create art and literature for their own age. In its vibrancy and vitality, this age was like a new birth for European culture, and so we now call it the Renaissance.

ren·e·gade (rĕn′ĭ-gād′)

noun

1. A person who rejects a cause, allegiance, religion, or group for another. **2.** An outlaw.

adjective

Of, relating to, or resembling a renegade; traitorous.

re·pose (rĭ-pōz′)

noun

1. The act of resting or the state of being at rest. **2.** Peace of mind; freedom from anxiety: *seeking security and repose.* **3.** Calmness; tranquility: *"It was the cool gray dawn, and there was a delicious sense of repose and peace in the deep pervading calm and silence of the woods"* (Mark Twain, *The Adventures of Tom Sawyer*).

verb

    Past participle and past tense: **re·posed**
    Present participle: **re·pos·ing**
    Third person singular present tense: **re·pos·es**

transitive verb
To lay (oneself) down to rest.

intransitive verb
1. To lie at rest; relax or sleep. **2.** To lie supported by something: *a dish reposing on the table.*

When Tom awoke in the morning, he wondered where he was. He sat up and rubbed his eyes and looked around. Then he comprehended. It was the cool gray dawn, and there was a delicious sense of **repose** and peace in the deep pervading calm and silence of the woods. Not a leaf stirred; not a sound obtruded upon great Nature's meditation. Beaded dewdrops stood upon the leaves and grasses. A white layer of ashes covered the fire, and a thin blue breath of smoke rose straight into the air. Joe and Huck still slept.

— Mark Twain,
The Adventures of Tom Sawyer

sac·ri·fice (săk′rə-fīs′)

noun

1. The act of giving up something highly valued for the sake of something else considered to be of greater value: *He was willing to make sacrifices in order to become a musician.* **2.** The act of offering something, such as an animal's life, to a deity in worship or to win favor or forgiveness. **3.** A victim offered this way. **4.** In baseball: **a.** A bunt that allows a runner to advance a base while the batter is retired. **b.** A fly ball enabling a runner to score after it is caught by a fielder.

verb
> Past participle and past tense: **sac·ri·ficed**
> Present participle: **sac·ri·fic·ing**
> Third person singular present tense: **sac·ri·fic·es**

transitive verb
1. To offer (something or someone) as a sacrifice to a deity. **2.** To give up (one thing) for another thing considered to be of greater value.

intransitive verb
1. To make or offer a sacrifice. **2.** In baseball, to hit a sacrifice bunt or sacrifice fly.

RELATED WORD:
> *adjective*—**sac′ri·fi′cial** (săk′rə-fĭsh′əl)

sil·hou·ette (sĭl'oo-ĕt')

noun

1. A drawing consisting of the outline of something, especially a human profile, filled in with a solid color. **2.** An outline of something that appears dark against a light background: *"A storm was coming up from the south, moving slowly. It looked something like a huge blue-gray shower curtain being drawn along by the hand of God. You could just barely see through it, enough to make out the silhouette of the mountains on the other side"* (Barbara Kingsolver, *The Bean Trees*).

transitive verb
> Past participle and past tense: **sil·hou·et·ted**
> Present participle: **sil·hou·et·ting**
> Third person singular present tense: **sil·hou·ettes**

To cause to be seen as a silhouette: *The lamp silhouetted his profile against the window shade.*

sol·stice (sŏl′stĭs *or* sōl′stĭs)

noun

Either of the times of year when the sun is farthest north or south of the equator. In the Northern Hemisphere, the summer solstice occurs on June 20 or 21 and the winter solstice occurs on December 21 or 22.

spec·trum (spĕk′trəm)

noun
   Plural: **spec·tra** (spĕk′trə) *or* **spec·trums**

1. A band of colors seen when white light is broken up according to wavelengths, as when passing through a prism or striking drops of water. **2.** The entire range of electromagnetic radiation, from gamma rays, which have the shortest wavelengths and highest frequencies, to radio waves, which have the longest wavelengths and lowest frequencies. Visible light, with intermediate wavelengths and frequencies, is near the center of the electromagnetic spectrum. **3.** A broad range of related qualities, ideas, or activities: *This class will cover a wide spectrum of ideas.*

---

solstice / strategy   **68**

ster·e·o·type (stĕr′ē-ə-tīp′)

noun

A conventional or oversimplified idea or image: *the stereotype of the meek librarian.*

transitive verb
> Past participle and past tense: **ster·e·o·typed**
> Present participle: **ster·e·o·typ·ing**
> Third person singular present tense: **ster·e·o·types**

To make a stereotype of: *a movie that stereotypes farmers as unsophisticated.*

RELATED WORD:
> *noun* — **ster′e·o·typ′er**

strat·e·gy (străt′ə-jē)

noun
> Plural: **strat·e·gies**

1. The science of using all the forces of a nation as effectively as possible during peace or war. **2.** A plan of action arrived at by means of this science or intended to accomplish a specific goal.

RELATED WORD:
> *adjective* — **stra·te′gic** (strə-tē′jĭk)

80
suf·frage (sŭf′rĭj)

noun

The right to vote in political elections: *Susan B. Anthony campaigned for women's suffrage.*

81
sym·bi·o·sis (sĭm′bē-ō′sĭs *or* sĭm′bī-ō′sĭs)

noun
Plural: **sym·bi·o·ses** (sĭm′bē-ō′sēz′ *or* sĭm′bī-ō′sēz′)

The close association between two or more different organisms of different species, often but not necessarily benefiting each member.

🖉 **NOTE:** Two organisms that live together in **symbiosis** may have one of three kinds of relationships: *mutualism, commensalism,* or *parasitism.* The *mutualism* shown by the rhinoceros and the tickbird benefits both. Riding on the rhino's back, the tickbird eats its fill of the ticks that bother the rhino while the rhino gets warning calls from the bird when it senses danger. In *commensalism,* one member benefits and the other is unaffected. The ocean fish known as the remora attaches to a shark by a suction disk on its head and gets to eat the scraps left after the shark feeds. But the shark is unaffected by the remora's presence. In *parasitism,* though, one species generally gets hurt, as when fleas infest a dog's coat and feed on its blood.

82

tar·iff (tăr′ĭf)

noun

1. A tax or duty imposed by a government on a category of imported or exported goods, such as automobiles or steel. **2.** A list or system of these taxes or duties. **3.** A list or table of prices or fees.

83

tech·nique (tĕk-nēk′)

noun

1. A procedure or method for accomplishing a complicated task, as in a science or an art: *a new technique for making computer chips.* **2.** Skill in handling such procedures or methods: *As a pianist, she has nearly perfect technique.*

84

tem·po (tĕm′pō)

noun
    Plural: **tem·pos** *or* **tem·pi** (tĕm′pē)

1. The speed at which music is or ought to be played. **2.** A characteristic rate or rhythm of something; a pace: *the rapid tempo of life in a city.*

tox·in (tŏk′sĭn)

noun

A poisonous substance produced by a living organism. Toxins can be products of ordinary metabolism (such as those found in urine), can be produced to kill or immobilize prey (such as the toxins in snake venom), or can be produced for self-defense (such as the cyanide produced by several plants). Toxins produced by bacteria cause disease.

RELATED WORD:
    adjective — **tox′ic**

tran·quil·i·ty (*also spelled* **tran·quil·li·ty**)
(trăng-kwĭl′ĭ-tē *or* trăn-kwĭl′ĭ-tē)

noun

The quality or condition of being free from disturbance; calmness; serenity: *"We the people of the United States, in order to form a more perfect union, establish justice, insure domestic tranquility . . . do ordain and establish this Constitution for the United States of America"* (Preamble to the Constitution of the United States of America).

We the people of the United States, in order to form a more perfect union, establish justice, insure domestic **tranquility**, provide for the common defense, promote the general welfare, and secure the blessings of liberty to ourselves and our posterity, do ordain and establish this Constitution for the United States of America.

— Preamble to the
Constitution of the
United States of America

tu·mult (tōo′mŭlt′)

noun

1. Noisy and disorderly activity; a commotion or disturbance; an uproar. **2.** Emotional or mental commotion or agitation.

RELATED WORD:
    adjective— **tu·mul′tu·ous** (tōo-mŭl′chōo-əs)

tun·dra (tŭn′drə)

noun

A cold, treeless, usually lowland area of far northern regions. The subsoil of tundras is permanently frozen, but in summer the top layer of soil thaws and can support low-growing mosses, lichens, grasses, and small shrubs: *"As I looked about me at the stark and cloud-topped hills, the waste of pressure-rippled ice, and, beyond the valley, to the desolate and treeless roll of tundra, I had no doubt that this was excellent wolf country"* (Farley Mowatt, *Never Cry Wolf*).

As I looked about me at the stark and cloud-topped hills, the waste of pressure-rippled ice, and, beyond the valley, to the desolate and treeless roll of **tundra**, I had no doubt that this was excellent wolf country. Indeed, I suspected that many pairs of lupine eyes were already watching me with speculative interest. I burrowed into my mountain of gear, found the revolver, and then took stock of the situation.

—Farley Mowatt,
Never Cry Wolf

89
ul·tra·vi·o·let (ŭl′trə-vī′ə-lĭt)

adjective

Of or relating to electromagnetic radiation having wavelengths shorter than those of visible light but longer than those of x-rays.

90
u·nan·i·mous (yōō-năn′ə-məs)

adjective

1. Sharing the same opinion; being fully in agreement: *"[N]eighborhood opinion was unanimous that Mrs. Dubose was the meanest old woman who ever lived"* (Harper Lee, *To Kill a Mockingbird*). **2.** Based on or characterized by complete agreement: *a unanimous vote.*

RELATED WORD:
   adverb — **u·nan′i·mous·ly**

Cecil Jacobs, who lived at the far end of our street next door to the post office, walked a total of one mile per school day to avoid the Radley Place and old Mrs. Henry Lafayette Dubose. Mrs. Dubose lived two doors up the street from us; neighborhood opinion was **unanimous** that Mrs. Dubose was the meanest old woman who ever lived.

— Harper Lee,
To Kill a Mockingbird

91

un·du·late (ŭn′jə-lāt′)

intransitive verb

    Past participle and past tense: **un·du·lat·ed**

    Present participle: **un·du·lat·ing**

    Third person singular present tense: **un·du·lates**

1. To move in waves or with a smooth wavy motion: *wheat undulating in the breeze.* **2.** To have a wavy appearance or form: *A line undulated across the chalkboard.*

RELATED WORD:

    noun — **un′du·la′tion**

---

undulate / vaccine   **78**

vac·cine (văk-sēn′)

noun

A substance that stimulates cells in the immune system to recognize and attack disease-causing agents, especially through the production of antibodies. Most vaccines are given by injection or are swallowed as liquids. Vaccines may contain a weaker form of the disease-causing virus or bacterium or even a DNA fragment or some other component of the agent.

RELATED WORD:

noun — **vac′ci·na′tion**

𝕊 **NOTE:** The word *vaccine* ultimately comes from Latin *vacca,* "cow," a word that may be familiar to you as French *vache* or Spanish *vaca.* Before the days of vaccination, the dread disease smallpox had long been a leading cause of death all over the world. In 1796, however, the English doctor Edward Jenner noticed that people who had caught cowpox, a mild disease contracted from dairy cows, did not get smallpox afterwards. Jenner took liquid from the cowpox sores of a milkmaid and injected a boy with it. Later, Jenner exposed the boy to smallpox, but the boy did not get sick. In this way, Jenner had discovered a safe way to prevent smallpox. From the Latin name for cowpox, *variolae vaccīnae* (literally, "smallpox of cows"), Jenner's technique became known as *vaccination,* and the liquid he injected as *vaccine.*

---

vac·il·late (văs′ə-lāt′)

intransitive verb

Past participle and past tense: **vac·il·lat·ed**
Present participle: **vac·il·lat·ing**
Third person singular present tense: **vac·il·lates**

To be unable to decide between one opinion or course of action and another; waver: *I vacillated between going on vacation with my family or going to summer camp.*

RELATED WORD:
   noun—**vac′il·la′tion**

ver·te·brate (vûr′tə-brĭt *or* vûr′tə-brāt′)

noun

Any of a large group of animals having a backbone, including the fishes, amphibians, reptiles, birds, and mammals.

adjective

1. Having a backbone: *vertebrate animals.* **2.** Of or characteristic of a vertebrate or vertebrates: *the vertebrate brain.*

95

vir·tu·o·so (vûr′chōō-ō′sō *or* vûr′chōō-ō′zō)

noun

Plural: **vir·tu·o·sos** *or* **vir·tu·o·si** (vûr′chōō-ō′sē)

1. A musical performer of great excellence, technique, or ability. **2.** A person of great skill or technique: *a chef who was a virtuoso in the kitchen.*

adjective

Exhibiting the ability, technique, or personal style of a virtuoso: *a virtuoso performance.*

vo·ra·cious (və-rā′shəs)

adjective

1. Eating or eager to eat great amounts of food; ravenous: *"Oliver Twist and his companions suffered the tortures of slow starvation for three months: at last they got so voracious and wild with hunger, that one boy . . . hinted darkly to his companions, that unless he had another basin of gruel per diem, he was afraid he might some night happen to eat the boy who slept next him. . . ."* (Charles Dickens, *Oliver Twist*). **2.** Having or marked by an insatiable appetite for an activity or occupation: *a voracious reader.*

RELATED WORDS:
> *adverb* — **vo·ra′cious·ly**
> *noun* — **vo·ra′cious·ness**

Boys have generally excellent appetites. Oliver Twist and his companions suffered the tortures of slow starvation for three months: at last they got so **voracious** and wild with hunger, that one boy, who was tall for his age, and hadn't been used to that sort of thing (for his father had kept a small cook-shop), hinted darkly to his companions, that unless he had another basin of gruel *per diem*, he was afraid he might some night happen to eat the boy who slept next him, who happened to be a weakly youth of tender age. He had a wild, hungry eye; and they implicitly believed him. A council was held; lots were cast who should walk up to the master after supper that evening, and ask for more; and it fell to Oliver Twist.

— Charles Dickens,
Oliver Twist

wretch·ed (rĕch′ĭd)

adjective

Comparative: **wretch·ed·er** *or* **more wretched**
Superlative: **wretch·ed·est** *or* **most wretched**

1. Very unhappy or unfortunate; miserable: *a wretched prisoner.* **2.** Characterized by or causing distress or unhappiness: *"But my night was wretched, my rest broken: the ground was damp, the air cold: besides, intruders passed near me more than once, and I had again and again to change my quarters: no sense of safety or tranquillity befriended me"* (Charlotte Brontë, *Jane Eyre*). **3.** Hateful or contemptible: *a bigot with a wretched personality.* **4.** Inferior in quality: *The movie was wretched.*

RELATED WORDS:
adverb — **wretch′ed·ly**
noun — **wretch′ed·ness**

I could not hope to get a lodging under a roof, and sought it in the wood I have before alluded to. But my night was **wretched**, my rest broken: the ground was damp, the air cold: besides, intruders passed near me more than once, and I had again and again to change my quarters: no sense of safety or tranquillity befriended me. Towards morning it rained; the whole of the following day was wet. Do not ask me, reader, to give a minute account of that day; as before, I sought work; as before, I was repulsed; as before, I starved; but once did food pass my lips. At the door of a cottage I saw a little girl about to throw a mess of cold porridge into a pig trough. "Will you give me that?" I asked.

—Charlotte Brontë,
Jane Eyre

98
xy·lem (zī′ləm)

noun

A plant tissue that carries water and dissolved minerals up from the roots through the stem to the leaves and provides support for the softer tissues. Xylem consists of various elongated cells that function as tubes. In a tree trunk, the innermost part of the wood is dead but structurally strong xylem.

99
yacht (yät)

noun

Any of various relatively small sailing or motor-driven vessels used for pleasure trips or racing.

NOTE: Many English words related to the sea or seafaring are borrowed from Dutch, including *brackish, corvette, deck, dock, freebooter, harpoon, hoist, maelstrom, mesh* (of a net), *reef, school* (of fish), *skipper, sloop, tackle, trawl,* and *walrus.* The word *yacht,* the only common English word in which *ch* is silent, was probably borrowed from Dutch *jaght,* now spelled *jacht.* Norwegian also has the word *jakt,* related to Dutch *jacht,* and possibly both languages contributed to the development of English *yacht.* These words ultimately come from Middle Low German *jachtschip,* or "hunting ship." The original Dutch *jacht,* a fast, light boat, actually served the practical purposes of pursuing smugglers. In 1660, the Dutch East India Company gave Charles II of England a *jacht* of this type. However, he used it for pleasure *cruises*—another word from Dutch!

In Dutch, the *ch* is actually pronounced as a separate sound, like the one you make when you clear your throat—it is like the *ch* at the end of the German pronunciation of the composer *Bach.* English used to have this sound, too. Everyone is familiar with silent *gh* from words such as *bought* and *thought.* This silent *gh* once spelled the same throat-clearing sound, which disappeared in English in the sixteenth century. By the time the English borrowed the Dutch word *jacht,* they could no longer say the *ch* very well, so it was left out of the pronunciation. But the spelling of the word stayed the same.

zo·ol·o·gy (zō-ŏl′ə-jē *or* zōō-ŏl′ə-jē)

noun

    Plural: **zo·ol·o·gies**

1. The branch of biology that deals with animals. **2.** The animals of a particular area or period: *The zoology of Australia is very different from the zoology of North America.*

Exercises
to Improve and
Enrich Your Vocabulary

Knowing and being able to use the *100 Words Every High School Freshman Should Know* is just one step that you can take to expand your vocabulary. Along with a good dictionary, such as the *American Heritage® Student Dictionary* or the *American Heritage® High School Dictionary*, you can use these 100 words as a starting point to discover new words. The exercises shown below are among the many ways you can become more familiar with your dictionary and improve your vocabulary.

Building your vocabulary is an ongoing process that you can continue throughout your life. If you feel discouraged because you can't retain the definitions of all the words that you encounter, approach the task of expanding your vocabulary more slowly. If learning ten words a week is too difficult, aim for three, or five.

What is important is not the quantity of words you're learning. Rather, what is important is your process behind learning the words and the commitment you make to yourself to strengthen your vocabulary over time.

Choose ten words from the list of *100 Words Every High School Freshman Should Know*. Look these ten words up in your dictionary.

On each page that these ten words are listed, choose a new word whose meaning you do not know. Create a document on your computer and type in that word along with its definition, or write the word down on paper with its definition.

For example, other words appearing on the same page as **bamboozle** in the *American Heritage Student Dictionary* that you might choose to learn include **balsam, balustrade,** or **banal**.

Keep a record of the new words that you learn. Every so often, go back and refresh your memory by rereading the definitions to these words. Create sentences that use these words so that you can become comfortable using them.

EXERCISE II

Choose a magazine or newspaper that you like to read at least once a week. Create a document on your computer or start a journal in a notebook. Every time you read a word whose meaning you're unsure of, add that word to your computer file or journal entry.

Look up the word in your dictionary, and write or type out the definition. Does knowing the precise definition of the word help you understand the article?

After you have acquired a list of ten words, memorize them until they are part of your active vocabulary.

EXERCISE III

Many of the words in the list of *100 Words Every High School Freshman Should Know* include terms from specific areas of study. For example, **ellipse** and **polygon** are both from the field of geometry. **Antibody** and **mutation** are from biology.

What fields of learning interest you? Create a list of ten words that you think people should know if they were to learn more about that topic. Think about how you would define those words, and compare your definitions with the definitions you find in your dictionary.

100

words every high school graduate should **know**

Guide to the Entries

ENTRY WORD The 100 words that constitute this section are listed alphabetically. The entry words, along with inflected and derived forms, are divided into syllables by centered dots. These dots show you where you would break the word at the end of a line. The pronunciation of the word follows the entry word. Please see the pronunciation guide and key on pages 98–99 for an explanation of the pronunciation system.

PART OF SPEECH At least one part of speech follows each entry word. The part of speech tells you the grammatical category that the word belongs to. Parts of speech include *noun, adjective, adverb, transitive verb,* and *intransitive verb.* (A transitive verb is a verb that needs an object to complete its meaning. *Wash* is transitive in the sentence *I washed the car.* The direct object of *wash* is *the car.* An intransitive verb is one that does not take an object, as *sleep* in the sentence *I slept for seven hours.* Many verbs are both transitive and intransitive.)

INFLECTIONS A word's inflected form differs from the main entry form by the addition of a suffix or by a change in its base form to indicate grammatical features such as number, person, or tense. They are set in boldface type, divided into syllables, and given pronunciations as necessary. The past tense, past participle, and the third person singular present tense inflections of all verbs are shown. The plurals of nouns are shown when they are spelled in a way other than by adding *s* to the base form.

LABELS A subject label identifies the special area of knowledge a definition applies to, as at **metamorphosis.** Information applicable only to a particular sense is shown after the number or letter of that sense; at **metamorphosis,** the biology sense is applicable to sense 2.

The *Usage Problem* label warns of possible difficulties involving grammar, diction, and writing style. A word or definition with this label is discussed in a Usage Note, as at **paradigm.**

Certain nouns are spelled as plurals but sometimes take a singular verb. This information is indicated in italic type, as at **thermodynamics.**

ORDER OF SENSES Entries having more than one sense are arranged with the central and often the most commonly sought meaning first. Senses and subsenses are grouped to show their relationships with each other. Boldface letters before senses indicate that two or more subsenses are closely related, as at **parameter.**

In an entry with more than one part of speech, the senses are numbered in separate sequences after each part of speech, as at **kowtow**.

EXAMPLES OF USAGE Examples often follow the definitions and are set in italic type. These examples show the entry words in typical contexts. Sometimes the examples are quotations from authors of books or newspaper articles. These quotations are shown within quotation marks and are followed by the quotation's author and source.

ETYMOLOGIES Etymologies appear in square brackets following the last definition. An etymology traces the history of a word as far back in time as can be determined with reasonable certainty. The stage most closely preceding Modern English is given first, with each earlier stage following in sequence. A language name, linguistic form (in italics), and brief definition of the form are given for each stage of the derivation. To avoid redundancy, a language, form, or definition is not repeated if it is identical to the corresponding item in the immediately preceding stage. Occasionally, a form will be given that is not actually preserved in written documents but which scholars are confident did exist—such a form will be marked by an asterisk (*). The word *from* is used to indicate origin of any kind: by inheritance, borrowing, or derivation. When an etymology splits a compound word into parts, a colon introduces the parts and each element is then traced back to its origin, with those elements enclosed in parentheses.

RELATED WORDS At the end of many entries, additional boldface words appear without definitions. These words are related in basic meaning to the entry word and are usually formed from the entry word by the addition of suffixes.

NOTES Some entries include Usage Notes or Word Histories. Usage Notes present important information and guidance on matters of grammar, diction, pronunciation, and nuances. Some refer to responses from our Usage Panel, a group of more than 200 respected writers, scholars, and critics. The editors of the *American Heritage Dictionaries* regularly survey these people on a broad range of usage questions. Word Histories are found at words whose etymologies are of particular interest. The bare facts of the etymology are explained to give a fuller understanding of how important linguistic processes operate, how words move from one language to another, and how the history of an individual word can be related to historical and cultural developments.

At the end of this section, there are exercises that are designed to help you further strengthen your vocabulary.

Pronunciation Guide

Pronunciations appear in parentheses after boldface entry words. If a word has more than one pronunciation, the first pronunciation is usually more common than the other, but often they are equally common. Pronunciations are shown after inflections and related words where necessary.

Stress is the relative degree of emphasis that a word's syllables are spoken with. An unmarked syllable has the weakest stress in the word. The strongest, or primary, stress is indicated with a bold mark (ˈ). A lighter mark (ʹ) indicates a secondary level of stress. The stress mark follows the syllable it applies to. Words of one syllable have no stress mark because there is no other stress level that the syllable is compared to.

The key on page 99 shows the pronunciation symbols used in this section. To the right of the symbols are words that show how the symbols are pronounced. The letters whose sound corresponds to the symbols are shown in boldface.

The symbol (ə) is called *schwa*. It represents a vowel with the weakest level of stress in a word. The schwa sound varies slightly according to the vowel it represents or the sounds around it:

a·bun·dant (ə-bŭnʹdənt)   **mo·ment** (mōʹmənt)

civ·il (sĭvʹəl)   **grate·ful** (grātʹfəl)

	PRONUNCIATION KEY			
Symbol	**Examples**		**Symbol**	**Examples**
ă	pat		oi	noise
ā	pay		ŏŏ	took
âr	care		ŏŏr	lure
ä	father		ōō	boot
b	bib		ou	out
ch	church		p	pop
d	deed, milled		r	roar
ĕ	pet		s	sauce
ē	bee		sh	ship, dish
f	fife, phase, rough		t	tight, stopped
			th	thin
g	gag		*th*	this
h	hat		ŭ	cut
hw	which		ûr	urge, term, firm, word, heard
ĭ	pit			
ī	pie, by			
îr	deer, pier		v	valve
j	judge		w	with
k	kick, cat, pique		y	yes
l	lid, needle		z	zebra, xylem
m	mum		zh	vision, pleasure, garage
n	no, sudden			
ng	thing			
ŏ	pot		ə	about, item, edible, gallop, circus
ō	toe			
ô	caught, paw			
ôr	core		ər	butter

The strong-bas'd promontory
Have I made shake, and by the spurs pluck'd up
The pine and cedar; graves at my command
Have wak'd their sleepers, op'd, and let 'em forth,
By my so potent art. But this rough magic
I here **abjure**.

—William Shakespeare,
The Tempest

1

ab·jure (ăb-jŏŏr′)

transitive verb
> Past participle and past tense: **ab·jured**
> Present participle: **ab·jur·ing**
> Third person singular present tense: **ab·jures**

1. To recant solemnly; renounce or repudiate: *"But this rough magic I here abjure"* (William Shakespeare, *The Tempest*). **2.** To renounce under oath; forswear: *The defendant abjured his previous testimony.*

[Middle English *abjuren*, from Old French *abjurer*, from Latin *abiūrāre* : *ab-*, away + *iūrāre*, to swear.]

RELATED WORDS:
> *noun*— **ab′ju·ra′tion** (ăb′jə-rā′shən)
> *noun*— **ab·jur′er**

2

ab·ro·gate (ăb′rə-gāt′)

transitive verb

> Past participle and past tense: **ab·ro·gat·ed**
> Present participle: **ab·ro·gat·ing**
> Third person singular present tense: **ab·ro·gates**

To abolish, do away with, or annul, especially by authority: "*In 1982, we were told that this amendment meant that our existing Aboriginal and treaty rights were now part of the supreme law of the land, and could not be abrogated or denied by any government*" (Matthew Coon-Come, *Native Americas*).

[Latin *abrogāre, abrogāt-* : *ab-*, away + *rogāre*, to ask.]

RELATED WORD:

> *noun*—**ab′ro·ga′tion** (ăb′rə-gā′shən)

3

ab·ste·mi·ous (ăb-stē′mē-əs *or* əb-stē′mē-əs)

adjective

1. Eating and drinking in moderation: "*Mr. Brooke was an abstemious man, and to drink a second glass of sherry quickly at no great interval from the first was a surprise to his system*" (George Eliot, *Middlemarch*). **2.** Characterized by abstinence or moderation: *The hermit led an abstemious way of life.*

[From Latin *abstēmius* : *abs-, ab-*, away + **tēmum*, liquor, variant of *tēmētum*.]

RELATED WORDS:

> *adverb*—**ab·ste′mi·ous·ly**
> *noun*—**ab·ste′mi·ous·ness**

4

ac·u·men (ăk′yə-mən *or* ə-kyoō′mən)

noun

Quickness and keenness of judgment or insight: *"'No, no, my dear Watson! With all respect for your natural acumen, I do not think that you are quite a match for the worthy doctor'"* (Arthur Conan Doyle, *The Adventure of the Missing Three-Quarter*).

[Latin *acūmen*, from *acuere*, to sharpen, from *acus*, needle.]

USAGE NOTE: The pronunciation (ə-kyoō′mən), with stress on the second syllable, is an older, traditional pronunciation reflecting the word's Latin origin. In recent years it has been supplanted as the most common pronunciation of the word by a variant with stress on the first syllable, (ăk′yə-mən). In our 1997 Usage Panel survey, 68 percent of the Panelists chose this as their pronunciation, while 29 percent preferred the pronunciation with stress on the second syllable. The remaining 3 percent said they use both pronunciations.

5

an·te·bel·lum (ăn′tē-běl′əm)

adjective

Belonging to the period before a war, especially the American Civil War: *While vacationing in Georgia, we took a tour of stately antebellum houses.*

[From Latin *ante bellum*, before the war : *ante*, before + *bellum*, war.]

6

aus·pi·cious (ô-spĭsh′əs)

adjective

1. Attended by favorable circumstances; propitious: *My boss was in a good mood, so I thought it was an auspicious time to ask for a raise.* **2.** Marked by success; prosperous: *The auspicious fundraiser allowed the charity to donate hundreds of toys to the orphanage.*

[From Latin *auspicium*, bird divination, from *auspex, auspic-*, one who foretold the future by watching the flights of birds.]

RELATED WORDS:
  adverb—**aus·pi′cious·ly**
  noun—**aus·pi′cious·ness**

7

be·lie (bē-lī′, bĭ-lī′)

transitive verb
  Past participle and past tense: **be·lied**
  Present participle: **be·ly·ing**
  Third person singular present tense: **be·lies**

1. To give a false representation to; misrepresent: *"He spoke roughly in order to belie his air of gentility"* (James Joyce, *Dubliners*). **2.** To show to be false; contradict: *Their laughter belied their outward anger.*

[Middle English *bilien*, from Old English *belēogan*, to deceive with lies.]

RELATED WORD:
  noun—**be·li′er**

He spoke roughly in order to **belie** his air of gentility, for his entry had been followed by a pause of talk. His face was heated. To appear natural he pushed his cap back on his head and planted his elbows on the table.

—James Joyce,
Dubliners

8

bel·li·cose (běl′ĭ-kōs′)

adjective

Warlike or hostile in manner or temperament: *The nations exchanged bellicose rhetoric over the border dispute.*

[Middle English, from Latin *bellicōsus*, from *bellicus*, of war, from *bellum*, war.]

RELATED WORDS:
> *adverb*— **bel′li·cose′ly**
> *noun*— **bel′li·cos′i·ty** (běl′ĭ-kŏs′ĭ-tē)
> *noun*— **bel′li·cose′ness**

9

bowd·ler·ize (bōd′lə-rīz′ *or* boud′lə-rīz′)

transitive verb
> Past participle and past tense: **bowd·ler·ized**
> Present participle: **bowd·ler·iz·ing**
> Third person singular present tense: **bowd·ler·iz·es**

To remove material that is considered objectionable or offensive from (a book, for example); expurgate: *The publisher bowdlerized the bawdy 18th-century play for family audiences.*

[After Thomas *Bowdler* (1754–1825), who published an expurgated edition of Shakespeare in 1818.]

RELATED WORDS:
> *noun*— **bowd′ler·ism**
> *noun*— **bowd′ler·i·za′tion**
> (bōd′lər-ĭ-zā′shən
> *or* boud′lər-ĭ-zā′shən)
> *noun*— **bowd′ler·iz′er**

---

chi·can·er·y (shĭ-kā**′**nə-rē *or* chĭ-kā**′**nə-rē)

noun

Deception by trickery or sophistry: *"The successful man . . . who has risen by conscienceless swindling of his neighbors, by deceit and chicanery, by unscrupulous boldness and unscrupulous cunning, stands toward society as a dangerous wild beast"* (Theodore Roosevelt, *The Strenuous Life*).

[From *chicane*, to deceive, from French *chicaner*, from Old French, to quibble.]

chro·mo·some (krō**′**mə-sōm**′**)

noun

1. A threadlike linear strand of DNA and associated proteins in the nucleus of eukaryotic cells that carries the genes and functions in the transmission of hereditary information: *Chromosomes occur in pairs in all of the cells of eukaryotes except the reproductive cells.* **2.** A circular strand of DNA in bacteria that contains the hereditary information of the cell.

[*chromo-*, colored (from Greek *khrōma*, color) + *-some*, body (from Greek *sōma*).]

RELATED WORDS:
adjective — **chro′mo·som′al** (krō′mə-sō′məl)
adjective — **chro′mo·som′ic** (krō′mə-sō′mĭk)

12

churl·ish (chûr′lĭsh)

adjective

1. Of, like, or befitting a churl; boorish or vulgar. **2.** Having a bad disposition; surly: *"He is as valiant as the lion, churlish as the bear"* (William Shakespeare, *Troilus and Cressida*).

[From *churl*, rude person, from Middle English, from Old English *ceorl*, peasant.]

RELATED WORDS:
    adverb—**chur′lish·ly**
    noun—**chur′lish·ness**

13

cir·cum·lo·cu·tion (sûr′kəm-lō-kyōō′shən)

noun

1. The use of unnecessarily wordy and indirect language: *"There lives no man who at some period has not been tormented, for example, by an earnest desire to tantalize a listener by circumlocution"* (Edgar Allan Poe, *The Imp of the Perverse*). **2.** Evasiveness in speech or writing. **3.** A roundabout expression: *"At such time as"* is a circumlocution for the word *"when."*

[Middle English *circumlocucioun*, from Latin *circumlocūtiō, circumlocūtiōn-*, from *circumlocūtus*, past participle of *circumloquī* : *circum-*, around + *loquī*, to speak.]

RELATED WORD:
    adjective—**cir′cum·loc′u·to′ry**
        (sûr′kəm-lŏk′yə-tôr′ē)

There lives no man who at some period has not been tormented, for example, by an earnest desire to tantalize a listener by **circumlocution**.

— Edgar Allan Poe,
The Imp of the Perverse

14

cir·cum·nav·i·gate (sûr′kəm-năv′ĭ-gāt′)

transitive verb

Past participle and past tense: **cir·cum·nav·i·gat·ed**
Present participle: **cir·cum·nav·i·gat·ing**
Third person singular present tense: **cir·cum·nav·i·gates**

1. To proceed completely around: *"The whale he had struck must also have been on its travels; no doubt it had thrice circumnavigated the globe"* (Herman Melville, *Moby-Dick*). **2.** To go around; circumvent: *I circumnavigated the downtown traffic by taking side streets on the west side of town.*

[*circum-*, around (from Latin) + *navigate*, to sail (from Latin *nāvigāre, nāvigāt-* : *nāvis*, ship + *agere*, to drive, lead).]

RELATED WORDS:
noun — **cir′cum·nav·i·ga′tion**
(sûr′kəm-năv′ĭ-gā′shən)
noun — **cir′cum·nav′i·ga′tor**

15

de·cid·u·ous (dĭ-sĭj′ōo-əs)

adjective

1. Shedding or losing foliage at the end of the growing season: *"Orange-picking begins in December and overlaps the pruning of the deciduous orchards"* (Mary Austin, *Art Influence in the West*). **2.** Falling off or shed at a specific season or stage of growth: *Male deer have deciduous antlers.* **3.** Not lasting; ephemeral.

[From Latin *dēciduus*, from *dēcidere*, to fall off : *dē-*, down from + *cadere*, to fall.]

RELATED WORDS:
> *adverb* — **de·cid′u·ous·ly**
> *noun* — **de·cid′u·ous·ness**

16

del·e·te·ri·ous (dĕl′ĭ-tîr′ē-əs)

adjective

Having a harmful effect; injurious: *"I will follow that system of regimen which, according to my ability and judgment, I consider for the benefit of my patients, and abstain from whatever is deleterious and mischievous"* (Hippocratic Oath).

[From Greek *dēlētērios*, from *dēlētēr*, destroyer, from *dēleisthai*, to harm.]

RELATED WORDS:
> *adverb* — **del′e·te′ri·ous·ly**
> *noun* — **del′e·te′ri·ous·ness**

---

dif·fi·dent (dĭf′ĭ-dənt *or* dĭf′ĭ-dĕnt′)

adjective

Lacking or marked by a lack of self-confidence; shy and timid: *"He was too diffident to do justice to himself; but when his natural shyness was overcome, his behaviour gave every indication of an open affectionate heart"* (Jane Austen, *Sense and Sensibility*).

[Middle English, from Latin *diffīdēns, diffīdent-*, present participle of *diffīdere*, to mistrust : *dis-*, not, do the opposite of + *fīdere*, to trust.]

RELATED WORD:
     adverb—**dif′fi·dent·ly**

en·er·vate (ĕn′ər-vāt′)

transitive verb
     Past participle and past tense: **en·er·vat·ed**
     Present participle: **en·er·vat·ing**
     Third person singular present tense: **en·er·vates**

To weaken or destroy the strength or vitality of: *"What is the nature of the luxury which enervates and destroys nations?"* (Henry David Thoreau, *Walden*).

[Latin *ēnervāre, ēnervāt-* : *ē-, ex-*, out of, from + *nervus*, sinew.]

RELATED WORDS:
     noun—**en′er·va′tion** (ĕn′ər-vā′shən)
     adjective—**en′er·va′tive**
     noun—**en′er·va′tor**

🖉 **USAGE NOTE:** Sometimes people mistakenly use *enervate* to mean "to invigorate" or "to excite" by assuming that this word is

---

diffident / enfranchise　　　　　　　　**112**

a close cousin of *energize*. In fact, *enervate* means essentially the opposite. *Enervate* comes from Latin *nervus*, "sinew," and thus means "to cause to become 'out of muscle'," that is, "to weaken or deplete of strength." *Enervate* has no historical connection with *energize*.

19

en·fran·chise (ĕn-frăn′chīz′)

transitive verb
>Past participle and past tense: **en·fran·chised**
>Present participle: **en·fran·chis·ing**
>Third person singular present tense: **en·fran·chis·es**

1. To endow with the rights of citizenship, especially the right to vote: *Many people who were enfranchised were nonetheless unable to vote because of onerous poll taxes.* **2.** To free, as from slavery or bondage.

[Middle English *enfraunchisen*, from Old French *enfranchir, enfranchiss-*, to set free : *en-*, intensive prefix + *franchir*, to free (from *franc*, free).]

RELATED WORD:
>*noun* — **en·fran′chise′ment**

e·piph·a·ny (ĭ-pĭf′ə-nē)

noun

Plural: **e·piph·a·nies**

1. Epiphany a. A Christian feast celebrating the manifestation of the divine nature of Jesus to the Gentiles as represented by the Magi. **b.** January 6, on which date this feast is traditionally observed. **2.** A revelatory manifestation of a divine being. **3.** A sudden manifestation of the essence or meaning of something; a revelation: *"I experienced an epiphany, a spiritual flash that would change the way I viewed myself"* (Frank Maier, *Newsweek*).

[Middle English *epiphanie,* from Old French, from Late Latin *epiphania,* from Greek *epiphaneia,* manifestation, from *epiphainesthai,* to appear : *epi-,* forth + *phainein, phan-,* to show.]

RELATED WORD:

    adjective — **ep′i·phan′ic** (ĕp′ə-făn′ĭk)

21

e·qui·nox (ē′kwə-nŏks′ *or* ĕk′wə-nŏks′)

noun
    Plural: **e·qui·nox·es**

1. Either of the two times during a year when the sun crosses the celestial equator and when the length of day and night are approximately equal: *The vernal equinox occurs on March 20 or 21, and the autumnal equinox occurs on September 22 or 23.* **2.** Either of two points on the celestial sphere at which the ecliptic intersects the celestial equator.

[Middle English, from Old French *equinoxe*, from Medieval Latin *aequinoxium*, from Latin *aequinoctium* : *aequi-*, equal + *nox, noct-*, night.]

RELATED WORD:
    adjective — **e′qui·noc′tial** (ē′kwə-nŏk′shəl
            or ĕk′wə-nŏk′shəl)

22

eu·ro or **Eu·ro** (yŏor′ō)

noun
    Plural: **eu·ros** or **Eu·ros**

The basic unit of currency among members of the European Monetary Union: *Italy and France are two countries that have adopted the euro.*

[After *Europe*.]

ev·a·nes·cent (ĕv′ə-nĕs′ənt)

adjective

Vanishing or likely to vanish like vapor: *"Most certainly I shall find this thought a horrible vision—a maddening, but evanescent dream"* (Mary Wollstonecraft Shelley, *The Last Man*).

[From Latin *ēvānēscere*, to vanish : *ē-, ex-*, away + *vānēscere*, to disappear (from *vānus*, empty).]

RELATED WORDS:
> *verb* — **ev′a·nesce′** (ĕv′ə-nĕs′)
> *adverb* — **ev′a·nes′cent·ly**

ex·pur·gate (ĕk′spər-gāt′)

transitive verb
> Past participle and past tense: **ex·pur·gat·ed**
> Present participle: **ex·pur·gat·ing**
> Third person singular present tense: **ex·pur·gates**

To remove erroneous, vulgar, obscene, or otherwise objectionable material from (a book, for example) before publication: *The R-rated movie was expurgated before it was shown on network television.*

[Latin *expūrgāre, expūrgāt-*, to purify : *ex-*, intensive prefix + *pūrgāre*, to cleanse (from *pūrus*, pure).]

RELATED WORDS:
> *noun* — **ex′pur·ga′tion** (ĕk′spər-gā′shən)
> *noun* — **ex′pur·ga′tor**

25

fa·ce·tious (fə-sē**′**shəs)

adjective

Playfully jocular; humorous: *The employee's facetious remarks were not appreciated during the meeting.*

[French *facétieux*, from *facétie*, jest, from Latin *facētia*, from *facētus*, witty.]

RELATED WORDS:
> *adverb* — **fa·ce′tious·ly**
> *noun* — **fa·ce′tious·ness**

26

fat·u·ous (făch**′**ōō-əs)

adjective

Foolish or silly, especially in a smug or self-satisfied way: *"'Don't you like the poor lonely bachelor?' he yammered in a fatuous way"* (Sinclair Lewis, *Main Street*).

[From Latin *fatuus*.]

RELATED WORDS:
> *adverb* — **fat′u·ous·ly**
> *noun* — **fat′u·ous·ness**

feck·less (fĕk′lĭs)

adjective

1. Lacking purpose or vitality; feeble or ineffective: *"She glowered at the rows of feckless bodies that lay sprawled in the chairs"* (Willa Cather, *The Song of the Lark*). **2.** Careless and irresponsible: *The feckless student turned in yet another late paper.*

[Scots *feck*, effect + *-less*.]

RELATED WORDS:
   adverb — **feck′less·ly**
   noun — **feck′less·ness**

fi·du·ci·ar·y (fĭ-dōō′shē-ĕr′ē *or* fĭ-dōō′shə-rē *or* fī-dōō′shē-ĕr′ē *or* fī-dōō′shə-rē)

adjective

1a. Of or relating to a holding of something in trust for another. **b.** Of or being a trustee or trusteeship. **c.** Held in trust. **2.** Of or consisting of legal tender, especially paper currency, authorized by a government but not based on or convertible into gold or silver.

noun
   Plural: **fi·du·ci·ar·ies**

One, such as a company director, that has a special relation of trust, confidence, or responsibility in certain obligations to others.

[Latin *fīdūciārius*, from *fīdūcia*, trust, from *fīdere*, to trust.]

She was going to have a few things before she died. She realized that there were a great many trains dashing east and west on the face of the continent that night, and that they all carried young people who meant to have things. But the difference was that *she was going to get them!* That was all. Let people try to stop her! She glowered at the rows of **feckless** bodies that lay sprawled in the chairs. Let them try it once!

—Willa Cather,
The Song of the Lark

fil·i·bus·ter (fĭl'ə-bŭs'tər)

noun

1a. The use of obstructionist tactics, especially prolonged speechmaking, for the purpose of delaying legislative action. **b.** An instance of the use of such tactics: *The senator's filibuster lasted over 24 hours.* **2.** An adventurer who engages in a private military action in a foreign country.

verb

> Past participle and past tense: **fil·i·bus·tered**
> Present participle: **fil·i·bus·ter·ing**
> Third person singular present tense: **fil·i·bus·ters**

intransitive: **1.** To use obstructionist tactics in a legislative body. **2.** To take part in a private military action in a foreign country.

transitive: To use a filibuster against (a legislative measure, for example).

[From Spanish *filibustero*, freebooter, from French *flibustier*, from Dutch *vrijbuiter*, pirate, freebooter, from *vrijbuit*, plunder : *vrij*, free + *buit*, booty (from Middle Dutch *būte*, of Middle Low German origin).]

RELATED WORD:
> *noun* — **fil'i·bus'ter·er**

30

gam·ete (găm′ēt′ *or* gə-mēt′)

noun

A reproductive cell having the haploid number of chromosomes, especially a mature sperm or egg capable of fusing with a gamete of the opposite sex to produce the fertilized egg.

[New Latin *gameta*, from Greek *gametē*, wife, and *gametēs*, husband, from *gamein*, to marry, from *gamos*, marriage.]

RELATED WORD:
    adjective — **ga·met′ic** (gə-mĕt′ĭk)

31

gauche (gōsh)

adjective

Lacking grace or social polish; awkward or tactless: *"A good man often appears gauche simply because he does not take advantage of the myriad mean little chances of making himself look stylish"* (Iris Murdoch, *The Black Prince*).

[French, awkward, lefthanded, from Old French, from *gauchir*, to turn aside, walk clumsily, of Germanic origin.]

RELATED WORDS:
    adverb — **gauche′ly**
    noun — **gauche′ness**

ger·ry·man·der (jĕr′ē-măn′dər *or* gĕr′ē-măn′dər)

transitive verb

Past participle and past tense: **ger·ry·man·dered**
Present participle: **ger·ry·man·der·ing**
Third person singular present tense: **ger·ry·man·ders**

To divide (a geographic area) into voting districts so as to give unfair advantage to one party in elections.

noun

1. The act, process, or an instance of gerrymandering.
2. A district or configuration of districts differing widely in size or population because of gerrymandering.

[After Elbridge *Gerry* + *(sala)mander* (from the shape of an election district created while Gerry was governor of Massachusetts).]

WORD HISTORY: *"An official statement of the returns of voters for senators give[s] twenty nine friends of peace, and eleven gerrymanders."* So reported the May 12, 1813, edition of the *Massachusetts Spy.* A gerrymander sounds like a strange political beast, which it is, considered from a historical perspective. This beast was named by combining the word *salamander,* "a small lizardlike amphibian," with the last name of Elbridge Gerry, a former governor of Massachusetts. Gerry was immortalized in this word because an election district created by members of his party in 1812 looked like a salamander. The word is first recorded in April 1812 in reference to the creature or its caricature, but it soon came to mean not only "the action of shaping a district to gain political advantage" but also "any representative elected from such a district by that method." Within the same year, *gerrymander* was also recorded as a verb.

33

he·gem·o·ny (hĭ-jĕm′ə′nē *or* hĕj′ə-mō′nē)

noun
>   Plural: **he·gem·o·nies**

The predominant influence of a state, region, or group, over others: *The hegemony of communism in Eastern Europe crumbled in the late 1980s.*

[Greek *hēgemoniā*, from *hēgemōn*, leader, from *hēgeisthai*, to lead.]

RELATED WORDS:
>   *adjective*—**heg′e·mon′ic** (hĕj′ə-mŏn′ĭk)
>   *noun & adjective*—**he·gem′o·nist** (hə-jĕm′ə-nĭst)

🐾 **USAGE NOTE:** *Hegemony* may be stressed on either the first or second syllable. In a 1988 survey of the Usage Panel, 72 percent of the Panelists preferred the latter pronunciation.

34

he·mo·glob·in (hē′mə-glō′bĭn)

noun

The iron-containing pigment in red blood cells of vertebrates, consisting of about 6 percent heme and 94 percent globin. In vertebrates, hemoglobin carries oxygen from the lungs to the tissues of the body and carries carbon dioxide from the tissues to the lungs.

[Ultimately short for *hematinoglobulin* : *hematin*, a compound formed from hemoglobin (*hemato-*, blood, from Greek *haima,* blood + *-in*, chemical suffix) + *globulin*, a kind of protein (*globule*, from French, from Latin *globulus,* diminutive of *globus*, sphere + *-in*, chemical suffix).]

There is no safety in unlimited technological **hubris**, none in simple-minded trust of the Kremlin, and none in a confident affection for expanding thermonuclear arsenals.

— McGeorge Bundy,
   New York Times Magazine

ho·mo·ge·ne·ous (hō′mō-jē′nē-əs
or hō′mō-jēn′yəs)

adjective

1. Uniform in structure or composition: *"Although the Vietnamese in America were at first a homogenous group, in the course of five separate waves of immigration they have encompassed a diverse cross-section of Vietnamese society"* (Lowell Weiss, *Atlantic Monthly*). **2.** Of the same or similar nature or kind. **3.** *Mathematics* Consisting of terms of the same degree or elements of the same dimension.

[From Medieval Latin *homogeneus,* from Greek *homogenēs* : *homo-,* same + *genos,* kind.]

RELATED WORDS:
> *adverb* — **ho′mo·ge′ne·ous·ly**
> *noun* — **ho′mo·ge′ne·ous·ness**

hu·bris (hyoō′brĭs)

noun

Overbearing pride or presumption; arrogance: *"There is no safety in unlimited technological hubris"* (McGeorge Bundy, *New York Times Magazine*).

[Greek, excessive pride, wanton violence.]

RELATED WORDS:
> *adjective* — **hu·bris′tic** (hyoō-brĭs′tĭk)
> *adverb* — **hu·bris′tic·al·ly**

hy·pot·e·nuse (hī-pŏt′n-ōos)

noun

The side of a right triangle opposite the right angle: *"You cannot write a textbook of geometry without reference to a hypotenuse and triangles and a rectangular parallelepiped. You simply have to learn what those words mean or do without mathematics"* (Hendrick Van Loon, *The Story of Mankind*).

[Latin *hypotēnūsa*, from Greek *hupoteinousa*, from feminine present participle of *hupoteinein*, to stretch or extend under : *hupo-*, under + *teinein*, to stretch.]

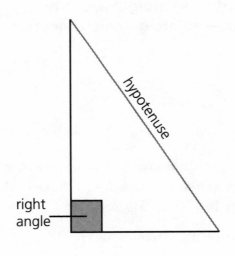

THE HYPOTENUSE
OF A RIGHT TRIANGLE

38

im·peach (ĭm-pēch′)

transitive verb
> Past participle and past tense: **im·peached**
> Present participle: **im·peach·ing**
> Third person singular present tense: **im·peach·es**

1a. To make an accusation against (a person). **b.** To charge (a public official) with improper conduct in office before a proper tribunal: *The House of Representatives impeached Andrew Johnson in 1868 and Bill Clinton in 1998; neither was convicted.* **2.** To challenge the validity of; try to discredit: *The lawyer impeached the witness's credibility with a string of damaging questions.*

[Middle English *empechen*, to impede, accuse, from Anglo-Norman *empecher*, from Late Latin *impedicāre*, to entangle : Latin *in-*, in + Latin *pedica*, fetter.]

RELATED WORDS:
> *adjective* — **im·peach′a·ble**
> *noun* — **im·peach′ment**

✍ **USAGE NOTE:** When an irate citizen demands that a disfavored public official be impeached, the citizen clearly intends for the official to be removed from office. This popular use of *impeach* as a synonym of "throw out" (even if by due process) does not accord with the legal meaning of the word. As recent history has shown, when a public official is impeached, that is, formally accused of wrongdoing, this is only the start of what can be a lengthy process that may or may not lead to the official's removal from office. In strict usage, an official is impeached (accused), tried, and then convicted or acquitted. The vaguer use of *impeach* reflects disgruntled citizens' indifference to whether the official is forced from office by legal means or chooses to resign to avoid further disgrace.

in·cog·ni·to (ĭn'kŏg-nē'tō)

adjective & adverb

With one's identity disguised or concealed: *The spy traveled incognito into enemy territory.*

noun
> Plural: **in·cog·ni·tos**

The identity assumed by a person whose actual identity is disguised or concealed.

[Italian, from Latin *incognitus*, unknown : *in-*, not + *cognitus*, past participle of *cognōscere*, to learn, recognize.]

in·con·tro·vert·i·ble (ĭn-kŏn'trə-vûr'tə-bəl *or* ĭn'kŏn-trə-vûr'tə-bəl)

adjective

Impossible to dispute; unquestionable: *The lawyer presented incontrovertible proof of her client's innocence.*

[*in-*, not + *controvertible*, able to be opposed by argument, from *controvert*, to oppose by argument, back-formation from *controversy* (on the model of such pairs as *inverse, invert*), from Middle English *controversie*, from Latin *contrōversia*, from *contrōversus*, disputed: *contrō-*, variant of *contrā-*, against + *versus*, past participle of *vertere*, to turn.]

RELATED WORDS:
> *noun*—**in·con'tro·vert'i·bil'i·ty**
> *adverb*—**in·con'tro·vert'i·bly**

41

in·cul·cate (ĭn-kŭl′kāt′ *or* ĭn′kŭl-kāt′)

transitive verb

Past participle and past tense: **in·cul·ca·ted**
Present participle: **in·cul·ca·ting**
Third person singular present tense: **in·cul·cates**

1. To impress (something) upon the mind of another by frequent instruction or repetition; instill: *"In the jungle might is right, nor does it take long to inculcate this axiom in the mind of a jungle dweller, regardless of what his past training may have been"* (Edgar Rice Burroughs, *The Son of Tarzan*). **2.** To teach (others) by frequent instruction or repetition; indoctrinate: *inculcate the young with a sense of duty.*

[Latin *inculcāre, inculcāt-*, to force upon : *in-*, on + *calcāre*, to trample (from *calx, calc-*, heel).]

RELATED WORDS:
    noun — **in′cul·ca′tion** (ĭn′kŭl-kā′shən)
    noun — **in·cul′ca′tor**

in·fra·struc·ture (ĭn′frə-strŭk′chər)

noun

1. The basic facilities, services, and installations needed for the functioning of a community or society, such as transportation and communications systems, water and power lines, and public institutions including schools, post offices, and prisons: *"To be fair, none of us really knows how much the country's infrastructure—services to the desperate underclass—had improved during the ten years from when we left until the Revolution"* (Terence Ward, *Searching for Hassan*). **2.** The basic system or underlying structure of an organization.

[*infra-*, below (from Latin *īnfrā*) + *structure* (from Middle English, the process of building, from Latin *strūctūra*, from *strūctus*, past participle of *struere*, to construct).]

Never in my life had I seen conditions as grim. To be fair, none of us really knows how much the country's **infrastructure** — services to the desperate underclass — had improved during the ten years from when we left until the Revolution. But one thing's certain. Whatever changes took place, it was too little, too late. Those forlorn dust heaps of villages, cut off from the world, with no medical facilities, no school, no decent roads to get goods to market. There seemed to be no hope at all.

— Terence Ward,
Searching for Hassan

in·ter·po·late (ĭn-tûr′pə-lāt′)

verb

Past participle and past tense: **in·ter·po·la·ted**
Present participle: **in·ter·po·la·ting**
Third person singular present tense: **in·ter·po·lates**

transitive: **1.** To insert or introduce between other elements or parts. **2a.** To insert (material) into a text. **b.** To insert into a conversation. **3.** To change or falsify (a text) with new or incorrect material. **4.** *Mathematics* To estimate a value of (a function or series) between two known values: *The researchers had actual statistics for the years 1998, 2000, and 2002, and they interpolated the values for 1999 and 2001.*

intransitive: To make insertions or additions.

[Latin *interpolāre, interpolāt-*, to touch up, refurbish, from *interpolis*, refurbished; akin to *polīre*, to polish.]

RELATED WORDS:
noun — **in·ter′po·la′tion** (ĭn-tûr′pə-lā′shən)
adjective — **in·ter′po·la′tive**
noun — **in·ter′po·la′tor**

i·ro·ny (ī′rə-nē *or* ī′ər-nē)

noun
Plural: **i·ro·nies**

1a. The use of words to express something different from and often opposite to their literal meaning. **b.** An expression or utterance marked by a deliberate contrast between apparent and intended meaning. **c.** A literary

---

style employing such contrasts for humorous or rhetorical effect. **2a.** Incongruity between what might be expected and what actually occurs. **b.** An occurrence, result, or circumstance notable for such incongruity. **3.** The dramatic effect achieved by leading an audience to understand an incongruity between a situation and the accompanying speeches, while the characters in the play remain unaware of the incongruity; dramatic irony.

[French *ironie*, from Old French, from Latin *īrōnīa*, from Greek *eirōneia*, feigned ignorance, from *eirōn*, dissembler, probably from *eirein*, to say.]

RELATED WORDS:

adjective — **i·ron′ic**

adverb — **i·ron′i·cal·ly**

🐾 **USAGE NOTE:** The words *ironic, irony,* and *ironically* are sometimes used of events and circumstances that might better be described as simply "coincidental" or "improbable," in that they suggest no particular lessons about human vanity or folly. The Usage Panel dislikes the looser use of these words; 78 percent reject the use of *ironically* in the sentence *In 1969 Susie moved from Ithaca to California where she met her husband-to-be, who, ironically, also came from upstate New York.* Some Panelists noted that this particular usage might be acceptable if Susie had in fact moved to California in order to find a husband, in which case the story could be taken as exemplifying the folly of supposing that we can know what fate has in store for us. By contrast, 73 percent accepted the sentence *Ironically, even as the government was fulminating against American policy, American jeans and videocassettes were the hottest items in the stalls of the market,* where the incongruity can be seen as an example of human inconsistency.

45

je·june (jə-jōōn′)

adjective

1. Not interesting; dull: *"Let a professor of law or physic find his place in a lecture room, and there pour forth jejune words and useless empty phrases, and he will pour them forth to empty benches"* (Anthony Trollope, *Barchester Towers*). **2.** Lacking maturity; childish: *The coach was dismayed at the players' jejune behavior after they won the game.* **3.** Lacking in nutrition: *The sickly child suffered from a jejune diet.*

[From Latin *iēiūnus*, meager, dry, fasting.]

RELATED WORDS:
> *adverb* — **je·june′ly**
> *noun* — **je·june′ness**

46

ki·net·ic (kə-nĕt′ĭk *or* kī-nĕt′ĭk)

adjective

1. Of, relating to, or produced by motion: *Any object that is moving has kinetic energy.* **2.** Relating to or exhibiting kinesis (movement or activity of an organism in response to a stimulus such as light).

[Greek *kīnētikos*, from *kīnētos*, moving, from *kīnein*, to move.]

RELATED WORD:
> *adverb* — **ki·net′i·cal·ly**

kow·tow (kou-tou′ *or* kou′tou′)

intransitive verb

> Past participle and past tense: **kow·towed**
> Present participle: **kow·tow·ing**
> Third person singular present tense: **kow·tows**

1. To kneel and touch the forehead to the ground in expression of deep respect, worship, or submission, as formerly done in China. **2.** To show servile deference: *Because everyone on staff was afraid of being laid off, they all kowtowed to their strict boss.*

noun

1. The act of kneeling and touching the forehead to the ground: *"We were always greeted in a grassy area near the headmen's fortresses, where tents were pitched especially for me to receive kowtows, enjoy good food, and watch singing and dancing"* (Alai, *Red Poppies*). **2.** An obsequious act.

[From Chinese (Mandarin) *kòu tóu* : *kòu*, to knock + *tóu*, head.]

48

lais·sez faire also **lais·ser faire**

(lĕs′ā fâr′ *or* lā′zā fâr′)

noun

1. An economic doctrine that opposes governmental regulation of or interference in commerce beyond the minimum necessary for a free-enterprise system to operate according to its own economic laws. **2.** Noninterference in the affairs of others.

[French : *laissez,* second person plural imperative of *laisser,* to let, allow (from Latin *laxāre,* to loosen, from *laxus,* loose) + *faire,* to do (from Latin *facere*).]

49

lex·i·con (lĕk′sĭ-kŏn′)

noun
    Plural: **lex·i·cons** or **lex·i·ca** (lĕk′sĭ-kə′)

1. A dictionary. **2.** A stock of terms used in a particular profession, subject, or style; a vocabulary: *The lexicon of anatomy includes terms such as "aorta" and "duodenum."*

[Medieval Latin, from Greek *lexikon (biblion),* word (book), neuter of *lexikos,* of words, from *lexis,* word, from *legein,* to speak.]

RELATED WORDS:
    adjective—**lex′i·cal**
    adverb—**lex′i·cal·ly**

50

lo·qua·cious (lō-kwā′shəs)

adjective

Very talkative; garrulous: *The loquacious barber always told stories while cutting the customers' hair.*

[From Latin *loquāx, loquāc-*, from *loquī*, to speak.]

RELATED WORDS:
    adverb — **lo·qua′cious·ly**
    noun — **lo·qua′cious·ness**
    noun — **lo·quac′i·ty** (lō-kwăs′ĭ-tē)

51

lu·gu·bri·ous (lo͞o-go͞o′brē-əs)

adjective

Mournful, dismal, or gloomy, especially to an exaggerated or ludicrous degree: *"This croak was as lugubrious as a coffin"* (Stephen Crane, *The Sergeant's Private Madhouse*).

[From Latin *lūgubris*, from *lūgēre*, to mourn.]

RELATED WORDS:
    adverb — **lu·gu′bri·ous·ly**
    noun — **lu·gu′bri·ous·ness**

met·a·mor·pho·sis (mĕt′ə-môr′fə-sĭs)

noun

Plural: **met·a·mor·pho·ses** (mĕt′ə-môr′fə-sēz′)

1. A marked change in appearance, character, condition, or function; a transformation: "*I sought out the myths of metamorphosis, tales of the weaver Arachne, who hanged herself and was changed by Athena into a spider*" (Jennifer Ackerman, *Chance in the House of Fate*). **2.** *Biology* Change in the form and often habits of an animal during normal development after the embryonic stage. Metamorphosis includes, in insects, the transformation of a maggot into an adult fly and a caterpillar into a butterfly, and, in amphibians, the changing of a tadpole into a frog.

[Latin *metamorphōsis*, from Greek, from *metamorphoun*, to transform : *meta-*, meta- + *morphē*, form.]

RELATED WORDS:
   adjective— **met′a·mor′phic** (mĕt′ə-môr′fĭk)
   verb— **met′a·mor′phose** (mĕt′ə-môr′fōz′ *or*
      mĕt′ə-môr′fōs′)
   adjective— **met′a·mor′phous**
      (mĕt′ə-môr′fəs)

53
mi·to·sis (mī-tō′sĭs)

noun
Plural: **mi·to·ses** (mī-tō′sēz)

The process in cell division by which the nucleus divides, typically consisting of four stages, prophase, metaphase, anaphase, and telophase, and normally resulting in two new nuclei, each of which contains a complete copy of the parental chromosomes. Division of the cytoplasm follows the division of the nucleus, resulting in the formation of two distinct cells.

[Greek *mitos*, warp thread + *-ōsis*, condition.]

RELATED WORDS:
adjective—**mi·tot′ic** (mī-tŏt′ĭk)
adverb—**mi·tot′i·cal·ly**

54
moi·e·ty (moi′ĭ-tē)

noun
Plural: **moi·e·ties**

1. A half: *"Tom divided the cake and Becky ate with good appetite, while Tom nibbled at his moiety"* (Mark Twain, *The Adventures of Tom Sawyer*). **2.** A part, portion, or share. **3.** Either of two kinship groups based on unilateral descent that together make up a tribe or society.

[Middle English *moite*, from Old French *meitiet, moitie*, from Late Latin *medietās*, from Latin, the middle, from *medius*, middle.]

nan·o·tech·nol·o·gy (năn′ə-tĕk-nŏl′ə-jē)

noun

The science and technology of building devices, such as electronic circuits, from individual atoms and molecules.

[*nano-*, at the molecular level (from Greek *nānos, nannos,* little old man, dwarf, from *nannās,* uncle) + *technology* (Greek *tekhnē,* art, skill + Greek *-logiā,* study, from *logos,* word).]

RELATED WORD:
    noun — nan′o·tech·nol′o·gist

ni·hil·ism (nī′ə-lĭz′əm *or* nē′ə-lĭz′əm)

noun

1. *Philosophy* **a.** An extreme form of skepticism that denies that existence is real: "*Nihilism is not only despair and negation, but above all the desire to despair and to negate*" (Albert Camus, *The Rebel*). **b.** The belief that all values are baseless and that nothing can be known or communicated. **2.** The rejection of all distinctions in moral or religious value and a willingness to repudiate all previous theories of morality or religious belief. **3.** The belief that destruction of existing political or social institutions is necessary for future improvement. **4.** also **Nihilism** A movement of mid-19th-century Russia that scorned authority and believed in reason, materialism, and radical change in society through terrorism and assassination. **5.** *Psychology* A delusion that the world or one's mind, body, or self does not exist.

[Latin *nihil*, nothing + *-ism.*]

RELATED WORDS:
    noun—**ni′hi·list**
    adjective—**ni′hi·lis′tic**
    adverb—**ni′hi·lis′ti·cal·ly**

no·men·cla·ture (nō′mən-klā′chər
or nō-mĕn′klə-chər)

noun

1. A system of names used in an art or science: *The nomenclature of mineralogy is a classification of types of rock.* **2.** The procedure of assigning names to organisms listed in a taxonomic classification: *Our biology teacher explained the rules of nomenclature for plants and animals.*

[Latin *nōmenclātūra*, from *nōmenclātor*, nomenclator, a slave who accompanied his master to tell him the names of people he met, variant of *nōmenculātor* : *nōmen*, name + *calātor*, servant, crier (from *calāre*, to call).]

non·sec·tar·i·an (nŏn′sĕk-târ′ē-ən)

adjective

Not limited to or associated with a particular religious denomination: *The airport chapel conducts nonsectarian services daily.*

[*non-*, not (from Middle English, from Old French, from Latin *nōn*) + *sectarian*, partisan (*sect*, sect, ultimately from Latin *sequī*, to follow + *-arian*, belonging to).]

RELATED WORD:
  noun—**non′sec·tar′i·an·ism**

59

no·ta·rize (nō′tə-rīz′)

transitive verb
> Past participle and past tense: **no·ta·rized**
> Present participle: **no·ta·riz·ing**
> Third person singular present tense: **no·ta·riz·es**

To certify or attest to (the validity of a signature on a document, for example) as a notary public: *Before I submitted the sales agreement at the real estate office, it had to be notarized.*

[*notar(y)* (from Middle English *notarie*, from Old French, from Latin *notārius*, relating to shorthand, shorthand writer, from *nota*, mark) + *-ize*.]

RELATED WORD:
> *noun*—**no′ta·ri·za′tion** (nō′tə-rĭ-zā′shən)

60

ob·se·qui·ous
> (ŏb-sē′kwē-əs *or* əb-sē′kwē-əs)

adjective

Full of or exhibiting servile compliance; fawning: *The movie star was surrounded by a large group of obsequious assistants.*

[Middle English, from Latin *obsequiōsus*, from *obsequium*, compliance, from *obsequī*, to comply : *ob-*, to; + *sequī*, to follow.]

RELATED WORDS:
> *adverb*—**ob·se′qui·ous·ly**
> *noun*—**ob·se′qui·ous·ness**

For they that are discontented under monarchy call it tyranny; and they that are displeased with aristocracy call it **oligarchy**: so also, they which find themselves grieved under a democracy call it anarchy.

— Thomas Hobbes,
Leviathan

ol·i·gar·chy (ŏl′ĭ-gär′kē *or* ō′lĭ-gär′kē)

noun
    Plural: **ol·i·gar·chies**

1a. Government by a few, especially by a small faction of persons or families: *"They that are displeased with aristocracy call it oligarchy"* (Thomas Hobbes, *Leviathan*). **b.** Those making up such a government. **2.** A state governed by a few persons.

[*olig(o)*-, few (from Greek *oligos*, little) + *-archy*, rule (from Greek *-arkhiā*, from *arkhein*, to rule).]

RELATED WORDS:
    adjective—**ol′i·gar′chic** (ŏl′ĭ-gär′kĭk
       or ō′lĭ-gär′kĭk)
    adjective—**ol′i·gar′chic·al**

62

om·nip·o·tent (ŏm-nĭp′ə-tənt)

adjective

Having unlimited or universal power, authority, or force; all-powerful: *"I began to instruct him in the knowledge of the true God . . . that He was omnipotent, and could do everything for us, give everything to us, take everything from us"* (Daniel Defoe, *Robinson Crusoe*).

noun

the Omnipotent God.

[Middle English, from Old French, from Latin *omnipotēns, omnipotent-* : *omni-,* all + *potēns,* present participle of *posse,* to be able.]

RELATED WORDS:
> *noun* — **om·nip′o·tence**
> *noun* — **om·nip′o·ten·cy**
> *adverb* — **om·nip′o·tent·ly**

or·thog·ra·phy (ôr-thŏg′rə-fē)

noun

Plural: **or·thog·ra·phies**

1. The art or study of correct spelling according to established usage. **2.** The aspect of language study concerned with letters and their sequences in words. **3.** A
method of representing a language or the sounds of
language by written symbols; spelling: *The orthography
of Spanish includes the letters í and ñ.*

[*ortho-*, straight, correct (from Greek *orthos*) + *-graphy*,
writing (from Greek *-graphiā*, from *graphein*, to write).]

RELATED WORDS:
>   *noun* — **or·thog′ra·pher**
>   *noun* — **or·thog′ra·phist**
>   *adjective* — **or′tho·graph′ic** (ôr′thə-grăf′ĭk)
>   *adverb* — **or′tho·graph′i·cal·ly**

64

ox·i·dize (ŏk′sĭ-dīz′)

verb

> Past participle and past tense: **ox·i·dized**
> Present participle: **ox·i·diz·ing**
> Third person singular present tense: **ox·i·diz·es**

transitive **1.** To combine with oxygen; make into an oxide: *The metal fender had begun to oxidize, as evidenced by the large rust stains.* **2.** To increase the positive charge or valence of (an element) by removing electrons. **3.** To coat with oxide.

intransitive To become oxidized.

[*oxid(e)*, compound containing oxygen (from French : *ox(ygène)*, oxygen + *(ac)ide*, acid) + *-ize.*]

RELATED WORDS:
> *adjective*— **ox′i·di′za·ble**
> *noun*— **ox′i·di·za′tion** (ŏk′sĭ-dĭ-zā′shən)

---

pa·rab·o·la (pə-răb′ə-lə)

noun

A plane curve formed by the intersection of a right circular cone and a plane parallel to an element of the cone or by the locus of points equidistant from a fixed line and a fixed point not on the line.

[New Latin, from Greek *parabolē*, comparison, application, parabola (from the relationship between the line joining the vertices of a conic and the line through its focus and parallel to its directrix), from *paraballein*, to compare : *para-*, beside + *ballein*, to throw.]

RELATED WORD:

adjective— **par′a·bol′ic** (păr′ə-bŏl′ĭk)

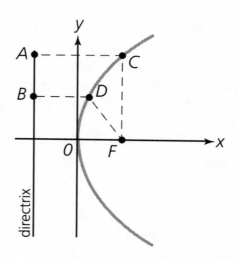

PARABOLA

Any point on a parabola is the same distance from the directrix as it is from the focus. *AC = CF* and *BD = DF.*

par·a·digm (păr′ə-dīm′ *or* păr′ə-dĭm′)

noun

1. One that serves as pattern or model. **2.** A set or list of all the inflectional forms of a word or of one of its grammatical categories: *The Latin textbook outlined the paradigms of the different sets of regular verbs.* **3.** A set of assumptions, concepts, values, and practices that constitutes a way of viewing reality for the community that shares them, especially in an intellectual discipline.

[Middle English, example, from Late Latin *paradīgma*, from Greek *paradeigma*, from *paradeiknunai*, to compare : *para-*, alongside + *deiknunai*, to show.]

RELATED WORD:

adjective— **par′a·dig·mat′ic** (păr′ə-dĭg-măt′ĭk)

🖋 **USAGE NOTE:** *Paradigm* first appeared in English in the 15th century, meaning "an example or pattern," and it still bears this meaning today: *Their company is a paradigm of small high-tech firms.* For nearly 400 years *paradigm* has also been applied to the patterns of inflections that are used to sort the verbs, nouns, and other parts of speech of a language into groups that are more easily studied. Since the 1960s, *paradigm* has been used in science to refer to a theoretical framework, as when Nobel Laureate David Baltimore cited colleagues' work that "*really established a new paradigm for our understanding of the causation of cancer.*" Thereafter, researchers in many different fields, including sociology and literary criticism, often saw themselves as working in or trying to break out of paradigms. Applications of the term in other contexts show that it can sometimes be used more loosely to mean "the prevailing view of things." In a 1994 Usage Panel survey, the Panelists split down the middle on these nonscientific uses of *paradigm*. Fifty-two percent disapproved of the sentence *The paradigm governing international competition and competitiveness has shifted dramatically in the last three decades.*

Paradigm of present tense Spanish verbs
with infinitives ending in -AR

-o	-amos
-as	-áis
-a	-an

hablar — to speak

First person singular:	*habl**o***
Second person singular:	*habl**as***
Third person singular:	*habl**a***

First person plural:	*habl**amos***
Second person plural:	*habl**áis***
Third person plural:	*habl**an***

pa·ram·e·ter (pə-răm′ĭ-tər)

noun

1. *Mathematics* **a.** A constant in an equation that varies in other equations of the same general form, especially such a constant in the equation of a curve or surface that can be varied to represent a family of curves or surfaces. **b.** One of a set of independent variables that express the coordinates of a point. **2a.** One of a set of measurable factors, such as temperature and pressure, that define a system and determine its behavior and are varied in an experiment. **b.** *(Usage Problem)* A factor that restricts what is possible or what results. **c.** A factor that determines a range of variations; a boundary: *The principal of the experimental school made sure that the parameters of its curriculum continued to expand.* **3.** *Statistics* A quantity, such as a mean, that is calculated from data and describes a population. **4.** *(Usage Problem)* A distinguishing characteristic or feature.

[New Latin *parametrum*, a line through the focus and parallel to the directrix of a conic : Greek *para-*, beside + Greek *metron*, measure.]

RELATED WORDS:
> *verb*— **pa·ram′e·ter·ize′** (pə-răm′ə-tə-rīz′)
> *adjective*— **par′a·met′ric** (păr′ə-mĕt′rĭk)
> *adjective*— **par′a·met′ri·cal**
> *adverb*— **par′a·met′ri·cal·ly**

✍ **USAGE NOTE:** The term *parameter*, which originates in mathematics, has a number of specific meanings in fields such as astronomy, electricity, crystallography, and statistics. Perhaps because of its ring of technical authority, it has been used more generally in recent years to refer to any factor that determines a range of variations and especially to a factor that restricts what

---

can result from a process or policy. In this use it often comes close to meaning "a limit or boundary." Some of these new uses have a clear connection to the technical senses of the word. For example, the provisions of a zoning ordinance that limit the height or density of new construction can be reasonably likened to mathematical parameters that establish the limits of other variables. Therefore one can say *The zoning commission announced new planning parameters for the historic district of the city.* But other uses go one step further and treat *parameter* as a high-toned synonym for *characteristic.* In the 1988 Usage Panel Survey, 80 percent of Panelists rejected this use of *parameter* in the example *The Judeo-Christian ethic is one of the important parameters of Western culture.*

Some of the difficulties with the nontechnical use of *parameter* appear to arise from its resemblance to the word *perimeter,* with which it shares the sense "limit," though the precise meanings of the two words differ. This confusion probably explains the use of *parameter* in a sentence such as *US forces report that the parameters of the mine area in the Gulf are fairly well established,* where the word *perimeter* would have expressed the intended sense more exactly. This example of a use of *parameter* was unacceptable to 61 percent of the Usage Panel.

There had come an improvement in their **pecuniary** position, which earlier in their experience would have made them cheerful. Jude had quite unexpectedly found good employment at his old trade almost directly he arrived, the summer weather suiting his fragile constitution; and outwardly his days went on with that monotonous uniformity which is in itself so grateful after vicissitude.

— Thomas Hardy,
Jude the Obscure

pe·cu·ni·ar·y (pĭ-kyōō′nē-ĕr′ē)

adjective

1. Of or relating to money: *"There had come an improvement in their pecuniary position, which earlier in their experience would have made them cheerful"* (Thomas Hardy, *Jude the Obscure*). **2.** Requiring payment of money: *A speeding ticket is generally a pecuniary offense.*

[Latin *pecūniārius*, from *pecūnia*, property, wealth, money.]

RELATED WORD:
> *adverb* — **pe·cu′ni·ar′i·ly**

pho·to·syn·the·sis (fō′tō-sĭn′thĭ-sĭs)

noun

The process by which green plants and certain other organisms synthesize carbohydrates from carbon dioxide and water using light as an energy source. Most forms of photosynthesis release oxygen as a byproduct.

[*photo-*, light (from Greek *phōto-*, from *phōs*, *phōt-*) + *synthesis*, the building of chemical compounds (from Latin, collection, from Greek *sunthesis*, from *suntithenai*, to put together : *sun-*, with, together + *tithenai*, *the-*, to put).]

RELATED WORDS:
> *verb* — **pho′to·syn′the·size′**
> (fō′tō-sĭn′thĭ-sīz′)
> *adjective* — **pho′to·syn·thet′ic**
> (fō′tō-sĭn-thĕt′ĭk)
> *adverb* — **pho′to·syn·thet′i·cal·ly**

pla·gia·rize (plā′jə-rīz′)

verb

Past participle and past tense: **pla·gia·rized**
Present participle: **pla·gia·riz·ing**
Third person singular present tense: **pla·gia·riz·es**

transitive **1.** To use and pass off (the ideas or writings of another) as one's own: *Gina plagiarized a science website by cutting and pasting large portions of its text into her paper.* **2.** To appropriate for use as one's own passages or ideas from (another): *Because Darren plagiarized Charles Dickens, the teacher could easily determine that he had cheated.*

intransitive To put forth as original to oneself the ideas or words of another: *Our teacher's policy is to fail any student who plagiarizes.*

[From Latin *plagiārius*, kidnapper, one who plagiarizes, from *plagium*, kidnapping, from *plaga*, net.]

RELATED WORD:
    noun— **pla′gia·riz′er**

---

plas·ma (plăz′mə) also **plasm** (plăz′əm)

noun

1. The clear yellowish fluid portion of blood or lymph in which cells are suspended. It differs from serum in that it contains fibrin and other soluble clotting elements. **2.** Blood plasma that has been sterilized and from which all cells have been removed, used in transfusions. **3.** The protoplasm or cytoplasm of a cell. **4.** The fluid portion of milk from which the curd has been separated by coagulation; whey. **5.** An electrically neutral state of matter similar to a gas but consisting of positively charged ions with most or all of their detached electrons moving freely about. Plasmas are produced by very high temperatures, as in the sun, and also by the ionization resulting from exposure to an electric current, as in a neon sign. Plasmas are distinct from solids, liquids, and normal gases.

[New Latin, from Late Latin, image, figure, from Greek, from *plassein*, to mold.]

RELATED WORDS:
      adjective— **plas·mat′ic** (plăz-măt′ĭk)
      adjective— **plas′mic** (plăz′mĭk)

72

pol·y·mer (pŏl′ə-mər)

noun

Any of numerous natural or synthetic compounds of usually high molecular weight consisting of repeated linked units, each a relatively light and simple molecule: *Some polymers, like cellulose, occur naturally, while others, like nylon, are artificial.*

[Greek *polumerēs*, consisting of many parts : *polu-*, many- + *meros*, part.]

73

pre·cip·i·tous (prĭ-sĭp′ĭ-təs)

adjective

1. Resembling a precipice; extremely steep. **2.** Having several precipices: *The hikers avoided the trail through the precipitous areas of the park.* **3.** *(Usage Problem)* Extremely rapid or abrupt; precipitate.

[Probably from obsolete *precipitious*, from Latin *praecipitium*, precipice, from *praeceps, praecipit-*, headlong : *prae-*, before, in front + *caput, capit-*, head.]

RELATED WORDS:
>   *adverb* — **pre·cip′i·tous·ly**
>   *noun* — **pre·cip′i·tous·ness**

☙ **USAGE NOTE:** The adjective *precipitate* and the adverb *precipitately* were once applied to physical steepness but are now used primarily of rash, headlong actions: *Their precipitate entry into the foreign markets led to disaster. He withdrew precipitately from the race.* Precipitous currently means "steep" in both literal and figurative senses: *the precipitous rapids of the upper river; a precipitous drop in commodity prices.* But *precipitous* and *precipi-*

tously are also frequently used to mean "abrupt, hasty," which takes them into territory that would ordinarily belong to *precipitate* and *precipitately*: *their precipitous decision to leave.* This usage is a natural extension of the use of *precipitous* to describe a rise or fall in a quantity over time: *a precipitous increase in reports of measles* is also an abrupt or sudden event. Though this extended use of *precipitous* is well attested in the work of reputable writers, it is still widely regarded as an error.

74

qua·sar (kwā′sär′)

noun

An extremely distant, and thus old, celestial object whose power output is several thousand times that of the entire Milky Way galaxy. Some quasars are more than ten billion light years away from earth.

[*quas(i-stellar)* + *(st)ar.*]

quo·tid·i·an (kwō-tĭd′ē-ən)

adjective

Commonplace or ordinary, as from everyday experience: *"There's nothing quite like a real ... train conductor to add color to a quotidian commute"* (Anita Diamant, *Boston Magazine*).

[Middle English *cotidien*, from Old French, from Latin *quōtīdiānus*, from *quōtīdiē*, each day : *quot*, how many, as many as + *diē*, ablative of *diēs*, day.]

re·ca·pit·u·late (rē′kə-pĭch′ə-lāt′)

verb

Past participle and past tense: **re·ca·pit·u·lat·ed**
Present participle: **re·ca·pit·u·lat·ing**
Third person singular present tense: **re·ca·pit·u·lates**

transitive **1.** To repeat in concise form: "*Uninitiated readers can approach this bewitching new rogue's tale as if nothing had happened. Whatever took place previously is recapitulated, now bathed in the warm light of memory*" (Janet Maslin, *New York Times*). **2.** *Biology* To appear to repeat (the evolutionary stages of the species) during the embryonic development of the individual organism.

intransitive To make a summary: *At the end of my presentation about the solar system, the teacher asked me to recapitulate.*

[Latin *recapitulāre, recapitulāt-* : *re-*, again + *capitulum*, main point, heading, diminutive of *caput, capit-*, head.]

RELATED WORDS:

noun — **re′ca·pit′u·la′tion**
(rē′kə-pĭch′ə-lā′shən)
adjective — **re′ca·pit′u·la′tive**
adjective — **re′ca·pit′u·la·to′ry**

re·cip·ro·cal (rĭ-sĭp′rə-kəl)

adjective

1. Existing, done, or experienced on both sides: *The two chess players showed reciprocal respect throughout the match.* **2.** Done, given, felt, or owed in return: *After hearing the emcee's kind remark, the guest of honor felt obliged to make a reciprocal compliment.* **3.** Interchangeable; complementary: *The hardware store stocks reciprocal electric outlets.* **4.** *Grammar* Expressing mutual action or relationship. Used of some verbs and compound pronouns. **5.** *Mathematics* Of or relating to the reciprocal of a quantity. **6.** *Physiology* Of or relating to a neuromuscular phenomenon in which the inhibition of one group of muscles accompanies the excitation of another. **7.** *Genetics* Of or being a pair of crosses in which the male or female parent in one cross is of the same genotype or phenotype as the complementary female or male parent in the other cross.

noun

1. Something that is reciprocal to something else. **2.** *Mathematics* A number related to another in such a way that when multiplied together their product is 1. For example, the reciprocal of 7 is 1/7; the reciprocal of 2/3 is 3/2.

[From Latin *reciprocus*, alternating.]

RELATED WORDS:

    noun—**re·cip′ro·cal′i·ty**
    adverb—**re·cip′ro·cal·ly**
    noun—**rec′i·proc′i·ty** (rĕs′ə-prŏs′ĭ-tē)

78

rep·a·ra·tion (rĕp′ə-rā′shən)

noun

1. The act or process of making amends for a wrong. **2.** Something done or money paid to compensate or make amends for a wrong. **3. reparations** Compensation or remuneration required from a defeated nation as indemnity for damage or injury during a war. **4.** The act or process of repairing or the condition of being repaired.

[Middle English *reparacion*, from Old French, from Late Latin *reparātiō*, *reparātiōn-*, restoration, from Latin *reparātus*, past participle of *reparāre*, to repair : *re-*, again + *parāre*, to prepare.]

res·pi·ra·tion (rĕs′pə-rā′shən)

noun

1a. The act or process of inhaling and exhaling; breathing: *"Every sudden emotion, including astonishment, quickens the action of the heart, and with it the respiration"* (Charles Darwin, *The Expression of the Emotions in Man and Animal*). **b.** The act or process by which an organism without lungs, such as a fish or a plant, exchanges gases with its environment. **2a.** The oxidative process in living cells by which the chemical energy of organic molecules is released in metabolic steps involving the consumption of oxygen and the liberation of carbon dioxide and water. **b.** Any of various analogous metabolic processes by which certain organisms, such as fungi and anaerobic bacteria, obtain energy from organic molecules.

[Latin *respīrātiō, respīrātiōn-*, from *respīrātus*, past participle of *respīrāre*, to breathe again : *re-*, again + *spīrāre*, to breathe.]

RELATED WORDS:
> *adjective*— **re′spi·ra′tion·al**
> *adverb*— **re′spi·ra′tion·al·ly**
> *verb*— **re·spire′** (rĭ-spīr′)

Every sudden emotion, including astonishment, quickens the action of the heart, and with it the **respiration**.

— Charles Darwin,
  *The Expression of the Emotions
  in Man and Animal*

san·guine (săng′gwĭn)

adjective

1. Cheerfully confident; optimistic: *"Haggard and red-eyed, his hopes plainly had deserted him, his sanguine mood was gone, and all his worst misgivings had come back"* (Charles Dickens, *The Mystery of Edwin Drood*). **2a.** In medieval physiology, having blood as the dominant humor. **b.** Having the temperament and ruddy complexion once thought to be characteristic of this humor; passionate. **3a.** Of the color of blood; red: *"This fellow here, with envious carping tongue / Up-braided me about the rose I wear / Saying the sanguine colour of the leaves / Did represent my master's blushing cheeks"* (William Shakespeare, *Henry VI, Part I*). **b.** Of a healthy reddish color; ruddy: *Because he worked out-doors, the farmer had a sanguine complexion.*

[Middle English, from Old French *sanguin*, from Latin *sanguineus*, from *sanguis, sanguin-*, blood.]

RELATED WORDS:

    adverb — **san′guine·ly**
    noun — **san′guine·ness**
    noun — **san·guin′i·ty**

WORD HISTORY: The similarity in form between *sanguine*, "cheerfully optimistic," and *sanguinary*, "bloodthirsty," may prompt one to wonder how they have come to have such different meanings. The explanation lies in medieval physiology with its notion of the four humors or bodily fluids (blood, bile, phlegm, and black bile). The relative proportions of these fluids was thought to determine a person's temperament. If blood was the predominant humor, one had a ruddy face and a disposition marked by courage, hope, and a readiness to fall in love. Such a temperament was called *sanguine,* the Middle English ancestor of our word *sanguine.* The source of the Middle English word was Old French *sanguin,* itself from Latin *sanguineus.* Both the Old French and Latin words meant "bloody," "blood-colored," Old French *sanguin* having the sense "sanguine in temperament" as well. Latin *sanguineus* was in turn derived from *sanguis,* "blood," just as English *sanguinary* is. The English adjective *sanguine,* first recorded in Middle English before 1350, continues to refer to the cheerfulness and optimism that accompanied a sanguine temperament but no longer has any direct reference to medieval physiology.

so·lil·o·quy (sə-lĭl′ə-kwē)

noun
> Plural: **so·lil·o·quies**

1. A dramatic or literary form of discourse in which a character talks to himself or herself or reveals his or her thoughts when alone or unaware of the presence of other characters: *Shakespeare employs soliloquy in most of his plays.* **2.** A specific speech or piece of writing in this form of discourse: *"To be or not to be" is the beginning of a famous soliloquy in* Hamlet.

[Late Latin *sōliloquium* : Latin *sōlus*, alone + Latin *loquī*, to speak.]

RELATED WORDS:
> *noun* — **so·lil′o·quist** (sə-lĭl′ə-kwĭst)
> *verb* — **so·lil′o·quize** (sə-lĭl′ə-kwīz′)
> *noun* — **so·lil′o·quiz′er** (sə-lĭl′ə-kwī′zər)

82

sub·ju·gate (sŭb′jə-gāt′)

transitive verb
> Past participle and past tense: **sub·ju·gat·ed**
> Present participle: **sub·ju·gat·ing**
> Third person singular present tense: **sub·ju·gates**

1. To bring under control; conquer: *The intention of the conquistadors was to subjugate the peoples of the New World.* **2.** To make subservient or submissive; subdue: *The new owners subjugated the defiant workers by threatening layoffs.*

[Middle English *subjugaten*, from Latin *subiugāre*, *subiugāt-* : *sub-*, under + *iugum*, yoke.]

RELATED WORDS:
> *noun*— **sub′ju·ga′tion** (sŭb′jə-gā′shən)
> *noun*— **sub′ju·ga′tor** (sŭb′jə-gā′tər)

83

suf·fra·gist (sŭf′rə-jĭst)

noun

An advocate of the extension of political voting rights, especially to women: *Tireless suffragists worked to ensure the passage of the Nineteenth Amendment in 1920.*

[*suffrag(e)* (ultimately from Latin *suffrāgium*, the right to vote, from *suffrāgārī*, to express support : *sub-*, under, in support of + *frāgārī*, to vote) + *-ist.*]

RELATED WORD:
> *noun*— **suf′fra·gism** (sŭf′rə-jĭz′əm)

84

su·per·cil·i·ous (soō′pər-sĭl′ē-əs)

adjective

Feeling or showing haughty disdain: *"Assuming his most supercilious air of distant superiority, he planted himself, immovable as a noble statue, upon the hearth, as if a stranger to the whole set"* (Fanny Burney, *Dr. Johnson and Fanny Burney*).

[Latin *superciliōsus*, from *supercilium*, eyebrow, pride : *super*, above + *cilium*, lower eyelid.]

RELATED WORDS:
    adverb—**su′per·cil′i·ous·ly**
    noun—**su′per·cil′i·ous·ness**

85

tau·tol·o·gy (tô-tŏl′ə-jē)

noun
    Plural: **tau·tol·o·gies**

1a. Needless repetition of the same sense in different words; redundancy. **b.** An instance of such repetition. **2.** *Logic* An empty or vacuous statement composed of simpler statements in a fashion that makes it logically true whether the simpler statements are factually true or false; for example, *Either it will rain tomorrow or it will not rain tomorrow.*

[Late Latin *tautologia*, from Greek *tautologiā*, from *tautologos*, redundant : *tauto-*, the same + *legein*, to say.]

RELATED WORDS:
    adjective—**tau′to·log′i·cal** (tôt′l-ŏj′ĭ-kəl)
    adverb—**tau′to·log′i·cal·ly**

---

tax·on·o·my (tăk-sŏn′ə-mē)

noun
Plural: **tax·on·o·mies**

1. The classification of organisms in an ordered system that indicates natural relationships. **2.** The science, laws, or principles of classification; systematics. **3.** Division into ordered groups or categories.

[French *taxonomie* : Greek *taxis*, arrangement + *-nomie*, method (from Greek *-nomiā*, from *nomos*, law).]

RELATED WORDS:
adjective— **tax′o·nom′ic** (tăk′sə-nŏm′ĭk)
adverb— **tax′o·nom′i·cal·ly**
noun— **tax·on′o·mist** (tăk-sŏn′ə-mĭst)

tec·ton·ic (tĕk-tŏn′ĭk)

adjective

1. Of or relating to the forces involved in forming the geological features, such as mountains, continents, and oceans, of the earth's lithosphere. The processes of plate tectonics, such as mountain building, are tectonic events. **2a.** Relating to construction or building. **2b.** Architectural.

[Late Latin *tectonicus*, from Greek *tektonikos*, from *tektōn*, builder.]

RELATED WORD:
adverb— **tec·ton′i·cal·ly**

88

tem·pes·tu·ous (tĕm-pĕs′chŏō-əs)

adjective

1. Of, relating to, or resembling a tempest: *"The 31st of January was a wild, tempestuous day: there was a strong north wind, with a continual storm of snow drifting on the ground and whirling through the air"* (Anne Brontë, *Agnes Grey*). **2.** Characterized by violent emotions or actions; tumultuous; stormy: *"For perhaps the first time in her life she thought of him as a man, young, unhappy, tempestuous, full of desires and faults"* (Virginia Woolf, *Night and Day*).

[Middle English, from Late Latin *tempestuōsus*, from *tempestūs*, tempest, variant of *tempestās*.]

RELATED WORDS:
  adverb — **tem·pes′tu·ous·ly**
  noun — **tem·pes′tu·ous·ness**

89

ther·mo·dy·nam·ics (thûr′mō-dī-năm′ĭks)

noun

1. *(used with a singular verb)* The branch of physics that deals with the relationships and conversions between heat and other forms of energy. **2.** *(used with a plural verb)* Thermodynamic phenomena and processes.

[*thermo-*, heat (from Greek *thermē*, heat, from *thermos*, warm) + *dynamics*, study of motion (from Greek *dunamikos*, powerful, from *dunamis*, power, from *dunasthai*, to be able).]

RELATED WORD:
  adjective — **ther′mo·dy·nam′ic**

She wondered what he was looking for; were there waves beating upon a shore for him, too, she wondered, and heroes riding through the leaf-hung forests? For perhaps the first time in her life she thought of him as a man, young, unhappy, **tempestuous**, full of desires and faults.

— Virginia Woolf,
Night and Day

to·tal·i·tar·i·an (tō-tăl′ĭ-târ′ē-ən)

adjective

Of, relating to, being, or imposing a form of government in which the political authority exercises absolute and centralized control over all aspects of life, the individual is subordinated to the state, and opposing political and cultural expression is suppressed: *"A totalitarian regime crushes all autonomous institutions in its drive to seize the human soul"* (Arthur M. Schlesinger, Jr., *Cycles of American History*).

noun

A practitioner or supporter of such a government.

[*total + (author)itarian*]

RELATED WORD:
  noun—**to·tal′i·tar′i·an·ism**
           (tō-tăl′ĭ-târ′ē-ə-nĭz′əm)

unc·tu·ous (ŭngk′chōo-əs)

adjective

1. Characterized by affected, exaggerated, or insincere earnestness: *I didn't believe a word that the unctuous spokesperson said.* **2.** Having the quality or characteristics of oil or ointment; slippery: *"They had march'd seven or eight miles already through the slipping unctuous mud"* (Walt Whitman, *Specimen Days*). **3.** Containing or composed of oil or fat.

[Middle English, from Old French *unctueus*, from Medieval Latin *ūnctuōsus*, from Latin *ūnctum*, ointment, from neuter past participle of *unguere*, to anoint.]

RELATED WORDS:
> *noun* — **unc′tu·os′i·ty** (ŭngk′chōō-ŏs′ĭ-tē)
> *adverb* — **unc′tu·ous·ly**
> *noun* — **unc′tu·ous·ness**

92
u·surp (yōō-sûrp′ *or* yōō-zûrp′)

verb
> Past participle and past tense: **u·surped**
> Present participle: **u·surp·ing**
> Third person singular present tense: **u·surps**

transitive **1.** To seize and hold (the power or rights of another, for example) by force and without legal authority: *"The principle that one class may usurp the power to legislate for another is unjust"* (Susan B. Anthony, quoted in Ida Husted Harper's *The Life and Work of Susan B. Anthony*). **2.** To take over or occupy without right: *The squatters illegally usurped the farmer's land.*

intransitive To seize another's place, authority, or possession wrongfully.

[Middle English *usurpen*, from Old French *usurper*, from Latin *ūsūrpāre*, to take into use, usurp.]

RELATED WORDS:
> *noun* — **u′sur·pa′tion** (yōō′sər-pā′shən
> *or* yōō′zər-pā′shən)
> *noun* — **u·surp′er**

vac·u·ous (văk′yoo-əs)

adjective

1a. Lacking intelligence; stupid. **b.** Devoid of substance or meaning; inane: *The interview with the celebrity produced a series of vacuous comments.* **c.** Devoid of expression; vacant: *"The narrow, swinelike eyes were open, no more vacuous in death than they had been in life"* (Nicholas Proffitt, *The Embassy House*). **2.** Devoid of matter; empty.

[From Latin *vacuus*, empty.]

RELATED WORDS:
> *adverb* — **vac′u·ous·ly**
> *noun* — **vac′u·ous·ness**

ve·he·ment (vē′ə-mənt)

adjective

Forceful or intense in expression, emotion, or conviction; fervid: *The senator issued a vehement denial regarding the report linking him to a scandal.*

[Middle English, from Old French, from Latin *vehemēns, vehement-*, perhaps from *vehere*, to carry.]

RELATED WORDS:
> *noun* — **ve′he·mence**
> *noun* — **ve′he·men·cy**
> *adverb* — **ve′he·ment·ly**

95

vor·tex (vôr′těks′)

noun

    Plural: **vor·tex·es** *or* **vor·ti·ces** (vôr′tǐ-sēz′)

1. A spiral motion of fluid, especially a whirling mass of water or air that sucks everything near it toward its center. Eddies and whirlpools are examples of vortexes. **2.** A place or situation regarded as drawing into its center all that surrounds it: *"Madam, is it not better that he showed repentance than that he never showed it at all? Better to atone for one minute than live in a vortex of despair?"* (Edna O'Brien, *In The Forest*).

[Latin *vortex, vortic-,* variant of *vertex,* from *vertere,* to turn.]

win·now (wĭn′ō)

verb

Past participle and past tense: **win·nowed**
Present participle: **win·now·ing**
Third person singular present tense: **win·nows**

transitive **1.** To separate the chaff from (grain) by means of a current of air. **2.** To blow (chaff) off or away. **3.** To examine closely in order to separate the good from the bad; sift: *The judges winnowed a thousand essays down to six finalists.* **4a.** To separate or get rid of (an undesirable part); eliminate: *The accountant was adept at winnowing out errors in the spreadsheet.* **b.** To sort or select (a desirable part); extract: *The investigators winnowed the facts from the testimony.* **5.** To blow on; fan: *A breeze winnowed the grass.*

intransitive **1.** To separate grain from chaff. **2.** To separate the good from the bad.

noun

1. A device for winnowing grain. **2.** An act of winnowing.

[Middle English *winnewen*, alteration of *windwen*, from Old English *windwian*, from *wind*, wind.]

RELATED WORD:
    noun—**win′now·er**

Such is thy pow'r, nor are thine orders vain,
O thou the leader of the mental train:
In full perfection all thy works are **wrought**
And thine the sceptre o'er the realms of thought.
— Phillis Wheatley,
"On Imagination"

wrought (rôt)

verb

A past tense and a past participle of **work**: *"In full per-fection all thy works are wrought / And thine the sceptre o'er the realms of thought"* (Phillis Wheatley, "On Imag-ination").

adjective

1. Put together; created: *The jewel thieves concocted a carefully wrought plan.* **2.** Shaped by hammering with tools. Used chiefly of metals or metalwork: *The horse-shoe was made of wrought iron.*

[Middle English *wroght*, from Old English *geworht*, past par-ticiple of *wyrcan*, to work.]

xen·o·phobe (zĕn′ə-fōb′ *or* zē′nə-fōb′)

noun

A person unduly fearful or contemptuous of that which is foreign, especially of strangers or foreign peoples.

[*xeno-*, a stranger (from Greek *xenos*) + *-phobe*, one who fears (from French, from Latin *-phobus*, from Greek *-phobos*, fearing, from *phobos*, fear).]

RELATED WORDS:
> *noun*—**xen′o·pho′bi·a** (zĕn′ə-fō′bē-ə
>   *or* zē′nə-fō′bē-ə)
> *adjective*—**xen′o·pho′bic** (zĕn′ə-fō′bĭk
>   *or* zē′nə-fō′bĭk)

99

yeo·man (yō′mən)

noun

Plural: **yeo·men**

1a. An attendant, servant, or lesser official in a royal or noble household. **b.** A yeoman of the guard. **2.** A petty officer performing chiefly clerical duties in the US Navy. **3.** An assistant or other subordinate, as of a sheriff. **4.** A diligent, dependable worker. **5.** A farmer who cultivates his own land, especially a member of a former class of small freeholders in England.

[From Middle English *yoman*, possibly alteration of *yong man*, young man, or possibly from Old English **gēaman* (compare Old Frisian *gāman*, villager) : **gēa-, *geā-*, region, district (akin to Old Frisian *gā*, region, district; German *Gau*, province) + *man*, man.]

RELATED WORD:

noun — **yeo′man·ry**

100

zig·gu·rat (zĭg′ə-răt′)

noun

A temple tower of the ancient Assyrians and Babylonians, having the form of a terraced pyramid with successively receding stories.

[Akkadian *ziqqurratu*, temple tower, from *zaqāru*, to build high.]

Exercises to Further Improve and Enrich Your Vocabulary

Knowing and being able to use the *100 Words Every High School Graduate Should Know* is just one step that you can take to actively expand your vocabulary. Along with a good dictionary, such as *The American Heritage College Dictionary* or *The American Heritage High School Dictionary*, you can use these 100 words as a starting point to discover new words. The exercises shown below are among the many ways you can become more familiar with your dictionary and improve your vocabulary.

Building your vocabulary is an ongoing process that you can continue throughout your life. If you feel discouraged because you can't retain the definitions of all the words that you encounter, approach the task of expanding your vocabulary more slowly. If learning ten words a week is too difficult, aim for three, or five.

What is important is not the quantity of words you're learning. Rather, what is important is your process behind learning the words and the commitment you make to yourself to strengthen your vocabulary over time.

Choose ten words from the list of *100 Words Every High School Graduate Should Know*. Look these ten words up in your dictionary.

On each page that these ten words are listed, choose a new word whose meaning you do not know. Create a document on your computer and type in that word along with its definition, or write the word down on paper with its definition.

For example, the word **auspicious** appears on page 95 of the fourth edition of *The American Heritage College Dictionary* and *The American Heritage High School Dictionary*. Other words on that page that you might choose to learn include **austerity, australopithecine, Austronesia,** or **authenticate**.

Keep a record of the new words that you learn. Every so often, go back and refresh your memory by rereading the definitions to these words. Create sentences that use these words so that you can become comfortable using them.

EXERCISE II

Choose a magazine or newspaper that you like to read at least once a week. Create a document on your computer or start a journal in a notebook. Every time you read a word whose meaning you're unsure of, add that word to your computer file or journal.

Look up the word in your dictionary, and write or type out the definition. Does knowing the precise definition of the word help you better understand the article?

After you have acquired a list of ten words, memorize them until they are part of your active vocabulary.

EXERCISE III

Many of the words in the list of *100 Words Every High School Graduate Should Know* include terms from specific areas of study. For example, **parabola** and **hypotenuse** are both from the field of geometry. **Hemoglobin** and **photosynthesis** are from biology.

What fields of learning interest you? Create a list of ten words that you think people should know if they were to learn more about that topic. Think about how you would define those words, and compare your definitions with the definitions you find in your dictionary.

100

words almost everyone confuses & misuses

Guide to the Entries

ENTRY WORD The 100 words that constitute this section are listed alphabetically. The entry words, along with inflected and derived forms, are divided into syllables by centered dots. These dots show you where you would break the word at the end of a line. The pronunciation of the word follows the entry word. Please see the key on page 189 for an explanation of the pronunciation system.

PART OF SPEECH At least one part of speech follows each entry word. The part of speech tells you the grammatical category that the word belongs to. Parts of speech include *noun, adjective, adverb, transitive verb,* and *intransitive verb.* (A transitive verb is a verb that needs an object to complete its meaning. *Wash* is a transitive verb in the sentence *I washed the car.* The direct object of *wash* is *the car.* An intransitive verb is one that does not take an object, as *sleep* in the sentence *I slept for seven hours.* Many verbs are both transitive and intransitive.)

INFLECTIONS A word's inflected forms differ from the main entry form by the addition of a suffix or by a change in the base form to indicate grammatical features such as number, person, or tense. They are set in boldface type, divided into syllables, and given pronunciations as necessary. The past tense, past participle, and the third person singular present tense inflections of all verbs are shown. The plurals of nouns are shown when they are spelled in a way other than by adding *s* to the base form.

LABELS The USAGE PROBLEM label warns of possible difficulties involving grammar, diction, or writing style. A word or definition with this label is discussed in a Usage Note, as at **flaunt.**

ORDER OF SENSES Entries having more than one sense are arranged with the central and often the most commonly sought meanings first. In an entry with more than one part of speech, the senses are numbered in separate sequences after each part of speech, as at **average.**

EXAMPLES OF USAGE Examples often follow the definitions and are set in italic type. These examples show the entry words in typical contexts. Sometimes the examples are quotations from authors of books. These quotations are shown within quotation marks, and the quotation's author and source are shown.

ETYMOLOGIES Etymologies appear in square brackets following the last definition. An etymology traces the history of a word as far back in time as can be determined with reasonable certainty. The stage most closely preceding Modern English is given first, with each earlier stage following in sequence. A language name, linguistic form (in italics), and brief definition of the form are given for each stage of the derivation. To avoid redundancy, a language, form, or definition is not repeated if it is identical to the corresponding item in the immediately preceding stage. Occasionally, a form will be given that is not actually preserved in written documents but which scholars are confident did exist—such a form will be marked by an asterisk (*). The word *from* is used to indicate origin of any kind: by inheritance, borrowing, or derivation. When an etymology splits a compound word into parts, a colon introduces the parts and each element is then traced back to its origin, with those elements enclosed in parentheses.

RELATED WORDS At the end of many entries, additional boldface words appear without definitions. These words are related in basic meaning to the entry word and are usually formed from the entry word by the addition of suffixes.

NOTES Some entries include Usage Notes that present important information and guidance on matters of grammar, diction, pronunciation, and nuances. Some refer to responses from our Usage Panel, a group of over 200 respected writers, scholars, and critics. The editors of the *American Heritage* dictionaries regularly survey these people on a broad range of usage questions.

Pronunciation Guide

Pronunciations appear in parentheses after boldface entry words. If a word has more than one pronunciation, the first pronunciation is usually more common than the other, but often they are equally common. Pronunciations are shown after inflections and related words where necessary.

Stress is the relative degree of emphasis that a word's syllables are spoken with. An unmarked syllable has the weakest stress in the word. The strongest, or primary, stress is indicated with a bold mark (**'**). A lighter mark (') indicates a secondary level of stress. The stress mark follows the syllable it applies to. Words of one syllable have no stress mark because there is no other stress level that the syllable can be compared to.

The key on page 189 shows the pronunciation symbols used in this book. To the right of the symbols are words that show how the symbols are pronounced. The letters whose sound corresponds to the symbols are shown in boldface.

The symbol (ə) is called *schwa*. It represents a vowel with the weakest level of stress in a word. The schwa sound varies slightly according to the vowel it represents or the sounds around it:

a·bun·dant (ə-bŭn**'**dənt)   **mo·ment** (mō**'**mənt)

civ·il (sĭv**'**əl)   **grate·ful** (grāt**'**fəl)

PRONUNCIATION KEY

Symbol	Examples	Symbol	Examples
ă	pat	oi	noise
ā	pay	o͝o	took
âr	care	o͝or	lure
ä	father	o͞o	boot
b	bib	ou	out
ch	church	p	pop
d	deed, milled	r	roar
ĕ	pet	s	sauce
ē	bee	sh	ship, dish
f	fife, phase, rough	t	tight, stopped
		th	thin
g	gag	*th*	this
h	hat	ŭ	cut
hw	which	ûr	urge, term, firm, word, heard
ĭ	pit		
ī	pie, by		
îr	deer, pier	v	valve
j	judge	w	with
k	kick, cat, pique	y	yes
l	lid, needle	z	zebra, xylem
m	mum	zh	vision, pleasure, garage
n	no, sudden		
ng	thing		
ŏ	pot	ə	about, item, edible, gallop, circus
ō	toe		
ô	caught, paw		
ôr	core	ər	butter

Then a dog began to howl somewhere in a farmhouse far down the road — a long, agonized wailing, as if from fear.... Then, far off in the distance, from the mountains on each side of us began a louder and a sharper howling — that of wolves — which **affected** both the horses and myself in the same way — for I was minded to jump from the caleche and run, whilst they reared again and plunged madly, so that the driver had to use all his great strength to keep them from bolting.

— Bram Stoker,
Dracula

ad·verse (ăd-vûrs′, ăd′vûrs′)

adjective

1. Acting or serving to oppose; antagonistic: *"And let thy blows, doubly redoubled,/Fall like amazing thunder on the casque/Of thy adverse pernicious enemy"* (William Shakespeare, *King Richard II*). **2.** Contrary to one's interests or welfare; harmful or unfavorable: *"[M]ost companies are fearful of adverse publicity and never report internal security breaches... to law enforcement agencies, security analysts contend"* (Peter H. Lewis, *New York Times*). **3.** Moving in an opposite direction: *As it ascended, the balloon was caught in an adverse current and drifted out to sea.*

[Middle English, from Old French *advers*, from Latin *adversus*, past participle of *advertere*, to turn toward : *ad-*, ad- + *vertere*, to turn.]

RELATED WORD:
adverb — **ad·verse′ly**

SEE NOTE AT **averse** (ON PAGE 206).

af·fect[1] (ə-fĕkt′)

transitive verb
> Past participle and past tense: **af·fect·ed**
> Present participle: **af·fect·ing**
> Third person singular present tense: **af·fects**

1. To have an influence on or effect a change in: *Inflation affects the buying power of the dollar.* **2.** To act on the emotions of; touch or move: *"Then, far off in the distance, from the mountains on each side of us began a louder and a sharper howling—that of wolves—which affected both the horses and myself in the same way"* (Bram Stoker, *Dracula*). **3.** To attack or infect, as a disease: *Rheumatic fever is one of many afflictions that can affect the heart.*

noun (ăf′ĕkt′)

1. Feeling or emotion, especially as manifested by facial expression or body language: *"The soldiers seen on television had been carefully chosen for blandness of affect"* (Norman Mailer, *Vanity Fair*). **2.** *Obsolete* A disposition, feeling, or tendency.

[Middle English *affecten*, from Latin *afficere, affect-,* to do to, act on : *ad-*, ad- + *facere,* to do.]

SEE NOTE AT **effect** (ON PAGE 223).

af·fect² (ə-fĕkt**′**)

transitive verb
   Past participle and past tense: **af·fect·ed**
   Present participle: **af·fect·ing**
   Third person singular present tense: **af·fects**

1. To put on a false show of; simulate: *"He wheedled, bribed, ridiculed, threatened, and scolded; affected indifference, that he might surprise the truth from her"* (Louisa May Alcott, *Little Women*). **2.** To have or show a liking for: *affects dramatic clothes.* **3.** To tend to by nature; tend to assume: *In my chemistry class, we study substances that affect crystalline form.* **4.** To imitate; copy: *"Spenser, in affecting the ancients, writ no language"* (Ben Jonson, *Timber*).

[Middle English *affecten,* from Latin *affectāre,* to strive after, frequentative of *afficere, affect-,* to affect, influence; see AFFECT¹.]

RELATED WORD:
   noun — **af·fect′er**

SEE NOTE AT **effect** (ON PAGE 224).

4

ag·gra·vate (ăg′rə-vāt′)

transitive verb
> Past participle and past tense: **ag·gra·vat·ed**
> Present participle: **ag·gra·vat·ing**
> Third person singular present tense: **ag·gra·vates**

1. To make worse or more troublesome: *"Drinking alcohol (especially heavy drinking) or taking tranquilizers or sedating antihistamines shortly before bedtime can aggravate snoring by reducing muscle tone"* (Jane E. Brody, New York Times). **2.** To rouse to exasperation or anger; provoke.

[Latin *aggravāre, aggravāt-* : *ad-*, ad- + *gravāre*, to burden (from *gravis*, heavy).]

RELATED WORDS:
> *adverb*—**ag′gra·vat′ing·ly**
> *adjective*—**ag′gra·va′tive**
> *noun*—**ag′gra·va′tor**

🖎 Some people claim that *aggravate* can only mean "to make worse," and not "to irritate," on the basis of the word's etymology. But in doing so, they ignore not only an English sense in use since the 17th century, but also one of the original Latin ones. *Aggravate* comes from the Latin verb *aggravāre*, which meant "to make heavier," that is, "to add to the weight of." The Latin word also had the extended senses "to annoy" and "to oppress." One-third of the Usage Panel does not approve of its use in the sentence *It's the endless wait for luggage that aggravates me the most about air travel.* When using *aggravate* in this sense, especially in formal writing, some of your readers may possibly view it as an error.

---

5 **al·leged** (ə-lĕjd′, ə-lĕj′ĭd)

adjective

Represented as existing or as being as described but not so proved; supposed: *"Cryptozoology is the study of un-explained and alleged sightings of strange creatures not documented by standard zoology"* (Chet Raymo, *Boston Globe*).

RELATED WORD:
adverb—**al·leg′ed·ly**

An *alleged* burglar is someone who has been accused of being a burglar but against whom no charges have been proved. An *alleged* incident is an event that is said to have taken place but has not yet been verified. In their zeal to protect the rights of the accused, newspapers and law enforcement officials sometimes misuse *alleged*. Someone arrested for murder may be only an *alleged* murderer, for example, but is a real, not an *alleged*, suspect in that his or her status as a suspect is not in doubt. Similarly, if the money from a safe is known to have been stolen and not merely mislaid, then we may safely speak of a theft without having to qualify our description with *alleged*.

6 all right (ôl rīt)

adjective

1. In good condition or working order; satisfactory: *The mechanic checked to see if the tires were all right.* **2.** Acceptable; agreeable: *"Men are all right for friends, but as soon as you marry them they turn into cranky old fathers, even the wild ones"* (Willa Cather, *My Ántonia*). **3.** Average; mediocre: *The performance was just all right, not remarkable.* **4.** Correct: *These figures are perfectly all right.* **5.** Uninjured; safe: *The passengers were shaken up but are all right.*

adverb

1. In a satisfactory way; adequately: *"Cobol was designed to be somewhat readable by nonprogrammers. The idea was that managers could read through a printed listing of Cobol code to determine if the programmer got it all right. This has rarely happened"* (Charles Petzold, *New York Times*). **2.** Very well; yes. Used as a reply to a question or to introduce a declaration: *All right, I'll go.* **3.** Without a doubt: *"They [Bonobos] are chimpanzees, all right, but almost the reverse of their more familiar cousins* (Phoebe-Lou Adams, *Atlantic Monthly*).

❧ Despite the appearance of the form *alright* in works of such well-known writers as Langston Hughes and James Joyce, the single word spelling has never been accepted as standard. This is peculiar, since similar fusions such as *already* and *altogether* have never raised any objections. The difference may lie in the fact that *already* and *altogether* became single words back in the Middle Ages, whereas *alright* has only been around for a little more than a century and was called out by language critics as a misspelling. Consequently, if you use *alright,* especially in formal writing, you run the risk that readers may view it as an error or as the deliberate breaking of convention.

al·to·geth·er (ôl′tə-gĕth′ər)

adverb

1. Entirely; completely; utterly: *The three-year-old, then, is a grammatical genius—master of most constructions... avoiding many kinds of errors altogether"* (Steven Pinker, *The Language Instinct*). **2.** With all included or counted; all told: *"There were altogether eight official Crusades"* (*The Reader's Companion to Military History*, Robert Cowley). **3.** On the whole; with everything considered: *Altogether, I'm sorry it happened.*

noun

A state of nudity. Often used with *the*: *The artist's model posed in the altogether.*

[Middle English *al togeder*.]

🌿 *Altogether* and *all together* do not mean the same thing. *Altogether* is an adverb that indicates totality or entirety: *I rarely eat tomatoes, and I avoid peppers altogether. All together* is an adverb that indicates that the members of a group perform or undergo an action collectively: *The nations stood all together. The prisoners were herded all together. All together* is used only in sentences that can be rephrased so that *all* and *together* may be separated by other words: *The books lay all together in a heap. All the books lay together in a heap.*

The three-year-old, then, is a grammatical genius—master of most constructions, obeying rules far more often than flouting them, respecting language universals, erring in sensible, adultlike ways, and avoiding many kinds of errors **altogether**.

— Steven Pinker,
The Language Instinct

a·mong (ə-mŭng′)
  also **a·mongst** (ə-mŭngst′)

preposition

1. In the midst of; surrounded by: *A tall oak tree grew among the pines.* **2.** In the group, number, or class of: *"Santería has a growing following among middle-class professionals, including white, black and Asian Americans"* (Lizette Alvarez, *New York Times*). **3.** In the company of; in association with: *I spent the summer in Europe traveling among a group of tourists.* **4.** By many or the entire number of; with many: *"It has long been a tradition among novel writers that a book must end by everybody getting just what they wanted, or if the conventional happy ending was impossible, then it must be a tragedy in which one or both should die"* (Molly Gloss, *Wild Life*). **5.** With portions to each of: *Distribute this among you.* **6.** With one another: *Don't fight among yourselves.*

[Middle English, from Old English *āmang* : *ā*, in + *gemang*, throng.]

SEE NOTE AT **between** (ON PAGE 208).

---

as·sure (ə-shŏŏr′)

transitive verb
> Past participle and past tense: **as·sured**
> Present participle: **as·sur·ing**
> Third person singular present tense: **as·sures**

1. To inform positively, as to remove doubt: *The ticket agent assured us that the train would be on time.* **2.** To cause to feel sure: *The candidate assured the electorate that he would keep his promises.* **3.** To give confidence to; reassure: *"Katharine assured her by nodding her head several times, but the manner in which she left the room was not calculated to inspire complete confidence in her diplomacy"* (Virginia Woolf, *Night and Day*). **4.** To make certain; ensure: *"Let every nation know, whether it wishes us well or ill, that we shall pay any price, bear any burden, meet any hardship, support any friend, oppose any foe, in order to assure the survival and the success of liberty"* (John F. Kennedy, Inaugural Address). **5.** *Chiefly British* To insure, as against loss.

[Middle English *assuren,* from Old French *assurer,* from Vulgar Latin **assēcūrāre,* to make sure : Latin *ad-,* ad- + Latin *sēcūrus,* secure.]

RELATED WORDS:
> *adjective—***as·sur′a·ble**
> *noun—***as·sur′er, as·sur′or**

SEE NOTE AT **insure** (ON PAGE 248).

10

au·ger (ô′gər)

noun

1a. Any of various hand tools, typically having a threaded shank and cross handle, used for boring holes in wood or ice: "[He] *can himself build a cabin with the three necessary implements: an ax, a broadax, and an auger*" (Michael Ennis, *Architectural Digest*). **b.** A drill bit. **2a.** A machine having a rotating helical shaft for boring into the earth. **b.** A rotating helical shaft used to convey material, as in a snow blower.

[Middle English, from *an auger*, alteration of *a nauger*, from Old English *nafogār*, auger.]

transitive verb
    Past participle and past tense: **au·gered**
    Present participle: **au·ger·ing**
    Third person singular present tense: **au·gers**

To bore by means of an auger: *The fishermen augered a hole in the ice.*

SEE NOTE AT **augur** (ON PAGE 203).

11 **au·gur** (ô′gər)

noun

1. One of a group of ancient Roman religious officials who foretold events by observing and interpreting signs and omens. **2.** A seer or prophet; a soothsayer.

verb
> Past participle and past tense: **au·gured**
> Present participle: **au·gur·ing**
> Third person singular present tense: **au·gurs**

transitive **1.** To predict, especially from signs or omens; foretell. **2.** To serve as an omen of; betoken: *Early returns augured victory for the young candidate.*

intransitive **1.** To make predictions from signs or omens. **2.** To be a sign or omen: *A smooth dress rehearsal augured well for the play.*

[Middle English, from Latin.]

RELATED WORD:
> *adjective*—**au′gu·ral** (ô′gyə-rəl)

✍ An *auger* is a tool used for boring holes. An *augur* is a seer or soothsayer. The verb *augur* means "to foretell or betoken," as in *A good, well-grounded education augurs success. Augur* is also commonly used in phrases such as *augur well* or *augur ill*, as in *The quarterback's injury augurs ill for the game.*

---

av·er·age (ăv′ər-ĭj, ăv′rĭj)

noun

1. The value obtained by dividing the sum of a set of quantities by the number of quantities in the set. Also called *arithmetic mean*: *The average of 2, 5, 8, and 11 is 6.5.* **2.** A number that is derived from and considered typical or representative of a set of numbers. **3.** A typical kind or usual level or degree: *"My basic athletic skills—quickness, speed, coordination, all those things— were a little above average, but what I could do better than anybody my age was anticipate what a pitcher was going to throw and where he was going to throw it"* (David Huddle, *The Story of a Million Years*). **4.** The ratio of a team's or player's successful performances such as wins, hits, or goals, divided by total opportunities for successful performance, such as games, times at bat, or shots: *The team finished the season with a .500 average.*

adjective

1. Computed or determined as an average: *"By ten o'-clock average windspeed is forty knots out of the north-northeast, spiking to twice that and generating a huge sea"* (Sebastian Junger, *The Perfect Storm*). **2.** Being intermediate between extremes, as on a scale: *The teacher offered extra help for students with average grades.* **3.** Usual or ordinary in kind or character: *The firm conducted a poll of average people.*

---

verb

> Past participle and past tense: **av·er·aged**
> Present participle: **av·er·ag·ing**
> Third person singular present tense: **av·er·ag·es**

transitive **1.** To calculate the average of: *The teacher explained how to average a set of numbers.* **2.** To do or have an average of: *The part-time employee averaged three hours of work a day.*

intransitive To be or amount to an average: *Our expenses averaged out to 45 dollars per day.*

[From Middle English *averay,* charge above the cost of freight, from Old French *avarie,* from Old Italian *avaria,* duty, from Arabic *'awārīya,* damaged goods, from *'awār,* blemish, from *'awira,* to be damaged.]

RELATED WORD:
> *noun* — **av'er·age·ness**

SEE NOTE AT **median** (ON PAGE 264).

13

a·verse (ə-vûrs′)

adjective

Having a feeling of opposition, distaste, or aversion; strongly disinclined: *"Cheating on schoolwork has simmered on as long as there have been students averse to studying"* (Christina McCarroll, *Christian Science Monitor*).

[Latin *āversus,* past participle of *āvertere,* to turn away.]

RELATED WORDS:
    adverb—**a·verse′ly**
    noun—**a·verse′ness**

🖎 Who isn't *averse* to getting *adverse* reactions to their ideas? *Averse* normally refers to people and means "having a feeling of distaste or aversion," as in *As an investor I'm averse to risk-taking.* People sometimes mistakenly slip in *adverse* for *averse* in these constructions with *to*. However, *adverse* normally does not refer to people, but rather to things that are antagonistic or contrary to someone's interests. Thus we say *We're working under very adverse* (not *averse) circumstances* and *All the adverse* (not *averse) criticism frayed the new mayor's nerves.*

be·tween (bǐ-twēn′)

preposition

1a. In or through the position or interval separating: *"The shapes of the shoulder bones indicate that the animal may have swung by its arms between the branches of trees"* (Lisa Guernsey, *Chronicle of Higher Education*); *"Between 1970 and 1995, the average American's yearly sugar consumption increased from 120 pounds to 150 pounds"* (Richard A. Knox, *Boston Globe*). **b.** Intermediate to, as in quantity, amount, or degree: *It costs between 15 and 20 dollars.* **2.** Connecting over or through a space that is separating: *I walked down the long path between the cabin and the lake.* **3.** USAGE PROBLEM Associating or uniting in a reciprocal action or relationship: *The mediator hammered out an agreement between workers and management. The professor noted a certain resemblance between the two essays.* **4.** In confidence restricted to: *Between you and me, he is not qualified.* **5a.** By the combined effort or effect of: *"Sickly, it began to occur to him that between them, they might have killed the old man by mistake"* (Jane Stevenson, *London Bridges*). **b.** In the combined ownership of: *They had only a few dollars between them.* **6.** As measured or compared against: *"[She] went to the butcher's to choose between steak and pork chops"* (Sinclair Lewis, *Main Street*).

adverb

In an intermediate space, position, or time; in the interim.

IDIOM:

in between In an intermediate condition or situation: *"The methane, however, cannot exist in its normal*

---

gaseous form at such pressures and temperatures, but is transformed into a 'supercritical fluid'—neither a gas nor a liquid but something in between" (Malcolm W. Browne, *New York Times*).

[Middle English *bitwene,* from Old English *betwēonum.*]

RELATED WORD:
noun — **be·tween′ness**

๖๖ According to a widely repeated but unjustified tradition, *between* is used for two, and *among* for more than two. It is true that *between* is the only choice when exactly two entities are specified: *the choice between* (not *among*) *good and evil, the rivalry between* (not *among*) *Great Britain and France.* When more than two entities are involved, however, or when the number of entities is unspecified, the choice of one or the other word depends on the intended sense. *Between* is used when the entities are considered as distinct individuals; *among,* when they are considered as a mass or collectivity. Thus in the sentence *The bomb landed between the houses,* the houses are seen as points that define the boundaries of the area of impact (so that we presume that none of the individual houses was hit). In *The bomb landed among the houses,* the area of impact is considered to be the general location of the houses, taken together (in which case it is left open whether any houses were hit). By the same token, we may speak of *a series of wars between the Greek cities,* which suggests that each city was an independent participant in the hostilities, or of *a series of wars among the Greek cities,* which allows for the possibility that the participants were shifting alliances of cities. To avoid this ambiguity, use *among* to indicate inclusion in a group: *She is among the best of our young sculptors. There is a spy among you.* Use *between* when the entities are seen as determining the limits or endpoints of a range: *They searched the area between the river, the farmhouse, and the woods. The truck driver had obviously been drinking between stops.*

15

bla·tant (blăt′nt)

adjective

1. Unpleasantly loud and noisy: *"There are those who find the trombones blatant and the triangle silly, but both add effective color"* (Musical Heritage Review). **2.** Us-AGE PROBLEM Thoroughly or offensively conspicuous or obtrusive: *The child was caught telling a blatant lie.*

[From Latin *blatīre,* to blab (on the model of words such as *rampant*).]

RELATED WORDS:
> *noun* — **bla′tan·cy**
> *adverb* — **bla′tant·ly**

It is not surprising that *blatant* and *flagrant* are often confused, since the words have overlapping meanings. Both attribute conspicuousness and offensiveness to certain acts. *Blatant* emphasizes the failure to conceal the act. *Flagrant,* on the other hand, emphasizes the serious wrongdoing inherent in the offense. Certain contexts may admit either word depending on what is meant. Thus, a violation of human rights might be either *blatant* or *flagrant.* If the act was committed with contempt for public scrutiny, it is *blatant.* If its barbarity was monstrous, it is *flagrant.*

    Blatant is sometimes used to mean simply "obvious," as in *the blatant danger of such an approach,* but this use has not been established and is widely considered an error.

cap·i·tal (kăp/ĭ-tl)

noun

1a. A town or city that is the official seat of government in a political entity, such as a state or nation: *Trenton is the capital of New Jersey.* **b.** A city that is the center of a specific activity or industry: *Many consider Milan to be the fashion capital of the world.* **2a.** Wealth in the form of money or property that is used or accumulated in a business by a person, partnership, or corporation, and is often used to create more wealth. **b.** Human resources considered in terms of their contributions to an economy: *"Castro's swift unveiling of his communist plans provoked a flight of human capital"* (George F. Will, *Newsweek*). **3.** The remaining assets of a business after all liabilities have been deducted; net worth. **4a.** The total amount of stock authorized for issue by a corporation, including common and preferred stock. **b.** The total stated or par value of the permanently invested capital of a corporation. **5.** An asset or advantage: *"He has profited from political capital accumulated by others"* (Michael Mandelbaum, *Foreign Affairs*). **6.** A capital letter.

adjective

1. First and foremost; principal: *We were faced with a decision of capital importance.* **2.** First-rate; excellent: *Planning a kayaking trip is a capital idea!* **3.** Relating to or being a seat of government: *Albany, New York, is a capital city.* **4.** Punishable by or involving death: *Treason is a capital offense.* **5.** Of or involving wealth and its use in investment: *"A multi-billion-dollar capital improvement plan has produced construction, physical*

---

capital / capitol

improvements, and repairs" (Peter Edelman, *Searching for America's Heart*).

[From Middle English, principal, from Old French, from Latin *capitālis,* from *caput,* head, money laid out.]

> ✍ *Capital* and *capitol* are terms that are often confused, mainly because they refer to things that are in some way related. The term for a town or city that serves as a seat of government is spelled *capital.* The term for the building in which a legislative assembly meets is spelled *capitol.*

17

cap·i·tol (kăp′ĭ-tl)

noun

1. A building or complex of buildings in which a state legislature meets. **2. Capitol** The building in Washington DC where the Congress of the United States meets.

[Middle English *Capitol,* Jupiter's temple in Rome, from Old French *capitole,* from Latin *Capitōlium,* after *Capitōlīnus,* Capitoline, the hill on which Jupiter's temple stood; perhaps akin to *caput*; see etymology at **capital** (#16).]

SEE NOTE AT **capital** (ABOVE).

The Pyncheon Elm, throughout its great circumference, was all alive, and full of the morning sun and a sweet-tempered little breeze, which lingered within this verdant sphere, and set a thousand leafy tongues a-whispering all at once. This aged tree appeared to have suffered nothing from the gale. It had kept its boughs unshattered, and its full **complement** of leaves; and the whole in perfect verdure, except a single branch, that, by the earlier change with which the elm-tree sometimes prophesies the autumn, had been transmuted to bright gold.

—Nathaniel Hawthorne,
The House of the Seven Gables

com·ple·ment (kŏm′plə-mənt)

noun

1a. Something that completes, makes up a whole, or brings to perfection. **b.** The quantity or number needed to make up a whole: "[The tree] *had kept its boughs unshattered, and its full complement of leaves* (Nathaniel Hawthorne, *The House of the Seven Gables*). **c.** Either of two parts that complete the whole or mutually complete each other. **2.** An angle related to another so that the sum of their measures is 90°. **3.** A word or words used after a verb to complete a predicate construction; for example, the phrase *to eat ice cream* is the complement of the predicate *We like to eat ice cream.* **4.** A complex system of proteins found in normal blood plasma that combines with antibodies to destroy pathogenic bacteria and other foreign cells.

transitive verb (kŏm′plə-mĕnt′)
> Past participle and past tense: **com·ple·ment·ed**
> Present participle: **com·ple·ment·ing**
> Third person singular present tense: **com·ple·ments**

To serve as a complement to: "*When chiles are dried, their flavor intensifies, and sometimes they take on a smoky, sweet flavor that complements the heat*" (Corby Kummer, *Atlantic Monthly*).

[Middle English, from Old French, from Latin *complēmentum*, from *complēre*, to fill out.]

✍ *Complement* and *compliment*, though quite distinct in meaning, are sometimes confused because they are pronounced the same. As a noun, *complement* means "something that completes or brings to perfection" *(The antique silver was a complement to the beautifully set table)*; used as a verb it means "to serve as a complement to" (*The neutral color of the paint complements the warmth of the oak floors*). The noun *compliment* means "an expression or act of courtesy or praise" (*They gave us a compliment on our beautifully set table*), while the verb means "to pay a compliment to" (*We complimented our hosts for the lovely dinner party*).

19

com·pli·ment (kŏm′plə-mənt)

noun

1. An expression of praise, admiration, or congratulation: *I took their interest in my screenplay as a compliment.* **2.** A formal act of civility, courtesy, or respect: *"You must give me leave to judge for myself, and pay me the compliment of believing what I say"* (Jane Austen, *Pride and Prejudice*). **3. compliments** Good wishes; regards: *Extend my compliments to your parents.*

transitive verb
> Past participle and past tense: **com·pli·ment·ed**
> Present participle: **com·pli·ment·ing**
> Third person singular present tense: **com·pli·ments**

To pay a compliment to: *The mayor complimented the volunteers who had cleaned up the park.*

[French, from Italian *complimento*, from Spanish *cumplimiento*, from *cumplir*, to complete, from Latin *complēre*, to fill out.]

SEE NOTE AT **complement** (ON PAGE 213).

com·prise (kəm-prīz′)

transitive verb

   Past participle and past tense: **com·prised**
   Present participle: **com·pris·ing**
   Third person singular present tense: **com·pris·es**

1. To consist of; be composed of: *"The French got what became known as French Equatorial Africa, comprising several territories"* (Alex Shoumatoff, *Vanity Fair*). **2.** To include; contain: *"The word 'politics' . . . comprises, in itself, a difficult study of no inconsiderable magnitude"* (Charles Dickens, *The Pickwick Papers*). **3.** USAGE PROBLEM To compose; constitute.

[Middle English *comprisen,* from Old French *compris*, past participle of *comprendre*, to include, from Latin *comprehendere, comprēndere.*]

🖉 The traditional rule states that the whole *comprises* the parts and the parts *compose* the whole. In strict usage: *The Union comprises 50 states. Fifty states compose* (or *constitute* or *make up*) *the Union.* Even though careful writers often maintain this distinction, *comprise* is increasingly used in place of *compose*, especially in the passive: *The Union is comprised of 50 states.* Our surveys show that opposition to this usage is abating. In the 1960s, 53 percent of the Usage Panel found this usage unacceptable; in 1996, only 35 percent objected.

21

con·sul (kŏn′səl)

noun

1. An official appointed by a government to reside in a foreign country and represent his or her government's commercial interests and assist its citizens there. **2.** Either of the two chief magistrates of the Roman Republic, elected for a term of one year. **3.** Any of the three chief magistrates of the French Republic from 1799 to 1804.

[Middle English *consul*, Roman consul, from Latin *cōnsul*; possibly akin to *cōnsulere*, to take counsel.]

RELATED WORDS:
adjective—**con′su·lar** (kŏn′sə-lər)
noun—**con′sul·ship′**

SEE NOTE AT **council** (ON PAGE 218).

22

con·vince (kən-vĭns′)

transitive verb
Past participle and past tense: **con·vinced**
Present participle: **con·vinc·ing**
Third person singular present tense: **con·vinc·es**

To bring by the use of argument or evidence to firm belief or a course of action: "*I was now quite convinced that she had made a fresh will, and had called the two gardeners in to witness her signature. Events proved that I was right in my supposition*" (Agatha Christie, *The Mysterious Affair at Styles*).

[Latin *convincere*, to prove wrong : *com-*, intensive prefix + *vincere*, to conquer.]

RELATED WORDS:

> *noun* — **con·vinc′er**
> *adjective* — **con·vinc′a·ble**

🙋 According to a traditional rule, one *persuades* someone to act but *convinces* someone of the truth of a statement or proposition: *By convincing me that no good could come of staying, he persuaded me to leave.* If the distinction is accepted, then *convince* should not be used with an infinitive: He *persuaded* (not *convinced*) me to go. In a 1981 Usage Panel survey, 61 percent rejected the use of *convince* with an infinitive. But the tide of sentiment against the construction appears to be turning. In a 1996 survey, 74 percent accepted it in the sentence *I tried to convince him to chip in a few dollars, but he refused.* Even in passive constructions, a majority of the Usage Panel accepted *convince* with an infinitive. Fifty-two percent accepted the sentence *After listening to the teacher's report, the committee was convinced to go ahead with the new reading program.* Persuade, on the other hand, is perfectly acceptable when used with an infinitive or a *that* clause in both active and passive constructions. An overwhelming majority of Panelists in the 1996 survey accepted the following sentences: *After a long discussion with her lawyer, she was persuaded to drop the lawsuit. The President persuaded his advisors that military action was necessary.* You can observe the traditional distinction between these words, but it is not very likely that readers will appreciate the effort.

23

coun·cil (koun′səl)

noun

1a. An assembly of persons called together for consultation, deliberation, or discussion. **b.** A body of people elected or appointed to serve as administrators, legislators, or advisors. **c.** An assembly of church officials and theologians convened for regulating matters of doctrine and discipline. **2.** The discussion or deliberation that takes place in such an assembly or body.

[Middle English *counceil,* from Old French *concile,* from Latin.]

❧ *Council, counsel,* and *consul* have similar pronunciations but are never interchangeable, although their meanings are related. *Council* refers principally to a deliberative assembly (such as a city council or student council), its work, and its membership. *Counsel* pertains chiefly to advice and guidance in general and to a person (such as a lawyer or camp counselor) who provides it. *Consul* denotes an officer in the foreign service of a country.

24

coun·sel (koun′səl)

noun

1. The act of exchanging opinions and ideas; consultation: *Frequent counsel among the members kept the committee informed.* **2.** Advice or guidance, especially as solicited from a knowledgeable person: *"I wish to engage your keener faculties, your logic and reason, so that you are able to discern a greater truth than I can. In short, I seek counsel and instruction"* (*Audubon's Watch,* John Gregory Brown). **3.** Private, guarded thoughts or opinions: *The quiet loner always kept his own counsel.* **4.** A lawyer or group of lawyers giving legal advice and especially conducting a case in court.

verb

> Past participle and past tense: **coun·seled** *or* **coun·selled**
>
> Present participle: **coun·sel·ing** *or* **coun·sel·ling**
>
> Third person singular present tense: **coun·sels**

transitive **1.** To give counsel to; advise: *"An Owl, in her wisdom, counseled the Birds that when the acorn first began to sprout, to pull it all up out of the ground and not allow it to grow"* (Aesop, *Fables: The Owl and the Birds*). **2.** To recommend: *counseled care in the forthcoming negotiations.*

intransitive To give or take advice.

[Middle English *counseil,* from Old French *conseil,* from Latin *cōnsilium*; akin to *cōnsulere,* to take counsel, consult.]

RELATED WORDS:

> *noun* — **coun′sel·or, coun′sel·lor**
>
> *noun* — **coun′sel·or·ship′**

SEE NOTE AT **council** (ON PAGE 218).

---

dis·creet (dĭ-skrēt′)

adjective

Marked by, exercising, or showing prudence and wise self-restraint in speech and behavior; circumspect: *"After-hours clubs are proliferating and are still the city's best-kept secrets. One need only make discreet inquiries as to the whereabouts of such places"* (Doris Pike, *Boston Magazine*).

[Middle English, from Old French *discret,* from Medieval Latin *discrētus,* from Latin, past participle of *discernere,* to separate, discern.]

RELATED WORDS:
> *adverb*—**dis·creet′ly**
> *noun*—**dis·creet′ness**

SEE NOTE AT **discrete** (ON PAGE 221).

26 dis·crete (dĭ-skrēt′)

adjective

Constituting a separate thing: *"Although hypertext may well turn out to be no more than an amusing detour in the history of the written word, its most ardent fans foresee a future in which traditional narratives would become obsolete, and discrete, self-contained books would also give way to vast interlinked electronic networks"* (Michiko Kakutani, *New York Times Magazine*).

[Middle English, from Old French, from Latin *discrētus*, past participle of *discernere*, to separate.]

RELATED WORDS:
> *adverb* — **dis·crete′ly**
> *noun* — **dis·crete′ness**

☙ Because they are pronounced the same way, *discreet* and *discrete* are sometimes confused in print. *Discreet* means "prudent in speech and behavior": *He told me the news but asked me to be discreet about it.* The related word *discrete* means "separate, distinct": *The summer science program consists of four discrete units.*

---

27 **dis·in·ter·est·ed** (dĭs-ĭn′trĭ-stĭd, dĭs-ĭn′tə-rĕs′tĭd)

adjective

1. Free of bias and self-interest; impartial: *"Debates on the fluoridation issue are passionate and polemical. For this reason disinterested scientific opinion on fluorides in the water supply, which is itself hard to come by, is not always the basis for public policy"* (Ellen R. Shell, *Atlantic Monthly*). **2.** USAGE PROBLEM Not interested or having lost interest; indifferent.

RELATED WORDS:

> *adverb* — **dis·in′ter·est·ed·ly**
> *noun* — **dis·in′ter·est·ed·ness**

℘ In traditional usage, *disinterested* can only mean "having no stake in an outcome," as in *Since the judge stands to profit from the sale of the company, she cannot be considered a disinterested party in the dispute.* But despite critical disapproval, *disinterested* has come to be widely used by many educated writers to mean "uninterested" or "having lost interest," as in *After she discovered skiing, she grew disinterested in her schoolwork.* Oddly enough, "not interested" is the oldest sense of the word, going back to the 17th century. This sense became outmoded in the 18th century but underwent a revival in the first quarter of the 20th. Despite its resuscitation, this usage is often considered an error. In a 1988 survey, 89 percent of the Usage Panel rejected the sentence *His unwillingness to give five minutes of his time proves that he is disinterested in finding a solution to the problem.* In a 2001 survey, 88 percent rejected a similar sentence, indicating continued strong resistance to this usage.

28

ef·fect (ĭ-fĕkt′)

noun

1. Something brought about by a cause or agent; a result: *"Every cause produces more than one effect"* (Herbert Spencer, *Essays on Education*). **2.** The power to produce an outcome or achieve a result; influence: *The drug had an immediate effect on the pain. The government's action had no effect on the trade imbalance.* **3.** A scientific law, hypothesis, or phenomenon: *the photovoltaic effect.* **4.** Advantage; avail: *The lawyer used the words of the witness to great effect in influencing the jury.* **5.** The condition of being in full force or execution: *This new regulation that goes into effect on January 1.* **6a.** Something that produces a specific impression or supports a general design or intention: *The strange lighting effects emphasized the harsh atmosphere of the drama.* **b.** A particular impression: *These large windows give an effect of spaciousness.* **c.** Production of a desired impression: *spent lavishly on dinner just for effect.* **7.** The basic or general meaning; import: *He said he was greatly worried, or words to that effect.* **8. effects** Movable belongings; goods.

transitive verb

Past participle and past tense: **ef·fect·ed**
Present participle: **ef·fect·ing**
Third person singular present tense: **ef·fects**

To produce as a result; cause to occur: *"It is known that the English pointer has been greatly changed within the last century, and in this case the change has, it is believed,*

---

been chiefly effected by crosses with the fox" (Charles Darwin, *On the Origin of Species*).

IDIOM:

in effect In essence; to all purposes: *testimony that in effect contradicted her earlier statement.*

[Middle English, from Old French, from Latin *effectus*, from past participle of *efficere*, to accomplish : *ex-*, ex- + *facere*, to make.]

RELATED WORDS:
> *noun* — **ef·fect′er**
> *adjective* — **ef·fect′i·ble**

🐝 The words *affect* and *effect* are often confused, in no small part because they often sound the same. What's worse, two different words are spelled *affect*. One is solely a verb and means "to put on a false show of," as in *The actor affected a British accent*. The other can be both a noun and a verb. The noun meaning "emotion" is a technical term from psychology that sometimes shows up in general writing, as in the quote *"The soldiers seen on television had been carefully chosen for blandness of affect"* written by Norman Mailer in a piece about the Gulf War. In its far more common role as a verb, *affect* usually means "to influence," as in *The Surgeon General's report outlined how much smoking affects health.*

Effect can also serve as a noun or a verb. The noun means "a result." Thus, if you *affect* something, you are likely to see an *effect* of some kind, and from this may arise further the confusion. As a verb, *effect* means "to bring about or execute." Thus, using *effect* in the sentence *These measures may effect savings* implies that the measures will cause new savings to come about. But using *affect* in the very similar sentence *These measures may affect savings* could just as easily imply that the measures may reduce savings that have already been realized.

29

en·er·vate (ĕn′ər-vāt′)

transitive verb
  Past participle and past tense: **en·er·vat·ed**
  Present participle: **en·er·vat·ing**
  Third person singular present tense: **en·er·vates**

1. To weaken or destroy the strength or vitality of: *"What is the nature of the luxury which enervates and destroys nations?"* (Henry David Thoreau, *Walden*). **2.** In medicine, to remove a nerve or part of a nerve.

[Latin *ēnervāre, ēnervāt-* : *ē-, ex-*, ex- + *nervus*, sinew.]

RELATED WORDS:
  noun — **en′er·va′tion**
  adjective — **en′er·va′tive**
  noun — **en′er·va′tor**

⚘ By mistakenly assuming that *enervate* is a close cousin of the verb *energize*, people sometimes use *enervate* incorrectly to mean "to invigorate" or "to excite" (as in *I was sleepy, so I took a cold shower hoping it would enervate me*). In fact, *enervate* does not come from the same source as *energize* (Greek *energos*, "active"). It comes from Latin *nervus*, "sinew." Thus *enervate* means "to cause to become 'out of muscle'," that is, "to weaken or deplete of strength."

e·nor·mi·ty (ĭ-nôr′mĭ-tē)

noun

Plural: **e·nor·mi·ties**

1. The quality of passing all moral bounds; excessive wickedness or outrageousness. **2.** A monstrous offense or evil; an outrage. **3.** Usage Problem Great size; immensity: *The enormity of the hot-air balloon amazed all the onlookers.*

[French *énormité*, from Old French, from Latin *ēnormitās*, from *ēnormis*, unusual, enormous.]

℅ *Enormity* is frequently used to refer simply to the property of being great in size or extent, but many would prefer that *enormousness* (or a synonym such as *immensity*) be used for this general sense and that *enormity* be limited to situations that demand a negative moral judgment, as in *Not until the war ended and journalists were able to enter Cambodia did the world really become aware of the enormity of Pol Pot's oppression.* According to this rule, the sentence *At that point, the engineers sat down to design an entirely new viaduct, apparently undaunted by the enormity of their task* would be considered incorrect. This distinction between *enormity* and *enormousness* has not always existed historically, but nowadays many observe it. You may want to avoid using *enormity* in phrases such as *the enormity of the support the mayor received in the election* as *enormity*'s sense of monstrousness may leave your audience misinterpreting what it is you are trying to say.

31

e·nor·mous·ness (ĭ-nôr′məs-nəs)

noun

The state or condition of being very great in size, extent, number, or degree: "[The whale] *seemed hardly to budge at all...good evidence was hereby furnished of the enormousness of the mass we moved*" (Herman Melville, *Moby-Dick*).

[enormous (from Latin *ēnormis,* unusual, huge, monstrous : *ē-, ex-,* ex- + *norma,* norm) + -ness (from Middle English *-nes,* from Old English).]

RELATED WORDS:
adjective—**e·nor′mous**
adverb—**e·nor′mous·ly**

SEE NOTE AT **enormity** (ON PAGE 226).

en·sure (ĕn-shoor′)

transitive verb

Past participle and past tense: **en·sured**
Present participle: **en·sur·ing**
Third person singular present tense: **en·sures**

To make sure or certain; insure: *"The world is still engaged in a massive armaments race designed to ensure continuing equivalent strength among potential adversaries"* (Jimmy Carter, Inaugural Address).

[Middle English *ensuren,* from Anglo-Norman *enseurer* : Old French *en-,* causative prefix + Old French *seur,* secure, variant of *sur.*]

SEE NOTE AT **insure** (ON PAGE 248).

The world is still engaged in a massive armaments race designed to **ensure** continuing equivalent strength among potential adversaries. We pledge perseverance and wisdom in our efforts to limit the world's armaments to those necessary for each nation's own domestic safety. And we will move this year a step toward ultimate goal—the elimination of all nuclear weapons from this Earth. We urge all other people to join us, for success can mean life instead of death.

— Jimmy Carter,
Inaugural Address

33
fac·toid (făk′toid)

noun

1. A piece of unverified or inaccurate information that is presented in the press as factual, often as part of a publicity effort, and that is then accepted as true because of frequent repetition: *"What one misses finally is what might have emerged beyond both facts and factoids—a profound definition of the Marilyn Monroe phenomenon"* (Christopher Lehmann-Haupt, *New York Times*). **2.** USAGE PROBLEM A brief, somewhat interesting fact.

RELATED WORD:
   adjective—**fac·toi′dal**

🖎 The *–oid* suffix normally imparts the meaning "resembling, having the appearance of" to the words it attaches to. Thus the *anthropoid apes* are the apes that are most like humans (from Greek *anthrōpos,* "human being"). In some words *–oid* has a slightly extended meaning—"having characteristics of, but not the same as," as in *humanoid,* a being that has human characteristics but is not really human. Similarly, *factoid* originally referred to a piece of information that appears to be reliable or accurate, as from being repeated so often that people assume it is true.

   Factoid has since developed a second meaning, that of a brief, somewhat interesting fact, that might better have been called a *factette,* as in *Each day the newspaper prints a list of factoids such as what kinds of condiments people prefer on ham sandwiches.* If you wish to avoid this usage, you can instead choose *statistics, trivia, useless facts,* and just plain *facts.*

few·er (fyōo′ər)

adjective

The comparative form of **few.** Amounting to or consisting of a smaller number: *The catcher played fewer innings than the shortstop did.*

pronoun

A smaller number of persons or things: *Chris ate six slices of pizza, and Lee had fewer.*

[Middle English, from Old English *fēawe* + Middle English *-er,* comparative suffix.]

✍ The traditional rule holds that *fewer* should be used for things that can be counted (*fewer than four players*), while *less* should be used with mass terms for things of measurable extent (*less paper; less than a gallon of paint*). However, *less* is used in some constructions where *fewer* would occur if the traditional rule were being followed. *Less than* can be used before a plural noun that denotes a measure of time, amount, or distance: *less than three weeks; less than $400; less than 50 miles.* *Less* is sometimes used with plural nouns in the expressions *no less than* (as in *No less than 30 of his colleagues signed the letter*) and *or less* (as in *Give your reasons in 25 words or less*).

35
fla·grant (flā′grənt)

adjective

Conspicuously bad, offensive, or reprehensible: *"[S]ome-times the very presence of received wisdom keeps blinders on us all, even when evidence of abuse of power or sloppy procedures is flagrant"* (Patricia Holt, *San Francisco Chronicle*).

[Latin *flagrāns, flagrant-*, present participle of *flagrāre*, to burn.]

RELATED WORDS:
> *noun*—**fla′grance**
> *adverb*—**fla′grant·ly**

SEE NOTE AT **blatant** (ON PAGE 209).

36
flam·ma·ble (flăm′ə-bəl)

adjective

Easily ignited and capable of burning rapidly; in-flammable: *"Until the early 1980's, many renderers had used flammable solvents to dissolve fats, and the solvents may have deactivated the agent that causes mad cow disease and scrapie"* (Sandra Blakeslee, *New York Times*).

[From Latin *flammāre*, to set fire to, from *flamma*, flame.]

RELATED WORDS:
> *noun*—**flam′ma·bil′i·ty**
> *noun*—**flam′ma·ble**
> *adverb*—**flam′ma·bly**

SEE NOTE AT **inflammable** (ON PAGE 247).

flaunt (flônt)

verb

> Past participle and past tense: **flaunt·ed**
> Present participle: **flaunt·ing**
> Third person singular present tense: **flaunts**

transitive **1.** To exhibit ostentatiously or shamelessly: *"In everything a prudent man acts with knowledge, but a fool flaunts his folly"* (Proverbs 13:16). **2.** USAGE PROBLEM To show contempt for; scorn.

intransitive **1.** To parade oneself ostentatiously; show oneself off. **2.** To wave grandly: *"Flaunt away, flags of all nations!"* (Walt Whitman, *Leaves of Grass*).

[Origin unknown.]

RELATED WORDS:
> *noun*— **flaunt′er**
> *adverb*— **flaunt′ing·ly**

☙ *Flaunt* as a transitive verb means "to exhibit ostentatiously": *They flaunted their wealth by wearing expensive clothing and jewelry.* To *flout* is "to show contempt for": *They flouted old civic traditions.* For some time now *flaunt* has been used in the sense "to show contempt for," even by educated users of English, but many people regard this usage as erroneous.

flout (flout)

verb

> Past participle and past tense: **flout·ed**
> Present participle: **flout·ing**
> Third person singular present tense: **flouts**

transitive To show contempt for; scorn: *"Considered on its face, suicide flouts the laws of nature, slashing through the sturdy instinct that wills all beings to fight for their lives until they can fight no longer"* (Natalie Angier, *The Beauty of the Beastly*).

intransitive To be scornful.

noun

A contemptuous action or remark; an insult: *"Bruise me with scorn, confound me with a flout; Thrust thy sharp wit quite through my ignorance; Cut me to pieces with thy keen conceit"* (William Shakespeare, *Love's Labours Lost*).

RELATED WORDS:
> *noun* — **flout′er**
> *adverb* — **flout′ing·ly**

[Perhaps from Middle English *flouten,* to play the flute, from Old French *flauter,* from *flaute,* flute.]

SEE NOTE AT **flaunt** (ON PAGE 233).

39

for·te (fôr′tā′, fôrt)

noun

1. Something in which a person excels: *"[O]ur senator had the misfortune to be a man who had a particularly humane and accessible nature, and turning away anybody that was in trouble never had been his forte"* (Harriet Beecher Stowe, *Uncle Tom's Cabin*). **2.** The strong part of a sword blade, between the middle and the hilt.

[French *fort*, from Old French, strong, from Latin *fortis*.]

🙣 Many claim that the word *forte,* coming from French *fort,* should properly be pronounced with one syllable, like the English word *fort.* Common usage, however, prefers the two-syllable pronunciation, (fôr′tā′), which has been influenced possibly by the music term *forte,* borrowed from Italian. Speakers can continue to pronounce it as one syllable knowing that the origin of the word supports this pronunciation, but they do so at an increasing risk of puzzling their listeners.

gen·der (jĕn′dər)

noun

1a. A grammatical category used in the classification of nouns, pronouns, adjectives, and, in some languages, verbs that may be arbitrary or based on characteristics such as sex or animacy and that determines agreement with or selection of modifiers, referents, or grammatical forms. **b.** The distinguishing form or forms used. **2.** Sexual identity, especially in relation to society or culture. **3a.** The condition of being female or male; sex. **b.** Females or males considered as a group: *The linguist studied expressions predominantly used by one gender.*

[Middle English *gendre,* from Old French, kind, gender, from Latin *genus, gener-.*]

☞ Traditionally, *gender* has been used primarily to refer to the grammatical categories of "masculine," "feminine," and "neuter," but in recent years the word has become well established in its use to refer to sex-based categories, as in phrases such as *gender gap* and *the politics of gender.* This usage is supported by the practice of many anthropologists and others concerned with the behaviors and attitudes of men and women. This distinction is sometimes summed up by the expression "Sex is who we are; gender is what we do." Accordingly, one would say *The effectiveness of the medication appears to depend on the sex* (not *gender*) *of the patient,* but *In peasant societies, gender* (not *sex*) *roles are likely to be more clearly defined.* This distinction is useful in principle, but it is by no means widely observed, and considerable variation in usage occurs at all levels.

hope·ful·ly (hōp′fə-lē)

adverb

1. In a hopeful manner. **2.** USAGE PROBLEM It is to be hoped: *Hopefully, it will stop raining before the game starts.*

If you use *hopefully* as a sentence adverb, as in *Hopefully the measures will be adopted,* be aware that the usage is unacceptable to many critics, including a large majority of the Usage Panel. It is not easy to explain why critics dislike this use of *hopefully.* The use is justified by analogy to similar uses of many other adverbs, as in *Mercifully, the lecture was brief* or *Frankly, I have no use for your suggestions.* And though this use of *hopefully* may have been a vogue word when it first gained currency back in the early 1960s, it has long since lost any hint of jargon or pretentiousness. The wide acceptance of the usage reflects popular recognition of its handiness; there is no precise substitute. Someone who says *Hopefully, the treaty will be ratified* makes a hopeful prediction about the fate of the treaty, whereas someone who says *I hope* (or *We hope* or *It is hoped*) *the treaty will be ratified* expresses a bald statement about what is desired. Only the latter could be continued with a clause such as *but it isn't likely.*

It might have been expected, then, that the initial flurry of objections to *hopefully* would have subsided once the usage became well established. Instead, critics appear to have become more adamant in their opposition. In the 1969 Usage Panel survey, 44 percent of the Panel approved the usage, but this dropped to 27 percent in our 1986 survey. (By contrast, 60 percent in the latter survey accepted the comparable use of *mercifully* in the sentence *Mercifully, the game ended before the opponents could add another touchdown to the lopsided score.*) Perhaps it is not the use of sentence adverbs per se that bothers critics; rather, it seems that the specific use of *hopefully* in this way has become a shibboleth, a marker of poor education or a lack of refinement.

42

im·pact (ĭm′păkt′)

noun

1. The striking of one body against another; collision: *The impact of the meteorite left a large crater.* **2.** The effect or impression of one thing on another: *The report gauges the impact of automation on the lives of factory workers.* **3.** The power of making a strong, immediate impression: *Unfortunately, the candidate gave a speech that lacked impact.*

verb (ĭm-păkt′)
Past participle and past tense: **im·pact·ed**
Present participle: **im·pact·ing**
Third person singular present tense: **im·pacts**

transitive **1.** To pack firmly together. **2.** To strike forcefully: *The astronomers observed meteorites impacting the lunar surface.* **3.** USAGE PROBLEM To have an effect or impact on: *The manufacturing industry has been impacted by recent trade agreements.*

intransitive USAGE PROBLEM To have an effect or impact.

[From Latin *impāctus*, past participle of *impingere*, to push against.]

RELATED WORD:
   noun—**im·pac′tion**

૪ૐ The use of impact as a verb meaning "to have an effect" often has a big impact on readers. Most language critics disapprove of the construction *to impact on*, as in *These policies are impacting on our ability to achieve success*, a sentence 85 percent of the Usage Panel found unacceptable in 2001. The use of *impact* as a transitive verb, as in the sentence *The court ruling will impact the education of minority students*, was unacceptable to 80 percent of the Panel.

It is unclear why this usage provokes such a strong response, but it cannot be because of novelty. *Impact* has been used as a verb since 1601, when it meant "to fix or pack in," and its modern, figurative use dates from 1935. It may be that its frequent appearance in the jargon-riddled remarks of politicians, military officials, and financial analysts continues to make people suspicious. Nevertheless, the verbal use of *impact* has become so common in the working language of corporations and institutions that many speakers have begun to regard it as standard.

43
im·peach (ĭm-pēch′)

transitive verb
> Past participle and past tense: **im·peached**
> Present participle: **im·peach·ing**
> Third person singular present tense: **im·peach·es**

1. To charge (a public official) with improper conduct in office before a proper tribunal: *The House of Representatives impeached Andrew Johnson in 1868 and Bill Clinton in 1998; neither was convicted.* **2.** To challenge the validity of; try to discredit: *The lawyer impeached the witness's credibility with a string of damaging questions.*

[Middle English *empechen*, to impede, accuse, from Anglo-Norman *empecher*, from Late Latin *impedicāre*, to entangle : Latin *in-*, in + Latin *pedica*, fetter.]

RELATED WORDS:
> *adjective*— **im·peach′a·ble**
> *noun*— **im·peach′er**
> *noun*— **im·peach′ment**

When an irate citizen demands that a disfavored public official be impeached, the citizen clearly intends for the official to be removed from office. This popular use of *impeach* as a synonym of "throw out" (even if by due process) does not accord with the legal meaning of the word. As recent history has shown, when a public official is impeached, that is, formally accused of wrongdoing, this is only the start of what can be a lengthy process that may or may not lead to the official's removal from office. In strict usage, an official is impeached (accused), tried, and then convicted or acquitted. The vaguer use of *impeach* reflects disgruntled citizens' indifference to whether the official is forced from office by legal means or chooses to resign to avoid further disgrace.

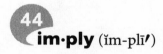

im·ply (ĭm-plī′)

transitive verb
 Past participle and past tense: **im·plied**
 Present participle: **im·ply·ing**
 Third person singular present tense: **im·plies**

1. To involve by logical necessity; entail: *"[S]chool would be a complete change: it implied a long journey, an entire separation from Gateshead, an entrance into a new life"* (Charlotte Brontë, *Jane Eyre*). **2.** To express or indicate indirectly: *"'Oh, shut up!' murmured his brother Dan. The manner of his words implied that this fraternal voice near him was an indescribable bore"* (Stephen Crane, *The Little Regiment*).

[Middle English *implien,* from Old French *emplier,* to enfold, from Latin *implicāre.*]

SEE NOTE AT **infer** (ON PAGE 246).

in·cred·i·ble (ĭn-krĕd′ə-bəl)

adjective

1. So implausible as to elicit disbelief: "*The next instant we were flying headlong through the air toward the surface of the lake a hundred feet below. Men have told me since that I never made that dive, or that I greatly overestimated the distance, and I admit that as I look back at it now it appears incredible*" (Rex Stout, *Under The Andes*).
2. Extraordinary: "*My father...became a busker and then a singing waiter and then a songwriter, and he felt incredible gratitude to this country for giving him the chance to become who he became*" (Mary Ellin Barrett, *Newsweek*).

[Middle English, from Latin *incrēdibilis* : *in-*, not + *crēdibilis*, believable.]

RELATED WORDS:
>   *noun* — **in·cred′i·bil′i·ty**
>   *noun* — **in·cred′i·ble·ness**
>   *adverb* — **in·cred′i·bly**

🙢 *Incredible* means "hard to believe, unbelievable": *His explanation of the cause of the accident was simply incredible.* It is often used more loosely to mean "extraordinary" or "astonishing," as in *The new pitcher has an incredible fastball. Incredulous* usually means "skeptical, disbelieving," as in *The incredulous reporters laughed at the manager's explanation of how the funds disappeared.* It is sometimes extended to mean "showing disbelief," as in *an incredulous stare.* You may occasionally see *incredulous* used where you would expect *incredible,* as in *an incredulous display of rudeness.* This usage is not well established, however, and is widely considered an error.

in·cred·u·lous (ĭn-krĕj'ə-ləs)

adjective

1. Disbelieving or doubtful; skeptical: *"[B]efore me the ice parted to reveal the cold, muddy swirl twisting below. . . . That's when common sense and terror hit and I headed for shore. . . . When I reached land, I looked back, incredulous that I'd thought I could actually make it across"* (William Least Heat-Moon, *River-Horse*). **2.** Expressive of or showing disbelief: *an incredulous stare.* **3.** Usage Problem Hard or impossible to believe.

[From Latin *incrēdulus* : *in-*, not + *crēdulus*, believing.]

RELATED WORDS:
 adverb — **in·cred'u·lous·ly**
 noun — **in·cred'u·lous·ness**

SEE NOTE AT **incredible** (ON PAGE 242).

I felt the floe I stood on begin to shake, then wobble, and before me the ice parted to reveal the cold, muddy swirl twisting below—a more fearsome thing I'd never seen. The frozen river wasn't locked in place as I'd supposed but was being forced slowly downstream, buckling, snapping, opening, closing, ready to swallow whatever came onto it. That's when common sense and terror hit and I headed for shore, unsure whether to go gently and slowly or hard and fast.... When I reached land, I looked back, **incredulous** that I'd thought I could actually make it across.

—William Least Heat-Moon,
River-Horse

47

in·fer (ĭn-fûr′)

transitive verb

> Past participle and past tense: **in·ferred**
> Present participle: **in·fer·ring**
> Third person singular present tense: **in·fers**

1. To conclude from evidence or reasoning: *"Unlike many other functions, reading cannot be studied in animals; indeed, for many years the cerebral localization of all higher cognitive processes could be inferred only from the effects of brain injuries on the people who survived them"* (Sally E. Shaywitz, *Scientific American*). **2.** To hint; imply.

[Latin *īnferre,* to bring in, adduce : *in-,* in + *ferre,* to bear.]

RELATED WORDS:

> *adjective*— **in·fer′a·ble**
> *adverb*— **in·fer′a·bly**
> *noun*— **in′fer·ence**

♈ *Infer* is sometimes confused with *imply,* but it makes good sense to keep these verbs distinct. Inference is the activity performed by a reader or interpreter in drawing conclusions that are not explicit in what is said: *When the mayor said that she would not rule out a tax increase, we inferred that she had been consulting with some new financial advisers, since her old advisers were in favor of tax reductions.* On the other hand, when we say that a speaker or sentence implies something, we mean that it is conveyed or suggested without being stated outright: *When the mayor said that she would not rule out a business tax increase, she implied* (not *inferred*) *that some taxes might be raised.*

---

in·flam·ma·ble (ĭn-flăm′ə-bəl)

adjective

Easily ignited and capable of burning rapidly; flammable: *"Slurry decomposes in storage and produces a mixture of gases.... All are unpleasant, some can be inflammable, and one in particular, hydrogen sulphide, is extremely poisonous to humans and animals alike"* (Edna O'Brien, *Wild Decembers*).

[Middle English, liable to inflammation, from Medieval Latin *īnflammābilis,* from Latin *īnflammāre.*]

RELATED WORDS:
> *noun —* **in·flam′ma·bil′i·ty**
> *noun —* **in·flam′ma·ble**
> *adverb—* **in·flam′ma·bly**

☞ Historically, *flammable* and *inflammable* mean the same thing. However, the presence of the prefix *in–* has misled many people into assuming that *inflammable* means "not flammable" or "noncombustible." The prefix *in–* in *inflammable* is not, however, the Latin negative prefix *in–,* which is related to the English *un–* and appears in such words as *indecent* and *inglorious.* Rather, this *in–* is an intensive prefix derived from the Latin preposition *in.* This prefix also appears in the word *inflame.* But many people are not aware of this derivation, and for clarity's sake it is advisable to use only *flammable* if you want to give a warning. If you wish to refer to the inability to catch on fire, use *nonflammable,* which is unambiguous.

in·sure (ĭn-shŏŏr′)

transitive verb

Past participle and past tense: **in·sured**
Present participle: **in·sur·ing**
Third person singular present tense: **in·sures**

1a. To provide or arrange insurance for: *"In the past two years, the number of patients [who are] insured by managed care plans has grown by about one-third"* (Lisa Belkin, *New York Times Magazine*). **b.** To acquire or have insurance for: *"More than 300,000 laptops were stolen last year alone, and so the company insures each bag with a computer compartment for up to $1,500 if it's stolen in the first year"* (Stephanie Cook, *Christian Science Monitor*). **2.** To make sure, certain, or secure: *"By relying primarily on voluntary cooperation and private enterprise...we can insure that the private sector is a check on the powers of the governmental sector and an effective protection of freedom of speech, of religion, and of thought"* (Milton Friedman, *Capitalism and Freedom*).

[Middle English *ensuren,* to assure, from Old French *enseurer,* possibly variant of *assurer.*]

RELATED WORDS:
   noun — **in·sur′a·bil′i·ty**
   adjective — **in·sur′a·ble**

⚘ *Assure, ensure,* and *insure* all mean "to make secure or certain." Only *assure* is used with reference to a person in the sense of "to set the mind at rest": *The ambassador assured the Prime Minister of his loyalty.* Although *ensure* and *insure* are generally interchangeable, only *insure* is now widely used in American English in the commercial sense of "to guarantee persons or property against risk."

i·ro·ny (ī′rə-nē, ī′ər-nē)

noun

Plural: **i·ro·nies**

1a. The use of words to express something different from and often opposite to their literal meaning. **b.** An expression or utterance marked by a deliberate contrast between apparent and intended meaning. **c.** A literary style employing such contrasts for humorous or rhetorical effect. **2a.** Incongruity between what might be expected and what actually occurs. **b.** An occurrence, result, or circumstance notable for such incongruity. **3.** The dramatic effect achieved by leading an audience to understand an incongruity between a situation in a play and its accompanying speeches, while the characters remain unaware of the incongruity; dramatic irony.

[French *ironie*, from Old French, from Latin *īrōnīa*, from Greek *eirōneia*, feigned ignorance, from *eirōn*, dissembler, probably from *eirein*, to say.]

RELATED WORDS:

    adjective—**i·ron′ic**
    adverb—**i·ron′i·cal·ly**

⌘ The words *ironic, irony,* and *ironically* are sometimes used of events and circumstances that might better be described as simply "coincidental" or "improbable," in that they suggest no particular lessons about human vanity or folly. The Usage Panel dislikes the looser use of these words; 78 percent rejected the use of *ironically* in the sentence *In 1969 Susie moved from Ithaca to California where she met her husband-to-be, who, ironically, also came from upstate New York.* Some Panelists noted that this particular usage might be acceptable if Susie had in fact moved to California in order to find a husband, in which case the story could be taken as exemplifying the folly of supposing that we can know what fate has in store for us. By contrast, 73 percent accepted the sentence *Ironically, even as the government was fulminating against American policy, American jeans and videocassettes were the hottest items in the stalls of the market,* where the incongruity of the government's statements and the practices it tolerates as necessary can be seen as an example of human inconsistency.

ir·re·gard·less (ĭr′ĭ-gärd′lĭs)

adverb

NONSTANDARD Regardless.

[Probably blend of *irrespective* and *regardless.*]

ℛ *Irregardless* is a word that many mistakenly believe to be correct usage in formal style, when in fact it is used chiefly in nonstandard speech or casual writing. Coined in the United States in the early 20th century, it has met with a blizzard of condemnation for being an improper yoking of *irrespective* and *regardless* and for the logical absurdity of combining the negative *ir–* prefix and *–less* suffix in a single term. Although one might reasonably argue that it is no different from words with redundant affixes like *debone* and *unravel,* it has been considered a blunder for decades and will probably continue to be so.

its (ĭts)

adjective

The possessive form of **it.** Used as a modifier before a noun: *The airline canceled its early flight to New York.*

[Alteration of *it's* : it + 's.]

SEE NOTE AT **it's** (ON PAGE 251).

53

it's (ĭts)

1. Contraction of *it is.* **2.** Contraction of *it has.*

🙋 *Its* is the possessive form of the pronoun *it* and is correctly written without an apostrophe: *The kitten licked its paws.* It should not be confused with the contraction *it's* (for *it is* or *it has*), which should always have an apostrophe: *It's snowing outside. It's been years since I've visited Chicago.*

54

ku·dos (ko͞o′dōz′, ko͞o′dōs′, ko͞o′dŏs′, kyo͞o′dōz′, kyo͞o′dōs′, kyo͞o′dŏs′)

noun

Acclaim or praise for exceptional achievement.

[Greek *kūdos*, magical glory.]

🙋 *Kudos* is one of those words like *congeries* that look like plurals but are etymologically singular. Acknowledging the Greek history of the term requires *Kudos is* (not *are*) *due her for her brilliant work on the score.* But *kudos* has often been treated as a plural, especially in the popular press, as in *She received many kudos for her work.* This plural use has given rise to the singular form *kudo.* These innovations follow the pattern whereby the English words *pea* and *cherry* were shortened from nouns ending in an (s) sound (English *pease* and French *cerise*), that were mistakenly thought to be plural. The singular *kudo* remains far less common than the plural use; both are often viewed as incorrect in more formal contexts.

It is worth noting that even people who are careful to treat *kudos* only as a singular often pronounce it as if it were a plural. Etymology would require that the final consonant be pronounced as a voiceless (s), as we do in *pathos,* another word derived from Greek, rather than as a voiced (z).

lay (lā)

verb

Past participle and past tense: **laid**
Present participle: **lay·ing**
Third person singular present tense: **lays**

transitive **1a.** To place or put, especially on a flat surface or in a horizontal position: *I laid the baby in the crib.* **b.** To put or place in a certain position or condition: *The remark laid him open to criticism.* **2.** To put in place; set down: *The workers are laying tiles down in the kitchen.* **3.** To produce (an egg or eggs). **4.** To cause to subside or become calm: *". . . chas'd the clouds, and laid the winds"* (John Milton, *Paradise Regained*). **5.** To put in order; prepare: *"He did not look at her but busied himself with his breakfast. . . He prepared coffee and laid the table"* (Carson McCullers, *The Heart Is a Lonely Hunter*). **6.** To spread over a surface: *The artist lays paint on the canvas.* **7.** To impose as a burden or punishment: *The police officer laid a fine on the offender.* **8.** To put forth; present for examination: *The lawyer laid the case before the court.* **9.** To place or give (importance, for example): *The teacher lays great value on correct grammar.* **10.** To assign; charge: *They laid the blame on us.* **11.** To place (a bet); wager: *At the race track, the gambler laid $100 on his favorite horse.*

intransitive To produce an egg or eggs: *The hens stopped laying suddenly.*

---

noun

The way in which something is situated or organized: *"Duane peered through the branches and studied the lay of the land"* (Zane Grey, *The Lone Star Ranger*).

[Middle English *leien,* from Old English *lecgan.*]

🙚 *Lay* ("to put, place, or prepare") and *lie* ("to recline or be situated") have been confused for centuries; evidence exists that *lay* has been used to mean "lie" since the 1300s. Why? First, there are two *lay*s. One is the base form of the verb *lay,* and the other is the past tense of *lie.* Second, *lay* was once used with a reflexive pronoun to mean "lie" and survives in the familiar line from the child's prayer *Now I lay me down to sleep; lay me down* is easily shortened to *lay down.* Third, *lay down,* as in *She lay down on the sofa* sounds the same as *laid down,* as in *I laid down the law to the kids.* It's not surprising that all this similarity of sound has produced confusion of usage, but traditional grammar requires that the two words be kept distinct.

Lay and *lie* are most easily distinguished by the following guidelines: *Lay* is a transitive verb and takes a direct object. *Lay* and its principal parts (*laid, laying*) are correctly used in the following examples: *He laid* (not *lay*) *the newspaper on the table. The table was laid for four. Lie* is an intransitive verb and cannot take an object. *Lie* and its principal parts (*lay, lain, lying*) are correctly used in the following examples: *She often lies* (not *lays*) *down after lunch. When I lay* (not *laid*) *down, I fell asleep. The garbage had lain* (not *laid*) *there a week. I was lying* (not *laying*) *in bed when he called.*

leave (lēv)

verb

> Past participle and past tense: **left**
> Present participle: **leav·ing**
> Third person singular present tense: **leaves**

transitive

1. To go out of or go away from: *After she finished the report, she left the office.* **2.** To end one's association with; withdraw from: *After ten years in the service, he left the navy for civilian life.* **3.** To go without taking or removing; forget: *I left my book on the bus.* **4.** To allow to remain unused: *I left some milk in the glass.* **5.** To allow to remain in a certain condition or place: *He left the lights on all night.* **6.** To give to another to control, act on, or use; entrust: *Leave all the details to us.* **7.** To give by will; bequeath: *"Jonah argued that men liked to make a surprise of their wills, while Martha said that nobody need be surprised if he left the best part of his money to those who least expected it"* (George Eliot, *Middlemarch*). **8.** To have as a result, consequence, or remainder: *The car left a trail of exhaust fumes. Two from eight leaves six.* **9.** NONSTANDARD To allow or permit; let.

intransitive To set out or depart; go: *We left after lunch.*

---

leave alone *or* **let alone** To refrain from disturbing or interfering with: *"'Leave my books alone!' he said. 'You might have thrown them aside if you had liked, but as to soiling them like that, it is disgusting!'"* (Thomas Hardy, *Jude the Obscure*).

[Middle English *leaven*, from Old English *lǣfan*.]

❧ In formal writing, *leave* is not an acceptable substitute for *let* in the sense "to allow or permit." Thus in the following examples, only *let* can be used: *Let me be. Let him go. Let it lie.*

Leave alone is an acceptable substitute for *let alone* in the sense "to refrain from disturbing or interfering with," as in *Left alone, he was quite productive.* However, there are some who do not accept this usage and feel that *leave alone* should mean simply "to depart from someone who remains in solitude," as in *They were left alone in the wilderness.*

less (lĕs)

adjective

A comparative of **little. 1.** Not as great in amount or quantity: *I have less money than I did yesterday.* **2.** Lower in importance, esteem, or rank: *The speaker was no less a person than the ambassador.* **3.** Consisting of a smaller number.

preposition

With the deduction of; minus: *Five less two is three.*

adverb

The comparative of **little. To** a smaller extent, degree, or frequency: *"We replaced and screwed down the lid, and, having secured the door of iron, made our way, with toil, into the scarcely less gloomy apartments of the upper portion of the house"* (Edgar Allan Poe, *The Fall of the House of Usher*).

noun

1. A smaller amount: *She received less than she asked for.* **2.** Something not as important as something else: *People have been punished for less.*

IDIOMS:

less than Not at all: *He had a less than favorable view of the matter.*

much less *or* **still less** Certainly not: *I'm not blaming anyone, much less you.*

[Middle English *lesse,* from Old English *lǣssa* (adjective), and *lǣs* (adverb).]

SEE NOTE AT **fewer** (ON PAGE 231).

let (lĕt)

verb

> Past participle and past tense: **let**
> Present participle: **let·ting**
> Third person singular present tense: **lets**

1. To give permission or opportunity to; allow: *I let them borrow the car. The inheritance money let us finally buy a house.* **2.** To cause to; make: *Let me know what happens.* **3.** Used as an auxiliary verb to express a command, request, or warning: *Let's finish the job!* **4.** Used as an auxiliary verb to express a proposal or assumption: *Let x equal 3.* **5.** To permit to enter, proceed, or depart: *"When we returned home, we let the dogs out, as we always did, to run around before they were shut in for the night"* (Lydia Davis, *St. Martin*). **6.** To permit escape; release: *Who let the air out of the balloon?* **7.** To rent or lease: *The landlord lets rooms to students.*

intransitive To become rented or leased: *The apartment lets for $900 a month.*

IDIOMS:

let alone 1. Not to mention; much less: *"Their ancestors had been dirt poor and never saw royalty, let alone hung around with them"* (Garrison Keillor, *Lake Wobegon Days*). **2.** *or* **leave alone** To refrain from disturbing or interfering: *"'Let me alone! let me alone!' sobbed Catherine. 'If I've done wrong, I'm dying for it. It is enough!'"* (Emily Brontë, *Wuthering Heights*).

let go To cease to employ; dismiss: *The factory let 20 workers go.*

[Middle English *leten*, from Old English *lǣtan*.]

SEE NOTE AT **leave** (ON PAGE 254).

---

lie (lī)

intransitive verb

> Past tense: **lay**
> Past participle: **lain**
> Present participle: **ly·ing**
> Third person singular present tense: **lies**

1. To place oneself at rest in a flat, horizontal, or resting position; recline: *He lay under a tree to sleep.* **2.** To be in a flat, horizontal, or resting position: *"I collected the instruments of life around me, that I might infuse a spark of being into the lifeless thing that lay at my feet"* (Mary Wollstonecraft Shelley, *Frankenstein*). **3.** To be or rest on a surface: *Dirty dishes lay on the table.* **4.** To be located: *The lake lies beyond this hill.* **5.** To remain in a certain position or condition: *The dust has lain undisturbed for years.* **6.** To consist or have as a basis: *"Eric was pleased, but he always reminded himself that his success lay in promoting the talent of others"* (Louis Auchincloss, *Her Infinite Variety*). **7.** To extend: *Our land lies between these trees and the river.* **8.** To be buried in a specified place: *His ancestors lie in the town cemetery.*

noun

The manner or position in which something is situated, as the surface or slope of a piece of land.

[Middle English *lien*, from Old English *licgan*.]

SEE NOTE AT **lay** (ON PAGE 253).

---

lie

It was on a dreary night of November that I beheld the accomplishment of my toils. With an anxiety that almost amounted to agony, I collected the instruments of life around me, that I might infuse a spark of being into the lifeless thing that **lay** at my feet. It was already one in the morning; the rain pattered dismally against the panes, and my candle was nearly burnt out, when, by the glimmer of the half-extinguished light, I saw the dull yellow eye of the creature open; it breathed hard, and a convulsive motion agitated its limbs.

—Mary Wollstonecraft Shelley,
Frankenstein

60
lit·er·al·ly (lĭt′ər-ə-lē)

adverb

1. In a literal manner; word for word: *The scholar translated the Greek passage literally.* **2.** In a literal or strict sense: *Don't take my remarks literally.* **3.** USAGE PROBLEM Really; actually. Used as an intensive before a figurative expression: *He was laughing so hard his sides literally burst.*

☙ For more than a hundred years, critics have remarked on the incoherency of using *literally* in a way that suggests the exact opposite of its primary sense of "in a manner that accords with the literal sense of the words." In 1926, for example, H.W. Fowler cited the example *"The 300,000 Unionists...will be literally thrown to the wolves."* The practice does not stem from a change in the meaning of *literally* itself—if it did, the word would long since have come to mean "virtually" or "figuratively"—but from a natural tendency to use the word as a general intensive, as in *They had literally no help from the government on the project,* where no contrast with the figurative sense of the words is intended.

61
mass (măs)

noun

1. A measure of the amount of matter contained in or constituting a physical body: *"The Sun will swallow the planet Mercury and its outer rim will reach beyond the present orbit of Venus. Our sister planet will no longer be there, however, because as the Sun has lost mass, its gravitational pull on Venus (and Earth) has become less, and these planets have moved away from the encroaching fires"* (James Trefil, *Smithsonian*). **2.** A unified body of

---

matter with no specific shape: *"Cooks throughout the many nations also use yams, cassavas, green bananas and plantains. These staples are tasty on their own or combined with other ingredients to make a starchy mass for scooping up savory dishes"* (Jonell Nash, *Essence*). **3.** A large but nonspecific amount or number: *A mass of people entered the stadium.* **4.** The principal part; the majority: *The mass of the continent was visible from the rocketship.* **5.** The physical bulk or size of a solid body: *The huge mass of the ocean liner crept into the harbor.* **6. masses** The body of common people or people of low socioeconomic status: *"Give me your tired, your poor, / Your huddled masses yearning to breathe free"* (Emma Lazarus, *The New Colossus*).

verb

> Past participle and past tense: **massed**
> Present participle: **mass·ing**
> Third person singular present tense: **mass·es**

transitive To gather into a mass: *"[T]he population massed itself and moved toward the river, met the children coming in an open carriage drawn by shouting citizens, thronged around it, joined its homeward march, and swept magnificently up the main street roaring huzzah after huzzah!"* (Mark Twain, *The Adventures of Tom Sawyer*).

intransitive To be gathered into a mass: *The hikers massed together to stay warm.*

adjective

1. Of, relating to, characteristic of, directed at, or attended by a large number of people: *mass communication.* **2.** Done or carried out on a large scale: *mass pro-*

duction. **3.** Total; complete: *The mass result is impressive.*

[Middle English *masse,* from Old French, from Latin *massa,* from Greek *māza, maza.*]

☙ Although most hand-held calculators can translate pounds into kilograms, an absolute conversion factor between these two units is not technically sound. A pound is a unit of force, and a kilogram is a unit of mass. When the unit pound is used to indicate the force that a gravitational field exerts on a mass, the pound is a unit of weight. Mistaking weight for mass is tantamount to confusing the electric charges on two objects with the forces of attraction (or repulsion) between them. Like charge, the mass of an object is an intrinsic property of that object: electrons have a unique mass, protons have a unique mass, and some particles, such as photons, have no mass. Weight, on the other hand, is a force due to the gravitational attraction between two bodies. For example, one's weight on the Moon is ¹⁄₆ of one's weight on Earth. Nevertheless, one's mass on the Moon is identical to one's mass on Earth. The reason that hand-held calculators can translate between units of weight and units of mass is that the majority of us use calculators on the planet Earth at or near sea level, where the conversion factor is constant for all practical purposes.

62

mean (mēn)

noun

1. Something having a position, quality, or condition midway between extremes; a medium. **2.** A number that typifies a set of numbers, especially an arithmetic mean or average. **3.** Either the second or third term of a proportion of four terms. In the proportion $^2\!/_3 = {}^4\!/_6$, the means are 3 and 4. **4. means** *(used with a singular or plural verb)* A method, a course of action, or an instrument by which an act can be accomplished or an end achieved: *The solar panels provide a practical means of using the sun's energy to generate electricity.* **5. means** *(used with a plural verb)* Money, property, or other wealth: *The mayor was a person of means and bankrolled his election campaign.*

adjective

1. Occupying a middle or intermediate position between two extremes: *The school district analyzed the mean test scores of each class.* **2.** Intermediate in size, extent, quality, time, or degree; average.

IDIOMS:

by any means In any way possible: *We must fix this problem by any means.*
by no means In no sense; certainly not: *By no means should you go sailing in rough weather.*

[Middle English *mene*, middle, from Old French *meien*, from Latin *mediānus*, from *medius*.]

֍ In the sense of "financial resources" *means* takes a plural verb: *His means are more than adequate.* In the sense of "a way to an end," *means* may be treated as either a singular or plural. It is singular when referring to a particular strategy or method: *The best means of securing the cooperation of the builders is to appeal to their self-interest.* It is plural when it refers to a group of strategies or methods: *The most effective means for dealing with the drug problem have generally been those suggested by the affected communities.*

   Means is most often followed by *of*: *a means of noise reduction.* But *for, to,* and *toward* are also used: *a means for transmitting sound; a means to an end; a means toward achieving equality.*

63 **me·di·an** (mē′dē-ən)

noun

1. Something that lies halfway between two extremes; a medium. **2.** The middle number of a sequence having an odd number of values or the average of the two middle values if the sequence has an even number of values. For example, in the sequence 1, 2, 5, 10, 19, the median is 5; in the sequence 7, 8, 12, 16, the median is 10. **3a.** A line that joins a vertex of a triangle to the midpoint of the opposite side. **b.** The line that joins the midpoints of the nonparallel sides of a trapezoid.

adjective

1. Located in or extending toward the middle: *The lanes of traffic were separated by a median barrier.* **2.** Constituting the middle value in a set of numbers: *The statisticians analyzed the median score.*

[Latin *mediānus,* from *medius,* middle.]

᭠ In statistics, the concepts of *average* and *median* are often confused. To calculate an average, you add up all the items under consideration, and then divide by the number of items. So, for example, if a real estate agent sells five houses worth $95,000, $115,000, $190,000, $260,000, and $800,000, the average sales price is $292,000. Determining the *median* involves looking at the middle value in a series of values (if the series contains an even number of values, you then take the average of the middle two values). Using the above prices, the median sales price of these homes was $190,000. Median prices are often reported because it tells you that the same number of items fall above that value as fall below it, whereas if one of the values is much greater or lower than the other values, reporting the average may seem skewed, as in the example above.

64 mis·chie·vous (mĭs′chə-vəs)

adjective

1. Causing mischief; naughty: *"I've left my young children to look after themselves, and a more mischievous and troublesome set of young imps doesn't exist, ma'am"* (Kenneth Grahame, *The Wind in the Willows*). **2.** Showing a tendency or intent to play pranks or tease: *The child cast a mischievous glance.* **3.** Causing injury or damage: *The hard drive was destroyed by a mischievous computer virus.*

[Middle English *mischevous*, from *mischef*, mischief, from Old French *meschief*, misfortune, from *meschever*, to end badly : *mes-*, badly + *chever*, to happen, come to an end (from Vulgar Latin **capāre*, to come to a head, from **capum*, head, from Latin *caput*).]

RELATED WORDS:
   adverb—**mis′chie·vous·ly**
   noun—**mis′chie·vous·ness**

The pronunciation (mĭs-chē′vē-əs) is considered nonstandard, and is an example of *intrusion*, a phonological process that involves the addition or insertion of an extra sound. *Mischievous* is properly pronounced with three syllables, with the accent on the first syllable. The word is often misspelled with the suffix *-ious*, which matches the mispronunciation.

nu·cle·ar (nōō′klē-ər, nyōō′klē-ər)

adjective

1. Of, relating to, or forming a nucleus: *The biologist studied the cell's nuclear membrane under a microscope.* **2.** Of or relating to atomic nuclei: *"December 2 [1942]: Scientists at the University of Chicago achieve the first sustained nuclear chain reaction in human history"* (Alan Brinkley & Davis Dyer, eds., *The Readers Companion to the American Presidency*). **3.** Using or derived from the energy of atomic nuclei: *"[A]n attack on a nuclear power plant would not automatically mean a disaster on the scale of Chernobyl"* (Sonya Yee, *Christian Science Monitor*). **4.** Relating to, having, or involving atomic or hydrogen bombs: *"In the early 1980s, the U.S. experienced a nuclear hysteria—a morbid, near panicked fear of nuclear apocalypse"* (Charles Krauthammer, *Time*).

[Adjectival form of *nucleus,* from Latin *nuculeus,* nucleus, kernel, from *nucula,* little nut, diminutive of *nux, nuc-,* nut.]

🙨 The pronunciation (nōō′kyə-lər), which is generally considered incorrect, is an example of how a familiar phonological pattern can influence an unfamiliar one. The usual pronunciation of the final two syllables of this word is (-klē-ər), but this sequence of sounds is rare in English. Much more common is the similar sequence (-kyə-lər), which occurs in words like *particular, circular, spectacular,* and in many scientific words like *molecular, ocular,* and *vascular.* Adjusted to fit into this familiar pattern, the (-kyə-lər) pronunciation is often heard in high places. It is not uncommon in the military, even among commanders, in association with nuclear weaponry, and it has been a notable characteristic of the speech of presidents Dwight Eisenhower, Jimmy Carter, and George W. Bush. The prominence of these speakers, however, has done little to brighten the appeal of (nōō′kyə-lər) for many others.

---

pa·ram·e·ter (pə-răm′ĭ-tər)

noun

1. A variable or an arbitrary constant appearing in a mathematical expression, each value of which restricts or determines the specific form of the expression. **2a.** One of a set of measurable factors, such as temperature and pressure, that define a system and determine its behavior and are varied in an experiment. **b.** USAGE PROBLEM A factor that restricts what is possible or what results. **c.** A factor that determines a range of variations; a boundary: *The principal of the experimental school made sure that the parameters of its curriculum continued to expand.* **3.** USAGE PROBLEM A distinguishing characteristic or feature.

[New Latin *parametrum*, a line through the focus and parallel to the directrix of a conic : Greek *para-*, beside + Greek *metron*, measure.]

RELATED WORDS:

> *verb* — **pa·ram′e·ter·ize′** (pə-răm′ə-tə-rīz′)
> *adjective* — **par′a·met′ric** (păr′ə-mĕt′rĭk)
> *adverb* — **par′a·met′ri·cal·ly**

☙ The term *parameter,* which originates in mathematics, has a number of specific meanings in fields such as astronomy, electricity, crystallography, and statistics. Perhaps because of its ring of technical authority, it has been used more generally in recent years to refer to any factor that determines a range of variations and especially to a factor that restricts what can result from a process or policy. In this use it often comes close to meaning "a limit or boundary." Some of these new uses have a clear connection to the technical senses of the word. For example, the provisions of a zoning ordinance that limit the height or density of new construction can be reasonably likened to mathematical parameters that establish the limits of other variables. Therefore one can say *The zoning commission announced new planning parameters for the historic district of the city.* But other uses go one step further and treat *parameter* as a high-toned synonym for *characteristic.* In 1988, 80 percent of the Usage Panel rejected this use of *parameter* in the example *The Judeo-Christian ethic is one of the important parameters of Western culture.*

Some of the difficulties with the nontechnical use of *parameter* appear to arise from its resemblance to the word *perimeter,* with which it shares the sense "limit," though the precise meanings of the two words differ. This confusion probably explains the use of *parameter* in a sentence such as *US forces report that the parameters of the mine area in the Gulf are fairly well established,* where the word *perimeter* would have expressed the intended sense more exactly. This example of a use of *parameter* was unacceptable to 61 percent of the Usage Panel.

67

pe·nul·ti·mate (pĭ-nŭl′tə-mĭt)

adjective

1. Next to last: *"His cause for beatification, the penultimate step before sainthood, is still on course"* (Alessandra Stanley, *New York Times*). **2.** Of or relating to the next-to-last syllable of a word: *The word* renewal *has penultimate stress.*

noun

The next to the last.

[From Latin *paenultimus,* next to last : *paene,* almost + *ultimus,* last.]

RELATED WORD:
  adverb —**pe·nul′ti·mate·ly**

✌ *Penultimate* is sometimes mistakenly used where the word *ultimate* is called for, especially in the sense of "representing or exhibiting the greatest possible development or sophistication" as in the sentence *This car is the penultimate in engineering design.* This mistake is probably due to a misconception that *pen-* is a prefix that acts as an intensifier of the word *ultimate,* when it actually derives from the Latin word *paene,* meaning "almost." Thus, people who know the correct meaning of *penultimate* would reject its use as a synonym of *ultimate* and they may view the speaker or writer as not only pretentious, but ignorant as well.

per·suade (pər-swād′)

transitive verb
> Past participle and past tense: **per·suad·ed**
> Present participle: **per·suad·ing**
> Third person singular present tense: **per·suades**

To cause (someone) to do or believe something by means of argument, reasoning, or entreaty: *"Lord cardinal, will your grace / Persuade the queen to send the Duke of York / Unto his princely brother presently?"* (William Shakespeare, *Richard III*).

[Latin *persuādēre* : *per-*, per- + *suādēre,* to urge.]

RELATED WORD:
> *adjective* —**per·suad′a·ble**
> *noun* —**per·suad′er**

SEE NOTE AT **convince** (ON PAGE 217).

Fie, what an indirect and peevish course
Is this of hers! Lord cardinal, will your grace
Persuade the queen to send the Duke of York
Unto his princely brother presently?
If she deny, Lord Hastings, go with him,
And from her jealous arms pluck him perforce.

—William Shakespeare,
Richard III

pe·ruse (pə-rōōz′)

transitive verb
> Past participle and past tense: **pe·rused**
> Present participle: **pe·rus·ing**
> Third person singular present tense: **pe·rus·es**

To read or examine, typically with great care: *"He that shall peruse the political pamphlets of any past reign, will wonder why they were so eagerly read, or so loudly praised"* (Samuel Johnson, *The Rambler*).

[Middle English *perusen,* to use up : Latin *per-*, per- + Middle English *usen,* to use.]

RELATED WORDS:
> *adjective* —**pe·rus′a·ble**
> *noun* —**pe·rus′al**
> *noun* —**pe·rus′er**

☙ *Peruse* has long meant "to read thoroughly." Seventy-eight percent of the Usage Panel accepts *She perused the pages, carefully looking for errors.* But the word is sometimes used loosely as a highfalutin synonym for *read,* and some people even use it to mean "to glance over, skim" as in *I only had a moment to peruse the manual quickly.* This sentence was unacceptable to 58 percent of the Panel in a 1999 survey, down somewhat from 66 percent in 1988, suggesting that resistance is still quite strong to this usage.

phe·nom·e·non (fə-nŏm′ə-nŏn)

noun

1. (Plural: **phe·nom·e·na**) An occurrence, circumstance, or fact that is perceptible by the senses or with aid of instrumentation: *"Typical manifestations of T cells at work include such diverse phenomena as the rejection of a foreign skin graft and the killing of tumor cells"* (Gary W. Litman, *Scientific American*). **2.** (Plural: **phe·nom·e·nons**) A remarkable, significant, or outstanding person or thing: *"In an industry famous for cutthroat competition, this summer's reality TV shows have become a pop culture phenomenon and left a string of stunned TV executives scrambling to catch up"* (Lauren Hunter, *cnn.com*).

[Late Latin *phaenomenon,* from Greek *phainomenon,* from neuter present participle of *phainesthai,* to appear.]

The word *phenomenon* comes to us from Greek via Latin and usually keeps its Greek plural form *phenomena* when it means "an occurrence, circumstance, or fact that is perceptible by the senses." You may sometimes come across *phenomena* used as a singular noun, as in *This is a very strange phenomena,* but this usage is widely considered incorrect. The plural *phenomenons* is used frequently in nonscientific writing when the meaning is "extraordinary things, occurrences, or persons," as in *The Beatles were phenomenons in the history of rock 'n' roll.*

plus (plŭs)

conjunction

1. Added to: *Three plus two equals five.* **2.** Increased by; along with: *Their strength plus their spirit makes them formidable.* **3.** Usage Problem And: *I bought a dining table, plus four chairs and a mirror.*

adjective

1. Positive or on the positive part of a scale: *a temperature of plus five degrees.* **2.** Added or extra: *a plus benefit.* **3.** *Informal* Increased to a further degree or number: *"At 70 plus, [he] is old enough to be metaphysical"* (Anatole Broyard, *New York Times Book Review*). **4.** Ranking on the higher end of a designated scale: *I received a grade of B plus in chemistry.* **5.** Relating to or designating an electric charge of a sign opposite to that of an electron; positive.

noun

Plural **plus·es** *or* **plus·ses**

1. The plus sign (+). **2.** A positive quantity. **3.** A favorable condition or factor: *The clear weather was a plus for the golf tournament.*

[Latin *plūs,* more.]

When mathematical equations are pronounced as English sentences, the verb is usually in the singular: *Two plus two is* (or *equals*) *four.* By the same token, subjects containing two noun phrases joined by *plus* are usually construed as singular: *The construction slowdown plus the bad weather has made for a weak market.* This observation has led some to argue that in these sentences, *plus* functions as a preposition meaning "in addition to." But if this were true, the *plus* phrase could be moved to the beginning of the sentence. Clearly, this is not the case—we do not say *Plus the bad weather, the construction slowdown has made for a weak market.* It makes more sense to view *plus* in these uses as a conjunction that joins two subjects into a single entity requiring a single verb by notional agreement, just as *and* does in the sentence *Chips and beans is her favorite appetizer.*

The usage *plus which,* as in: *The construction industry has been hurt by the rise in rates. Plus which, bad weather has affected housing starts* is not well established in formal writing; nor is *plus* accepted as correct in introducing an independent clause, as in *She has a great deal of talent, plus she is willing to work hard.*

pre·cip·i·tate (prĭ-sĭp′ĭ-tāt′)

verb

Past participle and past tense: **pre·cip·i·tat·ed**
Present participle: **pre·cip·i·tat·ing**
Third person singular present tense: **pre·cip·i·tates**

transitive **1.** To throw from or as if from a great height; hurl downward: *"[T]he finest bridge in all Peru broke and precipitated five travelers into the gulf below"* (Thornton Wilder, *The Bridge of San Luis Rey*). **2.** To cause to happen, especially suddenly or prematurely: *The political scandal precipitated a torrent of legislative reforms.* **3.** To cause (water vapor) to condense and fall from the air as rain, snow, sleet, or hail. **4.** To cause (a solid substance) to be separated from a solution: *The chemist precipitated the minerals from the water by adding borax.*

intransitive **1.** To condense and fall from the air as rain, snow, sleet, or hail. **2.** To be separated from a solution as a solid. **3.** To send into a sudden state or condition: *The ailing economy precipitated into ruin despite foreign intervention.*

---

precipitate   **276**

adjective (prĭ-sĭp′ĭ-tĭt)

1. Moving rapidly and heedlessly; speeding headlong: *The meteorologists tracked the tornado's precipitate course.* **2.** Acting with or marked by excessive haste and lack of due deliberation; reckless: *They soon came to regret the precipitate decisions.* **3.** Occurring suddenly or unexpectedly: *The pundits couldn't explain the precipitate rise in oil prices.*

noun (prĭ-sĭp′ĭ-tāt′, prĭ-sĭp′ĭ-tĭt)

A chemical solid or solid phase separated from a solution.

[Latin *praecipitāre, praecipitāt-*, to throw headlong, from *praeceps, praecipit-*, headlong : *prae-*, pre- + *caput, capit-*, head.]

RELATED WORDS:
> *adverb* —**pre·cip′i·tate·ly**
> *adjective* —**pre·cip′i·ta′tive**
> *noun* —**pre·cip′i·ta′tor**

SEE NOTE AT **precipitous** (ON PAGE 278).

pre·cip·i·tous (prĭ-sĭp′ĭ-təs)

adjective

1. Resembling a precipice; extremely steep. **2.** Having several precipices: *"The Duchy of Grand Fenwick lies in a precipitous fold of the northern Alps and embraces in its tumbling landscape portions of three valleys, a river, one complete mountain with an elevation of two thousand feet and a castle"* (Leonard Wibberley, *The Mouse That Roared*). **3.** Usage Problem Extremely rapid, hasty, or abrupt; precipitate.

[Probably from obsolete *precipitious*, from Latin *praecipitium*, precipice.]

RELATED WORDS:

  adverb —**pre·cip′i·tous·ly**
  noun —**pre·cip′i·tous·ness**

The adjective *precipitate* and the adverb *precipitately* were once applied to physical steepness but are now used primarily of rash, headlong actions: *Precipitous* currently means "steep" in both literal and figurative senses: *the precipitous rapids of the upper river; a precipitous drop in commodity prices.* But *precipitous* and *precipitously* are also frequently used to mean "abrupt, hasty," which takes them into territory that would ordinarily belong to *precipitate* and *precipitately: their precipitous decision to leave.* This usage is a natural extension of the use of *precipitous* to describe a rise or fall in a quantity over time: *a precipitous increase in reports of measles* is also an abrupt or sudden event. Although the extended use of *precipitous* is well attested in the work of reputable writers, it is still widely regarded as an error and was considered unacceptable to two-thirds of the Usage Panel in 2001.

74 pre·scribe (prĭ-skrīb′)

verb

> Past participle and past tense: **pre·scribed**
> Present participle: **pre·scrib·ing**
> Third person singular present tense: **pre·scribes**

transitive **1.** To set down as a rule or guide; impose or direct: *"In all well-governed states too, not only judges are appointed for determining the controversies of individuals, but rules are prescribed for regulating the decisions of those judges"* (Adam Smith, *The Theory of Moral Sentiments*). **2.** To order the use of (a medicine or other treatment): *The doctor prescribed antibiotics and plenty of bed rest.*

intransitive **1.** To establish rules, laws, or directions. **2.** To order a medicine or other treatment.

[Middle English *prescriben,* from Latin *praescrībere* : *prae-,* pre- + *scrībere,* to write.]

RELATED WORD:
> *noun* —**pre·scrib′er**

SEE NOTE AT **proscribe** (ON PAGE 284).

pres·ent·ly (prĕz**'**ənt-lē)

adverb

1. In a short time; soon: *"She thought she must have been mistaken at first, for none of the scarecrows in Kansas ever wink; but presently the figure nodded its head to her in a friendly way"* (L. Frank Baum, *The Wonderful Wizard of Oz*). **2.** USAGE PROBLEM At this time or period; now: *Springfield is presently the capital of Illinois.*

An original meaning of *presently* was "at the present time; currently." That sense is said to have disappeared from the literary language in the 17th century, but it has survived in popular usage and is widely found nowadays in literate speech and writing. Still, there is a lingering prejudice against this use. The sentence *General Walters is...presently the United States Ambassador to the United Nations* was acceptable to only 48 percent of the Usage Panel in the 1999 survey.

---

presently   **280**

While Dorothy was looking earnestly into the queer, painted face of the Scarecrow, she was surprised to see one of the eyes slowly wink at her. She thought she must have been mistaken at first, for none of the scarecrows in Kansas ever wink; but **presently** the figure nodded its head to her in a friendly way. Then she climbed down from the fence and walked up to it, while Toto ran around the pole and barked.

—L. Frank Baum,
The Wonderful Wizard of Oz

prin·ci·pal (prĭn′sə-pəl)

adjective

1. First, highest, or foremost in importance, rank, worth, or degree; chief: *The principal character in* Gone With the Wind *is Scarlett O'Hara.* **2.** Of, relating to, or being a financial principal, or a principal in a financial transaction.

noun

1. A person who holds a position of presiding rank, especially the head of an elementary school or high school: *The rowdy students were sent to the principal's office.* **2.** A main participant, as in a business deal. **3.** A person having a leading or starring role: *The director cast the chorus before casting the principals.* **4a.** A financial holding as distinguished from the interest or revenue from it. **b.** A sum of money owed as a debt, upon which interest is calculated.

[Middle English, from Old French, from Latin *prīncipālis,* from *prīnceps, prīncip-,* leader, emperor.]

RELATED WORDS:
> *adverb* —**prin′ci·pal·ly**
> *noun* —**prin′ci·pal·ship′**

♘ *Principal* and *principle* are often confused but have no meanings in common. *Principle* is only a noun and usually refers to a rule or standard: *The class was assigned to read an essay about the principles of democracy. Principal* is both a noun and an adjective. As a noun, in general usage it refers to a person who holds a high position or plays an important role: *A meeting was held among all the principals in the transaction.* As an adjective it has the sense of "chief" or "leading": *The coach's principal concern is the quarterback's health.*

---

principal / principle

prin·ci·ple (prĭn′sə-pəl)

noun

1. A basic truth or statement, especially a system of beliefs or ideals: *The senator swore to uphold the principles of democracy.* **2a.** A rule or standard, especially of good behavior: *The sheriff was a man of principle.* **b.** The general set of moral or ethical standards: *"He chose principle over partisanship and is respected by liberals and conservatives alike"* (Brent Staples, *New York Times Book Review*). **3.** A statement or set of statements describing the functioning of natural phenomena or mechanical processes: *"Quantum teleportation makes use of a strange aspect of quantum physics called the Heisenberg Uncertainty Principle, which says it is impossible to measure both the speed and position of an object at the same time"* (Peter O'Connor, *Star Tribune* [Minneapolis]).

IDIOMS:

in principle With regard to the basics: *"Monitoring systems can in principle be programmed to look for certain keywords, like* bomb *or* target, *within messages they capture"* (Susan Stellin, *New York Times*).

on principle According to or because of principle: *Because I am an environmentalist, I objected to the airport's expansion into the marsh on principle.*

[Middle English, alteration of Old French *principe,* from Latin *prīncipium,* from *prīnceps, prīncip-,* leader, emperor.]

SEE NOTE AT **principal** (ON PAGE 282).

pro·scribe (prō-skrīb′)

transitive verb
> Past participle and past tense: **pro·scribed**
> Present participle: **pro·scrib·ing**
> Third person singular present tense: **pro·scribes**

1. To forbid; prohibit: *The government proscribes the importation of certain plants.* **2.** To denounce; condemn: *"In June 1580, Philip II had proscribed William as 'the chief disturber of our state of Christendom' and offered twenty-five thousand ecus to anyone who might venture to kill him"* (Simon Schama, *American Scholar*). **3.** To banish; outlaw: *After the coup, the monarch was proscribed and ordered to leave the country.*

[Middle English *proscriben,* from Latin *prōscrībere,* to put up someone's name as outlawed : *prō-,* in front + *scrībere,* to write.]

RELATED WORD:
> *noun* —**pro·scrib′er**

🙪 Some senses of *prescribe* and *proscribe* are opposite in meaning. But because the two words sound similar, they're often confused. In its most common senses, *proscribe* means "to forbid" and "to denounce." *Prescribe,* on the other hand, means "to set down as a rule or guide," as in *The company handbook prescribes acceptable ways of reassigning an employee.* The medical sense, "to order the use of a medicine or treatment," as in *The doctor prescribed two aspirin,* is related to this sense.

re·nown (rĭ-noun′)

noun

The quality of being widely honored and acclaimed; fame.

[Middle English *renoun,* from Anglo-Norman, from *renomer,* to make famous : *re-,* repeatedly + *nomer,* to name (from Latin *nōmināre,* from *nōmen, nōmin-,* name).]

RELATED WORD:
adjective **—re·nowned′**

Because *renown* means "fame," and to be famous is to be well-known, *renown* is often misspelled with a *k.* For the same reasons, *renown* is often mispronounced as though it rhymed with *own. Renown* is properly pronounced with the same vowel sound as *noun* or *town.* The same holds true for the adjectival form, *renowned.*

ret·i·cent (rĕt′ĭ-sənt)

adjective

1. Inclined to keep one's thoughts, feelings, and personal affairs to oneself: *"The cowboy was usually soft-spoken and reserved of manner with strangers, so much so that he gained the reputation of being taciturn and reticent by nature, a conclusion which was erroneous"* (Ramon F. Adams, *Cowboy Lingo*). **2.** USAGE PROBLEM Reluctant; unwilling.

[Latin *reticēns, reticent-* present participle of *reticēre,* to keep silent : *re-,* re- + *tacēre,* to be silent.]

RELATED WORD:
    adverb —**ret′i·cent·ly**

✍ *Reticent* is generally used to indicate a reluctance to speak. Many people criticize its extended use as an all-purpose synonym for *reluctant.* In a 2001 survey, 83 percent of the Usage Panel found unacceptable the sentence *A lot of out-of-towners are reticent to come to the Twin Cities for a ballgame if there's a chance the game will be rained out.*

---

reticent / seasonable   **286**

81

sac·ri·le·gious (săk′rə-lĭj′əs, săk′rə-lē′jəs)

adjective

Grossly irreverent toward what is or is held to be sacred: *"Most sacrilegious murder hath broke ope/The Lord's anointed temple"* (William Shakespeare, *Macbeth*).

[From *sacrilege* (from Old French, from Latin *sacrilegium,* from *sacrilegus,* one who steals sacred things : *sacer,* sacred + *legere,* to gather) + *-ous,* adjectival suffix.]

RELATED WORDS:
>*noun* —**sac′ri·lege** (săk′rə-lĭj)
>*adverb* —**sac′ri·le′gious·ly**
>*noun* —**sac′ri·le′gious·ness**

✍ *Sacrilegious,* the adjective form of *sacrilege,* is often misspelled with the first *i* and the *e* switched, through confusion with the word *religious.*

82

sea·son·a·ble (sē′zə-nə-bəl)

adjective

1. In keeping with the time or the season: *"The weather was fair and seasonable, but Mary wore flannel underclothes beneath her dress and a heavy cloak as well"* (Michael Crummey, *River Thieves*). **2.** Occurring or performed at the proper time; timely: *The pundits praised the government's seasonable intervention in the trade dispute.*

RELATED WORD:
>*adverb* —**sea′son·a·bly**

SEE NOTE AT **seasonal** (ON PAGE 288).

---

sea·son·al (sē′zə-nəl)

adjective

Of or dependent on a particular season: *"Among the important soil properties are natural soil drainage, permeability, ... load bearing capacity, depth to water table, seasonal wetness, shrink-swell capacity and soil structure"* (Bobbi McDermott, *Yuma Sun*).

RELATED WORD:
>   *adverb* —**sea′son·al·ly**

ꧏ *Seasonal* and *seasonable,* though closely related, have different uses. *Seasonal* applies to what depends on or is controlled by the season of the year: *a seasonal increase in employment. Seasonable* applies to what is appropriate to the season (*seasonable clothing*) or timely (*seasonable intervention*). Rains are *seasonal* if they occur at a certain time of the year; they are *seasonable* at any time if they save the crops.

84

sen·su·al (sĕn′shoō-əl)

adjective

1. Of, relating to, given to, or providing gratification of the physical and especially the sexual appetites: *"The modern geisha is the aristocrat of the huge industry that has evolved through the centuries to cater to Japanese men's sensual desires"* (Jodi Cobb, *National Geographic*).
2. Relating to or affecting any of the senses or a sense organ; sensory.

RELATED WORDS:
   adverb —**sen′su·al·ly**
   noun —**sen′su·al·ness**

SEE NOTE AT **sensuous** (ON PAGE 290).

sen·su·ous (sĕn′shōō-əs)

adjective

1. Of, relating to, or derived from the senses: *"[T]hough he turned the pages with the sensuous joy of the book-lover, he did not know what he was reading, and one book after another dropped from his hand"* (Edith Wharton, *The Age of Innocence*). **2.** Appealing to or gratifying the senses: *The sculpture featured sensuous curves juxtaposed with sharp facial features.* **3.** Easily affected through the senses.

RELATED WORDS:
>   *adverb* —**sen′su·ous·ly**
>   *noun* —**sen′su·ous·ness**

🖉 Both *sensual* and *sensuous* mean "relating to or gratifying the senses." *Sensuous* can refer to any of the senses but usually applies to those involved in aesthetic enjoyment, as of art or music: *The critic lectured about the sensuous imagery in 19th century poems. Sensual* more often applies to the physical senses or appetites, particularly those associated with sexual pleasure.

[T]hough he turned the pages with the **sensuous** joy of the book-lover, he did not know what he was reading, and one book after another dropped from his hand. Suddenly, among them, he lit on a small volume of verse which he had ordered because the name had attracted him: "The House of Life." He took it up, and found himself plunged in an atmosphere unlike any he had ever breathed in books; so warm, so rich, and yet so ineffably tender, that it gave a new and haunting beauty to the most elementary of human passions.

—Edith Wharton,
The Age of Innocence

set (sĕt)

verb

> Past participle and past tense: **set**
> Present participle: **set·ting**
> Third person singular present tense: **sets**

transitive **1.** To put in a specified position; place: *I set the book on the shelf.* **2.** To put into a specified state: *With a push he set the wagon in motion.* **3.** To put into a stable position: *She set the fence post into a bed of concrete.* **4.** To restore to a proper and normal state when dislocated or broken: *The doctor set the broken bone.* **5.** To adjust for proper functioning: *We set the mouse traps to prevent infestation.* **6.** To adjust (an instrument, tool, or device) so that some desired condition of operation is established: *She set the alarm clock for 7:00.* **7.** To arrange tableware on or at in preparation for a meal: *"'Where's Papa going with that ax?' said Fern to her mother as they were setting the table for breakfast"* (E.B. White, *Charlotte's Web*). **8.** To arrange (hair) in a certain style, as by rolling it up with clips and curlers. **9a.** To arrange (type) into words and sentences in preparation for printing. **b.** To arrange (matter to be printed) into type. **10a.** To compose (music) to fit a given text. **b.** To write (words) to fit a melody. **11.** To represent the unfolding of (a drama or narrative, for instance) in a specific place: *The play* Romeo and Juliet *is set in Verona.* **12.** To make as a rule or guideline; establish: *You should set an example for your younger brother.* **13.** To decide on; appoint or designate: *They set June 6 as the day of the wedding.* **14.** To detail or assign (someone) to a particular duty, service, or station: *The guards were set around the perimeter.* **15a.** To put in a mounting; mount: *The jeweler set an emerald in a pendant.* **b.** To apply jewels to; stud: *The museum displayed a tiara*

---

that was set with diamonds. **16.** To cause to sit: *The host set the woozy guest on the couch.* **17.** To position (oneself) in such a way as to be ready to start running a race. **18.** To pass (a volleyball), usually with the fingertips, in an arc close to the net so that a teammate can drive it over the net. **19.** To fix at a given amount: *The judge set bail for the defendant at $50,000.* **20.** To point to the location of (game) by holding a fixed attitude. Used of a hunting dog.

intransitive **1.** To disappear below the horizon: *The sun set at seven that evening.* **2.** To sit on eggs. Used of fowl: *The hens were setting.* **3.** To become fixed; harden: *It will take 12 hours for the cement to set.* **4.** To become permanent. Used of dye. **5.** To become whole; knit. Used of a broken bone. **6.** NONSTANDARD To sit.

[Middle English *setten,* from Old English *settan.*]

🖉 The verbs *set* and *sit* have been confused since the Middle Ages, so it is not surprising that they sometimes get mixed up today. Throughout its history *set* has been a transitive verb. It originally meant "to cause (someone) to sit" and also "to cause (something) to be in a certain position." This second sense survives as a basic meaning of the verb today: *She set the book on the table.* But since about 1300, *set* has been used without an object to mean "to be in a seated position, sit." *Set* is still common as a nonstandard or regional word meaning "sit," especially in rural speech: *Stop on by and set a spell.* The most familiar of *set*'s intransitive uses describes the motion of the sun at the end of the day. The sun only *sets;* it never *sits.*

This would seem a bit anomalous, since *sit* is mainly an intransitive verb. Its basic meaning is "to rest supported on the hindquarters," as in *He sits at the table.* It has a variety of other uses that entail occupying a location (*The house sits on a small lot*) or existing in a resting or unused state (*The skis sat gathering dust*). Nevertheless, *sit* has its transitive uses, some of which date back to the 14th century. It has taken over the meaning that originally belonged to *set*, "to cause (someone) to sit," so that we can now say *They sat the winning ticket holder back in his chair.* A more recent transitive use of *sit* is "to provide seats for," as in *The theater sits 2,000.*

Fortunately, you don't have to worry about chickens. A hen can *sit* or *set* on her eggs, so in this usage you can't go wrong.

sex (sĕks)

noun

1a. The property or quality by which organisms are classified as female or male on the basis of their reproductive organs and functions: *Through amniocentesis, the sex of a developing fetus can be determined.* **b.** Either of the two divisions, designated female and male, of this classification: *The college's policy is that no student is allowed to have visitors of the opposite sex after midnight.* **2.** Females or males considered as a group. **3.** The condition or character of being female or male; the physiological, functional, and psychological differences that distinguish the female and the male. **4.** Sexual intercourse.

[Middle English, from Latin *sexus*.]

SEE NOTE AT **gender** (ON PAGE 236).

sit (sĭt)

verb
    Past participle and past tense: **sat**
    Present participle: **sit·ting**
    Third person singular present tense: **sits**

intransitive **1a.** To rest with the torso vertical and the body supported on the buttocks: *"I was leaning against a bar in a speak-easy on Fifty-second Street, waiting for Nora to finish her Christmas shopping, when a girl got up from the table where she had been sitting with three other people and came over to me"* (Dashiell Hammett, *The Thin Man*). **b.** To rest with the hindquarters lowered onto a supporting surface. Used of animals: *The dog sat at the foot of my bed.* **c.** To perch. Used of birds. **d.** To cover eggs for hatching; brood: *The hen sat on her eggs.* **2.** To be situated or located: *The farmhouse sits on a hill.* **3.** To lie or rest: *The dishes are sitting on a shelf.* **4.** To pose for an artist or photographer. **5.** To occupy a seat as a member of a body of officials: *Gerald Ford sat in Congress before becoming president.* **6.** To be in session: *The Supreme Court does not normally sit in the summer.* **7.** To remain inactive or unused: *Your expensive skis are sitting gathering dust in the corner.* **8.** To affect one with or as if with a burden; weigh: *Official duties sat heavily upon the governor's mind.* **9.** To fit, fall, or drape in a specified manner: *That jacket sits perfectly on you.* **10.** To be agreeable to one; please: *The idea didn't sit well with any of us.* **11.** To keep watch or take care of a child; babysit: *On weekends, I make extra money by sitting for the neighbors.*

intransitive **1.** To cause to sit; seat: *The ushers sat the wedding guests in the pews.* **2.** To sit on (eggs) for the purpose of hatching. **3.** To provide seating accommodation for: *This concert hall sits 1,000 people.*

[Middle English *sitten,* from Old English *sittan.*]

SEE NOTE AT **set** (ON PAGE 293).

that (*th̆at, th̆t*)

pronoun
> Plural **those** (*thōz*)

1. Used to refer to the one designated, implied, mentioned, or understood: *What kind of soup is that?* **2.** Used to indicate the farther or less immediate one: *That is for sale; this is not.* **3. those** Used to indicate an unspecified number of people: *The aide wrote down the names of those who refused to attend the meeting.* **4.** Used as a relative pronoun to introduce a clause, especially a restrictive clause: *They towed the car that had the flat tire.* **5.** In, on, by, or with which: *The director returns to New York City each summer that the concerts are performed.*

adjective
> Plural **those** (*thōz*)

1. Being the one singled out, implied, or understood: *Those mountains are seventy miles away.* **2.** Being the one further removed or less obvious: *That route is shorter than this one.*

adverb

1. To such an extent or degree: *Is your problem that complicated?* **2.** To a high degree; very: *No one took what he said that seriously.*

conjunction

1. Used to introduce a subordinate clause stating a result, wish, purpose, reason, or cause: *She hoped that he would arrive on time. He was saddened that she felt so little for him.* **2a.** Used to introduce an anticipated subordinate clause following the expletive *it* occurring as subject of the verb: *It is true that dental work is expensive.* **b.** Used to introduce a subordinate clause modifying an adverb or adverbial expression: *They will go anywhere that they are welcome.* **c.** Used to introduce a subordinate clause that is joined to an adjective or noun as a complement: *She was sure that she was right. It is his belief that rates will rise soon.* **3.** Used to introduce a noun clause that is usually the subject or object of a verb or a predicate nominative: *"That America is richer today* [as compared to 100 years ago] *almost goes without saying"* (Peter Grier, *Christian Science Monitor*).

IDIOM

that is To explain more clearly; in other words: *The bakery is on the first floor, that is, the floor at street level.*

[Middle English, from Old English *thæt*.]

🖉 The standard rule requires that *that* should be used only to introduce a restrictive (or defining) relative clause, which identifies the entity being talked about; in this use it should never be preceded by a comma. Thus, in the sentence *The house that Jack built has been torn down,* the clause *that Jack built* is a restrictive clause identifying the specific house that was torn down. Similarly, in *I am looking for a book that is easy to read,* the restrictive clause *that is easy to read* tells what kind of book is desired. A related rule stipulates that *which* should be used with nonrestrictive (or nondefining) clauses, which give additional information about an entity that has already been identified in the context; in this use, *which* is always preceded by a comma. Thus, we say *The students in Chemistry 101 have been complaining about the textbook, which* (not *that*) *is hard to follow.* The clause *which is hard to follow* is nonrestrictive in that it does not indicate which text is being complained about; even if the clause were omitted, we would know that the phrase *the textbook* refers to the text in Chemistry 101.

Some grammarians extend the rule and insist that, just as *that* should be used only in restrictive clauses, *which* should be used only in nonrestrictive clauses. Thus, they suggest that we should avoid sentences such as *I need a book which will tell me all about city gardening,* where the restrictive clause *which will tell me all about city gardening* indicates which sort of book is needed. But this extension of the rule is far from universally accepted, and the use of *which* with restrictive clauses is common. Furthermore, since *that* cannot be used with clauses introduced by a preposition (whether or not restrictive), *which* is used with both clauses when such a clause is joined by *and* or *or* to another that does not begin with a preposition, as in *It is a philosophy in which the common man may find solace and which many have found reason to praise.* Such constructions are often considered cumbersome, however, and it may be best to recast the sentence completely to avoid the problem.

That is often omitted in a relative clause when the subject of the clause is different from the word that the clause refers to. Thus, we may say either *the book that I was reading* or *the book I was reading.* In addition, *that* is commonly omitted before other kinds of subordinate clauses, as in *I think we should try again* where *that* would precede *we.* These constructions omitting *that* are entirely idiomatic, even in more formal contexts.

90

un·ex·cep·tion·a·ble (ŭn′ĭk-sĕp′shə-nə-bəl)

adjective

Beyond any reasonable objection; irreproachable: *Our accounting firm holds itself to the highest standards; therefore, any of its findings I believe to be unexceptionable.*

RELATED WORD:
> *adverb* —un′ex·cep′tion·a·bly

The confusion between *unexceptionable* and *unexceptional* is understandable, since both derive from the noun *exception*. *Unexceptionable* takes its meaning from *exception* in the sense "objection," as in the idiom *take exception to* ("find fault with, object to"). Thus *unexceptionable* is commendatory, meaning "not open to any objection or criticism," as in *A judge's ethical standards should be unexceptionable. Unexceptional,* by contrast, is related to the adjective *exceptional* ("outstanding, above average"), which takes its meaning from *exception* in the sense "an unusual case"; thus *unexceptional* generally has a somewhat negative meaning, "not superior, run-of-the-mill" as in *Some judges' ethical standards, sadly, have been unexceptional.*

91
un·ex·cep·tion·al (ŭn′ĭk-sĕp′shə-nəl)

adjective

Not varying from a norm; usual: *The professor gave the unexceptional paper a C.*

RELATED WORD:
   adverb —**un′ex·cep′tion·al·ly**

SEE NOTE AT **unexceptionable** (ABOVE).

un·in·ter·est·ed

(ŭn-ĭn**ʹ**trĭ-stĭd, ŭn-ĭn**ʹ**tər-ĭ-stĭd, ŭn-ĭn**ʹ**tə-rĕs**ʹ**tĭd)

adjective

1. Marked by or exhibiting a lack of interest: *Uninterested voters led to a low turnout on Election Day.* **2.** Having no stake or interest; impartial: *Both sides requested a mediator who was uninterested in the dispute.*

RELATED WORDS:
  adverb —**un·in***ʹ***ter·est·ed·ly**
  noun — **un·in***ʹ***ter·est·ed·ness**

SEE NOTE AT **disinterested** (ON PAGE 222).

SEE NOTE AT **disinterested** (ON PAGE 222).

u·nique (yoo͞-nēk**ʹ**)

adjective

1. Being the only one of its kind: *The scholar studied the unique existing example of the eighteenth-century author's handwriting.* **2.** Without an equal or equivalent; unparalleled: *The one-time offer presented them with a unique opportunity to buy a house.* **3.** Characteristic of a particular category, condition, or locality: *The marine biologist examined weather patterns unique to coastal areas.*

[French, from Old French, from Latin *ūnicus.*]

RELATED WORDS:
  adverb —**u·nique***ʹ***ly**
  noun —**u·nique***ʹ***ness**

For many grammarians, *unique* is the paradigmatic absolute term, a shibboleth that distinguishes between those who understand that such a term cannot be modified by an adverb of degree or a comparative adverb and those who do not. These grammarians would say that a thing is either unique or not unique and that it is therefore incorrect to say that something is *very unique* or *more unique* than something else. Most of the Usage Panel supports this traditional view. Eighty percent disapprove of the sentence *Her designs are quite unique in today's fashions.* But as the language of advertising in particular attests, *unique* is widely used as a synonym for "worthy of being considered in a class by itself, extraordinary," and if so construed it may arguably be modified. In fact, *unique* appears as a modified adjective in the work of many reputable writers. A travel writer states that *"Chicago is no less unique an American city than New York or San Francisco,"* for example, and the critic Fredric Jameson writes *"The great modern writers have all been defined by the invention or production of rather unique styles."* Although these examples of the qualification of *unique* are defensible, writers should be aware that such constructions are liable to incur the censure of some readers.

u·til·ize (yo͞ot′l-īz′)

transitive verb

Past participle and past tense: **u·til·ized**

Present participle: **u·til·iz·ing**

Third person singular present tense: **u·til·iz·es**

To put to use, especially for a practical purpose: "*The…* *group has genetically engineered the bacterium so that more glucose is diverted toward the other main chemical pathway within the organism that utilizes the sugar*" (Gary Stix, *Scientific American*).

[French *utiliser*, from Italian *utilizzare*, from *utile*, useful, from Latin *ūtilis*, from *ūtī*, to use.]

RELATED WORDS:

noun —**u′til·i·za′tion**

noun —**u′til·iz′er**

🙰 A number of critics have remarked that *utilize* is an unnecessary substitute for *use*. It is true that many occurrences of *utilize* could be replaced by *use* with no loss to anything but pretentiousness, for example, in sentences such as *They utilized questionable methods in their analysis* or *We hope that many commuters will continue to utilize mass transit after the bridge has reopened*. But *utilize* can mean "to find a profitable or practical use for." Thus the sentence *The teachers were unable to use the new computers* might mean only that the teachers were unable to operate the computers, whereas *The teachers were unable to utilize the new computers* suggests that the teachers could not find ways to employ the computers in instruction.

weight (wāt)

noun

1. A measure of the heaviness of an object: *The weight of the car is 3,000 pounds.* **2.** The force with which a body is attracted to Earth or another celestial body, equal to the product of the object's mass and the acceleration of gravity. **3a.** A unit measure of gravitational force: *Comprehensive reference works contain a table of weights and measures.* **b.** A system of such measures: *Gemstones are measured using a system of measurement called "troy weight."* **4.** An object used principally to exert a force by virtue of its gravitational attraction to Earth, such as a paperweight or a dumbbell. **5.** A load or burden; oppressiveness: *"Adding features to run complex software adds weight and bogs down portability"* (Eric C. Evarts, *Christian Science Monitor*). **6.** Influence, importance, or authority: *Her opinion carries great weight in the medical community.*

transitive verb
   Past participle and past tense: **weight·ed**
   Present participle: **weight·ing**
   Third person singular present tense: **weights**

1. To make heavy or heavier with a weight or weights: *"Marine mud [is] a blue-gray mud that settled 15,000 years ago while much of Maine was weighted down with glacial ice and Boston was underwater"* (Jamie Kageleiry & Christine Schultz, *Yankee Magazine*). **2.** To load down, burden, or oppress: *Until an extra associate was hired, I was weighted with heavy responsibilities at work.*

[Middle English *wight,* from Old English *wiht.*]

SEE NOTE AT **mass** (ON PAGE 262).

where·fore (hwâr′fôr′, wâr′fôr′)

adverb

For what purpose or reason; why: *"O Romeo, Romeo! wherefore art thou Romeo?"* (William Shakespeare, *Romeo and Juliet*).

noun

A purpose or cause: *The editorial explained all the whys and wherefores of the tax proposal.*

℘ Many people mistakenly assume that *wherefore* is a synonym of *where* based on a misreading of one of Shakespeare's most well-known lines. Many mistakenly interpret Juliet's balcony speech as questioning Romeo's location (who as it turns out happens to be just below the balcony). However, Juliet is not asking *where* Romeo is. She is asking *why* Romeo is Romeo—that is, she wants to know why her love is who he is: a member of the family with whom her family has been feuding.

O Romeo, Romeo! **wherefore** art thou Romeo?

Deny thy father and refuse thy name;

Or, if thou wilt not, be but sworn my love,

And I'll no longer be a Capulet.

— William Shakespeare,
Romeo and Juliet

which (hwĭch, wĭch)

pronoun

1. What particular one or ones: *Which of these books is yours?* **2.** The one or ones previously mentioned or implied, specifically: **a.** Used as a relative pronoun in a clause that provides additional information about the antecedent: *I want to renovate my house, which is small and old.* **b.** Used as a relative pronoun preceded by *that* or a preposition in a clause that defines or restricts the antecedent: *The clerk provided him with that which he requested. I was fascinated by the subject on which she spoke.* **c.** Used instead of *that* as a relative pronoun in a clause that defines or restricts the antecedent: *The movie which was shown later was better.* **3.** Any of the things, events, or people designated or implied; whichever: *Choose which you like best.* **4.** A thing or circumstance that: *They left early, which was wise.*

adjective

1. What particular one or ones of a number of things or people: *Which part of town do you mean?* **2.** Any one or any number of; whichever: *Use which door you please.* **3.** Being the one or ones previously mentioned or implied: *It started to rain, at which point we ran.*

[Middle English, from Old English *hwilc.*]

❧ The relative pronoun *which* is sometimes used to refer to an entire sentence or clause, rather than a noun or noun phrase, as in *They ignored me, which proved to be unwise. They swept the council elections, which could never have happened under the old rules.* While these examples are unexceptionable, using *which* in this way sometimes produces an ambiguous sentence. Thus *It emerged that Chris made the complaint, which surprised every-*

---

body leaves unclear whether it was surprising that a complaint was made or that Chris made it. The ambiguity can be avoided with paraphrases such as *It emerged that the complaint was made by Chris, a revelation that surprised everybody.*

ALSO SEE NOTE AT **that** (ON PAGE 297).

wreak (rēk)

transitive verb

Past participle and past tense: **wreaked**
Present participle: **wreak·ing**
Third person singular present tense: **wreaks**

1. To inflict (vengeance or punishment) upon a person: *"I at last devised a desperate plan that would not only blow my wedding to pieces but would wreak a terrible revenge on my parents and my betrothed"* (Louis Auchincloss, *DeCicco v. Schweizer*). **2.** To express or gratify (anger, malevolence, or resentment); vent: *"In his little evil brain he sought for some excuse to wreak his hatred upon Tarzan"* (Edgar Rice Burroughs, *Tarzan of the Apes*). **3.** To bring about; cause: *"A harmful recessive gene doesn't wreak havoc unless it exists in two copies"* (Jennifer Ackerman, *Chance in the House of Fate*).

[Middle English *wreken,* from Old English *wrecan.*]

🙊 *Wreak* is sometimes confused with *wreck,* perhaps because the wreaking of damage may leave a wreck: *The storm wreaked* (not *wrecked*) *havoc along the coast.* The past tense and past participle of *wreak* is *wreaked,* not *wrought,* which is an alternative past tense and past participle of *work.*

In the morning, looking towards the sea side, the tide being low, I saw something lie on the shore bigger than ordinary, and it looked like a cask; when I came to it, I found a small barrel, and two or three pieces of the **wreck** of the ship, which were driven on shore by the late hurricane; and looking towards the wreck itself, I thought it seemed to lie higher out of the water than it used to do.

—Daniel Defoe,
Robinson Crusoe

99 wreck (rĕk)

noun

1. Accidental destruction of a ship; a shipwreck: *The wreck of the Titanic occurred in the Atlantic Ocean in April of 1912.* **2a.** The stranded hulk of a severely damaged ship: *"I found a small barrel, and two or three pieces of the wreck of the ship, which were driven on shore by the late hurricane"* (Daniel Defoe, *Robinson Crusoe*). **b.** Fragments of a ship or its cargo cast ashore by the sea after a shipwreck; wreckage. **3.** The remains of something that has been wrecked or ruined: *"Up went the axe again...four times the blow fell;...it was not until the fifth, that the lock burst and the wreck of the door fell inwards on the carpet"* (Robert Louis Stevenson, *The Strange Case of Dr. Jekyll and Mr. Hyde*). **4.** A person who is physically or mentally broken down or worn out.

verb

Past participle and past tense: **wrecked**
Present participle: **wreck·ing**
Third person singular present tense: **wrecks**

transitive **1.** To cause the destruction of (something) in or as if in a collision: *"The morning after the storm that has wrecked the ship and drowned his companions, Crusoe wakes on shore with only a pocket knife, a pipe, and a tin of tobacco"* (Hilary Masters, *Making It Up*). **2.** To dismantle or raze; tear down: *The contractor wrecked the old building to make way for the new apartment complex.* **3.** To cause to undergo ruin or disaster: *"I will not go along with a huge tax cut for the wealthy at the expense of everyone else and wreck our good economy in the process"* (Al Gore, speech to the Democratic National Convention).

---

intransitive To suffer destruction or ruin; become wrecked: *The ship wrecked in the shoals off the shore.*

[Middle English *wrek,* from Anglo-Norman *wrec,* of Scandinavian origin; akin to Old Norse *rec,* wreckage.]

SEE NOTE AT **wreak** (ON PAGE 307).

100 zo·ol·o·gy (zō-ŏl′ə-jē, zōō-ŏl′ə-jē)

noun

1. The branch of biology that deals with animals and animal life, including the study of the structure, physiology, development, and classification of animals. **2.** The animal life of a particular area or period: *The professor lectured on the zoology of the Pleistocene.* **3.** The characteristics of a particular animal group or category: *In biology class, we had a unit on the zoology of mammals.*

RELATED WORD:
> *noun* **—zo·ol′o·gist**

℘ Traditionally, the first syllable of *zoology* has been pronounced as (zō), rhyming with *toe.* However, most likely due to the familiarity of the word *zoo* (which is merely a shortened form of *zoological garden*), the pronunciation of the first syllable as (zōō) is also commonly heard. In 1999, 88 percent of the Usage Panel found the (zō) pronunciation acceptable, and 60 percent found the (zōō) pronunciation acceptable. In their own speech, 68 percent of the Panelists use the (zō) pronunciation, and 32 percent use the (zōō) pronunciation. Thus, while both pronunciations can be considered acceptable, the (zō) pronunciation may be perceived as more scientific.

100 words every

word lover

should know

Guide to the Entries

ENTRY WORD The 100 words that constitute this section are listed alphabetically. The entry words, along with inflected and derived forms, are divided into syllables by centered dots. These dots show you where you would break the word at the end of a line. The pronunciation of the word follows the entry word. Please see the key on page 317 for an explanation of the pronunciation system.

PART OF SPEECH At least one part of speech follows each entry word. The part of speech tells you the grammatical category that the word belongs to. Parts of speech include *noun, adjective, adverb, transitive verb,* and *intransitive verb.* (A transitive verb is a verb that needs an object to complete its meaning. *Wash* is a transitive verb in the sentence *I washed the car.* The direct object of *wash* is *the car.* An intransitive verb is one that does not take an object, as *sleep* in the sentence *I slept for seven hours.* Many verbs are both transitive and intransitive.)

INFLECTIONS A word's inflected forms differ from the main entry form by the addition of a suffix or by a change in the base form to indicate grammatical features such as number, person, or tense. They are set in boldface type, divided into syllables, and given pronunciations as necessary. The past tense, past participle, and the third person singular present tense inflections of all verbs are shown. The plurals of nouns are shown when they are spelled in a way other than by adding *s* to the base form.

ORDER OF SENSES Entries having more than one sense are arranged with the central and often the most commonly sought meanings first. In an entry with more than one part of speech, the senses are numbered in separate sequences after each part of speech, as at **halcyon.**

EXAMPLES OF USAGE Examples often follow the definitions and are set in italic type. These examples show the entry words in typical contexts. Sometimes the examples are quotations from authors of books. These quotations are shown within quotation marks, and the quotation's author and source are shown in parentheses.

ETYMOLOGIES Etymologies appear in square brackets following the last definition. An etymology traces the history of a word as far back in time as can be determined with reasonable certainty. The stage most closely preceding Modern English is given first, with each earlier stage following in sequence. A language name, linguistic form (in italics), and brief definition of the form are given for each stage of the derivation. To avoid redundancy, a language, form, or definition is not repeated if it is identical to the corresponding item in the immediately preceding stage. Occasionally, a form will be given that is not actually preserved in written documents but which scholars are confident did exist—such a form will be marked by an asterisk (*). The word *from* is used to indicate origin of any kind: by inheritance, borrowing, or derivation. When an etymology splits a compound word into parts, a colon introduces the parts and each element is then traced back to its origin, with those elements enclosed in parentheses.

NOTES Many entries include Notes that present interesting information regarding the history of the word, including the process by which it entered English from other languages.

Pronunciation Guide

Pronunciations appear in parentheses after boldface entry words. If a word has more than one pronunciation, the first pronunciation is usually more common than the other, but often they are equally common. Pronunciations are shown after inflections and related words where necessary.

Stress is the relative degree of emphasis that a word's syllables are spoken with. An unmarked syllable has the weakest stress in the word. The strongest, or primary, stress is indicated with a bold mark (ˈ). A lighter mark (ˈ) indicates a secondary level of stress. The stress mark follows the syllable it applies to. Words of one syllable have no stress mark because there is no other stress level that the syllable can be compared to.

The key on page 317 shows the pronunciation symbols used in this book. To the right of the symbols are words that show how the symbols are pronounced. The letters whose sound corresponds to the symbols are shown in boldface.

The symbol (ə) is called *schwa*. It represents a vowel with the weakest level of stress in a word. The schwa sound varies slightly according to the vowel it represents or the sounds around it:

a·bun·dant (ə-bŭnˈdənt)   **mo·ment** (mōˈmənt)

civ·il (sĭvˈəl)   **grate·ful** (grātˈfəl)

PRONUNCIATION KEY			
Symbol	**Examples**	**Symbol**	**Examples**
ă	pat	oi	noise
ā	pay	ŏŏ	took
âr	care	ŏŏr	lure
ä	father	ōō	boot
b	bib	ou	out
ch	church	œ	*German* schön
d	deed, milled	p	pop
ĕ	pet	r	roar
ē	bee	s	sauce
f	fife, phase, rough	sh	ship, dish
		t	tight, stopped
g	gag	th	thin
h	hat	*th*	this
hw	which	ŭ	cut
ĭ	pit	ûr	urge, term, firm, word, heard
ī	pie, by		
îr	deer, pier		
j	judge	v	valve
k	kick, cat, pique	w	with
l	lid, needle	y	yes
m	mum	z	zebra, xylem
n	no, sudden	zh	vision, pleasure, garage
N	*French* bon		
ng	thing		
ŏ	pot	ə	about, item, edible, gallop, circus
ō	toe		
ô	caught, paw		
ôr	core	ər	butter

To visit one's lover, with tears and reproaches, at his own residence, was an image so agreeable to Mrs. Penniman's mind that she felt a sort of **aesthetic** disappointment at its lacking, in this case, the harmonious accompaniments of darkness and storm. A quiet Sunday afternoon appeared an inadequate setting for it; and, indeed, Mrs. Penniman was quite out of humour with the conditions of the time, which passed very slowly as she sat in the front-parlour, in her bonnet and her cashmere shawl, awaiting Catherine's return.

—Henry James,
Washington Square

aes·thet·ic *or* **es·thet·ic** (ĕs-thĕt′ĭk)

adjective

1. Relating to beauty or the appreciation of beauty: *"To visit one's lover, with tears and reproaches, at his own residence, was an image so agreeable to Mrs. Penniman's mind that she felt a sort of aesthetic disappointment at its lacking, in this case, the harmonious accompaniments of darkness and storm"* (Henry James, *Washington Square*).
2. Exhibiting beauty; pleasing in appearance: *The new website features a number of aesthetic enhancements.*
3. Relating to the branch of philosophy that deals with the nature and expression of beauty, as in the fine arts.

noun

A conception of what is artistically valid or beautiful: *The aesthetics of Modernism can be seen as a reaction to the staid conventions of Victorian culture.*

[German *ästhetisch*, from New Latin *aesthēticus*, from Greek *aisthētikos*, of sense perception, from *aisthēta*, perceptible things, from *aisthanesthai*, to perceive.]

---

al·che·my (ăl′kə-mē)

noun

1. A medieval chemical philosophy having as its asserted aims the transmutation of base metals into gold, the discovery of the panacea, and the preparation of the elixir of longevity. **2.** A seemingly magical power or process of transmuting: *"He wondered by what alchemy it* [a killed deer] *was changed, so that what sickened him one hour, maddened him with hunger the next"* (Marjorie K. Rawlings, *The Yearling*).

[Middle English *alkamie*, from Old French *alquemie*, from Medieval Latin *alchymia*, from Arabic *al-kīmiyā'* : *al-*, the + *kīmiyā'*, chemistry (from Late Greek *khēmeia, khumeia*, perhaps from Greek *Khēmia*, Egypt).]

al·le·go·ry (ăl′ĭ-gôr′ē)

noun
    Plural: **al·le·go·ries**

1a. The representation of abstract ideas or principles by characters, figures, or events in narrative, dramatic, or pictorial form. **b.** A story, picture, or play employing such representation. John Bunyan's *Pilgrim's Progress* and Herman Melville's *Moby-Dick* are allegories. **2.** A symbolic representation: *The blindfolded figure with scales is an allegory of justice.*

[Middle English *allegorie*, from Latin *allēgoria*, from Greek, from *allēgorein*, to interpret allegorically : *allos*, other + *agoreuein*, to speak publicly (from *agorā*, marketplace).]

a·nach·ro·nism (ə-năk**′**rə-nĭz**′**əm)

noun

1. The representation of someone as existing or something as happening in other than chronological, proper, or historical order. **2.** One that is out of its proper or chronological order, especially a person or practice that belongs to an earlier time: *"A new age had plainly dawned, an age that made the institution of a segregated picnic seem an anachronism"* (Henry Louis Gates, Jr., *Colored People: A Memoir*). *"Cavalry regiments of cuirassiers with glistening metal breastplates and long black horsehair tails hanging down from their helmets were conscious of no anachronism. Following them came huge crates housing airplanes and wheeled platforms bearing the long narrow gray-painted field guns, the* soixantequinzes *that were France's pride"* (Barbara W. Tuchman, *The Guns of August*).

[French *anachronisme,* from New Latin *anachronismus,* from Late Greek *anakhronismos,* from *anakhronizesthai,* to be an anachronism : Greek *ana-,* up, backward + Greek *khronizein,* to take time (from *khronos,* time).]

a·nath·e·ma (ə-năth′ə-mə)

noun
    Plural: **a·nath·e·mas**

1. An ecclesiastical ban, curse, or excommunication. **2.** A vehement denunciation or curse: *"If the children gathered about her . . . Pearl would grow positively terrible in her puny wrath, snatching up stones to fling at them, with shrill, incoherent exclamations that made her mother tremble, because they had so much the sound of a witch's anathemas in some unknown tongue"* (Nathaniel Hawthorne, *The Scarlet Letter*). **3.** One that is cursed or damned. **4.** One that is greatly reviled, loathed, or shunned: *"Essentialism—a belief in natural, immutable sex differences—is anathema to postmodernists, for whom sexuality itself, along with gender, is a 'social construct'"* (Wendy Kaminer, *Atlantic Monthly*).

[Late Latin *anathema,* accursed thing, from Greek, something dedicated, something devoted (to evil), from *anatithenai, anathe-,* to dedicate : *ana-,* up, backward- + *tithenai,* to put.]

bail·i·wick (bā′lə-wĭk′)

noun

1. A person's specific area of interest, skill, or authority: *"Tower liked people to be like himself: quick, sharp and to the point. A private school and a restricted cruise were his natural bailiwicks"* (Louis Auchincloss, "The Atonement"). **2.** The office or district of a bailiff: *"Another writ has been issued . . . and the defendant in that cause is the prey of the sheriff having legal jurisdiction in this bailiwick"* (Charles Dickens, *David Copperfield*).

[Middle English *bailliwik* : *baillif*, bailiff (ultimately from Latin *bāiulus*, carrier) + *wik*, town (from Old English *wīc*, from Latin *vīcus*).]

be·lea·guered (bĭ-lē′gərd)

adjective

1. Beset with troubles or problems: *"The beleaguered rider could do no better than cling to the horse's neck for dear life"* (Laura Hillenbrand, *Seabiscuit*). **2.** Surrounded with troops; besieged.

[Probably Dutch *belegeren* (*be-*, around + *leger*, camp) + *-ed*, past participle suffix.]

Seabiscuit didn't run, he rampaged. When the rider . . . tried to rein him in, the horse bolted, thrashing around like a hooked marlin. Asked to go left, he'd dodge right; tugged right, he'd dart left. The **beleaguered** rider could do no better than cling to the horse's neck for dear life.

— Laura Hillenbrand,
Seabiscuit

bro·mide (brō′mīd′)

noun

1a. A binary compound of bromine with another element, such as silver. **b.** Potassium bromide, a white crystalline solid or powder used as a sedative, in photographic emulsion, and in lithography. **2a.** A commonplace remark or notion; a platitude: *"The windows of buses and shops were adorned with bromides: 'The only magic to remove poverty—hard work, clear vision, iron will, strict discipline'"*(Katherine Frank, *Indira: The Life of Indira Nehru Gandhi*). **b.** A tiresome person; a bore.

[From *bromine* (from French *brome,* from Greek *brōmos,* stench + *-ine,* suffix used in names of chemical substances) + *-ide,* suffix in names of chemical compounds.]

℣ Several bromine compounds, especially potassium bromide, have been used medicinally as sedatives. In 1906 Gelett Burgess (the coiner of the word *blurb*) wrote a book entitled *Are You a Bromide?* in which he used *bromide* to mean a tiresome person of unoriginal thoughts and trite conversation, the sort of person who might put you to sleep. *Bromide* was soon after extended to include the kind of commonplace remarks that could be expected from a bromide, such as "You're a sight for sore eyes."

cap·puc·ci·no (kăp′ə-chē′nō, kä′pə-chē′nō)

noun

Plural: **cap·puc·ci·nos**

Espresso coffee mixed or topped with steamed milk or cream.

[Italian, Capuchin, cappuccino (from the resemblance of its color to the color of the monk's habit).]

℘ The history of the word *cappuccino* shows how words can develop new senses because of resemblances that the original coiners of the terms might not have dreamed possible. The Italian name of the Capuchin order of friars, established after 1525, came from the long pointed cowl, or *cappuccino,* that was worn as part of the order's habit. In Italian *cappuccino* went on to develop another sense, "espresso coffee mixed or topped with steamed milk or cream," probably because the color of the coffee resembled the color of the habit of a Capuchin friar.

10 **ca·price** (kə-prēs′)

noun

1a. An impulsive change of mind. **b.** An inclination to change one's mind impulsively. **c.** A sudden, unpredictable action, change, or series of actions or changes: *". . . six hours of alert immobility while the boat drove slowly or floated arrested, according to the caprice of the wind"* (Joseph Conrad, *Lord Jim*). **2.** *Music* An instrumental work with an improvisatory style and a free form; a capriccio.

[French, from Italian *capriccio,* from *caporiccio,* fright, sudden start : *capo,* head (from Latin *caput*) + *riccio,* curly (from Latin *ēricius,* hedgehog, from *ēr*).]

11 car·i·bou (kăr′ə-boo′)

noun
Plural: **caribou** *or* **car·i·bous**

Any of several large reindeer native to northern North America.

[Micmac *ĝalipu* (influenced by Canadian French *caribou,* also from Micmac), from Proto-Algonquin **mekālixpowa* : **mekāl-,* to scrape + **-ixpo-,* snow.]

12 chi·as·mus (kī-ăz′məs)

noun
Plural: **chi·as·mi** (kī-ăz′mī′)

A rhetorical inversion of the second of two parallel structures, as in *"Each throat / Was parched, and glazed each eye"* (Samuel Taylor Coleridge, *The Rime of the Ancient Mariner*).

[New Latin *chīasmus,* from Greek *khīasmos,* syntactic inversion, from *khīazein,* to invert or mark with an X.]

chor·tle (chôr′tl)

noun

A snorting, joyful laugh or chuckle.

intransitive and transitive verb
    Past participle and past tense: **chor·tled**
    Present participle: **chor·tling**
    Third person singular present tense: **chor·tles**

To utter a chortle or express with a chortle.

[Blend of *chuckle* and *snort*.]

  "'O frabjous day! Callooh! Callay!' He chortled in his joy." Perhaps Lewis Carroll would chortle a bit himself to find that people are still using the word *chortle*, which he coined in *Through the Looking-Glass*, published in 1872. In any case, Carroll had constructed his word well, combining the words *chuckle* and *snort*. This type of word is called a *blend* or a *portmanteau word*. In *Through the Looking-Glass* Humpty Dumpty uses *portmanteau* ("a large leather suitcase that opens into two hinged compartments") to describe the word *slithy*, saying, "It's like a portmanteau—there are two meanings packed up into one word" (the meanings being "lithe" and "slimy").

14 **coc·cyx** (kŏk′sĭks)

noun
Plural: **coc·cy·ges** (kŏk-sī′jēz, kŏk′sĭ-jēz′)

A small triangular bone at the base of the spinal column in humans and tailless apes, consisting of several fused rudimentary vertebrae. Also called *tailbone*.

[New Latin *coccyx,* from Greek *kokkūx,* cuckoo, coccyx (from its resemblance to a cuckoo's beak).]

15 **cres·cen·do** (krə-shĕn′dō)

noun
> Plural: **cres·cen·dos** *or* **cres·cen·di** (krə-shĕn′dē)

1. *Music* **a.** A gradual increase, especially in the volume or intensity of sound in a passage. **b.** A passage played with a gradual increase in volume or intensity. **2.** A steady increase in intensity or force: *"Then the sound came, a long, deep, powerful rumble increasing in crescendo until the windows rattled, cups danced in their saucers, and the bar glasses rubbed rims and tinkled in terror. The sound slowly ebbed, then boomed to a fiercer climax, closer"* (Pat Frank, *Alas, Babylon*).

intransitive verb
> Past participle and past tense: **cres·cen·doed**
> Present participle: **cres·cen·do·ing**
> Third person singular present tense: **cres·cen·does**

To build up to a point of great intensity, force, or volume.

[Italian, present participle of *crescere,* to increase, from Latin *crēscere.*]

---

cru·ci·ver·bal·ist (krōō′sə-vûr′bə-lĭst)

noun

1. A person who constructs crosswords. **2.** An enthusiast of word games, especially of crosswords.

[From Latin *crux, cruc-*, cross + Latin *verbum*, word (translation of English *crossword*).]

des·ul·to·ry (dĕs′əl-tôr′ē, dĕz′əl-tôr′ē)

adjective

1. Having no set plan; haphazard or random: *"[These] concert series, done mostly on a shoestring and involving many refugee musicians . . . were a beacon of enterprise on the desultory wartime musical scene"* (Meirion Bowen, *BBC Music Magazine*). **2.** Moving or jumping from one thing to another; disconnected: *"She had suddenly begun speaking, after sitting silently through several hours of desultory discussion with her husband about the Resistance"* (Adam Nossiter, *The Algeria Hotel*). *"Our conversation so far had been desultory, with lots of long silences and me staring fixedly out the window"* (Scott Anderson, *Men's Journal*).

[Latin *dēsultōrius*, leaping, from *dēsultor*, a leaper, from *dēsultus*, past participle of *dēsilīre*, to leap down : *dē-*, off + *salīre*, to jump.]

18
de·tri·tus (dĭ-trī′təs)

noun
Plural: **detritus**

1. Loose fragments or grains that have been worn away from rock. **2.** Disintegrated or eroded matter; debris: *Archaeologists study the detritus of past civilizations.*

[French *détritus*, from Latin *dētrītus*, from past participle of *dēterere*, to lessen, wear away.]

19
didj·er·i·doo *or* didg·er·i·doo
(dĭj′ə-rē-dōō′, dĭj′ə-rē-dōō′)

noun
Plural: **didj·er·i·doos** *or* **didg·er·i·doos**

A musical instrument of the Aboriginal peoples of Australia, consisting of a long hollow branch or stick that makes a deep drone when blown into while vibrating the lips.

[Imitative of its sound.]

20 **e·bul·lient** (ĭ-bŏōl′yənt′)

adjective

1. Zestfully enthusiastic: *"She was one of those intensely ebullient people who are great at the right kind of party but wearing in a small space"* (Deirdre McNamer, *My Russian*). **2.** Boiling or seeming to boil; bubbling.

[Latin *ēbulliēns, ēbullient-*, present participle of *ēbullīre*, to bubble up : *ē-, ex-*, out, away + *bullīre*, to bubble, boil.]

21 **ech·e·lon** (ĕsh′ə-lŏn′)

noun

1a. A formation of troops in which each unit is positioned successively to the left or right of the rear unit to form an oblique or steplike line. **b.** A flight formation or arrangement of craft in this manner. **c.** A similar formation of groups, units, or individuals: *"By asking the right questions and choosing the right tests and drawing the right conclusions the mechanic works his way down the echelons of the motorcycle hierarchy until he has found the exact specific cause or causes of the engine failure, and then he changes them so that they no longer cause the failure"* (Robert Pirsig, *Zen and the Art of Motorcycle Maintenance*). **2.** A subdivision of a military or naval force. **3.** A level of responsibility or authority in a hierarchy; a rank: *The recent graduate took a job in the company's lower echelon.*

[French *échelon*, from Old French *eschelon*, rung of a ladder, from *eschiele*, ladder, from Late Latin *scāla*, back-formation from Latin *scālae*, steps, ladder.]

---

22 e·gre·gious (ĭ-grē′jəs, ĭ-grē′jē-əs)

adjective

Conspicuously bad or offensive: *"This is a difficult chapter for me to write—not because my own youthful mistakes were so egregious . . . but because I may be making a mistake now"* (Wendy Lesser, *Nothing Remains the Same: Rereading and Remembering*).

[From Latin *ēgregius*, outstanding : *ē-*, *ex-*, out, away + *grex, greg-*, herd.]

23 e·phem·er·al (ĭ-fĕm′ər-əl)

adjective

1. Lasting for a markedly brief time: *"There remain some truths too ephemeral to be captured in the cold pages of a court transcript"* (Irving R. Kaufman, *New York Times Magazine*). *"Despite his position, Shah Zaman smiled like the Genie through his pearly beard and declared that Scheherazade was right to think love ephemeral. But life itself was scarcely less so, and both were sweet for just that reason—sweeter yet when enjoyed as if they might endure"* (John Barth, *Chimera*). **2.** Living or lasting only for a day, as certain plants or insects do.

noun

Something that is markedly short-lived.

[From Greek *ephēmeros* : *ep-*, *epi-*, upon, during + *hēmerā*, day.]

24
ep·i·cure (ĕp′ĭ-kyŏŏr′)

noun

1. A person with refined taste, especially in food and wine. **2.** A person devoted to sensuous pleasure and luxurious living.

[Middle English, an Epicurean, from Medieval Latin *epicūrus*, from Latin *Epicūrus*, Latin form of the name of *Epikouros*, Greek philosopher (341–270 BC) who advocated the pursuit of pleasure enjoyed in moderation.]

er·satz (ĕr′zäts′, ĕr-zäts′)

adjective

Being an imitation or a substitute, usually an inferior one; artificial: *"Now when she flips through memories, they have an ersatz quality, the sort of tint applied to enhance photos"* (Carol Anshaw, *Seven Moves*).

[German, replacement, from *ersetzen,* to replace, from Old High German *irsezzan* : *ir-,* out + *sezzan,* to set.]

Chris is not sure anymore who it is she's searching for. Now that the person she loved turns out to have been in great part concocted for her approval, who she is missing and who she might find are quite different people. Now when she flips through memories, they have an **ersatz** quality, the sort of tint applied to enhance photos — rose on the cheeks of the sallow graduate, blue on the muddy lake of the dilapidated resort.

— Carol Anshaw,
Seven Moves

26
fa·ce·tious (fə-sē′shəs)

adjective

Playfully jocular; humorous: *"He pointed out — writing in a foolish, facetious tone — that the perfection of mechanical appliances must ultimately supersede limbs"* (H.G. Wells, *The War of the Worlds*). *"[A]unty gave George a nudge with her finger, designed to be immensely facetious, and turned again to her griddle with great briskness"* (Harriet Beecher Stowe, *Uncle Tom's Cabin*).

[French *facétieux*, from *facétie*, jest, from Latin *facētia*, from *facētus*, witty.]

𝕱 *Facetious* is one of a very small number of English words that contain all five vowels in alphabetical order. (Another is *abstemious*.) The adverb *facetiously* contains all the vowels and *y* in order.

27 **fe·cun·di·ty** (fĭ-kŭn**′**dĭ-tē)

noun

1. The quality or power of producing abundantly; fruitfulness or fertility: *"In the Permian and Triassic periods, what is now the continent of Europe was dominated by endless sandy wastes, blasted by hot dry winds. Lifelessness, aridity and blistering heat suddenly took the place of all that Carboniferous moisture and fecundity"* (Simon Winchester, *The Map That Changed the World*). **2.** Productive or creative power: *fecundity of the mind.*

[From *fecund* (from Middle English, from Old French *fecond*, from Latin *fēcundus*, fertile, fruitful) + *-ity*, noun-forming suffix.]

28 **fo·cac·ci·a**
(fə-kä**′**chē**′**ə, fō-kä**′**chē**′**ə, fō-kä**′**chə)

noun

A flat Italian bread traditionally flavored with olive oil and salt and often topped with herbs, onions, or other items.

[Italian, hearth-cake, from Late Latin *focācia,* of the hearth, feminine of *focācius,* from Latin *focus,* hearth.]

fus·ty (fŭs′tē)

adjective
    Comparative: **fus·ti·er**
    Superlative: **fus·ti·est**

1. Smelling of mildew or decay; musty *"goggle-eyed headlines staring up at me on every street corner and at the fusty, peanut-smelling mouth of every subway"* (Sylvia Plath, *The Bell Jar*). **2.** Old-fashioned; antique.

[Middle English, from Old French *fust,* piece of wood, wine cask, from Latin *fūstis,* stick, club.]

It was a queer, sultry summer, the summer they electrocuted the Rosenbergs, and I didn't know what I was doing in New York. I'm stupid about executions. The idea of being electrocuted makes me sick, and that's all there was to read about in the papers — goggle-eyed headlines staring up at me on every street corner and at the **fusty,** peanut-smelling mouth of every subway. It had nothing to do with me, but I couldn't help wondering what it would be like, being burned alive all along your nerves.

— Sylvia Plath,
The Bell Jar

30 ge·müt·lich·keit

(gə-mo͞ot′lĭk-kīt′, gə-müt′lĭKH-kīt′)

noun

Warm friendliness; amicability.

[German *gemütlich,* congenial (from Middle High German *gemüetlich,* from *gemüete,* spirit, feelings, from Old High German *gimuoti,* from *muot,* mind, spirit, joy) + *-keit,* -ness.]

31 glos·so·la·li·a

(glô′sə-lā′lē-ə, glŏs′ə-lā′lē-ə)

noun

1. Fabricated and nonmeaningful speech, especially such speech associated with a trance state or certain schizophrenic syndromes. **2.** The ability or phenomenon to utter words or sounds of a language unknown to the speaker, especially as an expression of religious ecstasy. In this sense, also called *gift of tongues, speaking in tongues.*

[New Latin : Greek *glōssa,* tongue + Greek *lalein,* to babble.]

gos·sa·mer (gŏs′ə-mər)

adjective

1. Sheer, light, and delicate: *"[F]rom the looping cascades of communication and control emerge the particular parts of a body in perfect form, nearly every time: the needle nose of the narwhal, the gossamer wing of a butterfly, . . . the marvelous globe of the human eye somehow ready upon arrival out of a dark world instantly to receive light"* (Jennifer Ackerman, *Chance in the House of Fate*).
2. Tenuous; flimsy: *"He knew he was in trouble, but the trouble was glamorous, and he surrounded it with the gossamer lie of make-believe. He was living the storybook legend"* (Evan Hunter, "First Offense").

noun

1. A soft sheer gauzy fabric. **2.** Something delicate, light, or flimsy. **3.** A fine film of cobwebs often seen floating in the air or caught on bushes or grass.

[Middle English *gossomer* : *gos,* goose + *somer,* summer (probably from the abundance of gossamer during early autumn when geese are in season).]

gra·va·men (grə-vā′mən)

noun

Plural **gra·va·mens** *or*
gra·vam·i·na (grə-văm′ə-nə)

The part of a legal charge or an accusation that weighs most substantially against the accused.

[Medieval Latin *gravāmen,* injury, accusation, from Late Latin, encumbrance, obligation, from Latin *gravāre,* to burden, from *gravis,* heavy.]

hal·cy·on (hăl′sē-ən)

adjective

1. Calm and peaceful; tranquil: *"[I]t was the most halcyon summer I ever spent. We walked the river in the daytime, talking and watching and listening and holding hands, sitting in the dust, in the cool shade beneath the big oaks, and just listening to the mourning doves"* (Rick Bass, *The Sky, the Stars, the Wilderness*). **2.** Prosperous; golden: *"There is probably hardly a single American who does not yearn for a return to the halcyon years of the Eisenhower and Kennedy presidencies, when American manufacturers paid the highest wages in the world yet nonetheless almost effortlessly dominated world markets"* (Eammon Fingleton, *In Praise of Hard Industries*).

noun

1. A kingfisher, especially one of the genus *Halcyon*. **2.** A fabled bird, identified with the kingfisher, that was supposed to have had the power to calm the wind and the waves while it nested on the sea during the winter solstice.

[Middle English *alcioun*, from Latin *alcyōn, halcyōn*, from Greek *halkuōn*, a mythical bird, kingfisher, alteration (influenced by *hals*, salt, sea, and *kuōn*, conceiving, becoming pregnant) of *alkuōn*.]

They found a piglet caught in a curtain of creepers, throwing itself at the elastic traces in all the madness of extreme terror. . . . The three boys rushed forward and Jack drew his knife again with a flourish. He raised his arm in the air. There came a pause, a **hiatus,** the pig continued to scream and the creepers to jerk, and the blade continued to flash at the end of a bony arm. The pause was only long enough for them to understand what an enormity the downward stroke would be.

—William Golding,
Lord of the Flies

35 hi·a·tus (hī-ā′təs)

noun

Plural: **hi·a·tus·es** *or* **hiatus**

1. A gap or interruption in space, time, or continuity; a break: *"There came a pause, a hiatus, the pig continued to scream and the creepers to jerk, and the blade continued to flash at the end of a bony arm"* (William Golding, *The Lord of the Flies*). **2.** A slight pause that occurs when two immediately adjacent vowels in consecutive sylla-bles are pronounced, as in *reality* and *naïve*. **3.** A sepa-ration, aperture, fissure, or short passage in an organ or part of the body.

[Latin *hiātus*, from past participle of *hiāre*, to gape.]

hu·mu·hu·mu·nu·ku·nu·ku·a·pu·a·a
(hōō′mōō-hōō′mōō-nōō′kōō-nōō′kōō-ä′pōō-ä′ä′)

noun

Plural: **humuhumunukunukuapuaa** *or*
hu·mu·hu·mu·nu·ku·nu·ku·a·pu·a·as

Either of two triggerfishes, *Rhinecanthus aculeatus* or *R. rectangulus,* native to the outer reefs of Hawaii, the latter having a broad black band on the side and a black triangle at the beginning of the tail. The humuhumunukunukuapuaa is the state fish of Hawaii.

[Hawaiian *humuhumu-nukunuku-ā-pua'a,* trigger fish with a blunt snout like a pig's : *humuhumu,* small trigger fish (from reduplication of Proto-Polynesian **sumu,* trigger fish) + *nukunuku,* small snout, reduplication of *nuku,* snout + *ā,* like + *pua'a,* pig.]

i·con·o·clast (ī-kŏn′ə-klăst′)

noun

1. One who attacks and seeks to overthrow traditional or popular ideas or institutions: *"I think that nobody but a damned iconoclast could even conceive the atrocity you're proposing. I think you're one of those people who take pleasure in smashing apart anything that's stamped with tradition or stability"* (Stanley Ellin, "The Moment of Decision"). **2.** One who destroys sacred religious images.

[French *iconoclaste,* from Medieval Greek *eikonoklastēs,* smasher of religious images : *eikono-,* image + Greek *-klastēs,* breaker (from Greek *klān, klas-,* to break).]

Eikonoklastēs, the ancestor of our word *iconoclast*, was first formed in Medieval Greek from the elements *eikōn*, "image, likeness," and *-klastēs*, "breaker," from *klān*, "to break." The images referred to by the word are religious images, which were the subject of controversy among Christians of the Byzantine Empire in the eighth and ninth centuries, when iconoclasm was at its height. In addition to destroying many sculptures and paintings, those opposed to images attempted to have them barred from display and veneration. During the Protestant Reformation, images in churches were again felt to be idolatrous and were once more banned and destroyed. *Iconoclast*, the descendant of the Greek word, is first recorded in English (1641), with reference to the Byzantine iconoclasts.

in·sou·ci·ant (ĭn-sōō′sē-ənt)

adjective

Marked by blithe unconcern; nonchalant: *"No man, save the Texas Ranger, has ever carried it [the revolver] with the insouciant air and picturesque charm of the American cowboy"* (Ramon F. Adams, *Cowboy Lingo*).

[French : *in-*, not + *souciant*, present participle of *soucier*, to trouble (from Old French, from Vulgar Latin **sollicītāre*, alteration of Latin *sollicitāre*, to vex).]

in·ter·lop·er (ĭn′tər-lō′pər)

noun

1. One that interferes with the affairs of others, often for selfish reasons; a meddler: *"The Alexandria of my childhood was still a pure Southern culture, undiluted yet by suburban interlopers from up north"* (James Carroll, *An American Requiem*). **2.** One that intrudes in a place, situation, or activity. **3.** *Archaic* **a.** One that trespasses on a trade monopoly, as by conducting unauthorized trade in an area designated to a chartered company. **b.** A ship or other vessel used in such trade.

[From English *inter-* (from Latin, between) + probably Middle Dutch *lōper,* runner (from *lōpen,* to run).]

✒ The word *interloper* first appeared as England embarked on the course that led to the British Empire. First recorded around 1590 in connection with the Muscovy Company, the earliest major English trading company (chartered in 1555), *interloper* was soon used in connection with independent traders competing with the East India Company (chartered in 1600) as well. These monopolies held a dim view of independent traders, called *interlopers.* The term is probably partly derived from Dutch, the language of one of the great trade rivals of the English at that time. *Inter-* is simply the prefix *inter-,* meaning "between, among." The element *-loper* is probably related to the same element in *landloper,* "vagabond," a word adopted from Middle Dutch, where it is a compound of *land,* "land," and *lōper* (from *lōpen,* "to run, leap"). *Interloper* came to be used in the extended sense "busybody" in the 1600s.

in·ter·nec·ine

(ĭn′tər-nĕs′ēn′, ĭn′tər-nĕs′ĭn, ĭn′tər-nē′sīn′)

adjective

1. Of or relating to struggle within a nation, organization, or group: *"While he was becoming more and more closely drawn into the internecine politics of the Socialist party and its pro-Bolshevik and anti-Bolshevik offshoots, she was getting a broader sense of the country, of what the Russian experiment meant to various people"* (Mary V. Dearborn, *Queen of Bohemia*). **2.** Mutually destructive; ruinous or fatal to both sides. **3.** Characterized by bloodshed or carnage.

[Latin *internecīnus,* destructive, variant of *internecīvus,* from *internecāre,* to slaughter : *inter-,* intensive prefix + *nex, nec-,* death.]

🖙 Today, *internecine* usually means "relating to internal struggle," but in its first recorded use in English, in 1663, it meant "fought to the death," as did the Latin source of the word, derived from the verb *necāre,* "to kill." Here, the prefix *inter-* did not have the usual sense of "between, mutual" but rather that of an intensifier meaning "all the way, to the death." Samuel Johnson was unaware of this fact when he compiled his great dictionary in the 1700s. Misunderstanding the prefix, he defined *internecine* as "endeavoring mutual destruction." Johnson's dictionary was so popular and considered so authoritative that this error became widely adopted. It was further compounded when *internecine* acquired the sense "relating to internal struggle." Since the ultimate arbiter of language is how people use it, what was once a compounded error has long since become an acceptable usage.

41

in·vei·gle (ĭn-vā′gəl, ĭn-vē′gəl)

transitive verb
> Past participle and past tense: **in·vei·gled**
> Present participle: **in·vei·gling**
> Third person singular present tense: **in·vei·gles**

1. To win over by coaxing, flattery, or artful talk: *"Melmotte is, in short, a mighty con artist: we are on to him almost instantly. Our interest is not in finding out his scam, but in watching him inveigle and enmesh the gullible"* (Cynthia Ozick, *The New York Times Book Review*). **2.** To obtain by cajolery.

[Middle English *envegle,* alteration of Old French *aveugler,* to blind, from *aveugle,* blind, from Vulgar Latin **aboculus* : Latin *ab-,* away from + Latin *oculus,* eye (probably loan-translation of Gaulish *exsops* : *exs-,* from + *ops,* eye).]

42

jer·e·mi·ad (jĕr′ə-mī′əd)

noun

A literary work or speech expressing a bitter lament or a righteous prophecy of doom.

[French *jérémiade,* after *Jérémie,* Jeremiah, prophet to whom the biblical book of Lamentations is traditionally attributed, from Late Latin *Ieremiās,* from Hebrew *yirməyāhû,* Yahweh has established : *yirm,* he has established + *yāhû,* Yahweh.]

43
jux·ta·po·si·tion (jŭk′stə-pə-zĭsh′ən)

noun

The act or an instance of placing two items side by side, especially for comparison or contrast, or the state of being so placed: *"No human eye can isolate the unhappy coincidence of line and place which suggests evil in the face of a house, and yet somehow a maniac juxtaposition, a badly turned angle, some chance meeting of roof and sky, turned Hill House into a place of despair, more frightening because the face of Hill House seemed awake, with a watchfulness from the blank windows and a touch of glee in the eyebrow of a cornice"* (Shirley Jackson, *The Haunting of Hill House*).

[French *juxtaposition* : Latin *iūxtā*, close by + French *position*, position, from Latin *positiō, positiōn-*, placing, position, from *positus*, past participle of *pōnere*, to place.]

44
ko·an (kō′än′)

noun

A puzzling, often paradoxical statement or story, used in Zen Buddhism as an aid to meditation and a means of gaining spiritual awakening: *"Saskia will sit for an hour in the grass down by the shore, pondering a koan until she enters that space wherein silence and stillness press against her like solid walls"* (Brian Hall, *The Saskiad*).

[Japanese *kōan* : *kō*, public + *an*, matter for consideration, legal case.]

They were not welcomed home very cordially by their mother. Mrs. Bennet wondered at their coming, and thought them very wrong to give so much trouble, and was sure Jane would have caught cold again; but their father, though very **laconic** in his expressions of pleasure, was really glad to see them; he had felt their importance in the family circle.

— Jane Austen,
Pride and Prejudice

45 la·con·ic (lə-kŏn'ĭk)

adjective

Using few words; terse; concise: *"[T]heir father, though very laconic in his expressions of pleasure, was really glad to see them"* (Jane Austen, *Pride and Prejudice*).

[Latin *Lacōnicus,* Spartan, from Greek *Lakōnikos,* from *Lakōn,* a Spartan (from the reputation of the Spartans for brevity of speech).]

֎ The study of the classics allows us to understand the history of the term *laconic,* which comes to English via Latin from Greek *Lakōnikos.* The English word is first recorded in 1583 with the sense "of or relating to Laconia or its inhabitants." *Lakōnikos* is derived from *Lakōn,* "a Laconian, a person from Lacedaemon," the name for the region of Greece of which Sparta was the capital. The Spartans, noted for being warlike and disciplined, were also known for the brevity of their speech, and it is this quality that English writers still denote by the use of the adjective *laconic,* which is first found in this sense in 1589.

la·gniappe (lăn′yəp, lăn-yăp′)

noun
Chiefly southern Louisiana and Mississippi

1. A small gift presented by a storeowner to a customer with the customer's purchase. **2.** An extra or unexpected gift or benefit.

[Louisiana French, from American Spanish *la ñapa*, the gift : *la*, the + *ñapa* (variant of *yapa*, gift, from Quechua, from *yapay*, to give more).]

℘ *Lagniappe* derives from New World Spanish *la ñapa*, "the gift," and ultimately from Quechua *yapay*, "to give more." The word entered the rich Creole dialect mixture of New Orleans and there acquired a French spelling. It is still used in the Gulf states, especially southern Louisiana, to denote a little bonus that a friendly shopkeeper might add to a purchase. By extension, it may mean "an extra or unexpected gift or benefit."

lep·re·chaun (lĕp′rĭ-kŏn′, lĕp′rĭ-kôn′)

noun

One of a race of elves in Irish folklore who can reveal hidden treasure to those who catch them.

[Irish Gaelic *luprachán*, alteration of Middle Irish *luchrupán*, from Old Irish *luchorpán* : *luchorp* (*lú-*, small + *corp*, body, from *Latin* corpus) + *-án*, diminutive suffix.]

℘ Nothing seems more Irish than the leprechaun, yet hiding within the word *leprechaun* is a word from another language entirely. *Leprechaun* ultimately derives from Old Irish *luchorpán*, a compound of Old Irish *lú*, meaning "small," and the Old Irish word *corp*, "body." *Corp* is borrowed from Latin *corpus* (which can be seen in such words as *corporal*, "physical; relating to the body"). This fact is a piece of evidence attesting to the influence of Latin on the Irish language. Although *leprechaun* is old in Irish, it is fairly new in English, being first recorded in 1604.

48 li·to·tes (lī′tə-tēz′, lĭt′ə-tēz′, lī-tō′tēz)

noun
Plural: **litotes**

A figure of speech consisting of an understatement in which an affirmative is expressed by negating its opposite, as in *"I showed him over the establishment, not omitting the pantry, with <u>no little</u> pride, and he commended it highly"* (Charles Dickens, *David Copperfield*).

[Greek *lītotēs*, from *lītos*, plain.]

49 lu·cu·brate (lōō′kyōō-brāt′)

intransitive verb
Past participle and past tense: **lu·cu·brat·ed**
Present participle: **lu·cu·brat·ing**
Third person singular present tense: **lu·cu·brates**

To write in a scholarly fashion; produce scholarship.

[Latin *lūcubrāre*, to work at night by lamplight.]

50 mag·nan·i·mous (măg-năn′ə-məs)

adjective

Noble in mind and heart; generous and unselfish: *"[S]ophisticated and intellectually wise as I like to think I am now, I have to admit I'm still inspired by a poetic phrase, a magnanimous gesture, a promise of a better tomorrow"* (Norma Sherry, *Baltimore Chronicle & Sentinel*).

[From Latin *magnanimus* : *magnus*, great + *animus*, soul, mind.]

51 ma·ha·ra·jah *or* ma·ha·ra·ja
(mä′hə-rä′jə, mä′hə-rä′zhə)

noun

1. A king or prince in India ranking above a rajah, especially the sovereign of one of the former native states. **2.** Used as a title for such a king or prince.

[Sanskrit *mahārājaḥ* : *mahā-*, great + *rājā, rājaḥ*, king.]

℘ *Maharajah* comes from the Sanskrit word *mahārājaḥ*, meaning "great king." The element *mahā-* is related to Greek *mega-* and Latin *magnus*, both meaning the same thing as the Sanskrit term, "great." All three forms derive from an Indo-European root that also has descendants in Germanic, in particular, the Old English word *micel*, pronounced (mĭ′chəl). This survives today in *much* (shortened from Middle English *muchel*).

52 mal·a·prop·ism (măl′ə-prŏp-ĭz′əm)

noun

1. Ludicrous misuse of a word, especially by confusion with one of similar sound. **2.** An example of such misuse.

[After Mrs. Malaprop (from *malapropos*), a character in *The Rivals*, a play by Richard Brinsley Sheridan + *-ism*, nominal suffix.]

☞ "She's as headstrong as an allegory on the banks of the Nile" and "He is the very pineapple of politeness" are two of the absurd pronouncements from Mrs. Malaprop that explain why her name became synonymous with ludicrous misuse of language. A character in Richard Brinsley Sheridan's play *The Rivals* (1775), Mrs. Malaprop consistently uses language malapropos, that is, inappropriately. The word *malapropos* comes from the French phrase *mal à propos*, made up of *mal*, "badly," *à*, "to," and *propos*, "purpose, subject," and means "inappropriate." *The Rivals* was a popular play, and Mrs. Malaprop became enshrined in a common noun, first in the form *malaprop* and later in *malapropism*, which is first recorded in 1849. Perhaps that is what Mrs. Malaprop feared when she said, "If I reprehend any thing in this world, it is the use of my oracular tongue, and a nice derangement of epitaphs!"

mer·e·tri·cious (mĕr′ĭ-trĭsh′əs)

adjective

1a. Attracting attention in a vulgar manner: *"It was a platinum fob chain simple and chaste in design, properly proclaiming its value by substance alone and not by meretricious ornamentation — as all good things should do"* (O. Henry, "The Gift of the Magi"). **b.** Plausible but false or insincere; specious: *I saw through his meretricious arguments.* **2.** Of or relating to prostitutes or prostitution.

[Latin *meretrīcius*, of prostitutes, from *meretrīx*, *meretrīc-*, prostitute, from *merēre*, to earn money.]

54

mes·mer·ize (mĕz′mə-rīz′, mĕs′mə-rīz′)

transitive verb

    Past participle and past tense: **mes·mer·ized**
    Present participle: **mes·mer·iz·ing**
    Third person singular present tense: **mes·mer·iz·es**

1. To spellbind; enthrall: *"He could mesmerize an audience by the sheer force of his presence"* (Justin Kaplan). *"The other morning I watched five game shows in a row on television. I wanted to turn them off, but I was too mesmerized by the contestants"* (Erma Bombeck, *If Life Is a Bowl of Cherries, What Am I Doing in the Pits?*). **2.** To hypnotize.

[After Franz Mesmer (1734–1815), Austrian physician.]

  Franz Anton Mesmer, a visionary eighteenth-century physician, believed cures could be effected by having patients do things such as sit with their feet in a fountain of magnetized water while holding cables attached to magnetized trees. He then came to believe that magnetic powers resided in himself, and during highly fashionable curative sessions in Paris he caused his patients to have reactions ranging from sleeping or dancing to convulsions. These reactions were actually brought about by hypnotic powers that Mesmer was unaware he possessed. One of his pupils, named Puységur, then used the term *mesmerism* (first recorded in English in 1802) for Mesmer's practices. The related word *mesmerize* (first recorded in English in 1829), having shed its reference to the hypnotic doctor, lives on in the sense "to enthrall."

me·tic·u·lous (mǐ-tǐk′yə-ləs)

adjective

1. Extremely careful and precise: *"[H]is wardrobe seemed to consist entirely of meticulous reconstructions of garments of the previous century"* (William Gibson, *Neuromancer*). **2.** Extremely or excessively concerned with details.

[From Latin *metīculōsus*, timid, from *metus*, fear.]

Case had never seen him wear the same suit twice, although his wardrobe seemed to consist entirely of **meticulous** reconstructions of garments of the previous century. He affected prescription lenses, framed in spidery gold, ground from pink slabs of synthetic quartz and beveled like the mirrors in a Victorian dollhouse.

—William Gibson,
Neuromancer

mi·lieu (mĭl-yŏo′, mĭ-lyœ′)

noun
> Plural: **mi·lieus** *or* **mi·lieux** (mĭ-lyœ′)

An environment or a setting: *"I don't know that the arts have a milieu here, any of them; they're more like a very thinly settled outskirt"* (Edith Wharton, *The Age of Innocence*).

[French, from Old French, center : *mi,* middle (from Latin *medius*) + *lieu,* place (from Latin *locus*).]

mi·to·chon·dri·on (mī′tə-kŏn′drē-ən)

noun
> Plural **mi·to·chon·dri·a** (mī′tə-kŏn′drē-ə)

A structure that is found in the cytoplasm of all cells except bacteria; has an inner membrane enclosing a liquid that contains DNA (genetically different from nuclear DNA), RNA, small ribosomes, and solutes; and breaks down food molecules and converts them to usable energy in the presence of oxygen.

[New Latin : Greek *mitos,* warp thread + Greek *khondrion,* diminutive of *khondros,* grain, granule.]

nem·e·sis (nĕm′ĭ-sĭs)

noun
    Plural: **nem·e·ses** (nĕm′ĭ-sēz′)

1. A source of harm or ruin: *"The resolutions—calling for limitations on working hours, state support for education, nationalization of railways—were not very revolutionary. Reform was again showing itself to be the nemesis of revolution"* (John Kenneth Galbraith, *The Age of Uncertainty*). **2.** Retributive justice in its execution or outcome. **3.** An opponent that cannot be beaten or overcome. **4.** One that inflicts retribution or vengeance. **5. Nemesis** In Greek mythology, the goddess of retributive justice or vengeance.

[Greek, retribution, the goddess Nemesis, from *nemein,* to allot.]

nic·ti·tate (nĭk′tĭ-tāt′) *also* **nic·tate** (nĭk′tāt′)

intransitive verb
> Past participle and past tense: **nic·ti·tat·ed**
> Present participle: **nic·ti·tat·ing**
> Third person singular present tense: **nic·ti·tates**

To wink. Used especially in connection with the *nicti-tating membrane,* a transparent inner eyelid in birds, reptiles, and some mammals that closes to protect and moisten the eye.

[Medieval Latin *nictitāre,* frequentative of Latin *nictāre,* to wink.]

60 **nos·trum** (nŏs′trəm)

noun

1. A medicine whose effectiveness is unproved and whose ingredients are usually secret; a quack remedy: *"He was clearly a confirmed hypochondriac, and I was dreamily conscious that he was pouring forth interminable trains of symptoms, and imploring information as to the composition and action of innumerable quack nostrums, some of which he bore about in a leather case in his pocket"* (Arthur Conan Doyle, *The Sign of Four*). **2.** A favored but often questionable remedy: *"His economic nostrums of lowering taxes to feed the economy were the subject of furious debates"* (David Shribman, *Boston Globe*).

[From Latin *nostrum (remedium)*, our (remedy), neuter of *noster.*]

61 **nud·nik** *also* **nud·nick** (nŏŏd′nĭk)

noun

Slang An obtuse, boring, or bothersome person; a pest.

[Yiddish, from *nudne*, boring, from *nudyen*, to bore + *-nik*, -nik, nominal suffix.]

I find that all the fair and noble impulses of humanity, the dreams of poets and the agonies of martyrs, are shackled and bound in the service of organized and predatory Greed! And therefore I cannot rest, I cannot be silent; therefore I cast aside comfort and happiness, health and good repute — and go out into the world and cry out the pain of my spirit! Therefore I am not to be silenced by poverty and sickness, not by hatred and **obloquy,** by threats and ridicule — not by prison and persecution, if they should come — not by any power that is upon the earth or above the earth, that was, or is, or ever can be created.

— Upton Sinclair,
The Jungle

62 ob·lo·quy (ŏb′lə-kwē)

noun
Plural: **ob·lo·quies**

1. Abusively detractive language or utterance; calumny: *"Therefore I am not to be silenced by poverty and sickness, not by hatred and obloquy, by threats and ridicule"* (Upton Sinclair, *The Jungle*). **2.** The condition of disgrace suffered as a result of abuse or vilification; ill repute.

[Middle English *obloqui,* from Late Latin *obloquium,* abusive contradiction, from Latin *obloquī,* to interrupt : *ob-,* against + *loquī,* to speak.]

63 ob·strep·er·ous (ŏb-strĕp′ər-əs)

adjective

Noisily unruly or defiant: *"Nurse Hopkins ran the daycare center on the top floor of the agency building, and if from time to time she used tranquilizers on the more obstreperous children, she was at least trained and qualified to do so, and she knew what side effects to look out for"* (Faye Weldon, *The Life and Loves of a She-Devil*).

[From Latin *obstreperus,* noisy, from *obstrepere,* to make a noise against : *ob-,* against + *strepere,* to make a noise (of imitative origin).]

ox·y·mo·ron (ŏk′sē-môr′ŏn′)

noun

Plural: **ox·y·mo·rons**
or **ox·y·mo·ra** (ŏk′sē-môr′ə)

A rhetorical figure in which incongruous or contradictory terms are combined, as in *deafening silence.*

[Greek *oxumōron,* from neuter of *oxumōros,* pointedly foolish : *oxus,* sharp, + *mōros,* foolish, dull.]

⌇ Interestingly, the word *oxymoron* is itself etymologically an oxymoron. Combined, the Greek words *oxus* and *mōros,* which mean respectively "sharp" and "dull," form the compound *oxumōros,* "pointedly foolish."

pa·lav·er (pə-lăv′ər, pə-lä′vər)

noun

1a. Idle chatter. **b.** Talk intended to charm or beguile: *"The girl glanced back at him over her shoulder and said with great bitterness: —The men that is now is only all palaver and what they can get out of you"* (James Joyce, "The Dead," *Dubliners*). **2.** A parley between two groups, especially European explorers and representatives of local populations.

[Portuguese *palavra,* speech, alteration of Late Latin *parabola,* speech, parable.]

—O, then, said Gabriel gaily, I suppose we'll be going to your wedding one of these fine days with your young man, eh?

The girl glanced back at him over her shoulder and said with great bitterness:

—The men that is now is only all **palaver** and what they can get out of you.

— James Joyce,
"The Dead," *Dubliners*

66 pe·jor·a·tive

(pĭ-jôr′ə-tĭv, pĕj′ə-rā′tĭv, pē′jə-rā′tĭv)

adjective

Disparaging; belittling: *"Unfortunately, the word 'diet' has come to have a pejorative meaning for many people because it suggests denial, restriction, or limitations"* (James E. Marti, *The Ultimate Consumer's Guide to Diets and Nutrition*).

noun

A disparaging or belittling word or expression.

[From *pejorate*, to make worse (from Late Latin *pēiōrātus*, past participle of *pēiōrāre*, to make worse, from Latin *pēior*, worse), + *-ive*, adjectival suffix (from Latin *-īvus*).]

67 pre·car·i·ous (prĭ-kâr′ē-əs)

adjective

1. Dangerously lacking in security or stability: *"And the recurring sight of hitch-hikers waiting against the sky gave him the flash of a sensation he had known as a child: standing still with nothing to touch him, feeling tall and having the world come all at once into its round shape underfoot and rush and turn through space and make his stand very precarious and lonely"* (Eudora Welty, "The Hitch-Hikers"). **2.** Subject to chance or uncertain conditions: *The people eked out a precarious existence in the mountains.* **3.** Based on uncertain, unwarranted, or unproved premises: *a precarious solution to a difficult problem.*

[From Latin *precārius*, obtained by entreaty, uncertain, from *precārī*, to entreat.]

---

68 **pres·ti·dig·i·ta·tion** (prĕs'tĭ-dĭj'ĭ-tā'shən)

noun

1. Performance of or skill in performing magic or con-juring tricks with the hands; sleight of hand. **2.** Skill or cleverness, especially in deceiving others.

[French (influenced by *prestigiateur,* juggler, conjurer, from *prestige,* illusion), from *prestidigitateur,* conjurer : *preste,* nimble (from Italian *presto*) + Latin *digitus,* finger.]

69 **pre·ter·nat·u·ral**
(prē'tər-năch'ər-əl, prē'tər-năch'rəl)

adjective

1. Differing from what is normal or natural; abnor-mal or extraordinary: *"Dickens, with preternatural ap-prehension of the language of manners, and the varieties of street life, with pathos and laughter, with patriotic and still enlarging generosity, writes London tracts"* (Ralph Waldo Emerson, *English Traits*). **2.** Transcending the natural or material order; supernatural.

[Medieval Latin *praeternātūrālis,* from Latin *praeter nātūrām,* beyond nature : *praeter,* beyond + *nātūra,* nature.]

70 quark (kwôrk, kwärk)

noun

Any of a group of elementary particles supposed to be the fundamental units that combine to make up the subatomic particles known as hadrons (baryons, such as neutrons and protons, and mesons). Quarks have fractional electric charges, such as one-third the charge of an electron.

[From "Three quarks for Muster Mark!," a line in *Finnegans Wake* by James Joyce.]

✍ "Three quarks for Muster Mark!/Sure he hasn't got much of a bark/And sure any he has it's all beside the mark." This passage from James Joyce's *Finnegans Wake,* part of a poem directed against King Mark, the cuckolded husband in the Tristan legend, has left its mark on modern physics. Packed with names of birds and words suggestive of birds, the poem and accompanying prose are a squawk against the king that suggests the cawing of a crow. The word *quark* comes from the standard English verb *quark,* meaning "to caw, croak," and also from the dialectal verb *quawk,* meaning "to caw, screech like a bird." But why should *quark* have become the name for a group of hypothetical subatomic particles proposed as the fundamental units of matter? Murray Gell-Mann, the physicist who proposed this name for these particles, said in a private letter of June 27, 1978, to the editor of the *Oxford English Dictionary* that he had been influenced by Joyce's words: "The allusion to three quarks seemed perfect" (originally there were only three subatomic quarks). Gell-Mann, however, wanted to pronounce the word with (ô), not (ä), as Joyce seemed to indicate by rhymes such as *Mark*. Gell-Mann got around that "by supposing that one ingredient of the line 'Three quarks for Muster Mark' was a cry of 'Three quarts for Mister . . .' heard in H.C. Earwicker's pub," a plausible suggestion given the complex punning in Joyce's novel. It seems appropriate that this perplexing and humorous novel should have supplied the term for particles that come in six "flavors" and three "colors."

71 quix·ot·ic (kwĭk-sŏt′ĭk)

adjective

Caught up in the pursuit of unreachable goals; foolishly idealistic and impractical: *"[W]hat I like best in you is this particular enthusiasm, which is not at all practical or sensible, which is downright Quixotic"* (Willa Cather, *The Song of the Lark*).

[After Don Quixote, hero of a novel by Miguel de Cervantes Saavedra (1547–1616).]

red·o·lent (rĕd′l-ənt)

adjective

1. Fragrant; aromatic. **2.** Suggestive; reminiscent: *"There was a ripe mystery about it, a hint . . . of romances that were not musty and laid away already in lavender, but fresh and breathing and redolent of this year's shining motor-cars and of dances whose flowers were scarcely withered"* (F. Scott Fitzgerald, *The Great Gatsby*).

[Middle English, from Old French, from Latin *redolēns, redolent-*, present participle of *redolēre*, to smell : *re-, red-,* re-, intensive prefix + *olēre*, to smell.]

It amazed him — he had never been in such a beautiful house before. But what gave it an air of breathless intensity was that Daisy lived there — it was as casual a thing to her as his tent out at camp was to him. There was a ripe mystery about it, a hint of bedrooms upstairs more beautiful and cool than other bedrooms, of gay and radiant activities taking place through its corridors, and of romances that were not musty and laid away already in lavender, but fresh and breathing and **redolent** of this year's shining motor-cars and of dances whose flowers were scarcely withered.

— F. Scott Fitzgerald,
The Great Gatsby

73 re·pug·nant (rĭ-pŭg′nənt)

adjective

Arousing disgust or aversion; offensive or repulsive: "*There was her milk, untouched, forgotten, barely tepid. She drank it down, without pleasure; all its whiteness, draining from the stringing wet whiteness of the empty cup, was singularly repugnant*" (James Agee, *A Death in the Family*).

[Middle English, antagonistic, from Old French, from Latin *repugnāns, repugnant-*, present participle of *repugnāre*, to fight against : *re-, red-*, against + *pugnāre*, to fight, from *pugnus*, fist.]

74 ru·bric (roo′brĭk)

noun

1. A class or category: "*This mission is sometimes discussed under the rubric of 'horizontal escalation' . . . from conventional to nuclear war*" (Jack Beatty, *Atlantic Monthly*). **2.** A part of a manuscript or book, such as a title, heading, or initial letter, that appears in decorative red lettering or is otherwise distinguished from the rest of the text. **3.** A title or heading in a code of law. **4.** A direction in a missal, hymnal, or other liturgical book: "*This kind of answer given in a measured official tone, as of a clergyman reading according to the rubric, did not help to . . . justify the glories of the Eternal City, or to give her the hope that if she knew more about them the world would be joyously illuminated for her*" (George Eliot, *Middlemarch*). **5.** An authoritative rule or direction: "*The creative ferment of the Internet . . . is frequently in-*

voked by the legislative legions in Washington who want to extend some version of electronic networking to every home, school, library and hospital in the country under the rubric of a National Information Infrastructure" (Gary Stix, *Scientific American*). **6.** A form of hematite used as a red pigment.

adjective

1. Red or reddish. **2.** Written in red.

[Middle English *rubrike,* heading, title, from Old French *rubrique,* from Latin *rubrīca,* red chalk, from *ruber, rubr-,* red.]

75 **sang-froid** *or* **sang·froid** (säN-frwä′)

noun

Coolness and composure, especially in trying circumstances: "*For a moment his face became a white mask of horror, but he soon recovered his sang-froid and, looking up at Lady Windermere, said with a forced smile, 'It is the hand of a charming young man'*" (Oscar Wilde, *Lord Arthur Savile's Crime*).

[French : *sang,* blood (from Old French, from Latin *sanguis*) + *froid,* cold (from Old French, from Vulgar Latin **frigidus,* alteration of Latin *frīgidus).*]

sar·coph·a·gus (sär-kŏf′ə-gəs)

noun

> Plural: **sar·coph·a·gi** *or* **sar·coph·a·gus·es**
> (sär-kŏf′ə-jī′)

A stone coffin, often inscribed or decorated with sculpture.

[Latin, from Greek *sarkophagos,* coffin, from *(lithos) sarkophagos,* limestone that consumed the flesh of corpses laid in it : *sarx, sark-,* flesh + *-phagos,* eating, feeding on.]

> ℘ The macabre word *sarcophagus* comes to us from Latin and Greek, having been derived in Greek from *sarx,* "flesh," and *phagein,* "to eat." The Greek word *sarkophagos* meant "eating flesh," and in the phrase *lithos* ("stone") *sarkophagos,* it denoted a limestone that was thought to decompose the flesh of corpses placed in it. Used by itself as a noun the Greek term came to mean "coffin." The term was carried over into Latin, where *sarcophagus* was used in the phrase *lapis* ("stone") *sarcophagus,* referring to the same stone as in Greek. *Sarcophagus* used as a noun in Latin meant "coffin of any material." This Latin word was borrowed into English, first being recorded in 1601 with reference to the flesh-consuming stone and then in 1705 with reference to a stone coffin.

schwa (shwä)

noun

1. A vowel that is articulated with the tongue in the middle of the oral cavity, typically occurring in unstressed syllables as the first vowel of *about* or the final vowel of *sofa.* **2.** The symbol (ə) used to represent this

---

sound. In some phonetic systems it also represents the sounds of such vowels in stressed positions, as in *but*.

[German, from Hebrew, *šəwā'*, probably from Syriac *(nuqzē)* *šwayyā*, even (points), plural passive participle of *šwā*, to be even.]

78 ser·en·dip·i·ty (sĕr′ən-dĭp′ĭ-tē)

noun
   Plural: **ser·en·dip·i·ties**

1. The faculty of making fortunate discoveries by accident. **2.** The fact or occurrence of such discoveries. **3.** An instance of making such a discovery.

[From the characters in the Persian fairy tale *The Three Princes of Serendip,* who made such discoveries, from Persian *Sarandīp,* Sri Lanka, from Arabic *Sarandīb.*]

🙿 We are indebted to the English author Horace Walpole for the word *serendipity,* which he coined in one of the 3,000 or more letters that make up an important part of his literary legacy. In a letter of January 28, 1754, Walpole says that "this discovery, indeed, is almost of that kind which I call Serendipity, a very expressive word." Walpole formed the word on an old name for Sri Lanka, *Serendip.* He explained that this name was part of the title of "a silly fairy tale, called *The Three Princes of Serendip:* as their highnesses traveled, they were always making discoveries, by accidents and sagacity, of things which they were not in quest of. . . ."

ses·qui·pe·da·lian (sĕs′kwĭ-pĭ-dāl′yən)

adjective

1. Given to or characterized by the use of long words.
2. Having many syllables; polysyllabic: *"[R]ecently a strange whimsy has started to creep in among the sesquipedalian prose of scientific journals"* (Stephen S. Hall, *The New York Times*).

noun

A long word.

[From Latin *sēsquipedālis,* of a foot and a half in length : *sēsqui-, sesqui-* + *pēs, ped-,* foot + *-ian,* nominal and adjectival suffix.]

sha·man (shä′mən, shā′mən)

noun
    Plural: **sha·mans**

A member of certain tribal societies who acts as a medium between the visible world and an invisible spirit world and practices magic or sorcery for healing, divination, and control over natural events.

[Russian, from Evenki *šaman,* Buddhist monk, shaman, from Tocharian B *ṣamāne,* monk, from Prakrit *ṣamana,* from Sanskrit *śramaṇaḥ,* from *śrámaḥ,* religious exercise.]

  At first glance, *shaman* may seem to be a compound of *-man* and a mysterious prefix *sha-.* In fact, its far different and more remarkable history begins in India as the Sanskrit word *śramaṇaḥ,* "ascetic, Buddhist monk." In the Prakrit languages, which descended from Sanskrit, it developed into *ṣamana,* a term that spread with Buddhism over central Asia. It was borrowed into Tocharian B and probably from there into Evenki (a Tungusic language of Siberian reindeer herders), where the word referred to a healer or a person who communicated with the spirit world. The term was then borrowed into Russian and other European languages and then into English.

Shaman is probably the only English word that has come from or passed through a Tocharian language. The two closely related Tocharian languages, Tocharian A and Tocharian B, are now extinct. The Tocharians lived along the Silk Road in the eastern Turkistan (Xinjiang Uygur Autonomous Region in China). We know their languages from documents such as travelers' caravan passes and Buddhist sutras written around 600–800 AD. Together, Tocharian A and B constitute a separate branch of the family tree of the Indo-European languages, the family to which English also belongs.

81 **si·ne·cure** (sī′nĭ-kyŏŏr′, sĭn′ĭ-kyŏŏr′)

noun

1. A position or office that requires little or no work but provides a salary: *"Be it said, that in this vocation of whaling, sinecures are unknown; dignity and danger go hand in hand; till you get to be Captain, the higher you rise the harder you toil"* (Herman Melville, *Moby-Dick*).
2. *Archaic* An ecclesiastical benefice not attached to the spiritual duties of a parish.

[From Medieval Latin *(beneficium) sine cūrā*, (benefice) without spiritual care (of souls).]

82

snake·bit (snāk′bĭt′)
  also **snake·bit·ten** (snāk′bĭt′n)

adjective

Experiencing a period of misfortune or inability to succeed; unlucky: *Having lost four games in a row by one run, the pitcher was starting to feel a little snakebit.*

83

sop·o·rif·ic (sŏp′ə-rĭf′ĭk)

adjective

1. Inducing or tending to induce sleep: "*[T]he heavy supper she had eaten produced a soporific effect: she was already snoring before I had finished undressing*" (Charlotte Brontë, *Jane Eyre*). **2.** Drowsy.

noun

A drug or other substance that induces sleep; a hypnotic.

[From *sopor-*, sleep (from Latin *sopor*) + *-fic*, *-ific*, causing, making (from Latin *-ficus*, from *facere*, to make, do).]

I had to sit with the girls during their hour of study; then it was my turn to read prayers; to see them to bed: afterwards I supped with the other teachers. Even when we finally retired for the night, the inevitable Miss Gryce was still my companion: we had only a short end of candle in our candlestick, and I dreaded lest she should talk till it was all burnt out; fortunately, however, the heavy supper she had eaten produced a **soporific** effect: she was already snoring before I had finished undressing.

—Charlotte Brontë,
Jane Eyre

suc·co·tash (sŭk**′**ə-tăsh**′**)

noun

A stew consisting of kernels of corn, lima beans, and tomatoes.

[Narragansett *msíckquatash,* boiled whole-kernel corn.]

su·sur·ra·tion (soō′sə-rā**′**shən)

noun

A soft whispering or rustling sound; a murmur: *"The rain was now falling more steadily, with a low, monotonous susurration, interrupted at long intervals by the sudden slashing of the boughs of the trees as the wind rose and failed"* (Ambrose Bierce, *Can Such Things Be?*).

[Middle English *susurracioun,* from Late Latin *susurrātiō, susurrātiōn-,* from Latin *susurrātus,* past participle of *susurrāre,* to whisper, from *susurrus,* whisper, ultimately of imitative origin.]

syz·y·gy (sĭz**′**ə-jē**′**)

noun
    Plural: **syz·y·gies**

An alignment of three celestial bodies, especially the sun, the moon, and Earth, in which all three bodies lie along a single straight line: *After a solar eclipse, it is likely that there will be another eclipse somewhere on Earth at the next syzygy.* **2.** The combining of two feet into a single metrical unit in classical prosody.

[Late Latin *sȳzygia*, from Greek *suzugiā*, union, from *suzugos*, paired : *sun-*, *su-*, with, together + *zugon*, yoke.]

87 **tan·ta·lize** (tăn′tə-līz′)

transitive verb
>   Past participle and past tense: **tan·ta·lized**
>   Present participle: **tan·ta·liz·ing**
>   Third person singular present tense: **tan·ta·liz·es**

To excite (another) by exposing something desirable, especially while keeping it out of reach: *"Finer than human hair, lighter than cotton, and—ounce for ounce—stronger than steel, silk tantalizes materials researchers seeking to duplicate its properties or synthesize it for large-scale production"* (Richard Lipkin, *Science News*).

[From Latin *Tantalus*, Tantalus.]

🐚 *Tantalize* comes from *Tantalus*, the name of a mythical king of Lydia, a territory on the Aegean Sea in the west of Asia Minor (now Turkey). Tantalus, originally one of the luckiest of mortals, enjoyed the privilege of feasting with the gods, but he subsequently violated their hospitality. Some say he stole the food of the gods, the *nectar* and *ambrosia* that bestow eternal life, and gave it to mortals. Others say that he killed his own son Pelops and served him to the gods to test whether they could recognize the forbidden meat. Accordingly, the gods condemned Tantalus to suffer everlasting hunger and thirst. He stands in a pool of water that recedes when he bends to drink, and the branches of the trees above him move out of reach when he tries to pluck their fruit, *tantalizing* him for all eternity.

the·o·ry (thē′ə-rē, thîr′ē)

noun

   Plural: **the·o·ries**

1. A set of statements or principles devised to explain a group of facts or phenomena, especially one that has been repeatedly tested or is widely accepted and can be used to make predictions about natural phenomena. **2.** The branch of a science or art consisting of its explanatory statements, accepted principles, and methods of analysis, as opposed to practice: *He was a fine musician but had never studied theory.* **3.** A set of theorems that constitute a systematic view of a branch of mathematics. **4.** Abstract reasoning; speculation: *Her decision was based on experience rather than theory.* **5.** A belief or principle that guides action or assists comprehension or judgment: *The detectives staked out the house on the theory that criminals usually return to the scene of the crime.* **6.** An assumption based on limited information or knowledge; a conjecture.

[Late Latin *theōria,* from Greek *theōriā,* from *theōros,* spectator : probably *theā,* a viewing + *-oros,* seeing (from *horān,* to see).]

ℬ Hypothesis, law, and theory refer to different kinds of statements, or sets of statements, that scientists make about natural phenomena. A hypothesis is a proposition that attempts to explain a set of facts in a unified way. It generally forms the basis of experiments designed to establish its plausibility. Though a hypothesis can never be proven true (in fact, hypotheses generally leave some facts unexplained), it can sometimes be verified beyond reasonable doubt in the context of a particular theoretical approach. A scientific law is a hypothesis that is assumed to be universally true. A law has good predictive power, allowing a scientist to model a physical system and predict what will happen under various conditions. A theory is a set of statements, including laws and hypotheses, that explains a group of observations or phenomena in terms of those laws and hypotheses. A theory thus accounts for a wider variety of events than a law does. Broad acceptance of a theory comes when it has been tested repeatedly on new data and been used to make accurate predictions. Although a theory generally contains hypotheses that are still open to revision, sometimes it is hard to know where the hypothesis ends and the law or theory begins. Albert Einstein's theory of relativity, for example, consists of statements that were originally considered to be hypotheses (and daring at that). But all the hypotheses of relativity have now achieved the authority of scientific laws, and Einstein's theory has supplanted Newton's laws of motion. In some cases, such as the germ theory of infectious disease, a theory becomes so completely accepted, it stops being referred to as a theory.

89
tim·bre (tăm′bər, tĭm′bər)

noun

The combination of qualities of a sound that distinguishes it from other sounds of the same pitch and volume: *"John stared at Elisha all during the lesson, admiring the timbre of Elisha's voice, much deeper and manlier than his own"* (James Baldwin, *Go Tell It on the Mountain*).

[French, from Old French, drum, clapperless bell, probably from Medieval Greek *timbanon,* drum, from earlier Greek *tumpanon,* kettledrum.]

He was not much older than John, only seventeen, and he was already saved and was a preacher. John stared at Elisha all during the lesson, admiring the **timbre** of Elisha's voice, much deeper and manlier than his own, admiring the leanness, and grace, and strength, and darkness of Elisha in his Sunday suit, wondering if he would ever be holy as Elisha was holy.

— James Baldwin,
Go Tell It on the Mountain

90 **trog·lo·dyte** (trŏg′lə-dīt′)

noun

1a. A member of a fabulous or prehistoric race of people that lived in caves, dens, or holes: *"Awkward, red-faced, too big for his shrinking suit and towering over the room like some club-wielding troglodyte, O'Kane could only duck his head and mumble an apology"* (T. Coraghessan Boyle, *Riven Rock*). **b.** A person considered to be reclusive, reactionary, out of date, or brutish. **2a.** An anthropoid ape, such as a gorilla. **b.** An animal that lives underground.

[From Latin *Trōglodytae,* a people said to be cave dwellers, from Greek *Trōglodutai,* alteration (influenced by *trōglē,* hole, and *-dutai,* those who enter), of *Trōgodutai.*]

91 **ul·lage** (ŭl′ĭj)

noun

1. The amount of liquid within a container that is lost, as by leakage, during shipment or storage. **2.** The amount by which a container, such as a bottle, cask, or tank, falls short of being full: *The ullage allows wine to expand in response to the changes in temperature without pushing the cork out or bursting the bottle.*

[From Middle English *ulage,* from Old French *ouillage,* from *ouiller,* to fill up a cask, from *ouil,* eye, bunghole, from Latin *oculus,* eye.]

92 um·laut (o͝om′lout′)

noun

1a. A change in a vowel sound caused by partial assimilation especially to a vowel or semivowel in the following syllable. **b.** A vowel sound changed in this manner. **2.** The diacritic mark (¨) over a vowel, indicating an umlaut, especially in German.

[German : *um-*, around, alteration (from Middle High German *umb-*, from *umbe,* from Old High German *umbi*) + *Laut,* sound (from Middle High German *lūt,* from Old High German *hlūt*).]

🙞 The symbol ¨ is called an *umlaut* when it refers to change in the quality of a vowel, as in the German pair *Mann/Männer* ("man/men"), where the *a* is pronounced like the *a* in *father,* and the *ä* is pronounced like the *e* in *bet.* The same symbol is called a *dieresis* when it is placed over the second of two consecutive vowels, where it indicates that the two sounds are to be pronounced separately instead of as a diphthong, as in *Zoë* or *naïve.*

93
vi·cis·si·tude (vĭ-sĭs′ĭ-tōōd′, vĭ-sĭs′ĭ-tyōōd′)

noun

A sudden or unexpected change of fortune; a variation in one's life, activities or situation: "*The aspect of the venerable mansion has always affected me like a human countenance, bearing the traces not merely of outward storm and sunshine, but expressive, also, of the long lapse of mortal life, and accompanying vicissitudes that have passed within*" (Nathaniel Hawthorne, *The House of the Seven Gables*).

[Latin *vicissitūdō*, from *vicissim*, in turn, probably from *vicēs*, plural of **vix*, change.]

94
vis·cer·al (vĭs′ər-əl)

adjective

1. Immediate and emotional; not deliberate or thought out: "*People are wary of Dag when meeting him for the first time, in the same visceral way prairie folk are wary of the flavor of seawater when tasting it for the first time at an ocean beach*" (Douglas Coupland, *Generation X*). **2.** Relating to, situated in, or affecting the viscera.

[Medieval Latin *vīscerālis*: Latin *vīscus*, plural *vīscera*, internal organs, innards + *-ālis*, adjectival suffix.]

95 vo·lup·tu·ous (və-lŭp′chōō-əs)

adjective

1. Characterized by or arising from sensual pleasure: *"Once in my room, I spread my clothes on my bed. The cufflinks were beaten up and had someone else's initials on them, but they looked like real gold, glinting in the drowsy autumn sun which poured through the window and soaked in yellow pools on the oak floor—voluptuous, rich, intoxicating"* (Donna Tartt, *The Secret History*). **2.** Sexually attractive, especially from having a curvaceous figure. **3.** Devoted to or indulging in sensual pleasures.

[Middle English, from Old French *voluptueux,* from Latin *voluptuōsus,* full of pleasure, from *voluptās,* pleasure.]

was·sail (wŏs'əl, wŏ-sāl')

noun

1a. A salutation or toast given in drinking someone's health or as an expression of goodwill. **b.** The drink used in such toasting, commonly ale or wine spiced with roasted apples and sugar: *"When Duncan is asleep / . . . his two chamberlains / Will I with wine and wassail so convince / That memory, the warder of the brain, / Shall be a fume, and the receipt of reason / A limbeck only"* (William Shakespeare, *Macbeth*). **2.** A festivity characterized by much drinking: *"[L]ong had I nursed, in secret, the unnatural hatred—it blazed forth in an hour of drunken wassail"* (Walter Scott, *Ivanhoe*).

verb
>Past participle and past tense: **was·sailed**
>Present participle: **was·sail·ing**
>Third person singular present tense: **was·sails**

transitive To drink to the health of; toast.
intransitive To engage in or drink a wassail.

[Middle English, contraction of *wæshæil,* be healthy, from Old Norse *ves heill* : *ves,* imperative singular of *vera,* to be + *heill,* healthy.]

xer·o·phyte (zîr'ə-fīt')

noun

A plant adapted to living in an arid habitat; a desert plant.

[From *xero-,* dry (from Greek *xēro-,* from *xēros*) + *-phyte,* plant (from Greek *phuton,* from *phuein,* to make grow).]

yogh (yŏg)

noun

The Middle English letter ȝ, used to represent the sound (y) and the voiced and voiceless velar fricatives.

[Middle English, possibly from Old English *īw, ēoh,* yew.]

ℱᴧ In addition to the many grammatical differences and unfamiliar words, one of the things that modern readers find so difficult (or so charming) about Old and Middle English texts is the use of letters that have now become obsolete. These include yogh (ȝ), wynn or wen (ƿ), thorn (þ), edh (ð), and ash (æ). Yogh, originally the Old English form of the letter *g*, was used to represent several sounds, including the sound *ch* in Scottish *loch* that began to disappear from most varieties of English in the 1400s. The letters *y* or *gh* have replaced yogh in modern spelling. Wynn, which represented the sound (w), was borrowed by Old English scribes from the runes, the writing system of the early Germanic peoples. It was later superseded by the letter *w*, which was developed from two *u*'s or *v*'s written together. Both thorn (also a rune in origin) and edh were used indiscriminately to spell the two sounds (th) and (*th*)—the sounds in *breath* and *breathe,* respectively. The combination *th* now fills their role. Ash was used in Old English to represent the vowel (ă), as in the word *stæf*, meaning both "staff, stick of wood" and "letter (of the alphabet)." In this regard, it is interesting that several of the names for these old letters also relate to wood and trees, like *ash* and *thorn. Yogh* probably comes from Old English *īw* or *ēoh*, "yew tree."

Zeit·geist (tsīt′gīst′, zīt′gīst′)

noun

The spirit of the time; the taste and outlook character-istic of a period or generation: *"The prescription of psychoactive drugs for children has increased roughly threefold in the past decade, a particularly vivid demon-stration of the shift in the national Zeitgeist vis-à-vis psychological health"* (Arthur Allen, *Salon.com*).

[German : *Zeit*, time (from Middle High German *zīt*, from Old High German + *Geist*, spirit).]

ze·nith (zē′nĭth)

noun

1. The point on the celestial sphere that is directly above the observer: *"The sky stays clear, and when the sun reaches its zenith, I take a break and go down to the river"* (Sarah Pemberton Strong, *Burning the Sea*). **2.** The up-per region of the sky. **3.** The highest point above the observer's horizon attained by a celestial body. **4.** The point of culmination; the peak: *Her tenure as CEO was the zenith of her career.*

[Middle English *senith*, from Old French *cenith*, from Me-dieval Latin, from Arabic *samt* (*ar-ra's*), path (over the head), from Latin *sēmita*, path.]

The sky stays clear, and when the sun reaches its **zenith,** I take a break and go down to the river. The banks are always empty at noon. It's too hot to wash clothes, and all the cows are out grazing. In a few more hours, when the day will have cooled down, people will appear again to bathe, bringing pails to fill or leading their animals down to drink.

— Sarah Pemberton Strong,
Burning the Sea

thesaurus

HOW TO USE THE THESAURUS

Unlike a traditional thesaurus that prints exhaustive undifferentiated synonym lists, this thesaurus provides synonym studies on the most important meanings and ideas and discriminates among many of the most frequently used—and misused—words in the English language. Whether you are looking for the precise word to express a specific thought or for a synonym to express a simple thought, you will find that this is the handiest and most practical thesaurus available for the office or classroom.

What Is a Synonym?

Synonyms are words that are the same or nearly the same in meaning. Although all the synonyms entered in the individual lists in this thesaurus share an important aspect of meaning, there are often differences in shades of meaning. For example, consider *clean* and its synonyms *cleanly, immaculate*, and *spotless*. Basically all four words have the same meaning: they describe what is free from dirt, stains, or impurities. *Clean* is the most general word. *Immaculate* and *spotless* usually refer to what is "perfectly clean," but *immaculate* is a more formal term and *spotless* is a more conversational one. *Cleanly*, on the other hand, is most often used to describe what is "habitually neat and clean."

Synonym Studies

This thesaurus contains two kinds of synonym studies: relatively long paragraphs that discuss the synonyms in detail and short studies that focus on one central meaning of a number of common terms. These studies are organized alphabetically and present the synonyms in the following format: the entry word is given in boldface, followed by a part of speech (*adj.*, adjective; *adv.*, adverb; *n.*, noun; and *v.*, verb) and by the word's synonyms:

relevant *adj*. germane, material, pertinent.

Discriminated synonymies. The foundation of this thesaurus is a block of synonym paragraphs in which the meaning shared by all the words is supplemented by additional material that discriminates the various shades of meaning of each word:

relevant *adj.* germane, material, pertinent.

RELEVANT and its synonyms describe what is associated with a matter or situation at hand and has direct bearing on it: *Stick to relevant questions, please!* PERTINENT implies a logical and precise bearing: *The pertinent statistics do not confirm the press accounts of the accident.* GERMANE applies to what is so closely akin to the subject as to reinforce it: *statements germane to the topic of his speech.* MATERIAL has the sense of being needed to complete a subject: *material evidence.*

Antonyms—words that are opposite in meaning—are given at the end of many of the discriminated paragraphs. Not all antonyms given at a synonym study are themselves main entries. For example:

bare . . .
Antonym: covered.

Many words or senses of words have no true antonyms. For instance, the opposite of the verb *change* is best expressed by saying "to remain unchanged."

On the other hand, some words have more than one antonym:

generous . . .
Antonyms: cheap; stingy.

Such listings alert you to the fact that various shades of meaning are covered by the antonym given.

It should be emphasized that antonyms apply only to the entry words; they may apply to some of the synonyms, but often they do not.

Core-meaning synonymies. Interspersed with the discriminated synonymies are core-meaning studies that focus on a basic meaning shared by all the synonyms. In these the synonym list is followed by a definition and one or more examples using the main-entry word:

> **surpass** *v.* **exceed, excel, outdo, outshine, outstrip, pass, top, transcend.** *Core meaning:* To be greater or better than (*a wheat crop that surpassed last year's by two million bushels*).

Note that any of the other synonyms in the list can be substituted for *surpass* in the illustrative example.

Some of the core-meaning studies treat different forms of words that are dealt with in the discriminated studies and do not require additional discussion (such as *fair* and *fairly*). Most of these studies, however, deal with simple concepts; they offer an ample choice of synonyms for the most frequently used words—those words for which a person seeks an alternative to bring variety to his or her writing.

> **executive** *adj.* **administrative, managerial.** *Core meaning:* Of, for, or relating to administration (*an executive secretary; an executive committee*).

abandon *v.* desert, forsake, leave, quit.
Core meaning: To give up without intending to return or claim again (*abandoned his family*).

abandoned *adj.* derelict, deserted, forlorn, forsaken.
Core meaning: Having been given up or left alone (*an abandoned house; an abandoned strategy*).

aberrant See **abnormal.**

abeyance *n.* dormancy, latency, quiescence, remission, suspension.
Core meaning: The condition of being temporarily inactive (*hold a decision in abeyance*).

abhor See **hate.**

abhorrence See **hate.**

ability *n.* 1. capacity, skill, talent.
These words name qualities that enable one to do something desirable and usually rather difficult. ABILITY stresses the fact or power of accomplishment (*a person of great musical ability*), and CAPACITY the potential for such accomplishment (*a capacity for learning*). TALENT is usually regarded as a natural gift for achievement in a specific area: *artistic talent.* SKILL often implies proven expertness in an art or trade requiring practical, specialized knowledge: *skill in carpentry.*
2. See **expertise.**

able *adj.* capable, competent, qualified.
ABLE when it follows a verb like *be* or *feel* implies the capacity to serve in a given function but does not suggest any particular standard of performance: *He was able to ski.* When *able* precedes a noun, however, it indicates more than usual ability, skill, etc.: *an able skier.* CAPABLE implies the ability to meet usual required standards: *a capable teacher.* COMPETENT implies workmanlike standards: *a competent typist.* QUALIFIED connotes compliance with set standards of training or experience: *a qualified physician.*

---

abnormal *adj.* **aberrant, atypical, irregular.**

All of these refer to what deviates from a usual pattern, level, or type. ABNORMAL often suggests that something is strange (*an abnormal interest in bats*) or unhealthy (*an abnormal temperature*). ABERRANT and ATYPICAL both describe what differs from the normal or typical, but *aberrant* is the stronger term and sometimes even suggests a lapse in mental faculties: *aberrant behavior; an atypical response.* IRREGULAR has wide application; it can refer to what is not uniform, as in shape (*an irregular coastline*), does not follow a set pattern (*irregular rhythm*), or is unusual or improper (*a highly irregular procedure*).
Antonym: **normal.**

abolish *v.* **eradicate, exterminate, extinguish, extirpate, obliterate.**

These verbs mean to put an end to. ABOLISH is most often related to banning or outlawing existing conditions or regulations: *abolished Prohibition; abolish poll taxes.* EXTERMINATE refers to destruction of living things by deliberate, selective means: *exterminate rats.* To EXTINGUISH is to put out—a fire, for example, or something likened to a flame, such as human life or hope. ERADICATE and EXTIRPATE refer to extermination or to destruction of the whole of nonliving objects, as by rooting up or out; both imply wiping out by removing all trace, a sense that OBLITERATE makes more explicit: *villages obliterated by bombing.* See also **destroy.**

abominable See **unspeakable.**

aboriginal See **native.**

about See **approximately.**

absence *n.* **nonappearance, nonattendance.**
Core meaning: Failure to be present (*everyone at the meeting noticed her absence*).

absolute *adj.* **despotic, totalitarian, tyrannical.**
Core meaning: Having supreme, unlimited power and control (*an absolute ruler*).

absolve See **vindicate.**

absorb *v.* **assimilate, digest, imbibe.**
Core meaning: To take in and incorporate (*quickly absorbs new ideas*).

abstain See **refrain.**

abstinence *n.* **continence, sobriety, temperance.**
These nouns denote self-denial or self-restraint in the gratification of human appetites. ABSTINENCE is most often applied to voluntary refraining from food and drink considered harmful. CONTINENCE usually refers to self-denial in sexual activity. SOBRIETY is the absence of alcoholic intoxication. TEMPERANCE can mean complete refraining from alcoholic drink but more often denotes moderation in drinking.

abstract See **theoretical.**

abstruse See **ambiguous.**

absurd *adj.* **ludicrous, preposterous, ridiculous.**
These words all describe what obviously lacks sense or departs from logic. ABSURD is the most general: *an absurd suggestion.* PREPOSTEROUS is more intense than *absurd* and describes what is completely unreasonable: *a preposterous story.* LUDICROUS and RIDICULOUS often apply to absurdities that inspire laughter; *ridiculous* implies mockery: *a ludicrous costume; a ridiculous idea.*
Antonym: **sensible.**

abuse *v.* **maltreat, mistreat, misuse.**
ABUSE and its synonyms mean to treat or use wrongly. *Abuse* most often expresses action, by deed or word, that is harmful to persons; the injury may be calculated and malicious or may result from overindulgence in such things as alcohol, drugs, or a privilege: *abused his eyesight by reading in poor light; a child who had been abused by its parents.* MISUSE is generally applied to improper use of things resulting from ignorance or oversight: *misuse our natural resources.* MISTREAT and MALTREAT both imply rough handling, usually of persons or animals, that causes physical

injury; *maltreat* especially suggests deliberate cruelty: *an angry man who mistreated his son by boxing his ears; maltreating the dog by pulling his tail.*

abusive *adj.* **contumelious, invective, opprobrious, reviling, scurrilous, vituperative.**
Core meaning: Of, related to, or characterized by verbal abuse (*abusive remarks*).

academic See **theoretical.**

accelerate See **expedite.**

accept *v.* **1. embrace, take up, welcome.**
Core meaning: To receive something offered willingly and gladly (*accepted the award*).
2. admit, receive, take in.
Core meaning: To allow admittance (*accepted for membership in the club*).
3. See believe.

accessible See **convenient.**

accidental *adj.* **chance, fortuitous, haphazard, random.**
All of these words describe what is unexpected or unplanned. What is ACCIDENTAL happens unintentionally: *an accidental mistake.* CHANCE and FORTUITOUS imply lack of cause or design: *a chance* (or *fortuitous*) *meeting.* HAPHAZARD and RANDOM suggest the absence of patterns of selection or order: *a haphazard* (or *random*) *collection.*
Antonym: **intentional.**

acclaim See **praise.**

accompany *v.* **chaperon, conduct, escort.**
These verbs mean to be with or go with another. ACCOMPANY implies being or going on an equal footing with the other person or persons: *accompanied her friend on a trip to Europe.* CONDUCT stresses guidance of the other or others: *conducting a tour of the city.* ESCORT suggests either protective guidance (*police escorting the President during the parade*) or observance of social forms (*Jack escorted Mrs. Clark to the concert*). CHAPERON (or *chaperone*)

specifies protective accompaniment, usually of a young person by an adult: *chaperoned her friend's daughter during her travels.*

accomplice See **partner.**

accomplish See **reach.**

accord See **harmony.**

accountable See **liable.**

accredit See **attribute.**

accumulate See **gather.**

accuracy See **veracity.**

accurate See **true.**

accuse *v.* **arraign, charge, impeach, indict.**
These words share the general sense "to blame someone for a fault, error, or offense." ACCUSE and CHARGE are the most general and can be used in both legal and personal contexts. ARRAIGN, IMPEACH, and INDICT apply to formal legal procedure. To *arraign* is to call a prisoner before a court to answer an indictment; *impeach,* to charge with misconduct in office before a proper court of justice; and *indict,* to make a formal accusation against on the basis of the findings of a jury, especially a grand jury.
Antonym: **vindicate.**

achieve See **reach.**

acknowledge *v.* **admit, concede, confess, own.**
ACKNOWLEDGE and its synonyms refer to making a statement that grants the truth of something at issue. *Acknowledge* expresses that basic sense with fewer overtones than the other words. ADMIT more strongly implies reluctance to grant such a truth because the truth is to one's disadvantage: *admit a mistake.* CONCEDE also suggests a disadvantageous statement resulting from yielding under the pressure of contrary evidence: *conceded that his data were inconclusive.* CONFESS can be the mere equivalent of *admit* or *concede* but more strictly applies to formal disclosure of

wrongdoing: *confessed her crime* (or *her sins*). OWN also can have the force of *admit* or *concede* (*I own that I've made a mistake*), but in the combination *own up* it means to confess fully and openly: *owned up to a long record of falsehood.*

acme See **climax.**

acquit See **vindicate.**

active *adj.* **busy, dynamic, energetic, lively, vigorous.**
These mean taking part in some action or activity. ACTIVE suggests contribution: *an active member of the club.* BUSY implies sustained activity, without regard for its quality or worth: *busy playing cards.* DYNAMIC suggests forcefulness and intensity (*a dynamic salesman*); ENERGETIC, enthusiasm and unflagging strength (*an energetic campaigner*). LIVELY applies to what is full of life (*a lively baby*); VIGOROUS adds the implication of healthy strength: *a vigorous sportsman.* *Antonym:* **inactive.**

actually *adv.* **genuinely, indeed, really.**
Core meaning: In point of fact (*He said he was studying when actually he was at the movies*).

acute 1. See **critical. 2.** See **sharp.**

add *v.* **figure, sum (up), tally, total.**
Core meaning: To combine figures to form a sum (*adding the day's receipts*).

address See **send.**

adequate See **sufficient.**

adhere See **bond.**

ad-lib See **improvise.**

administer *v.* **administrate, direct, govern, head, manage, run, superintend.**
Core meaning: To have charge of the affairs of others (*administer a colony*).

administrate See **administer.**

administrative See **executive.**

admit 1. See **acknowledge. 2.** See **accept.**

admonish *v.* **rebuke, reprimand, reproach, reprove.**
These verbs mean to address someone disapprovingly in consequence of the person's fault or misdeed. ADMONISH refers to mild criticism (*admonished them for being late*); in a related sense the word means to counsel against—to warn as a means of rectifying or avoiding error (*admonished us to be careful*). REPROVE implies more pronounced disapproval, as does REPROACH, which often also suggests a feeling of injury and disappointment over another's conduct. REBUKE refers to sharp criticism, and REPRIMAND to severe criticism that is often a formal or official expression of disapproval by one in authority.

admonishment See **warning.**

admonition See **warning.**

adolescent See **young.**

adopt See **borrow.**

adore See **love.**

adroit See **graceful.**

adult See **mature.**

advance *v.* **1. proceed, progress.**
ADVANCE, PROCEED, and PROGRESS share the meaning of moving forward, literally or figuratively. *Advance* is often restricted to certain constructions, as: *The troops advanced at a rapid pace. He advanced a step. The editors advanced the deadline by two months. Proceed* emphasizes continuing motion: *She proceeded toward Boston by Route 2. Progress* suggests steady improvement or development: *His music studies progressed satisfactorily.*
Antonym: **recede.**
2. further, promote.
These verbs share the meaning of assisting in making something—such as a cause or a business venture—go forward: *Scientific and medical research advance knowledge.* PROMOTE and FURTHER in particular stress active support and

encouragement: *a campaign to promote a new product; promote a corporal to sergeant; furthering his career by attending classes at night school.*
Antonym: **hinder.**

adversary See **opponent.**

adverse See **unfavorable.**

advertise *or* **advertize 1.** *v.* **broadcast, disseminate, promulgate.**
Core meaning: To make information generally known (*advertised her engagement by wearing a diamond*).
2. build up, plug (*Informal*), **promote, publicize, push.**
Core meaning: to make known the positive features of a product (*advertise a new computer*).

affable See **amiable.**

affect *v.* **impress, influence, move, strike, touch.**
These verbs mean to produce a mental or emotional effect or response. AFFECT, TOUCH, and MOVE refer to arousing of emotions. *Affect* is nonspecific; *touch* implies a momentary sense of pity or tenderness (*a kindness that touched her*), and *move* a profound feeling capable of producing action: *a sight that moved them more than words.* What STRIKES one causes an immediate, abrupt mental response: *struck by her boldness.* What IMPRESSES has a marked, lasting effect, often favorable: *impressed the danger on us; impressed by her lack of fear.* What INFLUENCES produces a mental effect that controls a corresponding response: *influenced his decision to resign.*

affectation *n.* **air, airs, mannerism, pose.**
These are forms of human behavior that are often artificial and may serve to provide a false claim to distinction. AFFECTATION and POSE always denote something not true to one's nature. A mode of dress and a habit of speech can be examples of *affectation,* which applies to a particular trait. A *pose* is a series of such artificial devices or an attitude that may seek to mask one's unworthy nature or merely promote a notion of superiority. A MANNERISM is a distinctive

trait or idiosyncrasy, not necessarily false, that may strike another as distracting or foolish. An AIR is the sum of traits that contribute to an impressive personal bearing or manner, not necessarily false: *an air of mystery about him.* AIRS, however, always refers to an offensive and dubious claim to superiority: *putting on airs.*

affecting See **moving.**

affection See **love.**

affirm See **assert.**

affix See **attach.**

afflict *v.* **agonize, curse, plague, rack, scourge, torment, torture.**
Core meaning: To bring great harm or suffering to (*afflicted with chronic back problems*).

affluent See **rich.**

affront See **offend.**

after See **later.**

age *n.* **day(s), epoch, era, period, time(s).**
Core meaning: A particular time notable for its distinctive characteristics (*the Victorian age*).

aged See **old.**

agency See **means.**

agenda See **program.**

aggravate See **annoy.**

agonize See **afflict.**

agony See **distress.**

agree *v.* **coincide, conform, correspond.**
AGREE and its synonyms express compatibility between people or things. *Agree* may simply indicate freedom from difference or conflict (*His sisters agreed on the choice of his Christmas gift*), but it often suggests arriving at a settlement, and thus accommodation: *Management agreed to raise wages.* COINCIDE stresses exact agreement in space,

time, or thought: *The geometric figures coincided. Our political opinions coincide.* CONFORM stresses close resemblance, sometimes because of adjustment to established standards: *His behavior conformed with the family's wishes. He conformed his behavior to please his family.* CORRESPOND refers to similarity in form or nature or to similarity in function of dissimilar things: *Our ideas do not correspond. A modern stove corresponds to a sixteenth-century fireplace.*
Antonym: **disagree.**

agreeable 1. See **amiable. 2.** See **pleasant.**

aid See **help.**

air See **affectation.**

airs See **affectation.**

alarm See **frighten.**

alert *adj.* **1.** observant, open-eyed, vigilant, wary, watchful.
Core meaning: Vigilantly attentive (*alert to danger*).
2. See **clever.**

alien See **foreign.**

alienate See **estrange.**

alive *adj.* live, living.
These words all describe what has life or continuing existence: *Is the tree still alive? The victory kept their hopes alive. We saw a real live lizard. Drug abuse is a live topic. The living relatives all attended the funeral. The monument on his tomb is a living reminder of his achievements.*
Antonym: **dead.**

allege See **assert.**

all-out See **utter.**

allow See **permit.**

allowance See **permission.**

allure See **seduce.**

ally See **partner.**

almost See **approximately.**

alone *adj.* **lone, lonely, lonesome, solitary.**
These are applied to what is apart from others. ALONE describes such a condition in a manner that can range from matter-of-fact to very emphatic: *alone in her office; alone in the world.* LONE and SOLITARY stress singleness or lack of companionship: *a lone* (or *solitary*) *figure. Solitary* also can emphasize physical isolation or seclusion: *solitary confinement; a solitary nook.* LONELY and, less often, LONESOME are emphatic terms for describing isolation or the absence of others: *a lonely existence; that lonesome road.* More often they indicate a person's sense of dejection arising from general lack of companionship or the absence of specific companions: *a lonely boy; lonesome for old friends.*

aloneness *n.* **isolation, loneliness, loneness, solitude.**
Core meaning: The quality or state of being alone (*Aloneness often causes depression*).

alter See **change.**

alternative See **choice.**

amass See **gather.**

amateur *n.* **dilettante.**
An AMATEUR engages in an art, a science, or a sport for enjoyment rather than for money: *an orchestra made up of amateurs.* The word may imply a lack of professional skill: *a rambling novel written by an amateur.* A DILETTANTE is a person who has taken up an interest in an art or another branch of knowledge for amusement or pleasure; the interest is often merely superficial: *a dilettante in painting.*
Antonym: **professional.**

amazing See **fabulous.**

ambiguous *adj.* **abstruse, cryptic, enigmatic, equivocal, obscure, recondite, vague.**
These describe what is difficult to understand. AMBIGUOUS applies to what can be interpreted in several ways, usually because of faulty expression: *ambiguous directions.* EQUIV-

OCAL strongly implies that such multiple interpretation results from a deliberate attempt to evade, hedge, or cloud a matter at issue: *an equivocal reply*. Something VAGUE lacks clarity of form, owing to poor expression or fuzzy thought. Something OBSCURE is so little known that its meaning seems hardly worth investigating: *obscure legal details*. RECONDITE refers to what is deeply learned and beyond average understanding: *recondite scholarly pursuits*. To that sense ABSTRUSE adds the suggestion of complex expression. CRYPTIC and ENIGMATIC imply the tantalizing character of a riddle, whose meaning lies hidden under an inscrutable or misleading exterior: *a cryptic remark; an enigmatic smile*.

ambition *n.* **drive, enterprise, initiative, push** (*Informal*).
Core meaning: The wish or ability to begin and follow through with a plan or task (*a woman of great energy and ambition*).

ambush *v.* **bushwhack, surprise, waylay.**
Core meaning: To attack suddenly and without warning (*muggers ambushed them in the park*).

amend See **correct.**

amiable *adj.* **affable, agreeable, good-natured, obliging.**
These describe the dispositions and behavior of persons showing a tendency to please in social relations. AMIABLE suggests those qualities opposed to enmity, such as evenness of temper and sweetness of nature. AFFABLE describes one who is mild-mannered and pleasant, and GOOD-NATURED one who is easygoing and tolerant. AGREEABLE implies readiness to please others and comply with their wishes. OBLIGING suggests politeness and readiness to do favors.

amicable See **friendly.**

amid See **among.**

amiss See **awry.**

among *prep.* **amid, between.**
AMONG, AMID, and BETWEEN all indicate a middle or intermediate position in space, but in that sense are carefully

distinguished in usage. *Among* and *amid* (or *in the midst of*) connote a position in the company of other persons or things and usually also the state of being surrounded by them. *Among* implies that the persons or things are capable of being construed individually, as separable entities: *circulated among the delegates; gold nuggets among the pebbles. Amid* is sometimes used in the same way (*a nest amid the branches*), but the things surrounding or enveloping are often a collective mass rather than separable units: *poverty amid plenty. Between* indicates an intermediate location in the space separating two people, places, or things: *a stop between Pittsburgh and Philadelphia.*

amplitude See **bulk.**

amuse *v.* **divert, entertain.**
Amuse and its synonyms refer to actions that provide pleasure, especially as a means of spending leisure time. *Amuse* is the least specific when it refers to something done by and for oneself. Divert implies distraction from worry or care. Entertain suggests something done for others and thus often implies a certain degree of formality.
Antonym: **bore.**

amusement See **recreation.**

analysis *n.* **1. breakdown, dissection, resolution.**
Core meaning: The separation of a whole into its parts for study (*a harmonic analysis of a Bach fugue*).
2. examination, inspection, investigation, review, survey.
Core meaning: A close or systematic study (*an analysis of voting trends*).

ancestor *n.* **forebear, forefather, progenitor.**
These are all words for any person from whom one is descended directly, especially if that person is of a generation earlier than a grandparent.
Antonym: **descendant.**

ancient See **old.**

anger *n.* **fury, indignation, ire, rage, resentment, wrath.**
These name emotional states that may result when one is

greatly displeased. ANGER is the general term overlapping the others. RESENTMENT, which is ill will caused by a sense of being wronged or offended, most often suggests smoldering anger, whereas INDIGNATION implies overt display of grievance over injustice, meanness, or the like. RAGE is violent anger, as is FURY, which suggests even more strongly a wild, uncontrolled display. IRE, a literary term, and WRATH are approximately equivalent in suggesting extreme resentment that seeks expression as revenge or retribution.

anguish See **sorrow.**

animosity See **enmity.**

animus See **enmity.**

annoy *v.* **aggravate, bother, irk, irritate, peeve, provoke, rile, vex.**
ANNOY and its synonyms express the action of disturbing persons by causing mental discomfort of varying intensity. *Annoy* usually refers to minor disturbance. BOTHER suggests mild discomfort resulting from the imposition of a nuisance, and PEEVE a disturbance that produces a mildly resentful response. IRK implies imposition that wearies one. VEX often suggests repeated, petty impositions; sometimes it adds the related sense of confusing or baffling. IRRITATE applies to a stronger disturbance and angry response, as do PROVOKE and AGGRAVATE (informal in this sense); all suggest a taxing of patience, and *provoke* especially implies deliberate imposition. RILE refers to the stirring of strong anger, openly expressed. See also **displease.**

annul See **cancel.**

answer *v.* **reply, respond, retort.**
These refer to speaking or otherwise acting as a consequence of another's speech or act. ANSWER and REPLY, the most general, can refer to both language and action such as gesturing or bodily movement, but most often are applied to speech that follows a single direct question. When what follows is written, *reply* is the more common. RESPOND can

refer to spoken or written language; of all these words, it is in widest use to indicate an act or action that follows a stimulus of the kind noted, and in one sense it means to react in a particular or desired way: *respond to affection*. RETORT is largely limited to what is spoken—to a quick, direct statement sometimes noteworthy for wit, style of expression, etc.

answerable See **liable**.

antagonism See **enmity**.

antagonist See **opponent**.

antagonistic See **unfriendly**.

anticipate See **foresee**.

antipathy See **enmity**.

antique See **old**.

anxiety *n*. **care, concern, worry**.
These nouns express troubled states of mind. ANXIETY indicates a feeling of fear and apprehension, especially when what causes the feeling is unidentifiable: *anxiety about taking a plane*. CARE implies mental distress caused by heavy responsibilities: *the cares involved in raising a large family*. CONCERN stresses personal involvement in the source of mental unrest; it has more to do with serious thought than with emotion: *The doctor's gentle concern helped the patient recover*. WORRY implies persistent doubt or fear that disturbs one's peace of mind: *Business worries ruined her evening*.
Antonym: **tranquillity**.

apathetic *adj*. **disinterested, indifferent, insensible, lethargic, listless**.
Core meaning: Without emotion or interest (*apathetic voters*).

apathy See **disinterest**.

apex See **climax**.

apogee See **climax**.

appear *v.* **look, seem.**
Core meaning: To have the appearance of (*He appeared happy but really wasn't*).

appease See **pacify.**

appellation See **name.**

appendage See **branch.**

appreciable See **perceptible.**

appreciate *v.* **cherish, prize, treasure, value.**
All of these verbs express a favorable opinion of someone or something. APPRECIATE applies especially when high regard is based on critical assessment and judgment: *Many people appreciate the paintings of Renoir*. More loosely, it implies a sense of gratitude or warm response: *We appreciate your kindness to our parents*. CHERISH and TREASURE usually suggest affectionate regard: *She cherished her grandmother's teapot. Mr. Hubbard treasures his vintage Rolls Royce*. PRIZE emphasizes pride of possession: *She prized her collection of antiques*. The connotations of VALUE may range from mild appreciation or regard (*I value his opinion*) to what is rated above all else (*Ancient Romans often valued their honor more than life*).
Antonym: **despise.**

apprehend 1. See **arrest. 2.** See **comprehend.**

approach *n.* **advent, coming, convergence, imminence, nearness.**
Core meaning: The act or fact of coming near (*the advent of a new computer era*).

appropriate See **suitable.**

approve *v.* **certify, endorse, sanction.**
These are all used to signify satisfaction or acceptance. APPROVE, the most general, often means simply to consider right or good (*He approved of her decision*), though it is also used in the sense "to consent to officially" (*The legislature approved the bill*). CERTIFY implies official approval based on compliance with set requirements or standards:

The bank officials certified the check. ENDORSE implies the expression of support, especially by public statement: *The senator endorsed the candidate.* SANCTION usually implies not only approval (*The politician sanctioned the use of public-opinion polls in his campaign*) but also official authorization (*The city council sanctioned the opening of stores on Sundays*).
Antonym: **disapprove.**

approximately *adv.* **about, almost, nearly, roughly.**
Core meaning: Near to in quantity or amount (*There were approximately 50 people in the audience*).

apt See **suitable.**

arbiter See **judge.**

arbitrary See **dictatorial.**

arbitrator See **judge.**

archaic See **old.**

arctic See **cold.**

ardor See **passion.**

arduous See **difficult.**

area *n.* **belt, district, locality, region, zone.**
All of these nouns name extents of land varying widely in size but having recognizably separate identities. AREA is the least specific as to size and boundaries: *a blighted area in Los Angeles; state parks and recreation areas.* Most often REGION refers to an indefinitely large section with distinctive natural features (*tropical regions of South America*), but the term can denote a more precisely defined geographic unit (*polar regions*). ZONE is usually applied specifically (*the Torrid Zone*); sometimes arbitrarily created boundaries are implied (*a residential zone*). A BELT is distinctive in a single stated respect: *the wheat belt; the Bible Belt.* A DISTRICT is a component, generally rather small and distinguishable by its use (*a red-light district*) or by being a clearly defined administrative unit (*an election district*). A

LOCALITY, also small, is the site of a specific thing or of an event, such as a battle.

argue *v.* **bicker, dispute, haggle, quarrel, squabble, wrangle.**
These refer to verbal exchange expressing conflict of positions or opinions. ARGUE can be applied to the action of a debater or an advocate of a cause (*argue in favor of a law*), as well as to that of one engaged in an exchange on the lower level implied by most of these terms (*always arguing with his friends*). The same distinction applies to DISPUTE, but here there is often more suggestion of anger than of reasoning. QUARREL in this sense involves anger and usually hostility as well. WRANGLE stresses noisy display of anger. BICKER and SQUABBLE are applicable to minor quarrels; *squabble* suggests pettiness, and *bicker* implies persistent, bad-tempered exchange. HAGGLE applies to argument engaged in by one seeking the most favorable terms in arranging a bargain (*haggled over the price of the chair*) or in attempting to come to terms (*haggling over the site for peace talks*).

arm See **branch.**

aroma See **flavor.**

arouse See **provoke.**

arraign See **accuse.**

arrest *v.* **1. apprehend, detain.**
ARREST and APPREHEND mean to seize and hold under authority of the law: *arrest a criminal; apprehend a felon.* To DETAIN is to keep in custody: *detain a suspect.*
Antonym: **free.**
2. See **stop.**

artificial *adj.* **ersatz, synthetic.**
These three all refer to what is made by man rather than occurring in nature. ARTIFICIAL is the most neutral term and has widest application (*an artificial sweetener; artificial flowers; artificial pearls; an artificial respirator*); it also describes what is not genuine or natural (*an artificial display of affection*). What is ERSATZ suggests transparently inferior

imitation: *ersatz mink.* SYNTHETIC most often implies the use of a chemical process to produce a substance that will look or function like the original, often with certain advantages: *synthetic rubber; synthetic fabrics.*
Antonym: **natural.**

artsy See **arty.**

arty *adj.* **artsy, contrived, precious, pretentious.**
Core meaning: Pretentiously artistic (*an artsy film*).

ascend See **rise.**

ascribe See **attribute.**

assail See **attack.**

assault See **attack.**

assemble See **gather.**

assert *v.* **affirm, allege, declare.**
All of these words share the meaning of making a positive statement; they differ in emphasis. ASSERT implies that one states one's position boldly. AFFIRM stresses confidence in the validity of the statement. ALLEGE applies when the statement is apt to raise controversy and is made without proof. DECLARE has about the same force as *assert* but can suggest a formal manner or great authority.
Antonym: **deny.**

assign See **attribute.**

assimilate See **absorb.**

assist See **help.**

associate See **partner.**

association See **union.**

assuage See **pacify.**

assurance 1. See **certainty. 2.** See **confidence.**

astonishing See **fabulous.**

astute See **shrewd.**

atmosphere See **flavor.**

attach *v.* **affix, fasten.**
All of these denote the joining of one thing to another: *attach wires to an electrical plug; affix a label to a package; fasten a button to a skirt. Attach* and *affix* can also refer to adding on: *attach a signature to a document; affix a seal to a will. Fasten* often denotes making fast or secure: *fasten your seat belts.*
Antonym: **detach.**

attack *v.* **assail, assault, bombard.**
ATTACK and its synonyms refer to setting upon, literally or figuratively. *Attack* applies to any violent offensive action, physical or verbal: *The commandos attacked the outpost at dawn. She attacked any speaker whose views differed from hers.* ASSAIL implies repeated and violent attacks: *assailed the fortification; assailed by doubts.* ASSAULT usually—but not always—involves physical contact and sudden violence: *The mugger assaulted his victim in the park. The scientists assaulted the problem.* BOMBARD suggests showering with bombs or shells or, figuratively, with words: *ships bombarding Fort McHenry; bombarding the speaker with questions.*
Antonym: **defend.**

attain See **reach.**

attention See **notice.**

attire See **dress.**

attitude See **posture.**

attract *v.* **captivate, charm, enchant, fascinate.**
ATTRACT and its synonyms all mean to draw by some quality or action. *Attract* is the most general, simply implying the gravitation of objects, substances, or persons: *Light attracts insects. Her vitality attracted his interest.* CAPTIVATE, CHARM, ENCHANT, and FASCINATE all apply to strong, compelling attraction, often of one person to another. *Enchant* suggests an almost magical quality of attraction: *Her green eyes enchanted him. Captivate* and *charm* imply an ability or quality that pleases or delights: *a sense of drama*

that captivates audiences; courtesy that charms even the doubters. Fascinate includes not only the notion of irresistible attraction but also implies the ability to hold another's interest and attention: *The account of his trip to China fascinated his listeners.*
Antonym: **repel.**

attribute *v.* **accredit, ascribe, assign, charge, credit, impute.**
Core meaning: To regard as belonging to or resulting from another (*a painting attributed to Monet*).

atypical 1. See **abnormal. 2.** See **unconventional.**

audacious See **bold.**

augment See **increase.**

augury See **omen.**

auspicious See **favorable.**

austere See **plain.**

austerity See **severity.**

authentic *adj.* **bona fide, genuine, original, real, true, undoubted.**
Core meaning: Not counterfeit or copied (*an authentic Beethoven manuscript*).

authoritative See **dictatorial.**

authority 1. See **power. 2.** See **professional.**

authorization See **permission.**

automatic See **involuntary.**

aversion See **distaste.**

avid See **voracious.**

avoid *v.* **elude, escape, shun.**
AVOID and its synonyms share the sense of getting or staying away from something dangerous or unpleasant. *Avoid* and SHUN are close in meaning, and both imply a deliberate effort to remain out of the range of persons or things considered a source of difficulty: *avoid* (or *shun*) *nosy acquaintances; avoid* (or *shun*) *rich foods.* ELUDE suggests getting

away by cleverness or by a very small margin: *The fly eluded the spider.* Escape often suggests breaking loose from confinement (*escaped from jail*); it can also mean simply to remain unaffected by something harmful or unwanted (*escape injury*).
Antonym: **face.**

aware *adj.* **cognizant, conscious.**
These words all mean "being mindful of" and "having knowledge of." One is aware of something both through observation (*aware of his hostility*) and by means of information (*aware of the President's veto*). Cognizant, a more formal term, stresses having and recognizing sure knowledge: *I am cognizant of the objections of the faculty.* Conscious emphasizes the recognition of something sensed or felt: *conscious of an undercurrent of fear.*
Antonym: **unaware.**

awkward *adj.* **clumsy, inept, ungainly.**
All of these adjectives refer to lack of grace or skill in movement, manner, or performance. Awkward and clumsy, the most general, are often interchangeable. *Awkward*, however, applies both to physical movement (*an awkward dance*) and to embarrassing situations (*an awkward silence*), while *clumsy* emphasizes lack of dexterity in physical movements: *a clumsy juggler.* Inept applies to actions and speech showing a lack of skill or competence: *an inept performance; an inept remark.* Ungainly suggests a lack of grace in form or movement: *an ungainly teen-ager.*
Antonym: **graceful.**

awry *adj.* **amiss, wrong.**
Core meaning: Not in accordance with what is usual or expected (*knew something was awry when she failed to keep the appointment*).

axiom See **law.**

baby See **pamper.**

back *v.* **backtrack, fall back, retreat, retrograde, retrogress.**
Core meaning: To move in a reverse direction (*kept backing slowly toward the door*).

backtrack See **back.**

backward See **reactionary.**

badge See **sign.**

bald See **bare.**

ban See **forbid.**

barbarous See **cruel.**

bare *adj.* **bald, naked, nude.**
These apply to what lacks clothing or any usual or expected covering: *bare feet; a bare hillside; a bald head; mountains bald in the wintertime; a naked boy; naked feet; naked branches; a nude body.* Bare, bald, and sometimes *naked* can be used figuratively to describe what is blunt or without qualification: *the bare announcement that he had left; the bald truth; the naked facts.*
Antonym: **covered.**

barren *adj.* **sterile, unfruitful.**
BARREN, STERILE, and UNFRUITFUL describe what lacks the power to produce or support crops, plants, or offspring; figuratively they apply to what is not productive, effective, or rewarding: *barren soil; a barren desert; barren efforts; a desolate, sterile region; sterile pleasures; an unfruitful apple tree; an unfruitful discussion.*
Antonym: **fertile.**

bash See **hit.**

bashful See **shy.**

basic See **radical.**

bear See **carry.**

beautiful *adj.* **handsome, lovely, pretty.**
All these adjectives apply to what pleases the senses or the mind. BEAUTIFUL is the most comprehensive and the most widely applicable: *a beautiful day; a beautiful description; a beautiful sound.* LOVELY applies to what inspires ardent emotion rather than intellectual appreciation: *a lovely girl; a lovely thought.* PRETTY often implies a rather limited and superficial kind of beauty: *just another pretty face.* HAND-

SOME stresses visual appeal through regular and harmonious proportions: *a handsome design.*
Antonym: **ugly.**

befuddlement See **daze.**

begin *v.* **commence, initiate, start.**
These verbs all refer to coming or putting into operation, being, motion, etc. BEGIN and COMMENCE are equivalent in meaning, though *commence* is sometimes considered stronger in suggesting initiative: *a plant that is beginning to grow; a play that begins at eight o'clock; commenced composing his new symphony; festivities that commenced with the national anthem.* START is often interchangeable with *begin* and *commence* but can also imply setting out from a specific point (*started for New York early in the morning*), setting in motion (*start an engine*), or bringing about (*start an argument*). INITIATE suggests taking the first steps in a process: *initiated an advertising campaign.*
Antonym: **end.**

belief See **opinion.**

believe *v.* **accept, credit.**
To BELIEVE is simply to take as true or real: *I believe your statement.* ACCEPT implies satisfaction that a statement or explanation is in fact accurate (*I accept your word for it*), while CREDIT stresses trust (*Do not credit gossip*).
Antonym: **disbelieve.**

belittle *v.* **depreciate, derogate, detract (from), discount, disparage, downgrade, minimize.**
Core meaning: To think, represent, or speak of as small or unimportant (*belittled his rival's accomplishments*).

belt 1. See **area. 2.** See **hit.**

bend *v.* **1. bow, crook, curve**
These verbs all refer to changing from straightness to a curved or angular position: *bending his elbow; bend a wire; willows bending in the breeze; a back bowed by age; bowing under a heavy load; crooked his arm around the pack-*

age; a little finger that crooks; a road curving sharply just ahead; curve a metal band.
Antonym: straighten.
2. See **dispose.**

benevolent See **kind.**

benumb See **deaden.**

berate See **scold.**

betray See **deceive.**

between See **among.**

bias See **dispose.**

bicker See **argue.**

big *adj.* enormous, gigantic, great, huge, immense, large.
BIG and its synonyms all apply to what is of considerable size. *Big* is the most general and is often used interchangeably with LARGE. ENORMOUS, GIGANTIC, HUGE, and IMMENSE suggest that which is of extraordinarily large size. GREAT means "notably big"; in addition it has a number of extended senses that do not apply to physical dimension.
Antonym: little.

binary See **double.**

bind See **tie.**

bizarre 1. See **fantastic. 2.** See **strange.**

blame *v.* censure, condemn, criticize, denounce.
To BLAME is to find fault with: *didn't blame the children for being impatient to open their presents.* CENSURE, CONDEMN, and DENOUNCE all imply the expression of strong disapproval; *censure* is the weakest of the three: *a mayor censured by the press; a treaty that condemned war as a means of solving international problems; denouncing a proposed law.* To CRITICIZE is to judge severely; it often suggests a detailed account of one's objections: *We can criticize the government without fear of punishment.*
Antonym: praise.

blank See **empty.**

blast See **explode.**

bloc See **combine.**

block See **hinder.**

blow up See **explode.**

blue See **sad.**

bluff See **gruff.**

blunder See **botch.**

blunt 1. See **dull. 2.** See **gruff. 3.** See **deaden.**

blur See **confuse.**

boast *v.* **brag, crow, vaunt.**
Core meaning: To talk with excessive pride (*boasted about their wealth*).

boiling See **hot.**

bold *adj.* **1. audacious, daring.**
These all refer to what requires or shows courage and resoluteness: *a bold proposal; an audacious plan; a daring idea.* BOLD and DARING, as applied to persons, stress not only readiness to meet danger but also a desire to take initiative: *a bold executive; a daring explorer.* AUDACIOUS intensifies these qualities, often to the point of recklessness: *an audacious test pilot.*
Antonym: **timid.**
2. brash, brazen, forward, impudent, shameless.
All of these describe what shows boldness and effrontery. BOLD implies undue presumption: *a bold glance; a bold reply.* BRASH stresses what is shamelessly bold and even suggests arrogance: *a brash young man who thought he knew everything.* BRAZEN strongly implies open rudeness and insolence: *a brazen remark.* FORWARD applies to one who is unduly self-assertive (*a forward person*) or to what is presumptuous (*forward manners*). IMPUDENT suggests impertinence: *impudent comments made by the children to their grandfather.* SHAMELESS implies lack of a sense of de-

cency, together with contempt for the rights of others: *a shameless liar.*
Antonym: shy.

bombard See **attack.**

bona fide See **authentic.**

bond *v.* adhere (to), cleave, cling, adhere, stick.
Core meaning: To hold fast to (*plastics bonded with cement*).

bondage *n.* servitude, slavery.
These nouns refer to the condition of being involuntarily under the power of another. Bondage emphasizes being bound to another's service with virtually no hope of release: *The Israelites toiled in Egyptian bondage.* The term is also used figuratively: *Cocaine holds an addict in bondage.* Servitude stresses subjection or submission to a master: *involuntary servitude; sees his job as a form of servitude.* Slavery implies being owned as a possession and treated as property: *Lincoln abolished slavery in our country.*
Antonym: freedom.

bonus *n.* bounty, gratuity, reward, subsidy.
All of these designate some form of extra payment. Bonus usually applies to money given or paid in addition to what is normally received or strictly due, often in consideration of superior achievement. Bounty generally pertains to a sum of money given by a government for performing a specific service, such as capturing an outlaw or killing a destructive animal. A gratuity is a voluntary payment, such as a tip, in appreciation of services rendered. Reward refers broadly to payment for a specific effort or service, as the return of a lost article or the capture of a criminal. A subsidy is a large grant, usually by a government, in support of an enterprise considered to be in the public interest but not self-sustaining.

bony See **thin.**

---

book *v.* **engage, reserve.**
Core meaning: To claim or secure in advance (*book a function room*).

boost See **raise.**

border *n.* **borderline, brink, edge, fringe, margin, periphery, rim.**
Core meaning: A fairly narrow line or space forming a boundary (*the border of the property*).

borderline See **border.**

bore *v.* **fatigue, tire, weary.**
These apply to what generates tedium because it is uninteresting or monotonous. BORE implies dullness that causes listlessness and lack of interest. FATIGUE, TIRE, and WEARY suggest what makes one lose interest to the point of wanting to go to sleep.
Antonym: **amuse.**

borrow *v.* **adopt.**
To BORROW is to obtain or receive something with the understanding that it—or its equivalent in kind—will be returned: *borrow a book.* It also can mean taking up a word, gesture, attitude, etc., and using it as one's own (*English has many words borrowed from French*); ADOPT is a synonym of *borrow* only in this figurative sense (*adopted her sister's mannerisms*).
Antonym: **lend.**

botch *v.* **blunder, bungle, fumble, mishandle, mismanage, muff.**
Core meaning: To harm severely through inept handling (*a repair botched by an incompetent mechanic*).

bother See **annoy.**

bountiful See **generous.**

bow 1. See **bend.** 2. See **yield.**

brace See **couple.**

---

brag See **boast.**

branch *n.* appendage, arm, fork, offshoot.
Core meaning: Something resembling a tree branch (*the eastern branch of the company*).

brash See **bold.**

brave *adj.* courageous, fearless, valiant.
These are used to describe what has or shows resoluteness. BRAVE implies self-control and resolve in the face of danger: *a brave soldier.* COURAGEOUS and VALIANT emphasize moral strength and standing up for what is right and true: *a courageous social reformer; a valiant struggle against illness.* FEARLESS stresses absence of fear: *a fearless lion.* See also **face.**
Antonym: cowardly.

brazen See **bold.**

breach *n.* 1. infraction, infringement, transgression, trespass, violation.
Core meaning: An act or instance of breaking a law or regulation (*a breach in the security system*).
2. break, disaffection, estrangement, fissure, rent, rift, rupture, schism.
Core meaning: An interruption in friendly relations (*tried to repair the breach between the two brothers*).

break 1. See **opportunity.** 2. See **breach.**

breakable See **fragile.**

breakdown See **analysis.**

breed See **type.**

brief See **short.**

bright 1. See **cheerful.** 2. See **clever.** 3. See **intelligent.**

brilliant See **intelligent.**

brink See **border.**

brio See **spirit.**

brittle See **fragile.**

broad *adj.* **expansive, extensive, spacious, wide.**
BROAD and WIDE both indicate horizontal extent and are sometimes interchangeable. *Broad* is generally the choice when describing a surface or expanse (*a broad channel*), while *wide* is best for stressing space, such as the distance across a surface, especially when it is measured numerically (*a wide corridor*). EXPANSIVE stresses considerable sweep (*a calm, expansive lake*). EXTENSIVE focuses on the vast area of the space or topic under discussion (*extensive acreage; extensive coverage of the news*). SPACIOUS connotes greatness of size (*a spacious room*).
Antonym: **narrow.**

broadcast See **advertise.**

broker See **go-between.**

brusque See **gruff.**

build up See **advertise.**

bulk *n.* **amplitude, magnitude, mass, size, volume.**
Core meaning: Great amount or dimension (*the monstrous bulk of a supertanker*).

bungle See **botch.**

burden See **charge.**

burning See **hot.**

bushwhack See **ambush.**

business *n.* **commerce, industry, trade, traffic.**
BUSINESS applies broadly to all gainful activity, though it usually excludes the professions and farming. INDUSTRY is the production and manufacture of goods and commodities, especially on a large scale; COMMERCE and TRADE are the exchange and distribution of commodities. *Commerce* is often applied to exchange of commodities for money, as within a country, while *trade* refers to exchange of commodities for commodities, as between countries. TRAFFIC may suggest illegal trade, as in narcotics. See also **work.**

busy See **active**.

buy *v.* **purchase.**
BUY and PURCHASE, which are basically interchangeable, both mean "to obtain in exchange for money or something of equivalent value." *Purchase,* however, is often considered a more formal term, frequently implying that the transaction may be of some greater importance: *She buys food every Saturday in the supermarket. The entrepreneur purchased the* Queen Mary *as a tourist attraction.*
Antonym: **sell.**

bypass See **skirt**.

cadaverous See **ghastly**.

calamity See **disaster**.

calendar See **program**.

calm *adj.* **peaceful, placid, serene, tranquil.**
CALM and its synonyms describe absence of movement, noise, or disturbing emotion. *Calm* implies freedom from agitation: *a calm acceptance of the inevitable.* PEACEFUL refers to undisturbed serenity: *a peaceful family life.* PLACID suggests that a person is not easily shaken by emotion (*a placid disposition*); as a physical description it applies to surfaces that are unruffled (*a placid lake*). SERENE suggests a lofty, almost spiritual calm (*a serene smile*). TRANQUIL usually implies a calm that endures (*a tranquil lifestyle*). See also **tranquillity.**
Antonym: **upset.**

cancel *v.* **annul, erase, expunge, strike out.**
Core meaning: To remove or invalidate by or as if by wiping clean (*cancel an order*).

cant See **language**.

capable See **able**.

capacity See **ability**.

capital See **excellent**.

capitulate See **yield**.

---

capricious *adj.* changeable, erratic, fickle, inconstant, mercurial, temperamental, unpredictable, volatile.
Core meaning: Following no predictable pattern (*a capricious flirt; a capricious storm*).

captivate See **attract**.

care See **anxiety**.

careful *adj.* **1.** cautious, circumspect, prudent.
These all describe what has or shows caution. CAREFUL is most general: *a careful driver*. CAUTIOUS implies wariness, as if to avoid danger or harm: *a cautious pedestrian*. CIRCUMSPECT and PRUDENT suggest good judgment and discretion: *circumspect in shopping for a used car; a prudent decision*.
Antonym: careless.
2. conscientious, meticulous, painstaking.
These all describe what involves or shows effort and close attention. CONSCIENTIOUS also suggests seriousness of purpose and a sense of duty: *a conscientious clerk*. METICULOUS and PAINSTAKING both imply precision and thoroughness: *kept meticulous records; painstaking research*.
Antonym: careless.

careless *adj.* **1.** heedless, inadvertent.
All of these refer to actions or attitudes that show a lack of regard for consequences. CARELESS suggests lack of attentiveness: *a careless worker*. HEEDLESS implies inattentiveness to the point of recklessness: *heedless of their warnings*. INADVERTENT applies to unintentional actions: *an inadvertent mistake*.
Antonym: careful.
2. shoddy, slipshod, sloppy.
These all describe what is marked by neglect or insufficient attention: *careless typing; shoddy workmanship; slipshod bookkeeping; sloppy writing*.
Antonym: careful.

caress *v.* cuddle, fondle, pet.
Core meaning: To touch or stroke affectionately (*caressed the little boy*).

---

careworn See **haggard.**

carry *v.* **bear, have, possess.**
Core meaning: To hold on one's person (*I never carry cash*).

cartel See **combine.**

casual See **informal.**

cataclysm See **disaster.**

catalyst See **stimulus.**

catastrophe See **disaster.**

catch *v.* **clutch, grab, nab, seize, snatch.**
Core meaning: To get hold of something moving (*couldn't catch the ball*).

caustic See **sarcastic.**

caution See **warning.**

cautious See **careful.**

caveat See **warning.**

cease See **stop.**

censure 1. See **blame.** 2. See **disapprove.**

central See **middle.**

ceremonious See **formal.**

certainty *n.* **assurance, conviction.**
These all share the meaning "freedom from doubt." CER-
TAINTY stresses sureness (*the certainty that the team would win*); ASSURANCE, confidence and even self-confidence (*played tennis with assurance*); and CONVICTION, strong be-lief (*a conviction that patience would bring the best re-sults*).
Antonym: **uncertainty.**

certify See **approve.**

challenge See **objection.**

chance 1. See **accidental.** 2. See **opportunity.**

---

change *v.* **alter, convert, modify, transform, vary.**

These verbs all mean to make or become different. CHANGE, the most general, involves a basic difference (*change the colors in a picture*) or a substitution of one thing for another (*change clothes*). ALTER usually implies a smaller difference or one only in some given respect (*altered her appearance*). CONVERT can refer to change into another form, condition, etc. (*convert carbon dioxide into sugar*), or to change from one use to another (*convert a cellar into a playroom*). MOD-IFY often adds to *change* and *alter* the idea of making or becoming less extreme, severe, or strong: *weather that modified in the spring.* TRANSFORM refers to marked change in form, appearance, function, or condition: *A steam engine transforms heat into energy.* VARY implies not only change (*Temperature varies from day to day*) but also divergence (*behavior that varies from the expected*).

changeable See **capricious.**

chaperon See **accompany.**

character See **disposition.**

characteristic *adj.* **distinctive, individual, peculiar, typical.**

These indicate a trait, feature, or quality that identifies or sets apart someone or something. CHARACTERISTIC designates the identifying and especially the essential feature: *the zebra's characteristic stripes.* INDIVIDUAL lends to *characteristic* a personal quality that more definitely sets apart the person or thing: *students judged by individual performance.* DISTINCTIVE intensifies the meaning of *individual: Red berries are a distinctive feature of this plant.* PECULIAR emphasizes a trait belonging solely to one person or one thing; in this sense it does not necessarily imply oddness: *a mello sound peculiar to the cello.* TYPICAL, the most common of these terms, describes features, qualities, or behavior broadly applicable to a kind, group, or class: *a typical suburban community.*

charge 1. *n.* **burden, load, tax, weight.**

Core meaning: A heavy responsibility placed on a person

(*took his charge of the family budget very seriously*).
2. *v.* See **accuse. 3.** *v.* See **attribute.**

charlatan See **imposter.**

charm See **attract.**

chart See **table.**

chaste See **moral.**

chastise See **punish.**

cheap *adj.* **1. inexpensive.**
CHEAP and INEXPENSIVE describe what is low or relatively low in price: *a cheap dress; an inexpensive watch. Cheap* also has a figurative sense meaning "requiring little effort": *a cheap victory.*
Antonym: **expensive.**
2. shoddy.
These describe what is of poor or inferior quality: *cheap, badly made shoes; shoddy toys.*
3. stingy.
CHEAP and STINGY mean "not giving or spending generously": *a cheap escort; a stingy man.*
Antonym: **generous.**

check See **stop.**

cheerful *adj.* **1. cheery, happy, lighthearted.**
All of these describe persons who are in good spirits or behavior that indicates good spirits: *a cheerful waitress; a cheery smile; a happy baby; a lighthearted jest.* See also **glad.**
Antonym: **gloomy.**
2. bright, cheery.
These three describe what produces a feeling of cheer: *a cozy, cheerful room; a bright tune; a cheery fire.*
Antonym: **gloomy.**

cheery See **cheerful.**

cherish 1. See **appreciate. 2.** See **love.**

childish See **immature.**

chilly See **cold.**

choice *n.* **alternative, option, preference, selection.**
Each of these involves the privilege of choosing. CHOICE implies broadly the power, right, or possibility of choosing from a set of persons or things: *He left me no choice—he had already bought the green car.* ALTERNATIVE stresses choice between two possibilities or courses of action: *The alternative is between increased taxes and a budget deficit.* OPTION stresses the power or right of choosing: *having no option but to comply.* PREFERENCE indicates choice based on what one finds more desirable: *a preference for chocolate over vanilla.* SELECTION suggests a wide variety of things or persons to choose from: *a selection of books.*

choose *v.* **elect, pick, select.**
These all refer to taking one of several persons, things, or courses. CHOOSE implies the use of judgment: *chose a red hat; had to choose between working and studying.* ELECT strongly suggests careful thought in making a selection, usually between alternatives: *elects to go to London instead of Paris.* SELECT stresses care and comparison in choosing from a large variety: *select the right golf club for getting out of the trap.* PICK is the least precise of the group and often implies less deliberation than the others: *pick a pencil.*

chronic *adj.* **continuing, lingering, persistent, prolonged, protracted.**
Core meaning: Of long duration (*suffers chronic guilt feelings*).

chubby See **fat.**

circle 1. *n.* **clique, club, fraternity, set, society.**
CIRCLE and its synonyms denote a group of associates. *Circle* can describe almost any group having common interests or activities on a scale small or large: *a sewing circle; financial circles.* It can also designate the extent of personal relationships: *her circle of friends.* CLIQUE pertains to a small, exclusive group, usually social, that remains aloof

from others. CLUB can imply exclusiveness but often means only a group devoted to a common interest best pursued in company: *Rotary Club; a bridge club.* FRATERNITY most commonly denotes a social organization of male students; it can also refer to a group of people not actually organized but associated or linked by similar backgrounds, interests, occupations, etc.: *the medical fraternity.* SET suggests a large, loosely bound group defined by condition (*the younger set*), preoccupation with fashionable activity (*the smart set; the jet set*), etc. SOCIETY, in this sense, is usually a formally organized group with common interests, sometimes cultural: *a stamp-collecting society.*
2. *v.* See **surround.**

circuitous See **indirect.**

circumscribe See **limit.**

circumspect See **careful.**

circumspection See **prudence.**

circumvent See **skirt.**

civil See **polite.**

clandestine See **secret.**

clarify *v.* **elucidate, explain.**
These three mean to make clear or easier to understand: *clarify your argument; elucidate the meaning of a phrase; explain the rules of the game; explain the meaning of a poem.*
Antonym: **confuse.**

clash See **discord.**

clean *adj.* **cleanly, immaculate, spotless.**
CLEAN and its synonyms all describe what is free from dirt, stains, or impurities. *Clean* is the most general: *a clean glass; clean water.* CLEANLY means "habitually and carefully neat and clean": *A cat is a cleanly animal.* IMMACULATE and SPOTLESS are synonymous in meaning "perfectly

clean," but *immaculate* is the more formal term: *a spotless (or immaculate) coat.*
Antonym: **dirty.**

cleanly See **clean.**

clear *adj.* **distinct, unmistakable.**
These all apply to what is easily perceived by the eye, ear, or mind. CLEAR is the most general: *a clear picture; a clear voice; a clear statement.* DISTINCT suggests what is well defined: *a distinct outline.* UNMISTAKABLE emphasizes what is readily evident: *an unmistakable resemblance.*
Antonyms: **unclear; vague.**

cleave See **bond.**

clever *adj.* **alert, bright, smart.**
These describe persons who are quick to learn, think, understand, etc.: *a clever girl; an alert child; a bright, attractive freshman; a smart lawyer.* They can also be applied to actions, behavior, thoughts, etc., that reveal quick-wittedness: *a clever plan; alert driving; a bright idea; a smart decision.*
Antonym: **dull.**

climax *n.* **acme, apex, apogee, crest, culmination, peak, pinnacle, summit, zenith.**
Core meaning: The highest point or state (*a discovery that was the climax of her career*).

climb See **rise.**

cling See **bond.**

clip See **hit.**

clique See **circle.**

cloak See **hide.**

clobber See **hit.**

cloistered See **secluded.**

close 1. See **end.** 2. See **near.** 3. See **stingy.**

clothe See **dress.**

club See **circle.**

clumsy 1. See **awkward. 2.** See **tactless.**

clutch See **catch.**

coalition See **combine.**

coarse *adj.* **crude, gross, indelicate, obscene, vulgar.**
As it describes a material property COARSE means "rough in grain or texture." It has a figurative meaning that describes lack of refinement in manners, appearance, or expression (*coarse behavior; coarse language*); its synonyms share this meaning. CRUDE suggests lack of tact or taste: *a crude expression.* GROSS implies crudeness and vulgarity: *a gross remark.* INDELICATE describes what is offensive to propriety: *indelicate comments.* OBSCENE strongly stresses lewdness or indecency: *obscene jokes.* VULGAR emphasizes offensiveness and suggests boorishness and poor breeding: *a vulgar display of wealth.*
Antonym: **refined.**

coast See **slide.**

coax See **urge.**

coddle See **pamper.**

coercion See **force.**

coextensive See **parallel.**

cognizance See **notice.**

cognizant See **aware.**

coincide See **agree.**

cold *adj.* **arctic, chilly, cool, frigid, frosty, icy.**
Used literally, these words describe what has a low temperature; figuratively they also refer to lack of enthusiasm, cordiality, personal warmth, etc. COLD is the most general: *cold air; a cold person.* CHILLY and COOL suggest that something is moderately cold (*damp, chilly weather; a cool breeze*) or unenthusiastic (*a chilly reaction to the new plan; a cool reception*); *cool* can also imply that something is calm or unexcited: *a cool head in a crisis.* What is FROSTY is

cold enough for the formation of small ice crystals (*a frosty night*) or very cold and unfriendly in manner (*a frosty reply*). ARCTIC, FRIGID, and ICY all describe what is bitterly cold (*arctic weather; a frigid room; the icy waters of the sea in winter*); *frigid* and *icy* also apply to what is severe or very unfriendly (*frigid dignity; an icy stare*).
Antonym: **hot.**

collateral See **parallel.**

colleague See **partner.**

collect See **gather.**

collusion See **conspiracy.**

combat 1. See **conflict. 2.** See **repel. 3.** See **withstand.**

combine *n.* **bloc, cartel, coalition, faction, party.**
Core meaning: A group united by a common cause (*a combine of citizens against nuclear arms*).

comic See **laughable.**

comical See **laughable.**

command *v.* **1. direct, instruct, order.**
In the sense in which they are compared, these verbs all mean "to demand that a person or group do—or not do—something." COMMAND and ORDER are similar in emphasizing the official authority of the person making the demand: *commanded me to leave; order the staff to be punctual.* DIRECT and INSTRUCT are less imperative; *instruct* in particular suggests a mild order, often a mere direction that a person do something in a particular way: *direct the police to free the prisoners; instructed the soldiers to stand at attention.*
Antonym: **obey.**
2. See **expertise.**

commence See **begin.**

commentary See **review.**

commerce See **business.**

commodities See **goods.**

common *adj.* **familiar, ordinary, prevalent.**
These describe what is generally known or often seen, heard, or the like. COMMON applies to what is customary, takes place daily, or is widely used: *a common soldier; when filling stations became common.* FAMILIAR describes what is well known or quickly recognized through frequent occurrence or regular association: *the familiar voice of the announcer; a familiar sight.* ORDINARY refers to what is commonly encountered (*an ordinary day*) or what is average or of no exceptional quality (*ordinary parents whose child was a genius*). What is PREVALENT exists widely or occurs commonly: *Sickness is more prevalent in hot, humid areas than in dry, cool areas.* See also **familiar.**
Antonym: **uncommon.**

commonwealth See **nation.**

communicate See **say.**

companionable See **social.**

compass See **surround.**

compassionate See **kind.**

competent See **able.**

competitor See **opponent.**

complete 1. See **end. 2.** See **full. 3.** See **utter.**

complex *adj.* **complicated, intricate, involved.**
These describe things having parts so interconnected that the whole is difficult to understand. COMPLEX and COMPLICATED are similar in indicating a challenge to the mind: *complex ideas; a game with complicated rules. Complex,* however, often implies many varying parts (*a complex system of roads and highways*); *complicated* stresses elaborate relationship of parts rather than number (*yarn snarled into a complicated tangle*). INTRICATE refers to a pattern of intertwining parts that is difficult to follow: *an intricate design.* INVOLVED stresses confusion arising from the mixing together of parts and the difficulty of separating them: *a long, involved sentence.*
Antonym: **simple**

---

compliant See **submissive.**

complicated See **complex.**

comply See **obey.**

compose See **constitute.**

composure See **equanimity.**

comprehend *v.* **apprehend, grasp, understand.**
These verbs refer to the mental process of perceiving something. COMPREHEND and UNDERSTAND are often interchangeable in the sense of "know." *Understand* in particular specifies knowledge of the significance of a thing distinguished from its mere nature (*He doesn't pretend to understand the universe*); in related senses the word refers to knowledge or insight based on close contact or long experience (*really understands the Indians*) or to sympathy or tolerance (*understands their problems*). APPREHEND suggests mental awareness of something without necessarily implying the in-depth knowledge of understanding: *Do you apprehend my meaning?* GRASP usually implies such knowledge and stresses the process of visualizing or penetrating to the heart of a difficult matter: *grasps the principles of number theory.*

comprise See **constitute.**

compulsory *adj.* **mandatory, obligatory.**
COMPULSORY, MANDATORY, and OBLIGATORY describe what is required by laws, rules, or regulations: *compulsory military service; mandatory attendance; obligatory taxes.*
Antonym: **optional.**

compunction See **qualm.**

conceal See **hide.**

concede See **acknowledge.**

concentration *n.* **confluence, conflux, convergence.**
Core meaning: A converging at a common center (*heavy troop concentrations at the border*).

concern 1. See **anxiety. 2.** See **interest.**

---

conciliate See **pacify**.

concise *adj.* **laconic, pithy, succinct, terse.**
The idea of stating much in few words is contained in these adjectives. CONCISE implies clarity and compactness through the removal of all unnecessary words: *a concise paragraph*. TERSE adds to *concise* the sense that something is brief and to the point: *a terse reply*. LACONIC often suggests brevity that is almost rude: *a laconic response that merely answered the question*. PITHY implies that something is precisely meaningful and has a telling effect: *a pithy comment*. SUCCINCT strongly emphasizes compactness and the elimination of all elaboration: *a succinct explanation*.

conclude See **end**.

conclusive See **valid**.

concord See **harmony**.

concurrent 1. See **parallel. 2.** See **unanimous**.

condemn See **blame**.

conditional *adj.* **provisional, provisory, tentative.**
Core meaning: Depending on or containing a condition (*a conditional agreement*).

conduct See **accompany**.

confederate See **partner**.

confederation See **union**.

conference See **deliberation**.

confess See **acknowledge**.

confidence *n.* **1. assurance, self-confidence.**
CONFIDENCE and its synonyms imply faith in oneself or the state of mind that results from this. *Confidence* suggests faith in one's powers: *Her playing exhibited the confidence that comes from experience*. ASSURANCE even more strongly stresses a feeling of certainty and conviction: *managing a difficult situation with assurance*. SELF-CONFIDENCE denotes

trust in one's own abilities: *At the age of ten children often lack self-confidence.*
Antonym: **diffidence.**
2. reliance, trust.
These all imply a firm belief in the honesty, dependability, or power of someone: *I am placing my confidence in you. She put complete reliance in her friends. You must live up to the trust he has shown in you.* See also **trust.**
Antonym: **doubt.**

conflict *n.* **combat, contest, fight, melee, scuffle.**
These denote struggle between opposing forces. CONFLICT applies to large-scale physical struggle between hostile forces (*armed conflict*), to a struggle within a person (*in conflict about her sister*), and to a clash of opposing ideas, interests, etc. (*a conflict between the evidence and his testimony*). CONTEST can mean either friendly competition (*a skating contest*) or a struggle between rival or hostile forces (*a contest over a senatorial seat*). COMBAT implies armed encounter between two persons or groups (*killed in combat*). FIGHT usually refers to a clash involving two persons or a small group (*a fist fight*) or to a struggle for a cause (*the fight for civil rights*). MELEE and SCUFFLE denote generally impromptu and disorderly physical clashes; *melee* implies confused, hand-to-hand fighting, while *scuffle* suggests hand-to-hand fighting on a small scale. See also **discord.**

confluence See **concentration.**

conflux See **concentration.**

conform See **agree.**

conformist See **conventional.**

confuse *v.* **blur, muddle.**
These verbs share the meaning of making something unclear so that its features or elements cannot be distinguished: *Too many affidavits confused the record. Her distraction blurred her thoughts. The report muddled the issues.*
Antonym: **clarify.**

---

congress See **union.**

conjecture See **theory.**

connect See **join.**

conquest See **victory.**

conscientious See **careful.**

conscious See **aware.**

consecrate See **devote.**

consent See **permission.**

consequence See **effect.**

consequential See **important.**

conserve See **save.**

consider *v.* **deem, regard.**
These refer to holding opinions or views that reflect evaluation of a person or thing. CONSIDER suggests objective evaluation based on reflection and reasoning: *The committee met to consider her qualifications.* DEEM is more subjective through its emphasis on judgment distinguished from analytical thought: *deemed it advisable to wait.* REGARD may imply personal, subjective judgment: *regard him with skepticism.*

consist (of) See **constitute.**

consolidation See **unification.**

conspiracy *n.* **collusion, intrigue, machination, plot.**
CONSPIRACY and its synonyms denote secret plans or schemes. *Conspiracy* refers to such a plan by a group intent usually on an unlawful purpose: *a conspiracy to overthrow the government.* COLLUSION refers to secret agreement between persons or organizations, usually with intent to deceive or cheat others: *department stores acting in collusion to maintain high prices.* INTRIGUE usually implies selfish, petty actions rather than criminal ends: *office politics and intrigue.* MACHINATION, usually plural, strongly implies crafty, hostile dealing by one or more persons: *machinations that got his supervisor fired.* PLOT stresses sinister

means and motives but may be small or large in number of participants and scope: *a plot to kill the emperor.*

constant 1. See **continuous. 2.** See **faithful. 3.** See **true.**

constitute *v.* compose, comprise, consist (of), form, make, make up.
Core meaning: To be the constituent parts of (*Ten members constitute a quorum*).

constraint See **force.**

construct See **make.**

consultation See **deliberation.**

consume See **waste.**

consummate See **utter.**

contaminated See **impure.**

contemporary See **modern.**

contest See **conflict.**

continence See **abstinence.**

contingency See **possibility.**

continual See **continuous.**

continuation *n.* continuity, continuum, duration, endurance.
Core meaning: Uninterrupted existence or succession (*a continuation of the negotiations*).

continuing See **chronic.**

continuity See **continuation.**

continuous *adj.* constant, continual.
These have the common meaning of happening over and over during a long period of time. CONTINUOUS is the most inclusive; it implies either lack of interruption in time or unbroken extent in space: *a continuous supply of oxygen; a continuous line.* CONSTANT in this sense refers only to continuity in time: *Our television has a constant flicker.* CONTINUAL sometimes means "steady" (*a continual rumpus*), but it is more often used to describe regular and frequent

repetition: *the continual banging of the door.*
Antonym: **discontinuous.**

contract *v.* **shrink.**
CONTRACT and SHRINK share the meaning of drawing together or growing smaller: *The world seems to have contracted* (or *shrunk*) *with the invention of the communications satellite. Contract* frequently suggests a reversible process; it often implies the existence of a regular pattern of contraction and expansion or contraction and release: *He contracted his biceps. His biceps contracted. Shrink* often refers to an irreversible process: *The sweater shrank in the dryer. Shrink the material before you sew.*
Antonym: **expand.**

contradict See **deny.**

contradiction See **denial.**

contrary *adj.* **perverse, stubborn, willful.**
All of these refer to being in opposition to a prevailing order or to prescribed authority. CONTRARY applies especially to a person who is self-willed and given to resisting authority. PERVERSE implies obstinacy and a native disposition to depart from what is considered the right course of action. STUBBORN stresses inflexibility of mind or will and thus strongly implies resistance to authority. WILLFUL often implies unreasoning, headstrong self-determination and refusal to accept authority.

contrived See **arty.**

control See **power.**

contumelious See **abusive.**

convenient *adj.* **1. handy.**
These apply to what is suited to one's comfort, needs, or purpose: *a convenient appliance; a handy supply of pencils.*
2. accessible.
CONVENIENT and ACCESSIBLE refer to what is easy to get to: *a convenient shopping center; an accessible airport.*
Antonym: **inaccessible.**

conventional *adj.* conformist, establishmentarian, orthodox, square (*Informal*), straight (*Informal*), traditional.
Core meaning: Conforming to established practice or standards (*conventional dress; conventional social views*).

convergence See **concentration.**

convert See **change.**

convey See **say.**

conviction 1. See **certainty.** 2. See **opinion.**

convincing See **valid.**

convivial See **social.**

cool See **cold.**

core See **heart.**

corpulent See **fat.**

correct *v.* amend, rectify, redress, reform, remedy, revise.
All of these refer to making right or improving. CORRECT can apply broadly to any such act (*correct a wrong impression*) but usually refers to eliminating error or defect (*correcting an article before setting it in type*). RECTIFY stresses the idea of bringing something into conformity with a standard of what is right: *rectify a mistake in the records.* REMEDY involves repairing or removing something considered a cause of harm or damage: *legislation to remedy social inequities.* REDRESS usually refers to setting right something considered wrong or unjust: *redress a grievance.* REFORM implies broad change that improves character, as of a person or institution: *reform criminals; reform society.* REVISE suggests change as a result of reconsideration of an earlier course: *revised a paragraph.* AMEND adds to *revise* a more definite implication of improvement through alteration or addition: *amending his will.* See also **true.**

correctness See **veracity.**

correspond See **agree.**

corruption See **vice.**

---

cosmos See **universe**.

costly See **expensive**.

counsel See **deliberation**.

country See **nation**.

couple *n.* **brace, pair, yoke.**
These denote two of something in association. COUPLE refers to two of the same kind or sort; they are not necessarily—but often are—closely associated: *a couple of oranges; a married couple*. PAIR stresses close association and often reciprocal dependence of things (*a pair of gloves; a pair of pajamas*); sometimes it denotes a single thing with interdependent parts (*a pair of scissors; a pair of eyeglasses*). BRACE refers mainly to certain game birds, as partridges, and YOKE to two joined draft animals, as oxen.

courageous See **brave**.

courteous See **polite**.

covert See **secret**.

cowardly *adj.* **craven.**
These describe what lacks courage. Both COWARDLY and CRAVEN suggest a shameful show of fear, but *craven* implies an especially high degree of cowardice: *a cowardly lion; a craven liar*.
Antonym: **brave**.

coy See **shy**.

crack See **joke**.

craft See **expertise**.

craven See **cowardly**.

craving See **wish**.

create *v.* **establish, generate, produce.**
These verbs share the meaning of bringing into existence. CREATE often implies the production of something by invention and imagination: *create a musical composition*. To ESTABLISH is to set up or found: *established a chain of food*

---

stores. GENERATE is often used metaphorically: *generate ideas.* PRODUCE means both "to manufacture" (*produce parts for machines*) and "to give rise to" (*Poverty often produces despair*).

creation See **universe.**

credit 1. See **believe. 2.** See **attribute.**

crest See **climax.**

critical *adj.* **acute, crucial, serious.**
All of these adjectives are applied to conditions or situations to indicate degrees of intensity or significance. CRITICAL implies the arrival at a turning point and the imminence of decisive change, usually accompanied by considerable risk, peril, or suspense: *the critical point in the negotiations; a sick man in critical condition.* ACUTE applies to a somewhat earlier stage, when intensification of unfavorable conditions signals the approach of a crisis: *an acute need for money; acute appendicitis.* CRUCIAL and *critical* may apply to approximately the same point in time, but *crucial* emphasizes change that is likely to shape future events: *a crucial decision.* SERIOUS lacks the implication of great significance and immediate concern that is inherent in the other terms; rather, it suggests what is worthy of concern or anxiety: *a serious wound.*

criticism See **review.**

criticize 1. See **blame. 2.** See **disapprove.**

critique See **review.**

crook See **bend.**

crow See **boast.**

crucial See **critical.**

crude See **coarse.**

cruel *adj.* **barbarous, ferocious, inhuman, pitiless, sadistic, vicious.**
These apply to persons, their behavior, their attitudes, etc., when they cause pain, suffering, or hardship to others.

CRUEL implies satisfaction in or indifference to suffering: *a cruel man; a cruel remark.* What is FEROCIOUS is extremely cruel, even savage (*a ferocious attack*), and BARBAROUS adds the suggestion of brutality that befits only primitive or uncivilized men (*Hitler's barbarous acts*). INHUMAN refers to a marked lack of such desirable human qualities as sympathy for one's fellow man: *inhuman treatment.* SADISTIC implies the experiencing of satisfaction from inflicting cruelty on others. VICIOUS suggests native disposition to savage and dangerous behavior: *gave the boy a vicious beating.* PITILESS refers specifically to absence of mercy: *a pitiless massacre.*

cryptic See **ambiguous.**

cuddle See **caress.**

culmination See **climax.**

cultivate See **promote.**

cultivated See **refined.**

cultured See **refined.**

cumbersome See **heavy.**

curiosity See **interest.**

curious *adj.* **inquisitive, nosy.**
CURIOUS, INQUISITIVE, and NOSY share the meaning of having or showing a marked wish for information or knowledge. *Curious* most often suggests eagerness to enlarge one's knowledge, but it may also imply an urge to involve oneself unjustifiably in the affairs of others: *a curious scientist; curious about the contents of the letter. Inquisitive,* a more formal word, shares these implications: *an inquisitive mind; inquisitive to know what was in his will. Nosy* always implies excessive and impertinent personal curiosity. See also **strange.**
Antonym: **uninterested.**

current See **modern.**

curse See **afflict.**

---

curt See **gruff.**

curve See **bend.**

customary See **familiar.**

cut 1. *n.* **piece, portion, segment, slice.**
Core meaning: A part severed or taken from a whole (*a cut of beef*).
2. *v.* See **lower.**

danger *n.* **hazard, peril, risk.**
These nouns refer to exposure to harm or loss. DANGER is the least specific; it can be used to describe any potentially harmful situation: *At night the city is full of dangers.* HAZARD suggests a threat posed by chance or something largely beyond one's control: *the hazards of driving.* PERIL refers to an immediate threat: *His life will be in peril if the oxygen tank fails to work.* RISK stresses chance or uncertainty, but often from the standpoint of one who weighs it against possible gain; therefore it often suggests voluntary exposure to harm or loss: *This venture is a financial risk, but if we win, our troubles will be over forever.*
Antonym: **safety**

daring See **bold.**

dark *adj.* **dim, dusky, murky, shadowy, shady.**
DARK and its synonyms indicate the absence of light or clarity. *Dark,* the most widely applicable, can refer to insufficiency of illumination for seeing (*a dark tunnel*), to deepness of shade of a color (*dark blue*), or figuratively to absence of cheer (*a dark view of life*). DIM describes what is faintly lighted (*a dim corner of the hall*); it also suggests lack of clarity (*a dim memory of the accident*). DUSKY applies mainly to the dimness characteristic of twilight (*a dusky room*) or to deepness of shade of a color (*dusky brown*). MURKY usually implies darkness like that produced by smoke, sediment, etc.: *a murky sky; murky water.* SHADOWY implies obstructed light but suggests shifting illumination (*shadowy woods*) and indistinctness (*shadowy*

forms moving underwater). SHADY refers to what is shel-
tered from light, especially sunlight (*a shady street*), or,
figuratively, to what is covertly dishonest (*a shady deal*).
Antonym: **light.**

dash 1. See **spirit. 2.** See **trace.**

day(s) See **age.**

daze *n.* **befuddlement, fog, muddle, stupor, trance.**
Core meaning: A stunned or bewildered condition (*fell flat
and lay on the ground in a daze*).

dead *adj.* **1. deceased, extinct, lifeless.**
DEAD and its synonyms describe what is without life or
continuing existence. *Dead* has the widest use; it applies to
whatever once had—but no longer has—physical life (*a
dead leaf*), function (*a dead doorbell*), currency (*a dead
issue*), or usefulness (*a dead language*). DECEASED is a formal term that is used only for dead people. EXTINCT describes both what is burned out (*an extinct volcano*) and
what has died out (*The dodo is extinct, and so are the
Tudors*). LIFELESS can describe what once had physical life
(*a lifeless body*), what does not support life (*a lifeless
planet*), and what lacks spirit or brightness (*lifeless colors*).
Antonym: **alive.**
2. See **vanished.**

deaden *v.* **benumb, blunt, desensitize, dull, numb.**
Core meaning: To make less sensitive (*a topical anesthetic
to deaden the pain*).

deadly See **fatal.**

deathly See **ghastly.**

debacle See **disaster.**

decease See **die.**

deceased See **dead.**

deceitful See **false.**

deceitfulness See **dishonesty.**

---

deceive *v.* **betray, delude, double-cross, mislead.**
DECEIVE and its synonyms refer to misrepresentation used to victimize persons. *Deceive* itself involves lying or the deliberate concealment of truth in order to lead another into error or to disadvantage. BETRAY implies disloyalty or treachery that brings another into danger or to disadvantage: *betrayed his friend; betraying the confidence of the voters.* TO MISLEAD is to cause to gain a wrong impression (*misled by false rumors*); it does not always imply intent to harm. DELUDE refers to deceiving or misleading to the point of rendering a person unable to make sound judgments. DOUBLE-CROSS, a slang term, implies betrayal of a confidence or the willful breaking of a pledge.

decent 1. See **moral. 2.** See **sufficient.**

decide *v.* **determine, resolve, rule, settle.**
These verbs are compared as they refer to making conclusions or judgments. DECIDE, the least specific, overlaps the other terms without conveying their more special meanings. DETERMINE often involves somewhat narrower issues and more detailed solutions: *Determine whether this answer is true or false.* SETTLE stresses finality of decision (*settled the argument once and for all*), and RULE implies that the decision is handed down by someone having recognized authority (*The referee ruled that the play was fair*). RESOLVE implies deliberation and finality of decision or solution: *resolve a conflict; resolve a problem.*
Antonym: **hesitate.**

decision See **will.**

declare See **assert.**

decline See **reject.**

decorum See **manners.**

decrease *v.* **diminish, dwindle, lessen, reduce.**
All of these share the meaning of becoming or causing to become smaller or less, as in size, extent, or quantity. DECREASE is the most general; it implies gradual and steady

---

decline: *His appetite decreased daily. The pilot decreased the speed of the plane.* LESSEN can be used interchangeably with *decrease* in most contexts (*His appetite lessened daily*) but does not always stress gradualness (*The pain lessened immediately after the drug was administered*). DIMINISH suggests removal and consequent loss: *The king's authority diminished after the revolt. A drought diminished the nation's food supply.* DWINDLE connotes what decreases bit by bit to a vanishing point: *Their savings dwindled away.* REDUCE emphasizes the sense of coming or bringing down to a lower level: *The volume of noise gradually reduced. The workers reduced their wage demands.*
Antonym: increase.

dedicate See **devote.**

deem See **consider.**

deep *adj.* **profound.**
DEEP literally describes what lies or extends far below a surface: *a deep pit; a deep wound.* PROFOUND is no longer much used in this literal sense, but *deep* and *profound* share a figurative sense that describes what shows much wisdom and insight (*a deep knowledge; a profound philosophy*) or much feeling (*a deep love; a profound sigh*). See also **intense.**
Antonym: shallow.

defeat *n.* **rout.**
DEFEAT and ROUT refer to the fact or condition of being overcome by an adversary or opponent, as in war or in a competition. *Defeat,* the more general term, does not necessarily imply finality of outcome: *Napoleon's defeat at Waterloo changed the course of European history. The Bruins suffered defeat by the Canadiens but won the next game.* A *rout* is an overwhelming defeat, often followed by a disorderly retreat: *the rout of the Persian fleet at Salamis.*
Antonym: victory.

defective See **imperfect.**

---

defend *v.* **guard, preserve, protect, safeguard.**
These words mean to make or keep safe from danger or attack. DEFEND implies the use of actions taken to repel an attack: *defend the gates of the city; defended his reputation.* GUARD suggests keeping watch: *guarded the house against intruders.* PRESERVE implies measures taken to maintain something in safety: *Ecologists want to preserve our natural resources.* PROTECT suggests providing cover to repel discomfort, injury, or actual attack: *used a rain hat to protect her hair; a medieval city protected by strong walls.* SAFEGUARD stresses protection from danger and often implies action taken in advance: *safeguard valuables by keeping them in the bank.*
Antonym: **attack.**

defensible See **justifiable.**

defer See **yield.**

deference See **honor.**

deficiency *n.* **insufficiency, lack, shortage.**
These all denote the condition of being inadequate in amount or degree. DEFICIENCY and INSUFFICIENCY suggest that minimal requirements for a particular purpose are not being met: *The neglected child was suffering from vitamin deficiency. The bank had a temporary insufficiency of traveler's checks.* LACK can also imply that something is not available: *a lack of electricity.* SHORTAGE in addition suggests something that falls short of a required or expected amount: *a food shortage.*
Antonym: **excess.**

definite See **explicit.**

deft See **graceful.**

defunct See **vanished.**

dejected See **sad.**

delay *v.* **detain, retard, slow.**
These verbs share the meaning of holding back and hindering progress. DELAY applies to putting behind schedule or to

postponing action: *Business often delays his return home. His wife delays dinner then.* DETAIN stresses holding something up at a particular point along the way to completion: *detained by a phone call.* RETARD and SLOW imply a slackening of pace: *snow that retards traffic; winds that slow the car.*
Antonym: expedite.

delectable See **delicious.**

delegate See **representative.**

deliberate 1. See **slow. 2.** See **intentional. 3.** See **voluntary.**

deliberation *n.* conference, consultation, counsel, parley.
Core meaning: An exchange of views in an attempt to reach a decision (*the deliberations of the management committee*).

delicate See **fragile.**

delicious *adj.* delectable, luscious, scrumptious.
These all describe what is very pleasing or agreeable to the sense of taste. DELICIOUS, DELECTABLE, and LUSCIOUS can be used interchangeably: *a delicious apple; a delectable piece of cake; a luscious melon.* SCRUMPTIOUS has the same meaning but is informal: *a scrumptious peach.*

delight 1. See **joy. 2.** See **please.**

delimit See **limit.**

deliver See **save.**

delude See **deceive.**

dementia See **insanity.**

demise See **die.**

demolish See **destroy.**

demonstrate See **prove.**

denial *n.* contradiction, disclaimer, negation, rejection.
Core meaning: A refusal to grant the truth of a statement or charge (*issued a denial of the accusations*).

denomination See **name.**

denounce See **blame.**

dense See **dull.**

deny *v.* **contradict, gainsay, refute.**
These verbs have in common the sense of disputing the truthfulness of a statement or a speaker. DENY is the most general and usually implies an open declaration that something is untrue. To CONTRADICT is to assert that the opposite of a given statement is true. GAINSAY is generally used in negative constructions to stress the unlikelihood or impossibility of opposing or rejecting: *raised objections that could not be gainsaid.* REFUTE implies the use of evidence to disprove an opposing claim.
Antonym: **assert.**

depart See **die.**

dependable See **reliable.**

dependent See **subordinate.**

deplete See **waste.**

depravity See **vice.**

deprecate See **disapprove.**

depreciate See **belittle.**

depreciation *n.* **devaluation, markdown, reduction.**
Core meaning: A lowering in price or value (*another depreciation of the U.S. dollar*).

depress See **discourage.**

depressed See **sad.**

deputy See **representative.**

derelict See **abandoned.**

deride See **ridicule.**

derogate See **belittle.**

descend See **fall.**

descendant *n.* posterity, progeny.

A DESCENDANT is an individual considered as descended from specified ancestors. POSTERITY and PROGENY refer to descendants collectively.

Antonym: ancestor.

desensitize See **deaden.**

desert See **abandon.**

deserted See **abandoned.**

designation See **name.**

desire See **wish.**

desist See **stop.**

desolate See **sad.**

desperate See **upset.**

despise *v.* disdain, scorn.

These verbs all express a feeling that someone or something is inferior and undesirable. DESPISE emphasizes the simple fact of such a negative opinion; the person who despises need not express it to others: *despise unethical behavior.* DISDAIN implies that a feeling of contempt is communicated to others (*disdained her husband's cronies*); SCORN involves the expression of such an opinion, usually with some measure of anger, sarcasm, or ridicule: *scorned his ideas.*

Antonym: appreciate.

despotic See **absolute.**

destiny See **fate.**

destitute See **poor.**

destroy *v.* abolish, demolish, raze.

These all apply to the process of undoing or ruining completely. DESTROY has the broadest application. To ABOLISH is to put an end to: *abolish slavery.* DEMOLISH and RAZE suggest force. *Demolish* implies tearing down: *demolish a house; demolish an argument. Raze* means "to tear down

to the ground; to level": *razed old tenement buildings.*
Antonym: **create.**

detach *v.* **disengage, unfasten.**
These denote the separation of one thing from another: *detached the gold charm from her bracelet; tried to disengage his leg from the underbrush; unfastened the clasp of a necklace.*
Antonym: **attach.**

detain 1. See **arrest. 2.** See **delay.**

determination See **will.**

determine See **decide.**

detest See **hate.**

detestation See **hate.**

detonate See **explode.**

detract (from) See **belittle.**

detriment 1. See **harm. 2.** See **disadvantage.**

devaluation See **depreciation.**

devious See **underhand.**

devote *v.* **consecrate, dedicate, pledge.**
DEVOTE and its synonyms are compared mainly in the sense of giving oneself or one's effort for a particular end. *Devote,* the most general, implies loyal and close attention to a specific cause, activity, person, etc.: *devoted himself to the care of his mother.* DEDICATE adds the idea of a full and sometimes formal commitment: *a scientist who dedicates himself to research.* CONSECRATE stresses almost sacred commitment to some worthy purpose: *consecrate one's life to improving the lot of the poor.* PLEDGE refers to personal commitment backed by a solemn promise: *The girl's parents pledged their support.*

devotion See **love.**

devout See **holy.**

dextrous See **graceful.**

---

detach / different

dialect See **language**.

diatribe See **tirade**.

dictatorial *adj.* **arbitrary, authoritative, dogmatic, imperious, overbearing.**
All of these refer to what has or shows the tendency or disposition to assert authority or to impose control on others. DICTATORIAL suggests the idea of unlimited power and complete authority in the hands of one person; the term stresses a high-handed, absolute manner. ARBITRARY implies that something is based on whim, impulse, selfishness, hasty judgment, or anything other than sound reasoning. DOGMATIC suggests the imposition of one's will or opinion as though it were beyond challenge. IMPERIOUS suggests the manner of one accustomed to commanding. AUTHORITATIVE can apply to what arises from proper authority (*the general's authoritative manner*) or authority based on expert knowledge (*authoritative sources*). OVERBEARING implies a tendency to be domineering and arrogant.

diction See **wording**.

die *v.* **decease, demise, depart, expire, pass away, perish.**
Core meaning: To become dead (*died young*).

differ See **disagree**.

different *adj.* **disparate, divergent, diverse.**
DIFFERENT and its synonyms apply to things that are dissimilar or unlike. *Different* implies distinctness or separateness (*Different people like different things*), sometimes to the point of being unusual (*a really different hair style*). Things that are DISPARATE are entirely dissimilar: *disparate theories about the origin of man*. DIVERGENT suggests that things differ because they extend in different directions: *widely divergent trends*. DIVERSE strongly stresses distinctness in kind (*diverse points of view*); it often describes things that are of several or many kinds (*The United States is a land of diverse people*).
Antonym: **same**.

---

difficult *adj.* **arduous, hard, troublesome.**

All of these describe what requires great physical or mental effort. HARD and DIFFICULT are often interchangeable (*a hard—or difficult—climb; a hard—or difficult—task*), but *difficult* is frequently more appropriate when special skill or ingenuity is called for: *a difficult problem.* ARDUOUS suggests burdensome labor or persistent effort: *an arduous journey; arduous training.* TROUBLESOME implies demands that cause worry: *a troublesome child; a troublesome car that stalled often.*
Antonym: **easy.**

diffidence *n.* **shyness, timidity.**

These all denote lack of self-confidence: *diffidence that made it difficult for him to assert himself; shyness that made it painful for him to meet new people; timidity that prevented her from making friends.*
Antonym: **confidence.**

diffident See **shy.**

digest See **absorb.**

dilatory See **slow.**

dilemma See **predicament.**

dilettante See **amateur.**

dim See **dark.**

diminish See **decrease.**

diminutive See **little.**

direct 1. *adj.* **straight, straightforward.**

DIRECT and STRAIGHT share the meaning "not bending or curving": *a direct route; a straight line.* In a figurative sense *direct, straight,* and STRAIGHTFOWARD all describe what is not interrupted or does not deviate or swerve from the point: *a direct descendant; a straight answer; a straightforward explanation.* See also **command.**
Antonym: **indirect.**

2. *v.* See **administer.**

---

dirty *adj.* **filthy, foul, grimy, soiled.**
DIRTY is the most general of these words and describes anything that is physically unclean: *dirty clothes; a dirty floor*. FILTHY and FOUL are more intense and refer to what is extremely and offensively unclean: *a filthy* (or *foul*) *jacket*. *Dirty, filthy,* and *foul* also apply figuratively to what is obscene or indecent: *a dirty joke; a filthy picture; foul language*. GRIMY suggests something whose surface is smudged with soot or other dirt (*grimy hands*); SOILED, something partially stained or dirtied (*soiled laundry*).
Antonym: **clean.**

disadvantage *n.* **detriment, drawback, handicap, minus, shortcoming.**
Core meaning: An unfavorable condition, circumstance, or characteristic (*his lack of experience was a major disadvantage*).

disaffect See **estrange.**

disaffection See **breach.**

disagree *v.* **differ, dispute, dissent.**
These express incompatibility or lack of agreement. DISAGREE is the most general. DIFFER (*from*) denotes dissimilarity between persons or things that are being compared (*toothpaste differs from toothpowder*); *differ* (*with*), divergence of opinion (*He differed with her on the question*). DISPUTE and DISSENT share the sense of differing in opinion and saying so. *Dispute* implies disagreement expressed in debate or argument. *Dissent* suggests formal opposition to prevailing opinions.
Antonym: **agree.**

disagreeable See **unpleasant.**

disappointment *n.* **discontent, disgruntlement, dissatisfaction, letdown, regret.**
Core meaning: Unhappiness caused by the failures of one's hopes or expectations (*not getting the position was a disappointment*).

disapprove *v.* **censure, criticize, deprecate.**

These verbs are used to signify dissatisfaction or rejection. DISAPPROVE, the most general, often means simply to have an unfavorable opinion (*He disapproved of her smoking*), though it is also used in the sense "to refuse to approve" (*The faculty disapproved his request for an extension*). CENSURE implies the expression of strong disapproval: *The press censured the mayor.* To CRITICIZE is both to find fault with (*Newspapers criticized the tax bill*) and to voice criticism (*Jack seldom criticizes or praises*). DEPRECATE also implies the expression of disapproval, often with overtones of regret: *He deprecated the use of force to quell civil disturbances.*
Antonym: **approve.**

disaster *n.* **calamity, cataclysm, catastrophe, debacle, holocaust.**

DISASTER and its synonyms refer to grave occurrences having destructive results. *Disaster* generally implies great destruction, hardship, or loss of life, while CALAMITY emphasizes distress, grief, and suffering more than widespread destruction. A CATASTROPHE is a great and sudden calamity; the term especially stresses the sense of tragic outcome with irreparable loss. CATACLYSM refers to a sudden upheaval that brings an earthshaking change—physical, as an earthquake, or social, as a war. A DEBACLE is a sudden, disastrous collapse, downfall, or defeat. HOLOCAUST implies great or total destruction, especially by fire.

disbelieve *v.* **reject.**

DISBELIEVE, the more general of these terms, can simply imply withholding belief; it may also suggest—as REJECT invariably does—an active, conscious refusal to give credence: *The jury disbelieved* (or *rejected*) *his testimony.*
Antonym: **believe.**

discernible See **perceptible.**

discharge See **fulfill.**

discipline See **punish.**

---

disclaimer See **denial.**

discontent See **disappointment.**

discontinue See **stop.**

discontinuous *adj.* **intermittent.**
These describe what is marked by breaks or interruptions. DISCONTINUOUS is the more general term; it applies whether there is a single break or many: *a discontinuous line.* INTERMITTENT describes what stops and starts at intervals: *intermittent noises.*
Antonym: **continuous.**

discord *n.* **clash, conflict, dissension.**
These nouns denote a condition marked by disagreement. DISCORD implies sharply opposing positions within a group, preventing united action: *strife and discord within the government.* CLASH suggests sharp conflict involving ideas or interests: *a clash of cultures; a clash between political parties.* CONFLICT in this sense suggests antagonism that results in open hostility or divisiveness: *a personality conflict.* DISSENSION implies difference of opinion causing unrest that disrupts unity within a group: *Dissension prevented the union from accepting the fair settlement.*
Antonym: **harmony.**

discount See **belittle.**

discourage *v.* **1. depress.**
DISCOURAGE and DEPRESS share the meaning of making gloomy or less hopeful: *The sad news depressed everyone. The magnitude of the problem discouraged her.*
Antonym: **encourage.**
2. dissuade.
DISCOURAGE and DISSUADE both imply efforts to prevent someone from doing something: *Friends discouraged him from taking the trip. His invitation dissuaded her from leaving early.*
Antonym: **encourage.**

discourse See **speech.**

---

discourteous See **impolite.**

discretion See **prudence.**

disdain See **despise.**

disdainful See **proud.**

disengage See **detach.**

disfavor *n.* disgrace, disrepute.
These denote the condition of being held in low regard. DISFAVOR, the weakest of the terms, suggests mere lack of favor or approval: *His suggestion met with disfavor.* DISGRACE implies strong and general disapproval: *could not stand the disgrace of a divorce.* DISREPUTE involves the absence or loss of reputation: *held in disrepute because of shady business dealings.*
Antonym: **favor.**

disgrace 1. See **disfavor.** 2. See **dishonor.**

disgruntlement See **disappointment.**

disgust See **repel.**

dishonest See **false.**

dishonesty *n.* deceitfulness, duplicity, lying, mendacity, untruthfulness.
All of these nouns refer to a lack of honesty or integrity. DISHONESTY is the most general. DECEITFULNESS implies a deliberate effort to mislead by falsehood or by concealment of truth. DUPLICITY is both more formal and more emphatic than *deceitfulness;* it often connotes treachery. LYING and MENDACITY, which comes from Latin, both contain blunt accusations of untruth, but *mendacity* suggests a chronic inclination. UNTRUTHFULNESS is a word closely related to *lying* and *mendacity* but softer in tone.
Antonym: **honesty.**

dishonor *n.* disgrace, disrepute, ignominy, infamy, obloquy, odium, opprobrium, shame.
These nouns refer to the condition of being held in low regard. DISHONOR involves loss of esteem, respect, or repu-

tation: *the dishonor of impeachment.* DISGRACE implies strong and general disapproval: *a coward who lived in disgrace.* DISREPUTE denotes the absence or loss of a good name but is weaker then *dishonor* in suggesting descent from previous high regard: *held in disrepute for his bad conduct.* IGNOMINY often implies public contempt: *the ignominy of failure.* INFAMY is public disgrace or notoriety: *the infamy of the attack on Pearl Harbor.* OBLOQUY implies being subjected to abuse and vilification: *a deposed dictator faced with obloquy.* ODIUM adds to *disgrace* the sense of being widely detested: *the odium of the traffic in drugs.* OPPROBRIUM is the condition of being condemned with scorn: *a term of opprobrium.* SHAME suggests loss of status as a result of a moral offense: *felt shame for the crime he had committed.*
Antonym: honor.

disingenuous See **underhand.**

disinterest *n.* apathy, indifference.
DISINTEREST is merely lack of interest. APATHY is lack of interest in things that are generally found interesting, exciting, or moving: *viewed the great painting with complete apathy.* INDIFFERENCE is lack of any particular interest or marked feeling one way or another: *Whether he took the trip or not was a matter of indifference to him.*
Antonym: interest.

disinterested See **apathetic.**

dislike See **distaste.**

disloyal 1. See **faithless. 2.** See **false.**

dismal See **gloomy.**

disorderly *adj.* messy, sloppy, untidy.
These describe what is not neat or tidy: *a disorderly room; messy old clothes; a sloppy dresser; an untidy appearance.*
Antonym: neat.

disparage See **belittle.**

disparate See **different.**

dispatch See **send.**

dispel See **scatter.**

disperse See **scatter.**

display See **show.**

displease *v.* **annoy, offend.**
To DISPLEASE is to cause dissatisfaction, dislike, or disapproval: *an arrogant attitude that displeased his supervisor.*
ANNOY suggests bother or irritation: *Your constant complaints annoy your colleagues.* OFFEND applies to what causes anger, resentment, or annoyance: *Her brusqueness offends many people.*
Antonym: **please.**

dispose *v.* **bend, bias, incline, predispose, sway.**
Core meaning: To influence or be influenced in a certain direction (*Her openness disposed me to trust her*).

disposition *n.* **character, nature, personality, temperament.**
These terms all refer to the sum of traits that identify a person. DISPOSITION is approximately equivalent to one's usual mood, attitude, or frame of mind: *an affectionate disposition.* CHARACTER emphasizes moral and ethical characteristics: *a man of bad character.* NATURE suggests those fundamental qualities that determine characteristic behavior or emotional response in people: *It goes against her nature to be dishonest.* PERSONALITY is the sum of distinctive qualities and traits of a person that give him his own individuality: *a man of forceful personality.* TEMPERAMENT applies to the manner in which a person thinks, behaves, and reacts in general: *a nervous temperament.*

disprove *v.* **rebut, refute.**
These all share the sense of establishing that something is false, invalid, or in error by the presentation of opposing evidence or arguments: *disprove a theory; rebut legal arguments; refute a statement.* To *rebut* can also imply weakening the effect of an argument, contention, position, etc.,

without necessarily succeeding: *In a formal debate each side is given an opportunity to rebut the views of the opposition.*
Antonym: **prove.**

dispute 1. See **argue. 2.** See **disagree.**

disregard See **neglect.**

disrepute 1. See **disfavor. 2.** See **dishonor.**

disrespectful *adj.* **irreverent, uncivil.**
Core meaning: Having or showing a lack of respect (*disrespectful of government protocol*).

disrobe See **undress.**

dissatisfaction See **disappointment.**

dissection See **analysis.**

dissemble See **pretend.**

disseminate See **advertise.**

dissension See **discord.**

dissent See **disagree.**

dissipate 1. See **scatter. 2.** See **waste.**

dissolute See **immoral.**

dissuade See **discourage.**

distant See **far.**

distaste *n.* **aversion, dislike.**
These denote feelings of disinclination. DISLIKE is the most general of the three and can often be used interchangeably with the others. The implications of DISTASTE vary, ranging from mild dislike to repugnance. AVERSION suggests strong dislike bordering on repugnance.

distinct See **clear.**

distinctive See **characteristic.**

distraught See **upset.**

distress *n.* agony, hurt, misery, pain.
Core meaning: A state of suffering (*felt great distress over the death in the family*).

district See **area.**

distrust *n.* doubt, suspicion.
These denote a lack of trust or belief that something is true, reliable, etc.: *She regarded my proposal with distrust. He is in doubt over the existence of a supreme being. Your excuses inspire suspicion.*
Antonym: **trust.**

divergent See **different.**

diverse See **different.**

diversion See **recreation.**

diversity See **variety.**

divert See **amuse.**

divide See **separate.**

docket See **program.**

dogged See **obstinate.**

dogmatic See **dictatorial.**

dominant *adj.* predominant, preponderant.
All of these words describe what surpasses all others of its kind in power or importance. DOMINANT applies to what has the most influence or control (*the dominant person in a partnership*) or is unmistakably outstanding (*the dominant building in the skyline.*) PREDOMINANT has the same meanings as *dominant,* but it often suggests superiority that is only temporary (*the predominant city in a changing nation*). PREPONDERANT describes what is greater in weight, number, etc.: *A preponderant number of people voted for the bill, and it passed.*
Antonym: **subordinate.**

dormancy See **abeyance.**

dormant See **inactive.**

dote See **like.**

double *adj.* **binary, dual, duple, duplex, twofold.**
Core meaning: Composed of two parts or things (*a double window*).

double-cross See **deceive.**

doubt *n.* **misgiving, mistrust, suspicion.**
All of these denote a lack of certainty in the honesty, dependability, or power of someone. Doubt is the most general: *had doubt about Jack's willingness to help.* MISGIVING suggests a feeling of apprehension: *had misgivings about lending him her car.* MISTRUST implies a lack of trust: *mistrust of strangers.* SUSPICION, stronger than *mistrust,* implies the feeling that something is wrong: *eyed the stranger with suspicion.* See also **distrust; uncertainty.**
Antonym: **confidence.**

dour See **gloomy.**

douse See **extinguish.**

downgrade See **belittle.**

draft *n.* **outline, rough, skeleton, sketch.**
Core meaning: A preliminary plan or version (*a draft of the report*).

drain See **waste.**

drawback See **disadvantage.**

dreary See **gloomy.**

dress *v.* **attire, clothe.**
These verbs denote putting clothes on. DRESS is the least specific and most widely applicable: *He dressed the baby. She rarely dressed before breakfast.* CLOTHE often suggests providing clothes as well as putting them on: *It is difficult to feed and clothe such a large family.* ATTIRE suggests fine or formal clothing: *an emperor attired in ceremonial robes.*
Antonym: **undress.**

drill See **teach.**

drive See **ambition.**

---

drop 1. See **fall**. 2. See **lower**.

drudgery See **work**.

drunk *adj.* **inebriated, intoxicated, tipsy.**
DRUNK and its synonyms apply to people whose coordination and thinking are impaired by too much alcohol. *Drunk,* the most general, and INTOXICATED, a more formal word, mean the same thing; both can also be used to describe immoderate emotion: *drunk with power; intoxicated lovers.* INEBRIATED is rarely used figuratively. TIPSY means "slightly drunk."
Antonym: **sober.**

dual See **double**.

dull 1. *adj.* **dense, dumb, obtuse, slow, stupid.**
All of these describe persons who learn or understand slowly. When they are used in this sense, they are interchangeable, although DUMB is informal in tone and OBTUSE is formal: *brilliant thoughts wasted on a dull audience; a dense, confused pupil; a dumb child; too obtuse to see what the teacher meant; a man who was slow to grasp the drift of the conversation; a stupid boy. Dull, dumb,* and *stupid* can also apply to what is boring, silly, or unintelligent: *a dull book; a dumb play; a stupid solution to the problem.*
Antonym: **clever.**
2. *adj.* **blunt.**
DULL and BLUNT describe objects that are not sharp. *Dull* usually implies that sharpness has been lost through use: *a dull blade. Blunt* more often refers to what is thick-edged by design: *The murder weapon must have been a blunt instrument.*
Antonym: **sharp.**
3. *v.* See **deaden**.

dumb See **dull**.

duple See **double**.

duplex See **double**.

duplicitous See **underhand**.

---

drop / easy

duplicity See **dishonesty.**

duration See **continuation.**

duress See **force.**

dusky See **dark.**

dwindle See **decrease.**

dynamic See **active.**

early *adj.* **premature.**
Both of these words apply to what appears or takes place before its usual or expected time: *a few early robins hopping in the snow; a premature death. Premature* can also suggest undue haste: *a premature judgment.*
Antonym: **late.**

earn *v.* **deserve, get, merit, rate, win.**
Core meaning: To receive for one's labor or efforts (*earned a large salary*).

earnings See **wage(s).**

ease *n.* **facility.**
Ease and FACILITY share the sense of freedom from difficulty, hard work, or great effort: *play tennis with ease; read music with facility. Facility* emphasizes aptitude: *a facility for learning languages.*
Antonym: **effort.**

ease off See **relent.**

easy *adj.* **effortless, facile, light, simple.**
EASY and its synonyms describe what does not require or show much difficulty or expenditure of energy. *Easy* applies both to tasks requiring little exertion (*Dusting the house is easy*) and to persons who are not demanding (*A teacher who always gives high grades is an easy marker*). FACILE and EFFORTLESS stress aptitude and fluency: *a facile speaker; an effortless performance. Facile,* however, sometimes has unfavorable connotations, as of haste, lack of care, lack of sincerity, superficiality, etc.: *a facile solution to the problem.* LIGHT is applied to tasks or chores that involve little

effort: *light housekeeping*. S<small>IMPLE</small> describes what is not complex and hence not intellectually demanding: *a simple game*.
Antonym: **difficult.**

eccentric See **strange.**

eccentricity *n*. **idiosyncrasy, quirk.**
E<small>CCENTRICITY</small>, <small>IDIOSYNCRASY</small>, and <small>QUIRK</small> refer to peculiarity of behavior. *Eccentricity* implies deviation from what is normal, customary, or expected; the term may even suggest a disordered mind. An *idiosyncrasy* is more often such a deviation viewed as peculiar to the temperament of an individualistic person and serving as an identifying trait. *Quirk,* a milder term, merely suggests an odd trait or mannerism.

economical *adj*. **frugal, provident, prudent, thrifty.**
Core meaning: Careful in the use of material resources (*an economical shopper*).

edge See **border.**

edict See **law.**

educate See **teach.**

effect *n*. **consequence, issue, outcome, result, resultant.**
Core meaning: Something brought about by a cause (*high unemployment rates that are effect of the recession*).

effeminate See **female.**

effort *n*. **exertion, strain.**
These denote the use of physical or mental energy for the purpose of achieving a desired result. E<small>FFORT</small> has general application: *making an effort to get up; made an effort to move the piano*. E<small>XERTION</small> and <small>STRAIN</small> refer to major efforts, but *strain* often suggests excessive, hence debilitating, use of strength or will power: *Weightlifting involves exertion, but be careful to avoid strain.*
Antonym: **ease.**

effortless See **easy.**

egotistic See **selfish.**

elaborate *adj.* **fancy, ornate.**
ELABORATE applies to what is planned or made with great attention to numerous details; it often—but not always—connotes richness and luxury: *an elaborate dinner; an elaborate ball costume.* FANCY in this sense implies intricate and decorative design: *fancy clothes; a fancy bedroom.* ORNATE specifically refers to what is heavily, sometimes excessively, decorated: *ornate carving; an ornate apartment.* *Antonym:* **plain.**

élan See **spirit.**

elastic See **flexible.**

elderly See **old.**

elect See **choose.**

elective See **optional.**

elegant *adj.* **exquisite, graceful.**
Core meaning: So tastefully beautiful as to draw attention and admiration (*an elegant ball gown; an elegant lady*).

elevated See **high.**

eligibility See **qualification.**

elucidate See **clarify.**

elude See **avoid.**

emancipate See **free.**

embrace See **accept.**

eminent See **famous.**

emolument See **wage(s).**

employment See **work.**

empty *adj.* **blank, vacant.**
These three describe what contains nothing, literally and figuratively. EMPTY is the most general in its application: *an empty box; an empty room.* Figuratively it implies a lack of

purpose (*an empty life*), value or meaning (*empty promises*), and the like. BLANK also applies to what contains or is covered by nothing (*a blank wall*); figuratively it describes what lacks ideas or expression (*a blank mind; a blank stare*). VACANT is used to describe what is not occupied or taken: *a vacant mansion; a vacant position*. Figuratively it suggests lack of expression: *a vacant stare*.
Antonym: **full.**

enchant See **attract.**

encircle See **surround.**

enclose See **surround.**

encourage *v.* **1. hearten.**
ENCOURAGE and HEARTEN share the meaning of lending hope, confidence, or courage: *The doctor's report encouraged the patient's family. Her lawyer's presence heartened the nervous witness.*
Antonym: **discourage.**
2. urge.
ENCOURAGE and URGE both imply efforts to persuade: *Her husband encouraged her to take the bar examination. The Red Cross urges people to donate blood.*
Antonym: **discourage.**
3. See promote.

end *v.* **close, complete, conclude, finish, terminate.**
These words mean to bring or come to a stopping point or limit. FINISH and COMPLETE suggest reaching the final stage of a task, course, project, etc., and thus often stress accomplishment: *finish a novel; started but never finished; complete a voyage; completed work on his income tax. Complete* can also imply the addition of something missing or needed: *completing an employment application by filling in the blanks.* CLOSE applies to stopping an action, either when it is completed (*The church service closed with a benediction*) or when it cannot be continued (*Lack of support caused the play to close*). CONCLUDE and TERMINATE suggest

formality: *I suggest we terminate this discussion, and I am afraid we conclude on a note of hostility.* END emphasizes finality: *a nice way to end a trip.*
Antonym: begin.

endorse See **approve.**

endurance See **continuation.**

enduring See **permanent.**

energetic See **active.**

enfold See **wrap.**

engage See **book.**

enigmatic See **ambiguous.**

enjoy See **like.**

enjoyment See **joy.**

enlarge See **increase.**

enmity *n.* animosity, animus, antagonism, antipathy, hostility. *Core meaning:* Deep-seated hatred (*felt bitter enmity toward the oppressor*).

enormous See **big.**

enough See **sufficient.**

enterprise See **ambition.**

entertain See **amuse.**

entertainment See **recreation.**

enthusiasm See **passion.**

entice See **seduce.**

envelop See **wrap.**

envision See **foresee.**

epoch See **age.**

equal See **same.**

equality See **equivalence.**

equanimity *n.* **composure, nonchalance, serenity.**
EQUANIMITY is the condition or quality of being calm and even-tempered as a characteristic state. COMPOSURE is calmness and steadiness that suggest the exercise of self-control and maintenance of dignity. NONCHALANCE is the real or apparent absence not only of agitation but also of concern, usually shown by an indifferent or casual air. SERENITY is peace and tranquillity of nature that suggest immunity to agitation or turmoil.

equivalence *n.* **equality, par, parity.**
Core meaning: The state of being equivalent (*Einstein asserted the equivalence of mass and energy*).

equivalent See **same.**

equivocal See **ambiguous.**

era See **age.**

eradicate See **abolish.**

erase See **cancel.**

erratic See **capricious.**

erroneous See **false.**

error *n.* **mistake, oversight.**
All three of these terms refer to what is not in accordance with accuracy, truth, right, or propriety. ERROR and MISTAKE may often be used interchangeably: *an error* (or *mistake*) *in subtraction. Mistake* often implies poor judgment: *made the mistake of buying a fur coat when she had to borrow money to pay the rent.* An OVERSIGHT is an unintentional omission or faulty act.

ersatz See **artificial.**

erudition See **knowledge.**

escape See **avoid.**

escort See **accompany.**

esprit See **spirit.**

essence See **heart.**

essential See **necessary.**

establish 1. See **create. 2.** See **prove.**

establishmentarian See **conventional.**

estate See **holding(s).**

esteem See **favor.**

estrange *v.* **alienate, disaffect.**
These verbs refer to the disruption of love, friendship, or loyalty. ESTRANGE and ALIENATE apply when a harmonious relationship has given way to indifference or hostility. *Estrange* is most often used to describe married people and usually implies separation: *Through years of quarreling over money, the couple became estranged. Alienate* is often used in the same way but need not be: *He alienated everyone with his crude behavior.* DISAFFECT usually refers to the disruption or undermining of loyalty or allegiance within the membership of a group: *The revelations about the politician's shady deals disaffected his constituency. Antonym:* **reconcile.**

estrangement See **breach.**

eternal See **permanent.**

eternalize See **immortalize.**

ethical See **moral.**

ethos See **psychology.**

etiquette See **manners.**

even See **level.**

eventual See **last.**

eventuality See **possibility.**

everyday See **familiar.**

evil See **malevolent.**

exactitude See **veracity.**

examination See **analysis.**

exceed See **surpass.**

excel See **surpass.**

excellent *adj.* **capital, fine, first-class, great, prime, splendid, super** (*Slang*), **superb, topflight, topnotch.**
Core meaning: Exceptionally good of its kind (*an excellent picture; did an excellent job*).

excess *n.* **superfluity, surplus.**
These all denote the condition of exceeding what is normal or sufficient. EXCESS is the most general in this sense: *overcome by an excess of grief; enough oranges, an excess of apples.* SUPERFLUITY suggests abundance beyond need: *a superfluity of punctuation.* SURPLUS focuses on the amount or quantity beyond what is needed or used: *a surplus of coffee for export.*
Antonym: **deficiency.**

excite See **provoke.**

excusable See **justifiable.**

excuse See **pardon.**

execute See **fulfill.**

executive *adj.* **administrative, managerial**
Core meaning: Of, for, or relating to administration (*an executive secretary; an executive committee*).

exertion See **effort.**

exhaust See **waste.**

exhibit See **show.**

exhort See **urge.**

exigency See **need.**

exonerate See **vindicate.**

exotic See **foreign.**

expand 1. *v.* **swell.**
These words mean to increase in size, volume, etc. EXPAND, the more general, stresses growth or development

(*expanded her knowledge of French*) or an increase in physical dimensions (*Gases expand when heated*). SWELL often implies expansion beyond normal or usual limits: *The injured ankle swelled.*
Antonym: contract.
2. See **spread.**

expansive See **broad.**

expedite *v.* accelerate, hasten, speed.
These share the meaning of easing and helping progress along. EXPEDITE refers to action that makes for the quick and efficient accomplishment of a given project or purpose: *expedite a loan application.* ACCELERATE, HASTEN, and SPEED all suggest stepped-up activity, growth, progress, or production; *hasten* often adds the suggestion that time is short, while *speed* focuses on actual rapid movement: *measures to accelerate a tax reform; hastened the decision to move; speed delivery of the consignment.*
Antonym: delay.

expeditious See **fast.**

expend See **waste.**

expensive *adj.* costly.
EXPENSIVE and COSTLY describe what is high in price: *an expensive ring; costly jewelry.* They also have a figurative sense meaning "involving great loss or sacrifice": *an expensive* (or *costly*) *victory.*
Antonym: cheap.

expert See **professional.**

expertise *n.* ability, command, craft, expertness, mastery, proficiency.
Core meaning: Natural or acquired facility in a specific activity (*tremendous managerial expertise*).

expertness See **expertise.**

expire See **die.**

explain See **clarify.**

explanation *n*. account, justification, rationale, rationalization, reason.
Core meaning: A statement of causes or motive (*an explanation of the purpose of the project*).

explicit *adj*. definite, specific.
What is EXPLICIT is expressed with precision and in such a way that misunderstanding is difficult or impossible: *gave explicit instructions about selling her property*. DEFINITE refers to what is clearly defined and exact: *a definite plan; a definite time*. SPECIFIC describes what is precisely set forth and complete with any necessary details: *specific questions; specific qualifications*.
Antonym: implicit.

explode *v*. blast, blow up, burst, detonate.
Core meaning: To release energy violently and suddenly, especially with a loud noise (*a bomb that exploded in midair*).

expose See **show**.

express See **say**.

expunge See **cancel**.

exquisite See **elegant**.

extemporize See **improvise**.

extend See **spread**.

extended See **long**.

extensive See **broad**.

exterminate See **abolish**.

extinct See **dead**.

extinguish *v*. douse, quench.
These are compared as they refer to putting out a fire or light: *the wind extinguishing the candles; doused the campfire; dousing the lights in the living room; quenched the lamp*. See also **abolish**.
Antonym: ignite.

---

extirpate See **abolish.**

extraordinary See **uncommon.**

extreme See **intense.**

fabricate See **make.**

fabulous *adj.* amazing, astonishing, incredible, marvelous, miraculous, phenomenal, stupendous, unbelievable, wonderful, wondrous.
Core meaning: So remarkable as to cause disbelief (*the fabulous endurance of a long-distance runner*).

face *v.* brave, meet.
These share the meaning of confronting or dealing with something boldly or courageously. FACE and MEET are the most neutral: *She has faced danger many times. He meets adversity with fortitude.* BRAVE more strongly stresses self-control and resolve in the face of danger: *soldiers braving a bombardment by the enemy.*
Antonym: avoid.

facile 1. See **easy.** 2. See **glib.**

facility See **ease.**

faction See **combine.**

fail *v.* miscarry.
These two denote lack of success in a chosen activity or enterprise. FAIL applies generally: *He succeeded where all others had failed. The League of Nations failed to establish world peace.* MISCARRY means to go wrong or to be unsuccessful; it is a somewhat more formal word: *Our plans have all miscarried.*
Antonym: succeed.

failing See **weakness.**

fair *adj.* impartial, just.
FAIR and its synonyms describe persons, thoughts, and deeds that show proper and equal consideration for all parties and factors concerned in a matter. *Fair* has the widest

application. Impartial suggests lack of prejudice and freedom from favoritism or preconceived opinion: *an impartial judge*. Just implies honesty and impartiality (*a just decision*) and conformity to legal and ethical principles (*a just punishment*).
Antonym: **unfair.**

fairly *adv.* **impartially, justly.**
Core meaning: In a just way (*settled the dispute fairly*).

faith See **trust.**

faithful *adj.* **constant, loyal, staunch, steadfast.**
These refer to what is firm and unchanging in attachment to a person, cause, or the like. Faithful, constant, and loyal stress long and undeviating attachment: *faithful service; a constant friend; loyal followers*. Steadfast and especially staunch suggest both strong attachment and willingness to lend support when it is needed: *steadfast believers; a staunch ally*. See also **true.**
Antonym: **faithless.**

faithless *adj.* **disloyal, false, treacherous.**
These refer to what is unworthy of trust or in violation of it. Faithless implies failure to honor obligations or to fulfill promises: *a faithless husband*. Disloyal applies to those who do not give allegiance where it is due: *a traitor, disloyal to king and country*. False refers to persons who are neither loyal nor dutiful: *a false friend*. Treacherous applies to persons who knowingly betray a confidence or trust: *a treacherous ally*.
Antonym: **faithful.**

fake See **improvise.**

faker See **impostor.**

fall *v.* **descend, drop.**
These verbs denote a moving downward; fall and drop in particular have many extended senses. *Fall* often applies to descent caused by the pull of gravity: *The bombs fell, and the flames sparkled*. *Drop* implies falling or letting fall from

a higher to a lower place or position: *A penny dropped from his pocket. She dropped a dish on the floor. Fall* and *drop* are also used figuratively to indicate a decrease, as in value or intensity: *Prices on the stock exchange are falling* (or *dropping*). *Her fever dropped* (or *fell*). To DESCEND is simply to come or go down (*an airplane descending for the landing; descended the stairs*); it can also mean to arrive in an overwhelming manner (*relatives who descended on us for the weekend*), to come down from an origin (*an emperor descended from the gods*), and to pass by inheritance (*His estate descended to his daughters*).
Antonym: rise.

fallacious *adj.* **illogical, invalid, sophistic, specious, spurious.** *Core meaning:* Containing errors in reasoning (*fallacious logic*).

fall back See **back.**

false *adj.* **1. erroneous, inaccurate, incorrect, wrong.** These describe what is in error or contrary to fact or truth: *a false statement; a false answer; an erroneous conclusion; an inaccurate description; incorrect figures; a wrong answer.*
Antonym: true.
2. dishonest, untruthful. These words describe what shows or results from falseness or fraud: *a false accusation; a dishonest answer; untruthful testimony.*
Antonym: true.
3. deceitful. These two describe what is calculated to mislead: *false promises; deceitful advertising.*
Antonym: true.
4. disloyal, treacherous, unfaithful. These terms apply to persons who lack loyalty or betray a trust: *a false friend; a disloyal servant; a treacherous lawyer; an unfaithful wife.* See also **faithless.**
Antonym: true.

falsehood See **lie.**

falsity See **lie.**

falter See **hesitate.**

famed See **famous.**

familiar *adj.* **common, customary, everyday, frequent, ordinary, usual.**
FAMILIAR and its synonyms describe what is well known and encountered often: *a familiar sight; a familiar excuse; a common weed; the customary fee; an everyday occurrence; a frequent visitor; a dress of an ordinary size; the usual traffic jam during rush hour.* See also **common.**
Antonym: **strange.**

famous *adj.* **eminent, famed, renowned.**
These words describe what has attracted widespread and often favorable notice. FAMOUS and FAMED are the most neutral: *a famous soprano; a famous book; a famed author; a famed ocean liner.* EMINENT describes what is distinguished or outstanding in some respect (*an eminent scientist*); RENOWNED, what is widely honored and acclaimed (*a renowned orator; a renowned university*).
Antonym: **obscure.**

fancy **1.** See **elaborate.** **2.** See **imagination.** **3.** See **like.**

fantastic *adj.* **bizarre, grotesque.**
FANTASTIC and its synonyms apply to what is very strange or strikingly unusual. *Fantastic* often describes what seems to have slight relation to the real world because of its strangeness or extravagance: *all sorts of fantastic figures and designs.* BIZARRE stresses oddness of character or appearance that shocks or fascinates: *a bizarre hat.* GROTESQUE refers mainly to what is ludicrously distorted or odd in appearance or aspect: *a grotesque monster.*

fantasy See **imagination.**

far *adj.* **distant, remote.**
All of these refer to what is widely removed in space or, less often, in time. DISTANT can be used with a figure to indicate

a specific separation (*20 miles distant*), or it can indicate an indefinite but sizable separation (*the distant past; distant lands*). FAR implies a wide but indefinite distance: *a far country*. REMOTE suggests isolation as well as distance: *a remote Arctic island*.
Antonym: **near.**

fascinate See **attract.**

fashion 1. *n.* **style, vogue.**
All of these nouns refer to the prevailing or preferred practice in dress, manners, behavior, etc., at a given time. FASHION, the broadest term, applies to custom or practice that follows the conventions determined by those viewed as leaders: *the latest fashion.* STYLE is sometimes used interchangeably with *fashion* (*the latest style*), but *style* can also suggest what is elegant, distinguished, etc. (*living in style*). VOGUE is applied to what is fashionable or stylish at a given time (*Tiffany glass was in vogue in the early 1900's*); frequently the term suggests enthusiastic acceptance of something for a rather short period (*novels that enjoyed a vogue in the 1930's*). See also **method.**
2. *v.* See **make.**

fast *adj.* **expeditious, hasty, quick, rapid, speedy, swift.**
FAST, QUICK, RAPID, SPEEDY, and SWIFT describe what acts, moves, happens, or is accomplished in a brief space of time: *a fast runner; a fast train; a quick trip; rapid progress; a speedy reply; a swift response.* EXPEDITIOUS combines the senses of speed and efficiency: *The most expeditious transportation will be used for mail deliveries.* HASTY suggests hurried action and often lack of care and thought: *a hasty judgment.*
Antonym: **slow.**

fasten See **attach.**

fat *adj.* **chubby, corpulent, obese, plump, stout.**
These mean having an abundance of flesh, often to excess. FAT, CORPULENT, and OBESE always imply excessive bodily fat: *our fat friend; a corpulent executive; an obese patient.*

CHUBBY and PLUMP suggest pleasing roundness: *a chubby face; a plump figure.* STOUT describes a thickset, bulky figure: *a stout, stern-faced matron.*
Antonym: **thin.**

fatal *adj.* **deadly, lethal, mortal.**
FATAL describes conditions, circumstances, or events that have produced death or are destined inevitably to cause death or dire consequences: *a fatal illness; a fatal blow.* DEADLY applies to persons or things capable of killing or, in figurative usage, of producing severe hardship: *a deadly weapon; deadly strain.* MORTAL can describe a person likely to cause death (*a mortal enemy*) or a condition or action that has in fact produced death (*a mortal wound*). LETHAL refers to something that acts or can act as a sure agent of death: *a lethal dose of a drug; a lethal weapon.*

fate *n.* **destiny, kismet, lot, predestination.**
Core meaning: That which is inevitably destined (*Her fate was to lead a nation*).

fatigue See **bore.**

faultless See **perfect.**

faulty See **imperfect.**

favor *n.* **esteem, regard.**
These nouns denote the condition of holding or being held in good repute. FAVOR implies approval or support: *Her paper was received with favor. The idea of a national health plan is gaining favor with many legislators.* ESTEEM in addition suggests respect: *His accomplishments won him universal esteem.* REGARD adds the connotation of affection: *showed regard for her parents.*
Antonym: **disfavor.**

favorable *adj.* **auspicious, propitious.**
These three describe what is beneficial or points to a successful outcome. FAVORABLE has the widest application: *favorable winds; a favorable book review; a favorable impression; favorable signs of recovery.* AUSPICIOUS applies to what shows signs of a successful result: *an auspicious be-*

ginning for the business venture. PROPITIOUS suggests time, place, or circumstance considered as contributors to success: *a propitious spot for peace talks; a climate propitious to the growth of orchids.*
Antonym: **unfavorable.**

fearless See **brave.**

feasible See **possible.**

federation See **union.**

fee See **wage(s).**

feeling *n.* **1. idea, impression, intuition, suspicion.**
Core meaning: Intuitive cognition (*I have a feeling we'll get the contract*).
2. See **opinion.**

feign See **pretend.**

fellowship See **union.**

female *adj.* **effeminate, feminine, ladylike, womanly.**
FEMALE and FEMININE are essentially classifying terms. *Female* merely categorizes by sex; it is also applicable to animals, plants, and even things: *the female population; a female rabbit; a female socket. Feminine* can be used to categorize (*the feminine lead in a drama*), but it can also describe traits, good and bad, considered characteristic of women (*feminine allure; feminine wiles*). EFFEMINATE is almost always restricted in reference to men and things; it indicates lack of manliness or strength: *an effeminate walk.* LADYLIKE applies to what befits women of good breeding: *ladylike behavior.* WOMANLY describes things that become a woman: *womanly grace.*
Antonym: **male.**

feminine See **female.**

ferocious See **cruel.**

fertile *adj.* **fruitful, prolific.**
These all describe what has the power to produce or support crops, plants, and offspring; figuratively they apply to

what suggests growth and abundance, as of ideas, thoughts, and works. FERTILE is the most general term: *a fertile field; a fertile imagination.* FRUITFUL stresses what is conducive to productivity and beneficial results: *a fruitful rain; a fruitful discussion.* PROLIFIC emphasizes large and rapid output (*Rabbits are prolific animals*); used figuratively it is sometimes disparaging (*a prolific writer who turned out a novel a month*).
Antonym: **barren.**

fervor See **passion.**

festivity See **gaiety.**

feverish See **hot.**

fickle See **capricious.**

fiction See **lie.**

fiddle *v.* **fidget, fool, monkey, play, tinker, toy, trifle.**
Core meaning: To move one's fingers or hands in a nervous or aimless fashion (*fiddled with the papers on her desk*).

fidelity See **veracity.**

fidget See **fiddle.**

fiery See **hot.**

fight 1. See **conflict.** 2. See **repel.** 3. See **withstand.**

figure See **add.**

filthy See **dirty.**

final See **last.**

find *v.* **recover.**
As a synonym of *find,* RECOVER denotes getting back or regaining. *The police recovered the stolen car.* FIND shares this meaning (*Did you ever find your keys?*), but it is also used to mean coming upon something by chance or accident (*found the keys on the table*) and looking for and discovering (*Help me find my wallet*).
Antonym: **lose.**

fine See **excellent.**

finish See **end.**

firm See **hard.**

first *adj.* **foremost, inaugural, initial.**
FIRST and its synonyms refer to what marks a beginning. *First* itself applies to what comes before all others, as in a series, sequence, or any collection of like things: *the first month of the year; the first chapter in the book.* FOREMOST refers to what is first in rank or position and therefore leading: *the world's foremost authority on marine biology.* INAUGURAL is applied to what marks a formal beginning or introduction: *an inaugural flight.* INITIAL describes what occurs at the very beginning: *The initial reaction to the plan was unenthusiastic.*
Antonym: **last.**

first-class See **excellent.**

fissure See **breach.**

fit See **suitable.**

fitness See **qualification.**

fitting See **suitable.**

flagrant *adj.* **glaring, gross, rank.**
These refer to what is outstandingly bad, evil, erroneous, etc. FLAGRANT and GLARING both stress that what gives cause for concern or offense is unmistakable and conspicuous. *Glaring* is somewhat more emphatic in suggesting what cannot escape notice (*a glaring error*), but *flagrant* often implies that something is deliberately shocking (*a flagrant violation of the rules*). GROSS emphasizes that an offense or failing is so extreme that it cannot be overlooked or condoned: *a gross miscarriage of justice.* RANK, like *flagrant,* sometimes implies an affront to decency; it is often used as an intensifying term with the force of "complete" or "utter": *a rank amateur.* See also **outrageous.**

flash See **moment.**

flat 1. See **level.** 2. See **stale.**

---

flavor *n.* **aroma, atmosphere, savor.**
Core meaning: A distinctive yet intangible quality deemed typical of a given thing (*a city imbued with the flavor of the Orient*).

flawless See **perfect.**

fleeting See **temporary.**

flexible *adj.* **elastic, pliant, supple.**
FLEXIBLE and its synonyms describe what literally can be bent or what figuratively can undergo change or modification. *Flexible* and PLIANT are closely related in meaning: *flexible wire; a flexible administrator; flexible plans; pliant material; a pliant personality.* What is ELASTIC returns to its original or normal shape or arrangement after being stretched, compressed, etc. (*an elastic band*), can adapt or be adapted to differing circumstances (*an elastic clause in the contract*), and is quick to recover or revive, as from illness, misfortune, etc. (*an elastic spirit*). SUPPLE describes what is easily bent (*supple leather*), is agile or limber (*a supple body*), or is adaptable (*a supple mind*).
Antonym: **inflexible.**

flimsy See **implausible.**

flip See **glib.**

flourish See **succeed.**

flush See **level.**

fog See **daze.**

foible See **weakness.**

follow See **obey.**

fondle See **caress.**

fondness See **love.**

fool See **fiddle.**

foolish *adj.* **preposterous, silly.**
These three describe persons, ideas, deeds, etc., that have or show a lack of good sense or judgment. FOOLISH implies

poor judgment and lack of wisdom: *a foolish young fellow; a foolish investment of time and energy*. SILLY suggests that which shows lack of intelligence, purpose, meaning, etc.: *silly mistakes; a silly question; a silly child who constantly laughed for no reason*. PREPOSTEROUS describes what is completely unreasonable, to the point of being nonsensical: *the preposterous idea of wearing a bikini during a snow-storm*.

forbear See **refrain.**

forbearing See **patient.**

forbid *v.* **ban, prohibit.**
These three verbs all imply a refusal to allow something to be done or an order that prevents someone from doing something. FORBID, the least formal, is also most often used when personal relationships are involved; it suggests that compliance is expected: *The law forbids robbery. I forbid you to go.* PROHIBIT and BAN imply prevention by law or authority: *laws to prohibit discrimination; finally banning billboards on highways.*
Antonym: **permit.**

force *n.* **coercion, constraint, duress, pressure, strength, violence.**
Core meaning: Power used to overcome resistance (*used force to obtain a confession*).

forebear See **ancestor.**

forefather See **ancestor.**

foreign *adj.* **alien, exotic.**
All these describe what is of or from another country or part of the world: *a foreign language; alien workers; exotic birds. Alien* often carries connotations of unfamiliarity or strangeness (*an alien custom*), and *exotic* of the charm of the unfamiliar (*an exotic beauty*).
Antonym: **native.**

foreknow See **foresee.**

foremost See **first.**

---

foresee *v.* anticipate, envision, foreknow, see.
Core meaning: To know in advance (*difficulties no one could foresee*).

forewarning See **warning.**

forget *v.* repress.
To FORGET is to be unable or to fail to remember: *She forgets telephone numbers. He forgot where he put his cuff links.* Unlike *forget,* REPRESS implies a forcible effort to drive memories, fears, or thoughts from the conscious mind: *She repressed the details of the murder she had witnessed.*
Antonym: remember.

forgive See **pardon.**

fork See **branch.**

forlorn See **abandoned.**

form See **constitute.**

formal *adj.* ceremonious.
FORMAL and CEREMONIOUS describe what is in accordance with accepted forms, conventions, or rules. *Ceremonious* implies adherence to a set of prescribed rites: *a ceremonious midnight mass. Formal* is the less specific and more widely applicable term: *a formal discussion; a formal wedding announcement.*
Antonym: informal.

forsake See **abandon.**

forsaken See **abandoned.**

fortuitous See **accidental.**

fortunate *adj.* happy, lucky.
FORTUNATE and the less formal LUCKY can be used interchangeably to refer to what meets with or brings unexpected good fortune, success, etc.: *a fortunate* (or *lucky*) *girl; a fortunate* (or *lucky*) *choice.* HAPPY, which in this sense stresses that something is favorable, is rarely used to describe persons: *a happy circumstance; a happy outcome.*
Antonym: unfortunate.

---

forward See **bold.**

foster See **promote.**

foul See **dirty.**

fragile *adj.* **breakable, brittle, delicate, frangible.**
Core meaning: Easily broken or damaged (*a fragile crystal glass; a fragile economy*).

frailty See **weakness.**

frangible See **fragile.**

frantic See **upset.**

fraternity See **circle.**

free *v.* **emancipate, liberate, release.**
FREE and its synonyms share the sense of setting at liberty, as from confinement, oppression, the control of others, etc. *Free,* LIBERATE, and RELEASE are the most general and are often interchangeable: *free an innocent man; liberate slaves; releasing prisoners from an internment camp.* EMANCIPATE usually applies more narrowly to setting free from bondage or restraint: *emancipate serfs.*

freedom *n.* **liberty, license.**
These refer to the power to speak, think, and act without restraint. FREEDOM and LIBERTY are sometimes used interchangeably, but *freedom* is the more general term: *gave slaves their freedom; had the freedom to contradict the boss. Liberty* often denotes the political condition in which individual rights are defined and guaranteed by law: *The Magna Carta is known as the cornerstone of English liberty.* LICENSE implies the freedom to deviate from prevailing rules or standards: *poetic license.*

frequent See **familiar.**

fresh *adj.* **new, novel.**
FRESH, NEW, and NOVEL describe what has very recently been made, put into service, gathered, or the like. *Fresh* and *new* apply widely and generally: *fresh bread; fresh sheets; fresh vegetables; a new nation; new blankets; new corn.* Both words also describe what is recent, original, and

---

different: *a fresh approach to old problems; new techniques of typesetting. Novel* stresses striking originality: *a novel treatment of folk songs.* See also **new**.
Antonym: **stale.**

freshness See **novelty.**

friendly *adj.* **amicable.**
FRIENDLY describes what is marked by or shows friendship: *friendly cooperation; a friendly letter; a friendly gathering; a friendly official.* AMICABLE is a somewhat more formal term: *had an amicable discussion; parted on amicable terms.*
Antonym: **unfriendly.**

frighten *v.* **alarm, scare, startle, terrify.**
These verbs share the meaning of causing to feel or feeling fear. FRIGHTEN and SCARE are the most general terms; while *scare* is less formal, the two are often interchangeable: *The crash frightened us. Some children frighten easily. Loud noises scare me.* ALARM implies the sudden onset of fear or apprehension caused by the realization of danger: *Mrs. Danvers was alarmed when Betty's fever suddenly shot up to 104°.* STARTLE suggests sudden surprise or shock: *The doorbell startled me.* TERRIFY implies overwhelming, even paralyzing fear: *The sight of blood terrifies her.*

frightful See **unspeakable.**

frigid See **cold.**

fringe See **border.**

fritter See **waste.**

frosty See **cold.**

frugal See **economical.**

fruitful See **fertile.**

fulfill *v.* **discharge, execute, implement, perform.**
Core meaning: To carry out the functions or requirements of (*fulfilled my side of the bargain*).

full *adj.* **complete, replete.**
FULL describes what holds all that is normal or possible: *a full pail.* Together with COMPLETE it applies to what has everything necessary, usual, normal, wanted, etc.: *full* (or *complete employment; a complete* (or *full*) *meal. Full* (*of*) and REPLETE (*with*) describe what has a great number or quantity of something, but *replete* stresses plenty and abundance: *shelves full of books; an examination full of errors; a land replete with* (or *full of*) *streams and forests.*
Antonym: **empty.**

fulsome See **unctuous.**

fumble See **botch.**

fun See **gaiety.**

function See **operate.**

functional See **practical.**

fundamental See **radical.**

funny See **laughable.**

further See **advance.**

furtive See **secret.**

fury See **anger.**

gag See **joke.**

gaiety *n.* **1. glee, hilarity, jollity, merriment, mirth.**
Core meaning: A state of joyful exuberance (*a house that rang with Christmas gaiety*).
2. festivity, fun, merrymaking, revelry.
Core meaning: Joyful, exuberant activity (*invited the guests to join the gaiety*).

gain See **reach.**

gainsay See **deny.**

gape See **gaze.**

gather *v.* **accumulate, amass, assemble, collect.**
These five verbs denote bringing or coming together in a group or mass. GATHER is the most general term: *gather*

flowers; gather information; a crowd gathering for a picnic.
COLLECT is often interchangeable with *gather* (*collect*—or *gather*—*firewood; a crowd collecting*—or *gathering*—*for a picnic*), but it is also used to imply careful selection of related things that become part of an organized whole (*collect antiques; collect art*). ACCUMULATE and AMASS refer to the gradual increase of something over a period of time: *amass a fortune; amass knowledge; snow accumulating on the sidewalk; accumulated data.* ASSEMBLE suggests convening out of common interest or purpose: *classes that assembled in the auditorium.*
Antonym: **scatter.**

gaunt See **thin.**

gaze *v.* **gape, glare, ogle, peer, stare.**
All of these verbs refer to looking long and fixedly. To GAZE is usually to look intently and for a long time, as in wonder, fascination, awe, or admiration: *The tourists gazed at the wild beauty of the countryside.* GAPE suggests a prolonged, open-mouthed look reflecting amazement, stupidity, etc.: *gaping at the acrobats.* To GLARE is to fix another with a hard, hostile look: *glared at me with resentment.* To OGLE is to stare impertinently, often in a way that indicates improper interest: *ogling young girls on the street.* To PEER is to look narrowly and searchingly and seemingly with difficulty: *I peered at the small type of the telephone book.* STARE stresses steadiness of gaze and often indicates marked curiosity, boldness, surprise, etc.: *Bill stared at the candy.*

general See **public.**

generate See **create.**

generous *adj.* **bountiful, liberal.**
These adjectives describe what has or shows willingness to give or share. GENEROUS and LIBERAL are often interchangeable: *a generous* (or *liberal*) *contributor to worthy causes; a generous* (or *liberal*) *gift. Generous, liberal,* and BOUNTIFUL can all be used to describe what is generously sufficient: *a*

generous serving; a liberal portion; a bountiful supply.
Antonyms: **cheap, stingy.**

genteel See **refined.**

gentle *adj.* **mild.**
GENTLE and MILD can be used interchangeably to describe people who are kindly, peaceful, and patient in disposition, manner, or behavior: *Gentle people can be brave. Jack's father was a mild man who rarely punished his children. Gentle* can also suggest a soothing quality (*gentle hands; gentle words; a gentle breeze*); *mild* describes what is moderate in degree, force, or effect (*a mild reproach; mild soap*).
Antonym: **harsh.**

genuine 1. See **natural.** 2. See **true.** 3. See **authentic.**

genuinely See **actually.**

germane See **relevant.**

get See **earn.**

ghastly *adj.* **grim, grisly, gruesome, horrible, horrid, lurid, macabre.**
Core meaning: Shockingly repellent (*the ghastly sight of starving refugees*).
2. cadaverous, deathly, spectral.
Core meaning: Gruesomely suggestive of ghosts or death (*the ghastly figure of the Headless Horseman; the ghastly pallor of the dying patient*).

gibe See **ridicule.**

gigantic See **big.**

gird See **surround.**

gist See **heart.**

glad *adj.* **cheerful, happy, joyful.**
These describe what shows, is marked by, or expresses pleasure, good spirits, delight, etc. HAPPY is the most general: *a happy fellow; a happy day.* CHEERFUL suggests evident high spirits: *a girl who is cheerful even in the morning;*

a cheerful face; a cheerful tune. GLAD suggests pleasure that a wish has been gratified (*The children were glad to get the skis they had hoped for*) or satisfaction with immediate circumstances (*I am glad I found you*). JOYFUL, the strongest of these words, suggests extremely high spirits or a very strong sense of fulfillment or satisfaction: *felt joyful at the prospect of seeing him at last; a joyful smile.*
Antonym: **sad.**

glare See **gaze.**

glaring See **flagrant.**

glee See **gaiety.**

glib *adj.* **facile, flip** (*Informal*), **glossy, slick.**
Core meaning: Marked by ready but often insincere or superficial discourse (*a glib denial*).

glide See **slide.**

gloomy *adj.* **1. dour, glum, morose.**
All of these describe people who show a cheerless aspect or disposition. A GLOOMY person is by nature given to somberness or depression: *sullen and gloomy as he went about his tasks.* DOUR suggests a grim and humorless exterior: *a dour and ascetic minister.* GLUM often implies temporary low spirits: *When you are feeling glum, a talk with a friend can do a mountain of good.* MOROSE applies to those who are ill-humored and sullen: *a morose man who talked little with his neighbors.*
Antonym: **cheerful.**
2. dismal, dreary.
GLOOMY, DISMAL, and DREARY describe what produces a feeling of melancholy or depression: *a gloomy, deserted castle; a dismal fog; a dreary January rain.*
Antonym: **cheerful.**

glossy See **glib.**

glum See **gloomy.**

go See **operate.**

goad See **provoke.**

go-between *n.* broker, intercessor, intermediary, intermediate, middleman.

Core meaning: A person who acts as an intermediate agent in a transaction (*acted as the go-between in the labor dispute*).

godly See **holy.**

good-natured. See **amiable.**

goodness See **virtue.**

goods *n.* commodities, line, merchandise, wares.

Core meaning: Products bought and sold in commerce (*inventoried all the goods in the store*).

govern See **administer.**

grab See **catch.**

graceful *adj.* **1.** adroit, deft, dexterous, nimble.

Anything GRACEFUL shows beauty or charm of movement, form, or manner: *a graceful tango; a graceful figure; a graceful compliment.* The related words are more restricted in meaning. ADROIT, DEFT, DEXTEROUS, and NIMBLE apply to movement and manner. *Adroit* implies adeptness and skill, particularly under difficult conditions: *an adroit maneuver.* *Deft* suggests quickness, sureness, and lightness of touch: *a deft seamstress.* *Dexterous* applies to skilled manual activity: *a dexterous typist.* *Nimble* stresses quickness and liveliness in mental or physical performance: *nimble fingers.*

Antonym: awkward.

2. See **elegant.**

grand *adj.* grandiose, imposing, magnificent, majestic, stately.

GRAND and its synonyms apply to what is extremely impressive in some way. Both *grand* and MAGNIFICENT refer to what is fine, impressive, or splendid, as in appearance; *magnificent* especially suggests sumptuousness and excellence: *a grand coronation ceremony; a magnificent cathedral.* IMPOSING describes what is impressive with respect to size, bearing, power, etc.: *an imposing residence; an imposing officer.* STATELY refers mainly to what is impressive in size or proportions: *stately columns; a stately oak.* MA-JESTIC is applicable to manner, appearance, bearing, etc., and suggests dignity, nobility, or grandeur: *The queen gave a majestic wave of the hand.* GRANDIOSE refers principally to things that are on an exceedingly large scale (*a grandiose style of architecture*); in a related sense it often suggests pretentiousness, affectation, or pompousness (*full of grandiose ideas*).

grandiose See **grand.**

graphic *adj.* **lifelike, pictorial, realistic, vivid.**
Core meaning: Described verbally in accurate detail (*a graphic account of the battle*).

grasp See **comprehend.**

gratify See **please.**

gratifying See **pleasant.**

gratuitous *adj.* **supererogative, supererogatory, uncalled-for, wanton.**
Core meaning: Not required or warranted by the circumstances of the case (*gratuitous spending; the gratuitous killing of civilians by the conquering soldiers*).

gratuity See **bonus.**

great 1. See **big. 2.** See **excellent.**

grief See **sorrow.**

grim See **ghastly.**

grimy See **dirty.**

grin See **smile.**

grisly See **ghastly.**

gross 1. See **coarse. 2.** See **flagrant.**

grotesque See **fantastic.**

grown-up See **mature.**

gruesome See **ghastly.**

gruff *adj.* **bluff, blunt, brusque, curt.**
All of these adjectives refer to what is abrupt and sometimes markedly impolite in manner or speech. GRUFF implies roughness of manner and often harsh speech, but it does not necessarily suggest intentional rudeness. BRUSQUE emphasizes rude abruptness of manner. BLUNT stresses utter frankness and usually a disconcerting directness of speech. BLUFF refers to unpolished, unceremonious manner but usually implies good nature. CURT refers to briefness and abruptness of speech and manner and usually implies rudeness.

guard See **defend.**

guileful See **underhand.**

haggard *adj.* **careworn, wasted, worn.**
These adjectives describe what shows the effects of anxiety, disease, hunger, or fatigue. HAGGARD refers particularly to facial appearance and implies thinness, tiredness, and often the expression of one who has seemingly suffered or worried. CAREWORN is applicable to one whose physical appearance reveals the effects of worry, anxiety, or burdensome responsibility. WASTED stresses emaciation or marked loss of flesh, with consequent frailness or enfeeblement; the term is most often associated with illness or extreme physical hardship. WORN can refer to the effects of worry, sickness, or strain.

haggle See **argue.**

hale See **healthy.**

halt See **stop.**

hamper See **hinder.**

handicap See **disadvantage.**

handle *v.* **manipulate, ply, wield.**
These verbs refer to using, operating, or managing things or, less often, persons. HANDLE can refer to management or control of tools, implements, persons, or nonphysical things such as problems and situations; unless it is qualified

by an adverb, in every case the term suggests competence in gaining an end or objective. MANIPULATE connotes skillful or artful management of physical things, such as tools or instruments, or of persons or personal affairs, in which case it often implies deviousness. PLY refers principally to use of tools (*ply a broom in sweeping*) and to the regular and diligent engagement in a task (*ply the baker's trade*). WIELD implies that one has full command of what is used, principally tools and implements, weapons, means of expression such as the pen, or intangibles such as authority and influence.

handsome See **beautiful**.

handy See **convenient**.

hanging *adj*. **pendulous, pensile, suspended.**
Core meaning: Hung or appearing to be hung from a support (*a hanging plant*).

haphazard See **accidental**.

happy 1. See **cheerful**. **2.** See **fortunate**. **3.** See **glad**.

harangue See **tirade**.

hard *adj*. **firm.**
HARD and FIRM are often used interchangeably when they refer to what is resistant to pressure (*a hard surface; firm ground*). *Hard* can also suggest that something is physically toughened (*a hard palm with calluses*), while *firm* describes what shows the tone and resiliency characteristic of healthy tissue (*firm muscles*). See also **difficult**.
Antonym: **soft**.

harm *n*. **damage, detriment, hurt, injury.**
Core meaning: The action or result of inflicting loss or pain (*did harm to the hostages*).

harmony *n*. **accord, concord.**
These denote a condition marked by agreement in feeling, approach, action, disposition, etc.: *a community in perfect harmony; ideas in accord with my own; lived in peace and concord.*
Antonym: **discord**.

harsh *adj.* **rough, severe, stern.**
HARSH and its synonyms describe behavior, actions, etc., that affect the feelings unpleasantly or offensively: *a harsh remark; rough treatment; a severe tone of voice; a stern look of reproach. Harsh* and *rough* also apply to what is unpleasant to the senses: *harsh colors; rough wool. Severe* and *stern* can suggest that something is strict and inflexible: *a severe law; a severe teacher; stern discipline; a stern mother.*
Antonym: **gentle.**

harshness See **severity.**

hasten See **expedite.**

hasty See **fast.**

hate 1. *n.* **abhorrence, detestation, hatred, loathing.**
These nouns refer to intense feelings of dislike. HATE is often used as the abstract term: *Love and hate are opposites.* HATRED frequently refers more directly to the emotion as people experience it: *a hatred of liars.* For the differences in the meanings of the words ABHORRENCE, DETESTATION, and LOATHING, see the discussion below of the verbs from which they derive.
Antonym: **love.**
2. *v.* **abhor, detest, loathe.**
HATE, the most general of these terms, implies a feeling of aversion, enmity, or hostility: *"I hate you," he screamed at her.* ABHOR suggests a feeling of repugnance and even fear: *abhor violence in all forms.* DETEST and LOATHE imply intense dislike and scorn: *detest* (or *loathe*) *spinach; loathe* (or *detest*) *cheating.*
Antonym: **love.**

hatred See **hate.**

haughty See **proud.**

have See **carry.**

hazard See **danger.**

hazy See **vague.**

---

head See **administer.**

headstrong See **obstinate.**

healthy *adj.* **hale, sound, well.**
These adjectives describe persons who are in good physical or mental condition. WELL simply specifies the absence of disease: *He was sick for three days, but he is well now.* HEALTHY positively stresses a condition of good health and often suggests energy: *a healthy boy with a healthy appetite.* HALE stresses absence of infirmity, especially in elderly persons: *My grandmother is still hale and hearty.* SOUND emphasizes freedom from defect, decay, damage, injury, or sickness: *a sound mind in a sound body.*
Antonym: **sick.**

heart *n.* **core, essence, gist, kernel, marrow, nub, pith, root, substance.**
Core meaning: The most central and material part (*the heart of the matter*).

heartache See **sorrow.**

hearten See **encourage.**

heave See **raise.**

heavy *adj.* **cumbersome, hefty, massive, ponderous, weighty.**
HEAVY and its synonyms refer to what is of great or relatively great weight, size, etc. *Heavy* applies to what has great weight (*a heavy stone*); figuratively it describes what is burdensome or oppressive to the spirit: *heavy losses.* CUMBERSOME stresses difficulty of movement or operation caused by heaviness or bulkiness: *cumbersome luggage.* HEFTY refers mainly to heaviness or brawniness of physique: *a hefty sailor.* MASSIVE describes what is imposing in size (*a massive head*) or bulk (*a massive elephant*). PONDEROUS refers to what has great mass and weight and usually implies clumsiness: *ponderous prehistoric beasts.* WEIGHTY literally denotes having great weight (*a weighty package*); figuratively it describes what is very serious or important: *a weighty problem; a weighty decision.*
Antonym: **light.**

---

hedge See **skirt.**

heed See **notice.**

heedless See **careless.**

hefty See **heavy.**

help *v.* **aid, assist.**
These share the sense of contributing to the fulfillment of a need or the achievement of a purpose. HELP and AID are the most general: *helped with the farming; aids a friend in distress.* Sometimes *help* conveys a stronger suggestion of effective action: *Food helps the hungry more than advice on how to find work.* ASSIST usually implies making a lesser contribution or acting as a subordinate: *A crack team of trained guerrillas assisted the commander.*
Antonym: **hinder.**

helpless See **powerless.**

hem in See **surround.**

hesitate *v.* **falter, vacillate, waver.**
These verbs are used to express uncertainty or indecision. HESITATE implies slowness to act, speak, or decide. To FALTER is to act indecisively or ineffectually; it implies retreat from a course decided on or the inability to carry it out. VACILLATE implies swinging between alternative and often conflicting courses of action without making a decisive choice. WAVER suggests either inability to act, resulting from indecision, or tentative and ineffectual action once a choice has been made.
Antonym: **decide.**

heterogeneity See **variety.**

hide *v.* **cloak, conceal, secrete.**
These verbs refer to keeping from the sight or knowledge of others. HIDE and CONCEAL refer both to putting physical things out of sight (*hid the Christmas gifts in the closet; concealed the box under the bed*) and to withholding information or disguising one's feelings or thoughts (*hid the bad news; smiled and joked to conceal her hurt feelings*). *Con-*

---

ceal often implies a deliberate effort to keep from sight or knowledge, whereas *hide* also can refer to natural phenomena: *The thief hid* (or *concealed*) *the stolen money. Night hides the city's ugliness.* CLOAK usually refers to concealing thoughts, plans, etc.: *research cloaked in secrecy.* SECRETE refers chiefly to removing physical objects from sight and involves concealment in a place unknown to others: *secreted the money in a mattress.*
Antonym: **show.**

hideous See **ugly.**

high *adj.* **elevated, lofty, tall, towering.**
These refer to what stands out or is otherwise distinguished by reason of height. HIGH and TALL, the most general terms, are sometimes interchangeable. In general *high* refers to what rises a considerable distance from a base or is situated at a level well above another level considered as a base: *a high mountain; a high ceiling; a high shelf; high standards.* *Tall* describes what rises to a considerable extent; it often refers to living things and to what has great height in relation to breadth or in comparison with like things: *a tall man; tall trees; a tall building.* ELEVATED stresses height in relation to immediate surroundings; it refers principally to being raised or situated above a normal or average level (*an elevated plain*) but can also apply to something that is exalted in character or spirit (*elevated praise; elevated thought*). LOFTY describes what is imposingly or inspiringly high: *lofty mountains; lofty sentiments.* TOWERING suggests height that causes awe: *towering icebergs.*
Antonym: **low.**

hilarity See **gaiety.**

hinder *v.* **block, hamper, impede, obstruct.**
All of these share the sense of interfering with or preventing action or progress. HINDER and HAMPER are the most general; they apply to any restraining influence: *Diffidence hindered his ability to express himself. Rain hindered highway construction. Economic problems hamper the nation's de-*

---

velopment. Tight shoes hampered his freedom of movement. BLOCK and OBSTRUCT imply the setting up of obstacles: *The senator blocked passage of the bill for a week by filibustering. Guards blocked his entry. By withholding the documents the politician obstructed justice. Rocks obstructed the mountain pass.* To IMPEDE is to retard action or progress or make it so difficult that it is impossible: *Illogical thinking impedes the solution of geometry problems. Snow impeded the flow of traffic.*
Antonyms: advance; help.

hint 1. See **suggest. 2.** See **trace.**

hit *v.* **bash** (*Informal*), **belt** (*Informal*), **clip** (*Informal*), **clobber** (*Slang*), **paste** (*Slang*), **slam, slug** (*Slang*), **smack, smash, sock** (*Slang*), **strike, swat, wallop** (*Informal*), **whack.**
Core meaning: To deliver (a powerful blow) suddenly and sharply (*hit the other boxer in the jaw*).

hoard See **save.**

hoist See **raise.**

holding(s) *n.* **estate, possessions, property.**
Core meaning: Something, as land, legally possessed (*a company with vast holdings in South America*).

holocaust See **disaster.**

holy *adj.* **devout, godly, pious, religious.**
Core meaning: Concerned with God and religion (*a holy shrine*).

homage See **honor.**

honest See **true.**

honesty *n.* **honor, integrity, probity, veracity.**
HONESTY and its synonyms denote qualities closely associated with moral excellence. *Honesty* implies truthfulness (*Few doubted the President's honesty*), fairness in dealing (*treated his employees with absolute honesty*), and absence of fraud, deceit, and dissembling (*a banker of impeccable honesty*). HONOR suggests close adherence to a strict moral

or ethical code: *bound by his honor and his conscience.* INTEGRITY refers especially to moral soundness in individuals: *a man of integrity who never violated a trust.* PROBITY is proven integrity. VERACITY is truthfulness in expression: *doubted the veracity of the witness.*
Antonym: **dishonesty.**

honor *n.* **deference, homage, reverence, veneration.**
These are compared as they refer to the state, feeling, or expression of admiration, respect, or esteem. HONOR, the most general, applies both to the feeling (*hold in honor*) and to the expression (*displaying the flag to show honor to the United States*). DEFERENCE is respect or courteous regard that often takes the form of yielding to the wishes, judgment, condition, etc., of another: *In deference to his age he was permitted to remain seated.* HOMAGE is a public expression of high regard or respect: *paid homage to his king; a crowd cheering in homage to a great singer.* REVERENCE is a feeling of deep respect and devotion and often of love: *gazed at the cathedral with reverence.* VENERATION is both the feeling and worshipful expression of respect, love, and awe, especially for one whose wisdom, dignity, rank, age, etc., merits such attention: *viewed his great-grandfather with veneration.* See also **honesty.**
Antonym: **dishonor.**

honorable See **moral.**

hopeful See **optimistic.**

horizon See **ken.**

horrible See **ghastly.**

horrid See **ghastly.**

hostile See **unfriendly.**

hostility See **enmity.**

hot *adj.* **boiling, burning, feverish, fiery, scorching, sizzling, sultry, sweltering, torrid.**
Used literally, these words describe what has a high temperature; most of them also have figurative senses. HOT

---

applies most widely; its extended senses also describe what is warmer than usual (*a hot forehead*), highly spiced (*hot mustard*), or explosive or dangerous (*a hot dispute*). What is BOILING is heated to the boiling point (*boiling water*) or greatly excited, as with rage (*still boiling after their nasty fight*). BURNING calls up the image of fire; it refers to what is passionate (*a burning desire*) or urgent (*a burning issue*). FEVERISH suggests an abnormally high body temperature (*a feverish forehead*); it also applies to what is very active (*a feverish desire to win*). FIERY implies great heat, as of fire (*the fiery pavements of the city*); it can also describe what is high-spirited (*a fiery speech*) or easily stirred up (*a fiery temper*). SCORCHING applies literally to what is intensely hot (*a scorching summer day*) or figuratively to what is censorious or angry (*a scorching indictment of graft at city hall*). What is SIZZLING is so hot that it almost suggests the hissing sound characteristic of frying fat (*a tar sidewalk sizzling in the sun*); figuratively *sizzling* applies to something seething with anger or indignation (*sent a sizzling reply*). SULTRY means hot and humid (*a sultry day in August*); figuratively it refers to what is sensual and voluptuous (*gave him a sultry look*). SWELTERING, which implies oppressive and humid heat, has no figurative sense: *a sweltering apartment*. TORRID refers to what is very dry and hot (*torrid weather*) or to what is passionate (*a torrid romance*).
Antonym: **cold.**

huge See **big.**

human *adj.* **humane, humanitarian.**
These reflect concern with the welfare of people and the easing of suffering (*the alleviation of poverty—a human concern*). HUMAN is essentially a classifying term relating to individuals or people collectively (*human kindness*), while HUMANE stresses the qualities of kindness and compassion (*humane treatment*). HUMANITARIAN applies to what actively promotes the needs and welfare of people (*humanitarian considerations in the treatment of prisoners*).

humane See **human.**

---

humanitarian See **human.**

humble *adj.* **lowly, meek, modest.**
These refer mainly to demeanor or behavior. HUMBLE
stresses lack of pride, assertiveness, or pretense: *my
humble opinion.* MEEK implies patience, humility, and gen-
tleness; it sometimes suggests that a person is easily imposed upon: *a meek and dignified manner; the meekest of
men.* LOWLY combines the senses of *humble* and *meek: a
lowly beggar child.* MODEST implies lack of vanity, pretension, or forwardness: *modest despite his fame.*
Antonym: **proud.**

humdrum See **monotony.**

humor See **pamper.**

hurt 1. See **distress. 2.** See **harm.**

husband See **save.**

hypothesis See **theory.**

icy See **cold.**

idea See **feeling.**

ideal 1. *n.* **model, standard.**
IDEAL and the other two nouns refer to what serves as the
basis of direction or guidance in work or behavior. An *ideal*
is a goal of perfection in the form of a person or thing: *found
his ideal in the playing of Rubinstein.* A MODEL is a person
or thing imitated or worthy of imitation: *a model of honesty.*
A STANDARD is an established criterion or prevailing level of
quality, value, or achievement that is demanded or aimed
for: *an artist who set high standards for herself.*
2. *adj.* See **idealistic.**

idealistic *adj.* **1. ideal, utopian, visionary.**
Core meaning: Tending to envision things in a perfect but
unrealistic form (*an idealistic attitude toward foreign affairs*).
2. quixotic, romantic, unrealistic.
Core meaning: Not compatible with reality (*an idealistic
view of love*).

---

identical See **same.**

idiom See **language.**

idiosyncrasy See **eccentricity.**

idle See **inactive.**

ignite *v.* **kindle, light.**
These verbs mean to set fire to or catch fire: *ignite a match; a match that ignited; kindle a campfire; wood that kindles easily; light an oven; an oven that wouldn't light.*
Antonym: **extinguish.**

ignominy See **dishonor.**

ignorant *adj.* **illiterate, uneducated.**
Core meaning: Without education or knowledge (*ignorant teens who had quit school*).

ilk See **type.**

ill See **sick.**

illegal *adj.* **illegitimate, illicit, unlawful.**
All of these describe what conflicts with the law. ILLEGAL applies to what is prohibited by law or by official rules: *illegal gambling; an illegal move in a chess game.* ILLICIT stresses violation of accepted custom: *illicit relations.* ILLEGITIMATE describes what is not supported by the law: *an illegitimate deed to the property: illegitimate claims.* UNLAWFUL applies most often to what violates the law: *the unlawful possession of firearms.*
Antonym: **legal.**

illegitimate See **illegal.**

illicit See **illegal.**

illiterate See **ignorant.**

illogical 1. See **fallacious.** 2. See **unreasonable.**

imagination *n.* **fancy, fantasy.**
IMAGINATION, FANCY, and FANTASY refer to the ability of the mind to conceive ideas or to form images of something not present to the senses or within the actual experience of the

person involved. *Imagination* is broadly applicable to all such functions; it also applies to the creative use of that ability (*the lively imagination of the novelist*). *Fancy* suggests mental invention that is capricious, whimsical, or playful: *fact and fancy*. *Fantasy* is applied mainly to creative imagination (*Modern technology has turned fantasy into reality*) and to what exists only in the mind or imagination (*dismissed the idea as sheer fantasy*).

imbibe See **absorb.**

imitate *v.* **burlesque, mimic, parody.**
Core meaning: To copy (the manner or expression of another), often mockingly (*a comedian who imitated the President*).

immaculate See **clean.**

immaterial See **irrelevant.**

immature *adj.* **childish, infantile.**
These apply to what is thoughtless or foolish in a manner not suitable for a mature person: *an immature attitude toward work; childish, sulky behavior; an infantile outburst of rage.*
Antonym: **mature.**

immense See **big.**

immobile See **motionless.**

immoral *adj.* **1. unethical, unprincipled, unscrupulous.**
These describe that which is contrary to what is considered just, right, or good: *the immoral system of slavery; an unethical businessman; an unprincipled scoundrel; an unscrupulous politician.*
Antonym: **moral.**
2. dissolute, lecherous, lewd, profligate.
All of these apply to that which does not conform to accepted rules of propriety and morality in sexual matters. IMMORAL is the most general: *an immoral man; immoral behavior.* DISSOLUTE suggests moral corruption: *a dissolute life.* LECHEROUS and LEWD both imply a preoccupation with sexual desire and activity: *a lecherous glance; a lewd sug-*

---

gestion. PROFLIGATE, the strongest, means "completely given over to self-indulgence and vice."
Antonym: **moral.**

immorality See **vice.**

immortalize *v.* **eternalize, perpetuate.**
Core meaning: To cause to last forever (*immortalize her memory*).

impalpable See **imperceptible.**

impartial See **fair.**

impartially See **fairly.**

impatient *adj.* **restive.**
IMPATIENT applies to unwillingness or inability to wait patiently, endure irritation calmly, or show tolerant understanding: *impatient at the delay in the train's departure; a teacher impatient because Bill learned slowly.* RESTIVE applies more narrowly to impatience under restriction, pressure, or delay: *The crowd gradually grew restive while they waited for the speaker to appear.*
Antonym: **patient.**

impeach See **accuse.**

impeccable See **perfect.**

impede See **hinder.**

impel See **provoke.**

imperceptible *adj.* **impalpable, inappreciable, intangible.**
These adjectives describe what cannot—or can barely—be seen, measured, or detected by the senses or the mind even though it is present: *an imperceptible movement of her hand; an impalpable difference in meaning; an inappreciable amount; an intangible change.*
Antonym: **perceptible.**

imperfect *adj.* **defective, faulty.**
These describe what has defects, flaws, errors, etc.; they

can be used interchangeably: *imperfect speech; defective merchandise; a faulty memory.*
Antonym: **perfect.**

imperious See **dictatorial.**

implausible *adj.* **flimsy, improbable, inconceivable, unbelievable, weak.**
Core meaning: Not plausible or believable (*an implausible alibi*).

implement 1. *v.* See **fulfill. 2.** *n.* See **tool.**

implicit *adj.* **implied, tacit.**
What is IMPLICIT is understood without being directly expressed: *The author's opposition to the war is implicit throughout the book.* IMPLIED and TACIT describe what is conveyed indirectly or suggested without being spoken or written: *an implied consent; a tacit agreement.*
Antonym: **explicit.**

implied See **implicit.**

imply See **suggest.**

impolite *adj.* **discourteous, rude, unmannerly.**
These refer to lack of good behavior or manners. What is RUDE is offensive to the feelings of others; the word often connotes insolence: *apologized for his rude remarks.* IMPOLITE and DISCOURTEOUS imply lack of good manners and consideration for others: *too impolite to stand up when his grandmother came into the room; a discourteous guest who came for dinner two hours late.* UNMANNERLY suggests bad manners: *unmannerly behavior.*
Antonym: **polite.**

impolitic See **tactless.**

important *adj.* **consequential, momentous, significant, weighty.**
These all refer to what is able to determine or change the course of events or the nature of things. IMPORTANT is the most general term: *an important seaport; an important*

message; an important crop; an important composer. CON-
SEQUENTIAL describes what is important because of its possible outcome, result, etc.: *a consequential blunder.* What
is MOMENTOUS is of the utmost importance or significance: *a
momentous occasion; a momentous discovery.* SIGNIFICANT
applies to what is notable or adds important meaning: *a
significant battle; a significant look.* WEIGHTY implies great
seriousness: *a weighty decision.*
Antonym: **unimportant.**

imposing See **grand.**

impossible *adj.* **impracticable, impractical, unattainable, unfeasible, unrealizable, unthinkable, unworkable.**
Core meaning: Not capable of happening or being done
(*impossible dreams; an impossible plan*).

impostor *n.* **charlatan, faker, quack.**
IMPOSTOR and its synonyms denote persons who pretend to
be other than what they are or who otherwise practice deception for gain. An *impostor* assumes the identity of another person for the purpose of deceiving. A CHARLATAN
falsely claims to have expert skill or knowledge in a particular subject or field of activity. FAKER often refers to a person
who perpetrates a fraud. A QUACK usually practices
medicine without being qualified.

impotent See **powerless.**

impoverished See **poor.**

impracticable See **impossible.**

impractical See **impossible.**

impress See **affect.**

impression See **feeling.**

improbable 1. See **unlikely. 2.** See **implausible.**

improper See **unsuitable.**

improvise *v.* **ad-lib** (*Informal*), **extemporize, fake** (*Slang*),
make up.
Core meaning: To compose or do without preparation (*improvise a speech*).

---

impudent See **bold.**

impure *adj.* **contaminated, polluted, unclean.**
Core meaning: Rendered unfit by the addition of other substances (*impure drinking water*).

impute See **attribute.**

inaccurate See **false.**

inactive *adj.* **dormant, idle, inert, lazy.**
These all mean not involved in or disposed to action or movement. INACTIVE implies neither a favorable nor an unfavorable judgment: *an inactive attorney.* DORMANT refers chiefly to states of suspended activity but often implies the possibility of renewal: *a dormant snake in its winter hideaway.* IDLE refers to inactivity of persons, whether or not through choice (*employees idle because of the strike; idle boys who refuse to study*). When it comes about by choice and a negative judgment is implied, LAZY is more accurate: *too lazy to write a thank-you note.* INERT implies lethargy, especially of mind or spirit.

inadvertent See **careless.**

inappreciable See **imperceptible.**

inappropriate See **unsuitable.**

inapt See **unsuitable.**

inaugural See **first.**

incapable See **unable.**

incentive See **stimulus.**

inception See **origin.**

incite See **provoke.**

incline See **dispose.**

incompetent See **unable.**

inconceivable See **implausible.**

inconsequential See **unimportant.**

inconstant See **capricious.**

incorrect See **false.**

increase *v.* **augment, enlarge.**
These verbs share the meaning of becoming or causing to become greater, as in size, extent, or quantity. INCREASE has the greatest range of meanings. Used intransitively it suggests steady growth: *Her salary increased yearly. The mayor's political influence increased.* In transitive use *increase* does not necessarily connote such progressive growth; it can imply addition in any respect: *The director increased her salary. Illness increased his depression.* AUGMENT usually applies to what is already developed or well under way: *sadness that augments with every visit to the hospital; augmented his collection of books.* ENLARGE implies expansion, physical or other: *The landowner enlarged his property by repeated purchases. Fran's group of friends enlarged by leaps and bounds.*
Antonym: **decrease.**

incredible See **fabulous.**

incurious See **uninterested.**

indeed See **actually.**

indefinite See **vague.**

indelicate 1. See **coarse. 2.** See **tactless.**

indescribable See **unspeakable.**

indication See **sign.**

indict See **accuse.**

indifference See **disinterest.**

indifferent See **uninterested.**

indigenous See **native.**

indigent See **poor.**

indignation See **anger.**

indirect *adj.* **circuitous, roundabout.**
These describe what does not go straight to its destination: *an indirect path; a circuitous route home; a roundabout*

course that avoided heavy traffic. They are all used figuratively as well, in the meaning "not straight to the point." *Indirect* is the most general: *an indirect answer.* *Circuitous* and *roundabout* often imply an effort to evade or deceive.

Antonym: direct.

indispensable See **necessary.**

indisposed See **sick.**

indistinct See **vague.**

individual 1. See **characteristic. 2.** See **single.**

indulge See **pamper.**

industry See **business.**

inebriated See **drunk.**

inept See **awkward.**

inequitable See **unfair.**

inert See **inactive.**

inessential See **unnecessary.**

inestimable See **valuable.**

inexpensive See **cheap.**

infamous See **outrageous.**

infamy See **dishonor.**

infantile See **immature.**

inferior See **minor.**

infirmity See **weakness.**

inflame See **provoke.**

inflexible *adj.* **rigid, stiff.**
These three adjectives describe what literally is difficult to bend or stretch and to human behavior and attitudes that are not subject to modification or change. Anything STIFF cannot easily be bent (*a stiff board*); in reference to persons *stiff* suggests firmness of position and either lack of ease in manner or cold formality (*behavior that became stiff when*

she met new people; very stiff and proud around the children). INFLEXIBLE and RIGID refer to what cannot be bent physically, at least without damage or deformation (*an inflexible piece of steel; a rigid iron frame*); figuratively they describe unyielding positions or attitudes: *an inflexible rule; a rigid social structure; inflexible* (or *rigid*) *in his demands.* *Antonym:* **flexible.**

influence See **affect.**

informal *adj.* **casual**
These two adjectives describe what is not bound to or does not follow set ceremonies, rules, or conventions: *an informal agreement; an informal invitation; addressing his friends in a casual way; a casual survey.* *Antonym:* **formal.**

information See **knowledge.**

infraction See **breach.**

infringement See **breach.**

inhuman See **cruel.**

initial See **first.**

initiate See **begin.**

initiative See **ambition.**

injury See **harm.**

inquisitive See **curious.**

insanity *n.* **dementia, lunacy, madness, mania.**
All these terms denote conditions of mental disability. INSANITY, a social and legal term, is a serious and often prolonged condition of mental illness or disorder that renders a person not legally responsible for his actions. DEMENTIA implies mental deterioration brought on by organic disorders. LUNACY is sometimes used interchangeably with *insanity.* MADNESS, a more general term, often stresses the violent side of mental illness. MANIA refers mainly to the excited phase of manic-depressive psychosis. *Antonym:* **sanity.**

---

insensible See **apathetic.**

insignificant See **unimportant.**

insinuate See **suggest.**

inspection See **analysis.**

instability *n.* **precariousness, shakiness, unsteadiness.**
Core meaning: The quality or condition of being undependable and erratic (*the current instability of the stock market*).

instant See **moment.**

instinctive See **involuntary.**

instruct 1. See **command.** 2. See **teach.**

instrument 1. See **means.** 2. See **tool.**

insubordinate See **rebellious.**

insufficiency See **deficiency.**

insult See **offend.**

insurrection See **rebellion.**

intangible See **imperceptible.**

integrity See **honesty.**

intellectual See **intelligent.**

intelligent *adj.* **bright, brilliant, intellectual, smart.**
All of these refer to what has or shows the ability to learn, think, understand, or know. INTELLIGENT usually implies the ability to deal with demands created by novel situations and new problems, to apply what is learned from experience, and to use the power of reasoning effectively as a guide to behavior. BRIGHT, sometimes used interchangeably with *intelligent,* implies mental quickness in general; BRILLIANT suggests extreme and impressive intelligence. INTELLECTUAL stresses the working of the mind; *intellectual* persons show superior mental capacity. SMART is often a general term implying mental alertness; it can refer to practical knowledge or the ability to learn quickly.
Antonym: **unintelligent.**

intense *adj.* **deep, extreme.**
These describe what is of very great concentration, power, force, depth, etc.: *an intense blue; an intense light; a deep silence; a deep sleep; extreme caution; extreme cold.*

intentional *adj.* **deliberate, premeditated, voluntary.**
These adjectives describe what happens by plan or design. INTENTIONAL and DELIBERATE imply that something is done or said on purpose: *an intentional snub; a deliberate lie.* PREMEDITATED applies when one has planned on or thought out a course of action in advance: *premeditated murder.* VOLUNTARY describes action taken of one's own free will, without constraint: *a voluntary commitment to a cause.* See also **voluntary.**
Antonym: **accidental.**

intercessor See **go-between.**

interest *n.* **concern, curiosity.**
INTEREST and CONCERN refer to a feeling of involvement with or regard for something or someone: *The woman's father viewed her career with interest. The headlines triggered widespread concern among the public. Interest* and CURIOS-ITY agree in suggesting a desire to know or learn, in the case of *curiosity* often about something new or strange: *The beginning of the book failed to catch his interest. The articles about Laetrile sparked her curiosity.*
Antonym: **disinterest.**

interfere *v.* **meddle, tamper.**
INTERFERE, MEDDLE, and TAMPER are compared as they apply to concerning oneself in the affairs of others. *Interfere* and *meddle* are sometimes interchangeable. *Meddle* is the stronger in implying unwanted, unwarranted, or unnecessary intrusion: *meddling in matters that do not concern him.* It is somewhat weaker than *interfere* in implying action that seriously hampers, hinders, or frustrates: *interfered with her attempts to solve her personal problems. Tamper* refers to rash or harmful intervention: *tampered with his feelings.*

---

intermediary See **go-between.**

intermediate 1. *n.* See **go-between. 2.** *adj.* See **middle.**

intermittent See **discontinuous.**

intimate See **suggest.**

intimidate See **threaten.**

intoxicated See **drunk.**

intractable See **obstinate.**

intricate See **complex.**

intrigue See **conspiracy.**

introductory See **preliminary.**

intuition See **feeling.**

invalid *adj.* **1. null, void.**
INVALID, NULL, and VOID describe what is without legal force, foundation, effect, etc.: *an invalid will; a contract rendered null by a later agreement; declare a marriage null and void.*
Antonym: **valid.**
2. See **fallacious.**

invaluable See **valuable.**

invective See **abusive.**

inveigle See **seduce.**

invert See **reverse.**

invest See **wrap.**

investigation See **analysis.**

involuntary *adj.* **automatic, instinctive.**
These describe actions that are not based on conscious choice. INVOLUNTARY refers to what is not subject to the control of the will: *an involuntary muscle spasm.* What is AUTOMATIC is done or produced by the body without conscious control or awareness: *an automatic reflex in the face*

of danger. INSTINCTIVE actions are directed by unlearned inner drives: *The seasonal migration of birds is instinctive.* *Antonym:* voluntary.

involved See **complex.**

ire See **anger.**

irk See **annoy.**

ironic See **sarcastic.**

irrational See **unreasonable.**

irregular See **abnormal.**

irrelevant *adj.* **immaterial.**
IRRELEVANT and IMMATERIAL describe what has no relation to a subject or situation at hand: *We must stick to our subject and avoid irrelevant digressions. Immaterial* often suggests that something is unimportant: *If you aren't in the right place at the right time, your qualifications usually turn out to be immaterial.*
Antonym: relevant.

irreverent See **disrespectful.**

irreversible See **irrevocable.**

irrevocable *adj.* **irreversible, unalterable.**
Core meaning: That cannot be revoked or undone (*an irrevocable decision*).

irritate See **annoy.**

isolated See **secluded.**

isolation 1. See **solitude. 2.** See **aloneness.**

issue See **effect.**

iteration See **repetition.**

jeremiad See **tirade.**

jest See **joke.**

jiffy See **moment.**

job See **work.**

join *v.* **connect, link, unite.**
JOIN and its synonyms denote bringing or coming together. *Join* has the widest application, in both literal and figurative use: *join hands; join the ends of a chain; join in wedlock.* CONNECT and LINK imply a looser relationship in which individual units retain their identity while coming together at some point: *Capillaries connect the arteries and the veins. The Panama Canal links the Atlantic and the Pacific.* UNITE stresses the coherence or oneness that results from joining: *a plan to unite the colonies under one government; uniting for peace.*
Antonym: **separate.**

joke *n.* **crack, gag, jest, quip, sally, wisecrack, witticism.**
These refer to forms of humorous sayings or actions. JOKE and JEST, which can denote something said or done, are approximately interchangeable, though *jest* occurs infrequently in this sense. A WITTICISM is a cleverly worded, amusing remark. QUIP suggests a light, pointed, bantering remark, and SALLY a sudden, clever, or witty statement. CRACK and WISECRACK, informal terms, refer to flippant or sarcastic retorts. GAG, also informal, is principally applicable to a broadly comic remark.

joy *n.* **delight, enjoyment, pleasure.**
These terms denote states of happiness or satisfaction. DELIGHT applies to intense satisfaction: *The children opened their gifts with delight.* ENJOYMENT often suggests ongoing or sustained pleasure: *Books are a source of great enjoyment to him.* JOY implies an intense and sustained state and is often associated with self-realization, sharing, or high-mindedness: *the joy of cooking; the joys of motherhood.* PLEASURE is the least forceful of these terms; it often merely refers to a pleasant sensation, emotion, etc.: *She smiled with pleasure as she watched the robins build their nest.*
Antonym: **sorrow.**

joyful See **glad.**

judge *n.* **arbiter, arbitrator, referee, umpire.**
JUDGE and its synonyms denote persons empowered to make decisions that determine points at issue. A *judge* is

---

either the presiding officer in a court of justice or, in a nonlegal sense, anyone in a position to make decisions because he has authority or knowledge recognized as authoritative. An ARBITRATOR usually works, singly or with associates, to settle disputes, especially in labor-management relations, and derives his authority by advance consent of the parties to the dispute, who choose him or approve his selection for the job. An ARBITER is usually one who has no official status but is recognized as pre-eminent in a given nonlegal area, such as fashion or literature; less often, *arbiter* is used interchangeably with *arbitrator*. In legal terminology a REFEREE is an attorney appointed by a court to make a determination of a case or to investigate and report on it, and an UMPIRE is a person called upon to settle an issue that arbitrators are unable to resolve.

judgment See **opinion.**

judicious See **wise.**

just See **fair.**

justifiable *adj.* **defensible, excusable, tenable.**
Core meaning: Capable of being justified (*a justifiable reaction*).

justification See **explanation.**

justly See **fairly.**

juvenile See **young.**

keen See **sharp.**

ken *n.* **horizon, purview, range, reach, scope.**
Core meaning: The extent of one's understanding, knowledge, or vision (*written in technical language beyond my ken*).

kernel See **heart.**

kind 1. *adj.* **benevolent, compassionate, kindly.**
These describe persons and their actions when they show concern and sympathy for others. KIND and KINDLY are interchangeable when they describe persons and their na-

tures: *a kind man; a kindly, warm-hearted woman*. BENEVO-LENT suggests charitableness and a desire to promote others' welfare: *a benevolent ruler*. A COMPASSIONATE person is quick to sense another's suffering and often feels a wish to help or show mercy.
Antonym: **unkind.**
2. *n.* See **type.**

kindle 1. See **ignite. 2.** See **provoke.**

kindly See **kind.**

kismet See **fate.**

knowledge *n.* **erudition, information, learning, scholarship.**
These nouns refer to what one acquires and retains through study and experience. KNOWLEDGE is the broadest; it includes facts and ideas (*technical knowledge*), understanding (*our knowledge of the universe*), and the totality of what is known (*value knowledge for its own sake*). ERUDITION implies profound knowledge, often in a specialized area: *a scholar's erudition*. INFORMATION suggests a collection of facts and data about a certain subject or event: *An encyclopedia is a good source of information*. LEARNING refers to what is gained by schooling and study: *men of learning*. SCHOLARSHIP is the mark of one who has mastered some area of learning, which is reflected in the scope, thoroughness, and care of his work.
Antonym: **ignorance.**

labor See **work.**

lack See **deficiency.**

laconic See **concise.**

land See **nation.**

language *n.* **1. dialect, speech, tongue, vernacular.**
Core meaning: A system of terms used by a people sharing a history and culture (*Polish and Russian—two Slavic languages*).
2. cant, idiom, jargon, lexicon, terminology, vocabulary.
Core meaning: Specialized expressions characteristic of a

field, subject, trade, or subculture (*the language of electrical engineering; street language*).

large See **big.**

last *adj.* **eventual, final, terminal, ultimate.**
LAST and its synonyms refer to what marks an end or conclusion. *Last* applies to what brings a series, sequence, or any collection of like things to an end: *the last day of the month; the last piece of candy.* FINAL refers to what comes at the end of a progression or process and stresses the definiteness of the conclusion: *his final remark; our final offer.* TERMINAL is applied to what marks an end, a limit, or a boundary, as in space, time, development, etc.: *the terminal point of enemy penetration; the terminal stage of cancer.* EVENTUAL refers to what will occur at an unspecified future time: *the eventual date of publication; the eventual downfall of a corrupt government.* ULTIMATE is applied to what marks the end of a lengthy progression beyond which there exists no other: *our ultimate fate; an ultimate goal; the ultimate authority.*
Antonym: **first.**

late *adj.* **overdue, tardy.**
These apply to what fails to appear or take place at the usual, expected, or proper time. OVERDUE suggests a failure to meet an obligation when due: *Your rent is overdue!* TARDY is generally applied to persons who show up after an appointed time: *a tardy guest.* LATE fits either sense: *late returning your library books; late for the party.*
Antonym: **early.**

latency See **abeyance.**

later *adj.* **after, subsequent.**
Core meaning: Following something else in time (*later developments proved his predictions*).

laughable *adj.* **comic, comical, funny, laughing, risible.**
Core meaning: Deserving laughter (*a laughable matter*).

laughing See **laughable.**

lavish See **luxurious.**

law *n.* **1. canon, edict, precept, rule.**
Core meaning: A principle governing political affairs (*the law of nations*).
2. axiom, principle, theorem, universal.
Core meaning: A basic rule or truth (*the laws of decency*).

lawful See **legal.**

lax See **loose.**

lazy See **inactive.**

league See **union.**

lean See **thin.**

learning See **knowledge.**

leave See **abandon.**

leave off See **stop.**

lecherous See **immoral.**

lecture See **speech.**

legal *adj.* **lawful, legitimate.**
These describe what is authorized, established, recognized, approved, or permitted by law. In this sense LEGAL and LAWFUL are often interchangeable: *legal* (or *lawful*) *activities; his legal* (or *lawful*) *wife.* LEGITIMATE refers to what is in accordance with the law (*a legitimate political regime*), but it also applies to what is reasonable (*a legitimate reason for leaving*) and to what is authentic and genuine (*a legitimate complaint*).
Antonym: **illegal.**

legitimate See **legal.**

leisurely See **slow.**

lend *v.* **loan.**
To LEND is to give or allow the use of something temporarily on the condition that it—or its equivalent in kind—be returned (*lend a book*); it may also mean putting at another's disposal something that cannot be returned, as, for example, time or talent (*lend assistance*). LOAN is a synonym

of *lend* only in the first sense; in a financial transaction the payment of interest is usually implied.
Antonym: **borrow.**

lengthy See **long.**

lessen See **decrease.**

lesser See **minor.**

let See **permit.**

letdown See **disappointment.**

lethal See **fatal.**

lethargic See **apathetic.**

level *adj.* **even, flat, flush, plane, smooth.**
All of these apply to surfaces in which there are no, or no significant, variations in the form of elevations or depressions. LEVEL implies being horizontal or parallel with the line of the horizon: *level farmland.* FLAT often—but not always—refers to such a horizontal surface: *a flat geometric figure; a flat dish.* EVEN and PLANE refer to flat surfaces that are without elevations or depressions: *an even board; a plane figure.* FLUSH applies to a surface that is on an exact level with an adjoining one, forming a continuous surface: *a door that is flush with the wall.* SMOOTH describes a surface in which the absence of even slight irregularities can be established by sight or touch: *smooth wood; a smooth skin.*

lewd See **immoral.**

lexicon See **language.**

liable *adj.* **accountable, answerable, responsible.**
Core meaning: Legally obligated (*parents are liable for vandalism done by their children*).

liberal See **generous.**

liberate See **free.**

liberty See **freedom.**

license 1. See **freedom.** 2. See **permission.**

lie *n.* falsehood, falsity, fib, fiction, story, tale, untruth.
Core meaning: An untrue declaration (*spread lies about the senator's personal life*).

lifeless See **dead.**

lifelike See **graphic.**

lift See **raise.**

light 1. See **easy.** **2.** See **ignite.**

lighthearted See **cheerful.**

like *v.* dote, enjoy, fancy, relish.
LIKE and its synonyms mean to be attracted to or take pleasure in. *Like,* the least forceful, usually suggests only mild interest or regard: *She liked Jim a great deal but not enough to spend every evening with him.* DOTE (always used with *on*) implies foolish and extravagant attachment: *a woman who doted on her granddaughter.* ENJOY is applied to what gives pleasure (*enjoyed the movie*) or fulfillment (*enjoys living in the country*); FANCY, to what appeals to one's taste, inclination, caprice, etc. (*didn't fancy chocolates*); and RELISH, to what moves one to keen or zestful appreciation (*relished compliments*).
Antonym: dislike.

likely *adj.* probable.
LIKELY and PROBABLE refer to what shows a strong probability of happening or of being true: *It is likely to rain at any moment. Carelessness was the probable cause of the accident.* Both also describe what seems to be true but is not certain: *a likely excuse; a probable explanation.*
Antonym: unlikely.

limit *v.* circumscribe, delimit, restrict.
Core meaning: To specify the greatest amount or number allowed (*limited the number of free passes*).

line See **goods.**

lingering See **chronic.**

link See **join.**

---

listless See **apathetic.**

little *adj.* diminutive, miniature, minute, small, tiny.

LITTLE and its synonyms all apply to what is not large in size. *Little* is the most general and is often used interchangeably with SMALL. DIMINUTIVE, MINUTE, and TINY suggest that which is of extremely small size. MINIATURE can also be used loosely to mean "exceedingly small" but strictly refers to something that is on a scale greatly reduced from the usual.

Antonym: **big.**

live See **alive.**

livelihood See **living.**

liveliness See **spirit.**

lively See **active.**

living *n.* livelihood, maintenance, subsistence, support.

LIVING and its synonyms refer to what provides the necessities of life. *Living* and LIVELIHOOD often specify the occupation, work, or other means by which one earns his income: *Eskimos make their living by hunting and trapping. Jackson practiced medicine as a livelihood.* SUBSISTENCE often refers to what barely supports life: *earned his daily subsistence from the soil.* MAINTENANCE and SUPPORT are usually reckoned as the equivalent in money of what is needed for necessities such as food, lodging, and clothing: *a divorced man who provides maintenance* (or *support*) *for his family.* See also **alive.**

load See **charge.**

loan See **lend.**

loathe See **hate.**

loathing See **hate.**

locality See **area.**

lofty See **high.**

logic *n.* ratiocination, rationality, reason.

Core meaning: Exact, valid, and rational reasoning (*his logic was unassailable*).

logical See **sensible.**

lone See **alone.**

loneliness See **aloneness.**

lonely See **alone.**

loneness See **aloneness.**

lonesome See **alone.**

long *adj.* **extended, lengthy.**
Long describes what has great length or is of relatively great duration or extent: *a long river; a long novel; a long wait; a long journey.* Lengthy is often interchangeable with *long: a lengthy explanation; a lengthy journey.* What is extended continues for a long period of time: *extended peace talks.*
Antonym: **short.**

loose *adj.* **lax, slack.**
Loose and slack can be used interchangeably to refer to what is literally insufficiently stretched: *a loose* (or *slack*) *rope. Loose* also describes what is not tight-fitting (*a loose robe*), tightly fitted (*loose sleeves*), or tightly fastened (*loose shoelaces*). *Slack* and lax suggest carelessness or negligence: *a slack performance; lax about paying bills.*
Antonym: **tight.**

lose *v.* **mislay.**
To lose is to fail to find in the usual place (*lost my dictionary*). To mislay is to put in a place that one cannot remember: *She mislaid her hat.*
Antonym: **find.**

lost See **vanished.**

lot See **fate.**

love 1. *n.* **affection, devotion, fondness.**
All of these refer to feelings of attraction and attachment experienced by persons. Love suggests an intense feeling: *a husband's love for his wife; love of reading.* Affection is a steady feeling of warm regard: *motherly affection; an affec-*

tion for animals. DEVOTION is dedication, attachment, and loyalty to a person or thing: *his devotion to his mother; devotion to the cause.* FONDNESS, in its most common sense, is rather strong liking for a person or thing: *a fondness for his friends; a fondness for grapes.*
Antonym: **hate.**
2. *v.* adore, cherish.
These all refer to feelings of love or strong affection. LOVE is the most neutral: *loved her husband; loves reading.* ADORE stresses devotion (*adored her mother*); used in an informal sense, it merely means "to like very much" (*adores skiing*). CHERISH emphasizes tender care: *The old man cherished the foundling as if she were his own. The collector cherishes his paintings.*
Antonym: **hate.**

lovely See **beautiful.**

lower 1. *v.* drop.
To LOWER is to let, bring, or move something down to a lower level: *lowered her eyelids; lower the flag; lower your head.* To DROP is to let fall: *She dropped her glasses.*
Antonym: **raise.**
2. *v.* cut, reduce, slash.
These words all mean to decrease, as in amount, value, etc. LOWER, CUT, and REDUCE are often interchangeable in this sense: *lowering taxes; cut prices; reduced costs.* SLASH implies great reduction: *slashed prices for the sale.*
Antonym: **raise.**
3. *adj.* See minor.

lowly See **humble.**

loyal 1. See **faithful. 2.** See **true.**

lucky See **fortunate.**

ludicrous See **absurd.**

lunacy See **insanity.**

lure See **seduce.**

lurid See **ghastly.**

luscious See **delicious.**

lush See **luxurious.**

luxurious *adj.* **lavish, lush, luxuriant, opulent, palatial, plush, rich.**
Core meaning: Marked by extravagant, ostentatious magnificence (*a luxurious yacht*).

lying See **dishonesty.**

macabre See **ghastly.**

machination See **conspiracy.**

macrocosm See **universe.**

madness See **insanity.**

magnificent See **grand.**

magnitude See **bulk.**

maintenance See **living.**

majestic See **grand.**

make *v.* **1. construct, fabricate, fashion, manufacture, shape.**
Core meaning: To create by forming, combining, or altering materials (*made a house from logs; make a sandwich*).
2. See **constitute.**

make up 1. See **constitute. 2.** See **improvise.**

male *adj.* **manful, manly, mannish, masculine, virile.**
MALE and MASCULINE are essentially classifying terms. *Male* merely categorizes by sex; it is also applicable to animals, plants, and even things: *a male voice; a male rabbit; a male thread on a bolt. Masculine* can be used to categorize (*the masculine lead in a play*), but it can also describe traits, good and bad, considered characteristic of men: *masculine strength; masculine pride.* MANFUL and MANLY suggest such traits as braveness and resoluteness: *a manful* (or *manly*) *attempt.* MANNISH almost always indicates affectation of masculine traits or style by women: *a mannish haircut.* VIRILE stresses physical and sexual power.
Antonym: **female.**

malevolent *adj.* evil, malicious, malign, malignant, mean, nasty, poisonous, venomous, wicked.
Core meaning: Marked by ill will and spite (*a malevolent hatred of his rival*).

malicious See **malevolent**.

malign See **malevolent**.

malignant See **malevolent**.

maltreat See **abuse**.

manage See **administer**.

managerial See **executive**.

mandatory See **compulsory**.

maneuver See **move**.

manful See **male**.

mania See **insanity**.

manipulate See **handle**.

manly See **male**.

manner See **method**.

mannerism See **affectation**.

manners *n.* decorum, etiquette, proprieties.
Core meaning: Socially correct behavior (*had to mind his manners at the party*).

mannish See **male**.

manufacture See **make**.

margin See **border**.

mark 1. See **sign**. 2. See **notice**.

markdown See **depreciation**.

market See **sell**.

marriage *n.* matrimony, nuptials, wedding, wedlock.
MARRIAGE is applied broadly to the state or process of being married, to the ceremony involved, and to any close union (*a marriage of minds; opera, a marriage of music and*

drama). MATRIMONY applies to the condition of being married, often with emphasis on its religious nature. WEDLOCK pertains to the condition, primarily from a legal standpoint. WEDDING applies to the ceremony or celebrating, with connotations of social festivity. NUPTIALS applies most often to a wedding ceremony and may emphasize the religious aspect.

marrow See **heart.**

marvelous See **fabulous.**

masculine See **male.**

massive See **heavy.**

master See **professional.**

mastery See **expertise.**

material 1. See **relevant. 2.** See **matter.**

matrimony See **marriage.**

matter *n.* **material, stuff, substance.**
Core meaning: That from which things are made (*interesting matter for a novel*).

mature *adj.* **adult, grown-up.**
These apply to what has or shows the mental and emotional qualities associated with adults: *mature judgment; adult behavior; grown-up for her age.*
Antonym: **immature.**

maybe *adv.* **perchance, perhaps.**
Core meaning: Possibly but not certainly (*Maybe he'll come, and maybe not*).

mean See **malevolent.**

meaning *n.* **sense, significance, signification.**
MEANING is nonspecific and overlaps each of the following. SENSE, in this context, may be used to indicate the meaning conveyed by speech or writing (*Paragraphs often mark a break in the sense*) or to denote a particular meaning of a single word or phrase (*Words that are synonyms are usually alike in some senses*). SIGNIFICANCE stresses underlying or

---

long-range meaning; it implies evaluation: *a historical event of great significance*. SIGNIFICATION applies to accepted or established meaning, conveyed directly: *the dictionary signification of a word*.

means *n.* agency, instrument, mechanism, medium.
Core meaning: That by which something is accomplished (*increase sales by means of a new advertising campaign*).

measure See **move**.

mechanism See **means**.

meddle See **interfere**.

meditative See **pensive**.

medium See **means**.

meek See **humble**.

meet See **face**.

melancholy See **sad**.

melee See **conflict**.

menace See **threaten**.

mendacity See **dishonesty**.

mentality See **psychology**.

merchandise 1. See **sell**. 2. See **goods**.

mercurial See **capricious**.

merit See **earn**.

merriment See **gaiety**.

merrymaking See **gaiety**.

messy See **disorderly**.

method *n.* fashion, manner, mode, system, way.
These all refer to the procedures or plans followed to accomplish a given task. METHOD often suggests regularity of procedure; it emphasizes detailed, logically ordered plans: *Three methods of purifying water are to filter it, to distill it, and to add chemicals to it*. SYSTEM stresses order and regularity affecting all parts and details of a procedure: *a system*

for improving production. MANNER, FASHION, and MODE refer more to individual and distinctive procedure, as that dictated by preference, tradition, custom, etc.: *taught in an innovative manner; sings in an interesting fashion; an unusual mode of painting*. WAY is the most neutral and general of these terms and is often an inclusive synonym for them: *a better way of working out accounting problems*.

meticulous See **careful.**

mid See **middle.**

middle *adj.* **central, intermediate, mid, midway.**
Core meaning: Not extreme (*took the middle course in the negotiations*).

middleman See **go-between.**

midway See **middle.**

mild See **gentle.**

mimic See **imitate.**

mind 1. See **obey. 2.** See **psychology.**

miniature See **little.**

minimize See **belittle.**

minor *adj.* **inferior, lesser, lower, secondary.**
Core meaning: Of subordinate standing or importance (*a minor consideration*).

minus See **disadvantage.**

minute 1. See **little. 2.** See **moment.**

miraculous See **fabulous.**

mirth See **gaiety.**

miscarry See **fail.**

miserable See **sad.**

miserly See **stingy.**

misery See **distress.**

misgiving 1. See **doubt. 2.** See **qualm.**

mishandle See **botch.**

mislay See **lose.**

mislead See **deceive.**

mismanage See **botch.**

mistake See **error.**

mistreat See **abuse.**

mobile See **moving.**

mock See **ridicule.**

mode See **method.**

model See **ideal.**

modern *adj.* **contemporary, current, present-day.**
These all refer to what belongs to the moment in time intermediate between the past and the future: *modern life; a contemporary composer; current developments; present-day living.* MODERN can also stress a break with tradition and bold new experimentation and originality: *modern art; modern dance.*
Antonym: **old.**

modernize *v.* **refurbish, rejuvenate, restore, update.**
Core meaning: To make modern in appearance or style (*modernized the factory*).

modest 1. See **humble. 2.** See **plain. 3.** See **shy.**

modify See **change.**

mollify See **pacify.**

moment *n.* **flash, instant, jiffy, minute, second, trice.**
MOMENT pertains to a brief but usually not insignificant period; the sense of importance is strengthened when the term specifies a point in time: *a great moment in history.* MINUTE, used strictly, is specific; informally it is interchangeable with *moment: Wait a minute* (or *moment*). An INSTANT is a period of time almost too brief to detect; though the term is imprecise, it implies haste and usually urgency, especially as a specific point in time: *Come this instant!* SECOND may be used specifically or it may be used loosely, as

the equivalent of *instant* (*Come this second!*). TRICE, a literary term, and FLASH and the informal JIFFY appear in combinations preceded by *in a* (as *in a trice*—or *flash* or *jiffy*); they are imprecise but approximately equal in duration to *instant;* they imply haste but not necessarily urgency.

momentary See **temporary.**

momentous See **important.**

monkey See **fiddle.**

monotony *n.* **humdrum, tediousness, tedium.**
Core meaning: A tiresome lack of variety (*The monotony of office routine*).

monstrous See **outrageous.**

moral *adj.* **1. decent, ethical, honorable.**
These describe what conforms to accepted standards of what is considered just, right, or good: *made a moral choice; decent behavior; ethical business practices; an honorable man.*
Antonym: **immoral.**
2. chaste, pure, virtuous.
These four apply to what conforms to accepted rules of propriety and morality, especially in sexual matters: *moral behavior; a virtuous woman.* CHASTE and PURE often imply virginity or celibacy: *a chaste nun; a pure child.*
Antonym: **immoral.**

morality See **virtue.**

morose See **gloomy.**

mortal See **fatal.**

motionless *adj.* **immobile, still.**
These all apply to what is not in motion. MOTIONLESS is the most general: *stood motionless in front of his boss's desk.* IMMOBILE can refer to what is not moving (*paused immobile beside the tree*) or to what is fixed and not movable (*a statue immobile on its pedestal*). STILL implies lack of motion, noise, or disturbance: *still water; a still night.*
Antonym: **moving.**

motivate See **provoke.**

motivation See **stimulus.**

mount See **rise.**

movable See **moving.**

move 1. *n.* maneuver, measure, procedure, step, tactic.
Core meaning: An action calculated to achieve an end (*trying to decide their next move*).
2. *v.* See **affect.**
3. *v.* See **provoke.**

moving *adj.* **1.** mobile, movable.
MOVING applies to what changes or can change position: *a moving truck; moving parts.* What is MOBILE can move (*An animal's tail is mobile*) or be moved from place to place (*a mobile hospital*). MOVABLE implies only the capability of being moved: *movable type.*
Antonym: **motionless.**
2. affecting, pathetic, poignant, stirring, touching.
All of these refer to emotional reaction. MOVING applies to what calls forth any deeply felt emotion: *a moving love story.* STIRRING stresses strong emotion and is related to stimulation and inspiration: *a stirring anthem.* POIGNANT describes what is piercing or penetrating (*poignant criticism*); it also applies to what is keenly distressing or painful (*poignant grief*) and what appeals to the emotions (*poignant memories*). TOUCHING emphasizes sympathy and compassion: *a touching letter.* PATHETIC stresses pity (*a pathetic old woman*) and sometimes mild scorn for what is hopelessly inept or inadequate (*a pathetic attempt at humor*). AFFECTING applies to anything capable of moving the feelings but often pertains to what inspires pity and tenderness: *an affecting tale of woe.*

muddle 1. See **confuse. 2.** See **daze.**

muff See **botch.**

multifariousness See **variety.**

multiformity See **variety.**

multiplicity See **variety.**

murky See **dark.**

musing See **pensive.**

mutinous See **rebellious.**

mutiny See **rebellion.**

mutual *adj.* **reciprocal, reciprocative.**
Core meaning: Having the same relationship each to the other (*mutual affection*).

nab See **catch.**

nag See **scold.**

naked See **bare.**

name *n.* **appellation, denomination, designation, nickname, title.**
NAME is the general term among these related words. A DESIGNATION is a name given to classify or identify: *The correct designation for "heavy hydrogen" is "deuterium."* A DENOMINATION is also a categorizing name; it is applied to persons or things, often religious groups or monetary units, having close relationship: *people of all denominations; bills of small denomination.* A TITLE, applied to persons, indicates rank, office, vocation, etc., and generally connotes distinction; applied to things, such as literary or musical works, it serves to identify. An APPELLATION is a name, other than a proper one, that describes or characterizes and that gains currency more through use than through a formal act of designation: *Abraham Lincoln is known by the appellation "The Great Emancipator."* A NICKNAME is an informal, unofficial, or affectionate name, often a shortened form of a proper name: *Joseph's nickname is Joey.*

nasty See **malevolent.**

nation *n.* **commonwealth, country, land, people, race, state.**
NATION primarily signifies a political body—a group of human beings organized under a single government, without close regard for their origins (*the new nations of Africa*); it

also denotes the territory occupied by a political body (*All across the nation new industries are developing*). STATE even more specifically indicates governmental organization, generally on a sovereign basis and in a well-defined area: *the state of Israel.* COMMONWEALTH is used in a political sense to denote the people of a nation or state; it also refers to a nation or state governed by the people: *Australia is a commonwealth.* COUNTRY signifies the territory of one nation (*the country of France*) and is also used in the sense of *nation* (*all the countries of the world*). LAND is a term for a region (*the land of the bison and beaver*); it also can be used to mean *nation* (*the highest elective office in the land*). PEOPLE, in this context, signifies a group united over a long period by common cultural, religious, linguistic, and social ties (*primitive peoples*); it also denotes a body of persons living in the same country under one national government (*the American people*). RACE refers to those recognizable physical traits, stemming from common ancestry, that succeeding generations have in common: *the Caucasian race.*

native *adj.* **aboriginal, indigenous.**
NATIVE indicates birth or immediate origin in a specific place: *a native Englishman.* ABORIGINAL describes those who are the first known to have lived in a given region: *aboriginal peoples.* INDIGENOUS specifies that something or someone is of a kind originally living or growing in a region rather than coming or being brought from another part of the world: *The bison is indigenous to North America. The Ainu are indigenous to the northernmost islands of Japan.* *Antonym:* **foreign.**

natural *adj.* **1. genuine, real.**
NATURAL, GENUINE, and REAL all refer to what is not man-made but is present in or produced by nature: *the moon, a natural satellite of the earth; genuine leather; real sable.* *Antonym:* **artificial.**
2. genuine, real, simple, unaffected.
These refer to what shows lack of artifice and affectation. NATURAL stresses spontaneity: *a natural way of speaking.*

GENUINE and REAL suggest that something is free of pretense or falseness: *genuine affection; real humility*. What is SIMPLE is utterly sincere and lacking in deviousness or deceit: *a simple, direct answer*. UNAFFECTED emphasizes lack of affectation: *unaffected behavior*.
Antonym: **affected.**

nature 1. See **disposition.** 2. See **universe.**

nauseate See **repel.**

near *adj.* **close, nearby.**
NEAR, CLOSE, and NEARBY refer to what is not far, as in space, time, position, or degree. *Nearby* is the most restricted in application, since it almost always refers to what is located a short distance away: *a nearby city*. *Near* and *close* can be used in this sense, often interchangeably: *The airport is near* (or *close to*) *town*. Both can also imply intimacy of relationship (*near relatives; close friends*).
Antonym: **far.**

nearby See **near.**

nearly See **approximately.**

neat *adj.* **orderly, tidy, trim.**
NEAT and its synonyms all describe what is in good or clean condition. *Neat* is the most general: *a neat room; neat handwriting*. ORDERLY implies that which is well arranged or managed and therefore efficient: *an orderly kitchen*. What is TIDY is precisely arranged: *a tidy room; a tidy closet*. TRIM stresses especially pleasing or smart appearance resulting from neatness and tidiness: *looked very trim in his new suit*.
Antonym: **disorderly.**

necessary *adj.* **essential, indispensable, vital.**
NECESSARY and its synonyms describe what is needed to achieve a certain result or fulfill a certain requirement. *Necessary* implies that which fills an urgent but not invariably all-compelling need: *fill out the necessary forms*. ESSENTIAL and VITAL refer to what is basic and therefore of crucial importance: *The microscope is an essential tool of science.*

Irrigation was vital to early civilization. INDISPENSABLE even more strongly applies to what cannot be left out or done without: *Oxygen is indispensable for human life.*
Antonym: **unnecessary.**

necessity See **need.**

need *n.* **exigency, necessity, requisite.**
NEED is the most general of these nouns and the least strong in signifying urgency. NECESSITY greatly intensifies urgency; what is a *necessity* is required for the existence, success, or functioning of something: *The sun is a necessity to life on the earth.* EXIGENCY, which is usually plural in this sense, stresses great urgency brought about by particular conditions or circumstances: *the exigencies of war.* REQUISITE specifies need closely associated with the attainment of a given goal: *The first requisite for a successful novel is a good plot.*

needless See **unnecessary.**

negation See **denial.**

neglect *v.* **disregard, shirk, slack.**
Core meaning: To avoid the fulfillment of (*neglected their duty*).

nervous See **upset.**

new *adj.* **fresh, recent.**
NEW applies to what has just been produced or made (*a new movie; a new car*) or has never been used or worn (*a new typewriter; new clothes*). What is FRESH is not yet old; the term suggests unspoiled quality: *fresh eggs.* RECENT stresses the fact that something has been in existence for a short time: *a summary of recent events.* See also **fresh; strange.**
Antonym: **old.**

nickname See **name.**

nimble See **graceful.**

nonappearance See **absence.**

nonattendance See **absence.**

nonchalance See **equanimity.**

nonessential See **unnecessary.**

normal *adj*. **regular, standard, typical.**
NORMAL refers to what conforms to or constitutes a usual pattern, level, or category (*his normal weight; normal room temperature*); more specifically it describes what functions in a natural, healthy way (*normal digestion; normal growth*). REGULAR and STANDARD indicate conformity to a pattern in an impersonal sense: *sold radios at 25 per cent off the regular price; a standard sort of horror movie.* TYPICAL stresses the traits or characteristics peculiar to a kind, group, or category: *a typical college professor.*
Antonym: **abnormal.**

nosy See **curious.**

note 1. See **sign.** 2. See **notice.**

notice *n*. **attention, cognizance, heed, mark, note, regard.**
Core meaning: The act of observing or taking into account (*took notice of the young executive's drive*).

noticeable See **perceptible.**

novel 1. See **fresh.** 2. See **unconventional.**

novelty *n*. **freshness, originality.**
Core meaning: The quality of being new and different (*acclaimed the novelty of his ideas*).

nub See **heart.**

nude See **bare.**

null See **invalid.**

numb See **deaden.**

nuptials See **marriage.**

obedient See **submission.**

obese See **fat.**

obey *v*. **comply, follow, mind.**
OBEY and COMPLY both mean to act in accordance with a request, rule, order, or the like. *Obey* suggests the accep-

tance of authority (*obeying traffic regulations*); *comply,* the disposition to yield without protest (*The singer complied with the audience's request by singing an encore*). FOLLOW suggests adherence to a prescribed course of action: *followed the doctor's orders.* MIND applies particularly to children on good behavior: *He minds his mother.*
Antonym: **command.**

objection *n.* **challenge, protest, remonstrance.**
Core meaning: The act of expressing strong or reasoned opposition (*a decision made despite the objections of the staff*).

objectionable See **unpleasant.**

obligatory See **compulsory.**

obliging See **amiable.**

obliterate See **abolish.**

obloquy **1.** See **dishonor. 2.** See **tirade.**

obscene See **coarse.**

obscure *adj.* **unknown.**
These two describe what has not attracted widespread notice: *obscure members of the clergy; unknown legal treatises.* See also **ambiguous.**
Antonym: **famous.**

observant See **alert.**

obstinate *adj.* **dogged, headstrong, intractable, intransigent, refractory.**
Core meaning: Tenaciously unwilling to yield (*an obstinate man who never apologized*).

obstruct See **hinder.**

obtuse See **dull.**

occasion See **opportunity.**

occupation See **work.**

odd See **strange.**

odium See **dishonor.**

offbeat See **unconventional.**

offend *v.* **affront, insult, outrage.**
OFFEND is the least emphatic of these verbs, which denote the act of giving displeasure; it often makes no implication regarding intent. To INSULT is to speak to or treat with contempt; it implies a deliberate act calculated to cause humiliation. AFFRONT strengthens this sense of open insult. OUTRAGE, stronger still, emphasizes what causes extreme resentment by flagrant violation of standards of right and decency. See also **displease.**

offer *v.* **present, proffer, tender.**
OFFER is the basic, general term among this group of verbs, which all refer to putting something forward for acceptance or refusal. PROFFER is somewhat more emphatic through its implication of voluntary action motivated by courtesy or generosity: *proffered her help to a blind man at a street corner.* TENDER, in business or legal usage, may stress formality (*tender one's resignation*), or it may apply specifically to discharge of an obligation (*tender payment*); in more general usage it emphasizes formality and observance of amenities (*tender one's respects*). PRESENT stresses formality: *The ambassador presented his credentials to the king.*

offshoot See **branch.**

ogle See **gaze.**

oily See **unctuous.**

old *adj.* **1. aged, elderly, venerable.**
These terms apply to persons. OLD, while the most general, often strongly stresses advanced years: *an old man with a white beard.* ELDERLY specifies the period past late middle age without necessarily implying decline: *an elderly gentleman.* AGED emphasizes advanced years and sometimes suggests infirmity: *an aged couple living in retirement.* VENERABLE implies dignity and qualities associated with age that are worthy of great respect: *a venerable senator.*
Antonym: **young.**

---

2. used, worn.

OLD applies to what is not of recent make (*a collection of old paperweights*); USED, to what is secondhand (*a used car; used clothing*); and WORN, to what is damaged by wear or use (*worn, faded trousers*).

Antonym: **new.**

3. ancient, antique, archaic, olden.

These all describe what belongs to an earlier time or period. OLD is the general term: *an old Roman bronze.* ANCIENT suggests the remote past (*ancient history*); ARCHAIC refers to primitive times (*an archaic religion*) or to what is not current (*archaic laws*). ANTIQUE is applied both to what is very old and to what has acquired added value through age: *antique furniture.* OLDEN often suggests a note of nostalgia: *in olden days.*

Antonym: **modern.**

olden See **old.**

omen *n.* **augury, portent, presage.**

Core meaning: A sign or warning of some future good or evil (*saw omens of trouble to come*).

omnivorous See **voracious.**

open See **spread.**

open-eyed See **alert.**

opening See **opportunity.**

operate *v.* **function, go, run, work.**

Core meaning: To act effectively (*The machine doesn't operate half the time*).

opinion *n.* **belief, conviction, feeling, judgment, persuasion, sentiment, view.**

An OPINION is any conclusion held with confidence but not supported by positive knowledge or proof: *a man who mistook opinion for fact.* VIEW stresses individuality of outlook as a determinant of the conclusion: *her views on education.* SENTIMENT and especially FEELING are views or attitudes based on emotion rather than reason: *public sentiment against foreign wars; his religious feelings.* A BELIEF is a conclusion to which one subscribes strongly: *It is my belief that justice will prevail.* CONVICTION is belief that excludes doubt: *my conviction that he is a dishonest person.* PERSUASION applies to a strong belief but does not necessarily suggest an intellectual basis: *of a certain political persuasion.* JUDGMENT, strictly, is opinion based on reasoning and evaluation rather than emotion or will: *In my judgment now is the time to sell.*

opponent *n.* **adversary, antagonist, competitor, rival.**
All of these nouns refer to persons engaged in contests or struggles. An OPPONENT is a person or group that opposes another, as in a battle, controversy, etc. ADVERSARY suggests a more formidable opponent, while an ANTAGONIST is an actively hostile opponent. COMPETITOR, a milder word, suggests a person trying to outdo one or more opponents, as in sports or business. RIVAL most frequently implies a single, more personal opponent who is competing for the same objective.

opportunity *n.* **break, chance, occasion, opening.**
OPPORTUNITY and its synonyms refer to a favorable or suitable time or circumstance. An *opportunity* is the right moment to take action toward a certain purpose: *taking the opportunity to go to Europe.* OCCASION, weaker than *opportunity,* suggests the appropriate time for action: *took the occasion to ask her to the celebration.* An OPENING is either an unexpected or an awaited opportunity, as to embark on a new career, launch an enterprise, etc.: *waited for an opening in the conversation to make known his opinion.* CHANCE often implies luck or accident in the arrival of an opportunity: *never had the chance to study photography.* BREAK adds to *chance* the idea that adverse circumstances have unexpectedly become favorable: *had a lucky break and was promoted.*

oppose 1. See **repel. 2.** See **withstand.**

opprobrious See **abusive.**

---

opprobrium See **dishonor.**

optimistic *adj.* **hopeful, rosy, sanguine.**
Core meaning: Expecting a favorable outcome (*optimistic about the future of the company*).

option See **choice.**

optional *adj.* **elective, voluntary.**
These three describe what is not required by laws, rules, or regulations. OPTIONAL often suggests that something may be included or not as one wishes: *Whitewall tires and bucket seats are optional.* ELECTIVE implies free choice: *The school offers a wide selection of elective courses.* VOLUNTARY applies to what one does of one's own accord: *voluntary military service.*
Antonym: **compulsory.**

opulent See **luxurious.**

oration See **speech.**

order 1. See **command.** 2. See **union.**

orderly See **neat.**

ordinary 1. See **common.** 2. See **familiar.**

organization See **union.**

origin *n.* **inception, root, source.**
ORIGIN and its synonyms relate to beginnings. *Origin,* applicable to persons as well as to things, indicates the often remote time and place when something began: *the origin of life; the origin of a word.* INCEPTION is more specific and marks the actual start of an action or process: *the inception of the space program.* ROOT usually refers to beginning in the sense of fundamental cause or basic reason: *Money is the root of all evil.* SOURCE stresses a place or thing from which something is derived or comes into being (*used the sea as a source of food*); it may also denote a person or printed work considered as a giver of information (*used newspaper articles as the source for his report*).

original See **authentic.**

---

originality See **novelty.**

ornate See **elaborate.**

orthodox See **conventional.**

outcome See **effect.**

outdo See **surpass.**

outline See **draft.**

outlook 1. See **posture. 2.** See **view.**

output See **production.**

outrage See **offend.**

outrageous *adj.* **flagrant, infamous, monstrous.**
These adjectives describe behavior that is grossly offensive or revolting to society; they are often used interchangeably. OUTRAGEOUS applies to what is so distasteful or appalling as to be shocking or intolerable: *an outrageous remark; outrageous prices*. FLAGRANT often adds to *outrageous* the idea of defiance of recognized authority: *a flagrant violation of the law*. INFAMOUS has a personal sense, suggesting bad reputation and notoriety: *an infamous murderer*. MONSTROUS describes actions so outrageous as to be almost inhuman: *Kidnapping is a monstrous act.*

outright See **utter.**

outshine See **surpass.**

outstretch See **spread.**

outstrip See **surpass.**

overbearing See **dictatorial.**

overdue See **late.**

oversight See **error.**

overthrow *v.* **overturn, topple, tumble.**
Core meaning: To bring about the downfall of (*rebels trying to overthrow the government*).

overturn See **overthrow.**

own See **acknowledge.**

---

pacify *v.* appease, assuage, conciliate, mollify, placate, propitiate.
Core meaning: To ease the anger or agitation of (*managed to pacify the irate customer*).

pain See **distress.**

painstaking See **careful.**

pair See **couple.**

palatial See **luxurious.**

palpable See **perceptible.**

pamper *v.* baby, coddle, humor, indulge, spoil.
These all refer to catering excessively to another's—or one's own—desires or feelings. INDULGE is applied principally to desires, appetites, and special pleasures, sometimes without very strong condemnation: *indulged my craving for candy.* To PAMPER is to treat with extreme indulgence; it often suggests overattentiveness to physical comforts: *pampered their only child.* HUMOR implies short-term compliance with another's wishes, mood, or idiosyncrasies: *good-naturedly humoring her aunt.* SPOIL usually implies a long-term oversolicitude that badly affects a person's character: *spoiling his son by giving him a big allowance and no responsibilities.* CODDLE points to tender, often overtender care: *coddled his young wife.* BABY suggests bestowing on someone the indulgence and attention appropriate to an infant; it is always unfavorable: *annoyed her grown son by hovering over him and babying him.*

par See **equivalence.**

parallel *adj.* coextensive, collateral, concurrent.
Core meaning: Lying in the same plane but not intersecting (*parallel roads*).

pardon *v.* excuse, forgive.
These verbs denote withholding punishment or blame for an offense or fault. To PARDON is to pass over an offense without demanding punishment or subjecting to disfavor: *The queen pardoned a dozen offenders in honor of her birthday.*

Forgive implies giving up all resentment as well as all claim to retribution: *forgave him for stealing the family silver.* Excuse suggests making allowance for or overlooking an offense: *Excuse me for what I said yesterday.*
Antonym: **punish.**

parity See **equivalence.**

parlance See **wording.**

parley See **deliberation.**

parody See **imitate.**

part See **separate.**

partner *n.* **accomplice, ally, associate, colleague, confederate.** Partner and its synonyms all denote one who cooperates in a venture, occupation, or challenge. *Partner* implies a relationship, frequently between two people, in which each has equal status and a certain independence but also has implicit or formal obligation to the other or others. A colleague is a fellow member of a profession, staff, or organization. An ally is one who, out of a common cause, has taken one's side and can be relied upon, at least temporarily. Confederate, in this sense, and accomplice are both derogatory; they are usually applied to alleged criminals and suggest guilt by willful association. *Confederate* is the more general, signifying any collaborator in a suspicious relationship or venture. An *accomplice* is more specifically somebody who assists a lawbreaker in a crime, without necessarily being present at the time of the crime. An associate is broadly anyone who works in the same place (as distinct from the same field) as another, usually in direct contact with him.

party See **combine.**

pass See **surpass.**

pass away See **die.**

passion *n.* **ardor, enthusiasm, fervor, zeal.** All of these nouns denote strong feeling, either sustained or passing, for or about something or somebody. Passion is a deep, overwhelming feeling or emotion; when directed toward a person, it usually connotes love as well as sexual desire, although it can also refer to hostile emotions such as anger and hatred (*loathe with passion*). Used lightly, it suggests an avid interest, as in an activity or hobby: *a passion for music.* ARDOR can suggest intense devotion to a cause but commonly connotes a warm, rapturous feeling directed toward persons (*The couple embraced with ardor*). ENTHUSIASM reflects excitement and responsiveness to specific or concrete things: *supported the hockey team with enthusiasm.* FERVOR is a highly intense, sustained emotional state, frequently (like *passion*) with a potential loss of control implied: *He fought with fervor.* ZEAL, which sometimes reflects strong, forceful devotion to a specific cause, expresses a driving attraction to something that grows out of motivation or attitude: *studied philosophy with zeal.*

passive See **submissive.**

paste See **hit.**

pathetic See **moving.**

patient *adj.* **forbearing, resigned.**
All of these refer to what is marked by or shows tolerance of trouble, hardship, delay, etc., over a period of time, usually without complaint though not necessarily without annoyance. PATIENT often implies calm that comes from understanding: *a patient teacher who realizes how difficult it is to learn to read.* FORBEARING suggests restraint, often in the face of considerable provocation: *the forbearing parents of a rebellious teenager.* RESIGNED implies a feeling of failure or of passive acceptance: *resigned to his lot in life.* *Antonym:* **impatient.**

pay See **wage(s).**

peace See **tranquillity.**

peaceful See **calm.**

peak See **climax.**

peculiar 1. See **characteristic.** 2. See **strange.**

peddle See **sell.**

peer See **gaze.**

peeve See **annoy.**

penalize See **punish.**

pendulous See **hanging.**

pensile See **hanging.**

pensive *adj.* meditative, musing, wistful.
Core meaning: Suggestive of or expressing deep thoughtfulness (*a pensive mood*).

people See **nation.**

pep See **spirit.**

perceptible *adj.* appreciable, discernible, noticeable, palpable. These describe what can be seen, measured, or detected. PERCEPTIBLE applies to what can be apprehended by the senses or the mind: *a perceptible improvement in the patient's condition.* APPRECIABLE refers to what is considerable in a quantitative sense: *an appreciable amount of atomic waste.* What is DISCERNIBLE can be recognized through scrutiny: *no discernible progress in the negotiations.* NOTICEABLE applies to what is adequately revealed or observable: *a noticeable tremor in his voice.* PALPABLE refers to what can be touched or felt (*a palpable oil*) and to what is easily perceived, even obvious (*a palpable feeling of anger*).
Antonym: imperceptible.

perchance See **maybe.**

perfect *adj.* faultless, flawless, impeccable.
These describe what has no defects, flaws, errors, etc.; they can be used interchangeably: *a perfect piece of marble; a faultless performance of the sonata; a flawless diamond; impeccable table manners.*
Antonym: imperfect.

perhaps See **maybe.**

peril See **danger.**

period See **age.**

periphery See **border.**

perish See **die.**

permanent *adj.* **enduring, eternal, perpetual.**
These all apply to what is lasting or meant to last indefinitely. PERMANENT is the most general. ENDURING usually suggests what is not dimmed or changed by the passage of time: *enduring fame.* ETERNAL and PERPETUAL imply uninterrupted existence unaffected by time: *eternal truths; the perpetual ice and snow of the polar regions.*
Antonym: **temporary.**

permission *n.* **allowance, authorization, consent, license, sanction.**
Core meaning: Approval for an action (*received permission to go ahead with the project*).

permit *v.* **allow, let.**
These are compared in the meaning "to consent to something." Inherent in both PERMIT and ALLOW is the ability to prevent an act. *Permit,* however, suggests authoritative consent (*permit smoking*); *allow,* mere refraining from any hindrance (*Please allow me to finish*). LET often suggests weak consent or failure to prevent something: *His mother let him go to the rock concert even though she disapproved.*
Antonym: **forbid.**

perpendicular See **vertical.**

perpetual See **permanent.**

perpetuate See **immortalize.**

persistent See **chronic.**

personal See **private.**

personality See **disposition.**

perspective See **view.**

persuasion See **opinion.**

pertinent See **relevant.**

perverse See **contrary.**

pet See **caress.**

phenomenal See **fabulous.**

phraseology See **wording.**

phrasing See **wording.**

pick See **choose.**

pictorial See **graphic.**

piece See **cut.**

pinnacle See **climax.**

pious See **holy.**

pith See **heart.**

pithy See **concise.**

pitiless See **cruel.**

placate See **pacify.**

placid See **calm.**

plague See **afflict.**

plain *adj.* **austere, modest, severe, simple.**
PLAIN and its synonyms apply to what is not showy, elaborate, or luxurious. *Plain* and SIMPLE can be used interchangeably in this meaning: *a plain* (or *simple*) *dress; plain* (or *simple*) *food.* AUSTERE and SEVERE imply extreme simplicity, even to the point of total lack of decoration or ornamentation: *austere living quarters; a severe black dress.* MODEST stresses lack of pretension: *a modest summer cottage.*
Antonym: **elaborate.**

plane See **level.**

play See **fiddle.**

plead See **urge.**

pleasant *adj.* **agreeable, gratifying, pleasing, welcome.**
These words describe what gives delight or satisfaction: *a pleasant guest; a pleasant visit; an agreeable hostess; an*

agreeable aroma; a gratifying response to the offer; election results that were gratifying; a pleasing personality; a pleasing furniture arrangement; a welcome visitor; a welcome change.
Antonym: unpleasant.

please *v.* **delight, gratify.**
To PLEASE is to give enjoyment or satisfaction: *The island pleased the vacationers. The new employee was eager to please.* DELIGHT suggests great pleasure or enjoyment: *I was delighted to run into my old friend after all these years.* GRATIFY especially emphasizes satisfaction, as from deserved recognition, fulfillment of a need, etc.: *His scientific achievements gratified his father.*
Antonym: displease.

pleasing See **pleasant.**

pleasure See **joy.**

pledge *v.* **1. promise, swear, vow.**
Core meaning: To guarantee by a solemn promise (*pledged financial assistance*).
2. See **devote.**

pliant See **flexible.**

plight See **predicament.**

plot See **conspiracy.**

plug See **advertise.**

plump See **fat.**

plush See **luxurious.**

ply See **handle.**

poignant See **moving.**

poisonous See **malevolent.**

polite *adj.* **civil, courteous.**
These apply to proper and mannerly persons and behavior. POLITE is the least specific: *a polite boy; polite applause.* CIVIL suggests reserve, formality, and a minimum of friend-

liness and tact: *Can't you give me a civil answer?* COURTE-
OUS implies kind and warm graciousness: *a courteous host.*
See also **refined.**
Antonym: **impolite.**

polluted See **impure.**

ponderous See **heavy.**

poor *adj.* **destitute, impoverished, indigent.**
All of these refer to persons who have little or no money,
wealth, or income. POOR and INDIGENT, the more formal
term, can be used interchangeably: *a poor* (or *indigent*)
family who cannot afford to buy groceries. IMPOVERISHED
suggests that someone has been reduced to poverty but may
once not have been poor: *impoverished people who had to
sell the family silver.* DESTITUTE, the strongest of these
words, implies complete poverty: *left destitute after the
flood. Poor* and *impoverished* can be used figuratively to
describe something that lacks natural richness or strength:
poor (or *impoverished*) *soil.*
Antonym: **rich.**

popular See **public.**

portent See **omen.**

portion See **cut.**

pose See **affectation.**

position See **posture.**

possess See **carry.**

possessions See **holdings.**

possibility *n.* **contingency, eventuality.**
Core meaning: Something that may occur or be done (*Rain
is a real possibility tonight*).

possible *adj.* **feasible, practicable.**
POSSIBLE applies to what can be realized or accomplished: *It
may be possible to get there by helicopter.* Something is
FEASIBLE if it is clearly possible and likely to be carried out:
a feasible plan for new housing. PRACTICABLE describes

what is fitted for actual application: *a practicable solution to the problem.*
Antonym: **impossible.**

posterity See **descendant.**

posture *n.* **attitude, outlook, position, stance.**
Core meaning: A frame of mind affecting one's thoughts or behavior (*a defeatist posture*).

power *n.* **authority, control.**
These nouns denote the right or ability to dominate or rule others. POWER is the most general; it applies whether it is based on rank, position, character, or other advantages: *the absolute power of an emperor; a general with the power to send troops into action.* AUTHORITY suggests legitimate and recognized power: *The mayor had the authority to dismiss the dishonest commissioner.* CONTROL stresses the right to regulate or direct as well as dominate: *the conductor's control over the orchestra.*

powerless *adj.* **helpless, impotent.**
POWERLESS and HELPLESS describe what lacks power or authority, as to act or resist: *powerless people at the mercy of their enemies; helpless to combat superior forces.* IMPOTENT in addition suggests weakness and the inability to act: *a ruler impotent to right a wrong.*
Antonym: **powerful.**

practicable See **possible.**

practical *adj.* **functional, serviceable, useful.**
PRACTICAL and its synonyms describe what serves or is capable of serving some purpose. *Practical* often refers to what is designed to serve a purpose, without being decorative (*practical low-heeled shoes*); often it stresses efficiency (*a practical machine*). USEFUL stresses the capacity to be used advantageously: *a useful map; a useful reminder.* FUNCTIONAL applies especially to what is designed for a particular purpose: *functional clothing for infants.* SERVICEABLE often suggests durability and sturdiness: *serviceable work boots.*
Antonym: **impractical.**

---

praise *v.* **acclaim, commend.**
These are words for expressing approval. To PRAISE is to express one's esteem or admiration: *The customers all praised the restaurant highly. Everyone praised her good sense and learning.* ACCLAIM is often—but not always— used literally to indicate actual applause or cheering: *The audience acclaimed the artist's performance of Chopin. The critics are all acclaiming her new novel.* COMMEND implies speaking well of and is usually more formal and official: *The mayor commended the commission for its thorough report.*
Antonym: **blame.**

precariousness See **instability.**

precept See **law.**

precious 1. See **arty. 2.** See **valuable.**

predestination See **fate.**

predicament *n.* **dilemma, plight, quandary.**
A PREDICAMENT is a difficult or embarrassing situation; it often suggests that one has a puzzling or troublesome decision to make and is considering the problem rationally. A PLIGHT is a serious condition or a situation of difficulty or peril, with the appropriate course of action being less clear. DILEMMA more abstractly denotes a problem that requires a person to choose between courses of action that are equally difficult or unpleasant. QUANDARY, somewhat more formal, suggests a complicated condition of uncertainty or doubt.

predispose See **dispose.**

predominant See **dominant.**

prefatory See **preliminary.**

preference See **choice.**

preliminary *adj.* **introductory, prefatory, preparatory.**
Core meaning: Prior to or preparing for the main action or matter (*preliminary remarks*).

premature See **early.**

---

premeditated See **intentional.**

preparatory See **preliminary.**

preponderant See **dominant.**

preposterous 1. See **absurd.** 2. See **foolish.**

presage See **omen.**

present See **offer.**

present-day See **modern.**

preserve See **defend.**

press See **urge.**

pressure See **force.**

pretend *v.* **dissemble, feign, simulate.**
These all refer to the false assumption of an identity, manner, or skill. PRETEND is mild in force, implying no evil end, but it can suggest an unsuccessful or transparent attempt to fool others: *pretending to be interested in their conversation.* FEIGN implies more strongly the false assumption of some condition, often to evade the responsibilities incurred by being sincere: *She feigned illness and left early.* DISSEMBLE suggests artful deception in speech or manner to conceal one's true purposes or feelings: *dissembled his disappointment with a show of gaiety.* To SIMULATE is to make a pretense of (*simulated lack of interest*); in another sense the term refers to imitation that closely resembles reality (*a device that simulates space flight*).

pretentious See **arty.**

pretty See **beautiful.**

prevalent See **common.**

priceless See **valuable.**

prime See **excellent.**

principle See **law.**

private *adj.* **personal.**
PRIVATE and PERSONAL both apply to what pertains to or is confined to one particular person: *my private opinion; a*

personal experience. Both can suggest what is intimate or even secret: *a private thought; a personal letter*. *Private* also refers to what is not available for public use or participation (*a private club; a private party*) and to what is owned by a person or group rather than the public or government (*a private house; private property*).
Antonym: **public.**

prize See **appreciate.**

probable See **likely.**

procedure See **move.**

proceed See **advance.**

produce See **create.**

product See **production.**

production *n*. **output, product, yield.**
Core meaning: The amount or quantity produced (*keeping production up to meet the demand*).

professional *n*. **authority, expert, master.**
A PROFESSIONAL is someone who follows or makes a living at an occupation requiring training and specialized study: *The actors in this troupe are all professionals*. An AUTHORITY is someone who is an accepted source of expert information: *an authority on medieval history*. An EXPERT is a person with great knowledge, skill, and experience in a given field: *a leading foreign-policy expert*. A MASTER is someone who has gained complete command of a skill or craft: *a master in cabinetmaking*.
Antonym: **amateur.**

proffer See **offer.**

proficiency See **expertise.**

profligate See **immoral.**

profound See **deep.**

progenitor See **ancestor.**

progeny See **descendant.**

---

program *n.* agenda, calendar, docket, schedule.
Core meaning: An organized list of activities, events, etc.
(*A visit to the factory is on today's program*).

progress See **advance.**

prohibit See **forbid.**

prolific See **fertile.**

prolixity See **wordiness.**

prolonged See **chronic.**

promise See **pledge.**

promote *v.* 1. cultivate, encourage, foster.
Core meaning: To help bring about (*Does TV promote violence?*).
2. See **advance.**
3. See **advertise.**

promulgate See **advertise.**

proper See **suitable.**

property See **holding(s).**

propitiate See **pacify.**

propitious See **favorable.**

prospect See **view.**

prosper See **succeed.**

protect See **defend.**

protest See **objection.**

protracted See **chronic.**

proud *adj.* arrogant, disdainful, haughty, supercilious.
These words imply self-esteem, most of them to the degree of belief in one's superiority over others. PROUD applies to persons who feel justifiable satisfaction over something they own, make, do, or are a part of (*proud to be named to the Olympic team; proud to be an American*); it sometimes suggests conceit or arrogance (*too proud to talk to those who had less education*). ARROGANT refers to those who

assume excessive and unpleasant self-importance: *the arrogant manners of the maître d'*. DISDAINFUL suggests scorn and contempt: *a cold, disdainful stare*. HAUGHTY refers to an attitude of superiority, often because of one's birth or station: *a haughty aristocrat*. SUPERCILIOUS combines the meanings of *haughty* and *disdainful: a supercilious smile*.
Antonym: **humble.**

prove *v.* **demonstrate, establish.**
These verbs share the sense of establishing that something is true or valid by presenting evidence or arguments: *proved the charge of murder at the trial; demonstrate* (or *establish*) *one's innocence of an accusation*. They can also be used to mean "show convincingly": *proved he could lift 400 pounds; demonstrated his ability to do the job; establishing that the earth moves around the sun*.
Antonym: **disprove.**

provident See **economical.**

provisional 1. See **temporary. 2.** See **conditional.**

provisory See **conditional.**

provoke *v.* **1. arouse, excite, goad, impel, incite, inflame, kindle, motivate, move, rouse, spur, stimulate.**
Core meaning: To stir to action or feeling (*carelessness that provoked anger*).
2. See **annoy.**

prudence *n.* **circumspection, discretion.**
These nouns are compared as they express caution and wisdom. PRUDENCE, the most comprehensive, implies not only caution but also the capacity to judge in advance the probable results of one's actions. DISCRETION suggests prudence coupled with self-restraint and sound judgment. CIRCUMSPECTION adds to *discretion* the implication of wariness in one's actions out of heedfulness for circumstances or consequences.

prudent 1. See **careful. 2.** See **economical. 3.** See **wise.**

psyche See **psychology.**

psychology *n.* **ethos, mentality, mind, psyche.**
Core meaning: The thought processes characteristic of an individual or group (*the psychology of today's youth*).

public *adj.* **general, popular.**
These adjectives describe what pertains to, affects, or represents the people at large: *public opinion; public safety; the general welfare; the popular vote. Public* also applies to what is supported by, used by, or open to the people or community: *the public library; a public telephone. General* and *popular* refer to what is widespread or prevalent: *general discontent; a popular idea.*
Antonym: **private.**

punish *v.* **chastise, discipline, penalize.**
These verbs refer to different ways of causing someone to undergo a penalty for a crime, fault, or misbehavior. PUNISH applies whether the penalty takes the form of money, time in jail, or physical pain. CHASTISE often refers specifically to physical punishment, but it also means to criticize severely. DISCIPLINE stresses punishment designed to control an offender and to eliminate unacceptable conduct: *discipline an unruly child.* PENALIZE is the weakest of these terms; it usually involves the forfeit of money or privileges for breaking a code of fair play or established conduct.
Antonym: **pardon.**

purchase See **buy.**

pure See **moral.**

purview See **ken.**

push 1. See **sell. 2.** See **advertise. 3.** See **ambition.**

quack See **impostor.**

quaint See **strange.**

quake See **shake.**

qualification *n.* **eligibility, fitness, suitableness.**
Core meaning: The quality or state of being eligible (*had all the qualifications for the job*).

qualified See **able.**

---

qualm *n.* compunction, misgiving, reservation, scruple.

QUALM and its synonyms denote varying degrees of uncertainty felt by a person about his or her judgment in taking action. *Qualm* can be as slight as a feeling of uneasiness or as strong as a queasy sensation in its implication of self-doubt. SCRUPLE is hesitation—or a feeling producing hesitation—based on one's conscience. COMPUNCTION stresses the importance of conscience in deciding the rightness or wrongness of one's acts; it often refers to a feeling that one has done something one ought not to have done. MISGIVING implies doubt or concern as to one's ability or fear that one has made a mistake. RESERVATION also connotes doubt about the fitness or correctness of an action; it refers to a rather well-defined limiting condition that one has arrived at (*has reservations about the proposal*).

quandary See **predicament.**

quarrel See **argue.**

queer See **strange.**

quench See **extinguish.**

quick See **fast.**

quick-witted See **shrewd.**

quiet *adj.* restrained, subdued, unobtrusive.

Core meaning: Not showy or obtrusive (*a room decorated in a quiet, pleasing style*).

quip See **joke.**

quirk See **eccentricity.**

quiver See **shake.**

quixotic See **idealistic.**

race See **nation.**

rack See **afflict.**

radical *adj.* basic, fundamental, underlying.

Core meaning: Arising from or going to the root or source (*radical differences about the very purpose of the organization*).

---

rage See **anger.**

rail See **scold.**

raise *v.* **boost, heave, hoist, lift.**
These verbs mean to move or bring something from a lower level to a higher one, often in a figurative sense. RAISE implies movement to a higher position (*raise the window slightly; raise a drawbridge*); figuratively it suggests movement to a higher plane or level (*raise the tone of a discussion*). LIFT stresses the effort involved: *a suitcase that is too heavy to lift.* HOIST is applied chiefly to the lifting of heavy objects, often by mechanical means (*hoist a sunken ship*), and HEAVE, to lifting or raising that requires great exertion (*heaved the pack onto his back*). BOOST refers to upward movement effected by pushing from below (*boosted her into the saddle*); figuratively it applies to an increase or advance in amount, degree, status, etc.: *boost sales; boost morale.*
Antonym: **lower.**

random See **accidental.**

range See **ken.**

rank See **flagrant.**

rapacious See **voracious.**

rapid See **fast.**

rare See **uncommon.**

rate See **earn.**

ratiocination See **logic.**

rationale See **explanation.**

rationality See **logic.**

rationalization See **explanation.**

ravenous See **voracious.**

raze See **destroy.**

reach 1. *v.* **accomplish, achieve, attain, gain.**
These verbs refer to the attainment of certain objectives. REACH connotes arriving at a goal through effort or progress: *jets reaching supersonic speeds; reaching old age.* ACCOMPLISH implies successful completion: *accomplish an assignment.* ACHIEVE suggests the successful accomplishment of something important, as through skill or initiative: *achieved the desired effect; achieve recognition.* ATTAIN may imply great effort: *Correct grammar is a tool for attaining confidence in writing and speaking.* GAIN connotes arriving at a goal despite considerable effort in surmounting obstacles: *The troops gained the hill.*
2. *n.* See **ken.**

reactionary *adj.* **backward, unprogressive.**
Core meaining: Clinging to obsolete ideas (*reactionary views on civil rights*).

real 1. See **natural. 2.** See **authentic.**

realistic See **graphic.**

really See **actually.**

reason See **logic.**

reasonable See **sensible.**

rebellion *n.* **insurrection, mutiny, revolt, revolution, riot, uprising.**
These terms pertain in varying degree to opposition to existing order or authority. REBELLION is defiance of authority in general or open but unorganized disobedience (*teen-age rebellion*); it is also open, armed, and organized opposition to constituted political authority that often fails in its purpose (*Shays' Rebellion*). A REVOLUTION is a radical alteration in a system or in social conditions (*the industrial revolution*); it is also the overthrow by open, organized armed force of a government and its replacement with another (*the American Revolution*). REVOLT is widespread opposition to prevailing standards (*a taxpayers' revolt*); like INSURRECTION and UPRISING, it is also an armed attempt to change authority. A RIOT is a sudden, violent, disorganized uprising, fre-

quently unarmed and unplanned. MUTINY is open rebellion against constituted authority, especially by subordinates in the armed forces.

rebellious *adj.* **insubordinate, mutinous.**
These apply to what resists authority. REBELLIOUS is the least specific: *a rebellious child; a rebellious prisoner.* INSUBORDINATE specifically implies the refusal or failure to recognize the authority of a superior: *The general demoted his aide for his insubordinate behavior.* MUTINOUS pertains to rising up against lawful authority, especially that of a naval or military command: *The mutinous seamen were sent to walk the plank.*
Antonym: **submissive.**

rebuff See **reject.**

rebuke See **admonish.**

rebut See **disprove.**

recall See **remember.**

recede *v.* **regress, retire, retreat, withdraw.**
These verbs describe motion backward, literally or figuratively. RECEDE suggests motion backward from a limit, point, or mark: *a hairline that is receding; a tide that receded, exposing barnacle-covered rocks.* REGRESS suggests a return to an earlier condition, often even the reversal or undoing of progress: *Under hypnosis he regressed to childhood.* RETIRE implies moving back either in space or from a social environment: *He retired to his study. He retired early from his career.* WITHDRAW denotes moving back but also applies to getting out of a commitment or obligation: *He withdrew from the campaign.* RETREAT suggests withdrawal, often to avoid danger or attack: *The troops retreated rapidly.*
Antonym: **advance.**

receive See **accept.**

recent See **new.**

reciprocal See **mutual.**

reciprocative See **mutual.**

reclaim See **save.**

recollect See **remember.**

reconcile *v.* **reunite.**
These refer to the restoration of harmonious relations after a period of anger or discontent. RECONCILE focuses on the renewed state of peace or affection: *The politicians reconciled after the election. After they realized what fools they had been, the lovers were quickly reconciled.* REUNITE often suggests no more than coming together after a separation (*The friends were reunited years after the shipwreck*), but as a synonym of *reconcile* it suggests the mending of a split: *Three years after their divorce his parents were reunited.*
Antonym: **estrange.**

recondite See **ambiguous.**

recoup See **recover.**

recover *v.* **recoup, regain, retrieve.**
To RECOVER is to get back something lost: *a crusade to recover the Holy Land.* REGAIN suggests efforts to get back something lost or taken from one, usually a quality or status rather than an object: *regaining his health; regained her freedom.* RECOUP means getting back the equivalent of something lost or damaged: *losses that can never be recouped.* RETRIEVE emphasizes effort and very often pertains to the physical recovery of a thing (*retrieved the ball in the end zone*); it can also refer to making good or putting right what is bad, wrong, etc. (*retrieving an error*). See also **find.**

recreation *n.* **amusement, diversion, entertainment.**
These nouns refer to activity that refreshes the mind or body after work. RECREATION implies something that restores one's strength, spirits, or vitality: *played tennis for recreation.* AMUSEMENT suggests that which occupies in an agreeable or pleasing fashion: *performed music for their own amusement.* DIVERSION suggests something to take one's attention off customary affairs: *went shopping for*

diversion. ENTERTAINMENT shares these meanings but especially suggests a performance or show that is designed to amuse or divert.

rectify See **correct.**

recur See **return.**

redeem See **save.**

redress See **correct.**

reduce 1. See **decrease. 2.** See **lower.**

reduction See **depreciation.**

referee See **judge.**

refined *adj.* **cultivated, cultured, genteel, polite.**
As it describes a material property REFINED means "free of impurities." It has a figurative meaning that describes freedom from coarseness or vulgarity (*a refined young woman*); its synonyms share this meaning. CULTIVATED and CULTURED both imply refinement, good manners, and the appreciation of what is beautiful and civilized: *a cultivated person; a cultured gentleman who collects paintings.* GENTEEL describes a person who is both well-bred and polite: *a poor but genteel family.* POLITE stresses good manners, tact, and consideration for others: *a polite child; a polite letter.*
Antonym: **coarse.**

reform See **correct.**

refractory See **obstinate.**

refrain *v.* **abstain, forbear, withhold.**
Core meaning: To hold oneself back (*Please refrain from applauding*).

refurbish See **modernize.**

refuse See **reject.**

refute 1. See **deny. 2.** See **disprove.**

regain See **recover.**

regard 1. See **consider. 2.** See **favor. 3.** See **notice.**

---

region See **area.**

regress See **recede.**

regret 1. See **sorrow. 2.** See **disappointment.**

regular See **normal.**

reiteration See **repetition.**

reject *v.* **decline, rebuff, refuse, spurn.**
These all refer to turning down what is available or offered. REJECT, DECLINE, and REFUSE are the most neutral of the group: *rejected his request for an extension on the loan; declined her invitation; refuse permission to leave early.* REBUFF suggests a blunt or abrupt refusal (*rebuffing his advances*); SPURN, a disdainful or scornful one (*spurn a suitor*). See also **disbelieve.**
Antonym: **accept.**

rejection See **denial.**

rejuvenate See **modernize.**

release See **free.**

relent *v.* **ease off, slacken, soften, weaken, yield.**
Core meaning: To moderate or change a position or course of action (*would not relent despite public opinion*).

relevant *adj.* **germane, material, pertinent.**
RELEVANT and its synonyms describe what is associated with a matter or situation at hand and has direct bearing on it: *Stick to relevant questions, please!* PERTINENT implies a logical and precise bearing: *The pertinent statistics do not confirm the press accounts of the accident.* GERMANE applies to what is so closely akin to the subject as to reinforce it: *statements germane to the topic of his speech.* MATERIAL has the sense of being needed to complete a subject: *material evidence.*
Antonym: **irrelevant.**

reliable *adj.* **dependable, trustworthy.**
RELIABLE implies complete confidence in the honesty or truthfulness of a person (*a reliable witness*) or in the ability

of a person or thing to perform ably (*a reliable doctor; a reliable stove*). DEPENDABLE suggests confidence in the support or strength of a person or thing (*a dependable friend; a dependable elevator*). TRUSTWORTHY applies less often to things; it usually refers to a person who has established his or her right to be considered worthy of another's confidence: *a trustworthy husband.*
Antonym: **unreliable.**

reliance See **confidence.**

religious See **holy.**

relish See **like.**

remedy See **correct.**

remember *v.* **recall, recollect.**
REMEMBER and its synonyms mean to bring back to memory or think of again: *She remembered all the old songs of her childhood. I can never recall names. Do you recollect her address?* More specifically, to *remember* is often to keep something in mind: *Remember to phone your parents! Recall* and *recollect* frequently suggest a deliberate effort to bring something back to mind: *The boy could not recall the circumstances of the accident. It took her a few moments to recollect why she had refused the job offer.*
Antonym: **forget.**

remission See **abeyance.**

remonstrance See **objection.**

remote See **far.**

renowned See **famous.**

rent See **breach.**

repel *v.* **1. combat, fight, oppose, resist.**
These all share the meaning "to struggle against": *repel an invasion; combat an enemy; combat crime; fight an opponent; fight illness; oppose corruption; resist an attack; resist change.*

2. disgust, nauseate, revolt, sicken.
All of these mean "to cause aversion in," whether the strong dislike is physical or emotional: *The shrillness of the voice repelled her. His behavior disgusted his friends. His opinions nauseated his colleagues. His taking advantage of the handicapped revolted everyone who knew about it. The dictator's cruelty sickened liberal citizens.*
Antonym: **attract.**

repetition *n.* **iteration, reiteration, restatement.**
Core meaning: The act or process of repeating (*a repetition of past mistakes*).

replete See **full.**

reply See **answer.**

representative *n.* **delegate, deputy.**
Core meaning: One who stands or acts for another (*representatives at a convention*).

repress See **forget.**

reprimand See **admonish.**

reproach See **admonish.**

reprove See **admonish.**

requisite See **need.**

rescue See **save.**

resentment See **anger.**

reservation See **qualm.**

reserve See **book.**

resigned See **patient.**

resist 1. See **repel.** 2. See **withstand.**

resolution 1. See **analysis.** 2. See **will.**

resolve 1. See **decide.** 2. See **will.**

respond See **answer.**

responsible See **liable.**

restatement See **repetition.**

restive See **impatient.**

restore See **modernize.**

restrained See **quiet.**

restrict See **limit.**

result See **effect.**

resultant See **effect.**

retail See **sell.**

retard See **delay.**

retire See **recede.**

retort See **answer.**

retreat 1. See **recede. 2.** See **back.**

retrieve See **recover.**

retrograde See **back.**

retrogress See **back.**

return *v.* **recur, revert.**
RETURN, the least specific of these terms, denotes going or coming back to a former place, position, condition, etc. RECUR applies to repeated occurrences of the same thing: *an area where earthquakes recur.* REVERT refers to returning to an earlier and sometimes less desirable condition, belief, interest, etc.: *a neglected garden reverting to a weedy wilderness.*

reunite See **reconcile.**

reveal See **show.**

revelry See **gaiety.**

revengeful See **vindictive.**

reverence See **honor.**

reverse *v.* **invert, transpose.**
REVERSE implies a complete turning about to a contrary position with reference to action, direction, or policy. To IN-VERT is basically to turn something upside down (*invert a jar*), but it may imply placing something in a contrary order

(*invert a sentence by placing the predicate first*). TRANSPOSE applies to altering position in a sequence by reversing or changing the order: *transpose the letters of a word.*

revert See **return.**

review *n.* **1. commentary, criticism, critique.**
Core meaning: Evaluative and critical discourse (*The new book received rave reviews*).
2. See **analysis.**

revile See **scold.**

reviling See **abusive.**

revise See **correct.**

revolt 1. See **rebellion. 2.** See **repel.**

revolting See **unspeakable.**

revolution See **rebellion.**

reward See **bonus.**

rich *adj.* **affluent, wealthy.**
All of these refer to persons who have a great deal of money or income. RICH is the most general and straightforward word (*a rich family*); it can also be used figuratively to describe something that is abundant in natural resources (*rich land*). A WEALTHY person is often a person of substance in a community: *a wealthy patron of the arts.* AFFLUENT sometimes connotes continually increasing prosperity: *an affluent landowner.*
Antonym: **poor.**

ridicule *v.* **deride, gibe, mock, taunt, twit.**
These verbs concern the efforts of one person to find amusement or delight at the expense of another; they vary from mere mischief to sheer malice. RIDICULE refers to the attempt to arouse laughter or merriment at another's expense by making fun of or belittling him. To MOCK is to make fun of a person, often by imitating him or depicting him in an insulting way. TAUNT suggests insult with contempt. DERIDE implies both scorn and contempt in demeaning a person. To TWIT is to tease, especially by calling attention

to something embarrassing. To GIBE is to make heckling or jeering remarks.

ridiculous See **absurd.**

rift See **breach.**

right See **true.**

righteousness See **virtue.**

rigid See **inflexible.**

rigor See **severity.**

rile See **annoy.**

rim See **border.**

ring See **surround.**

riot See **rebellion.**

rise *v.* **ascend, climb, mount, soar.**
These verbs denote a moving upward, but they differ widely in both their literal and their figurative meanings. RISE is applied to a great range of events, chiefly involving steady or customary upward movement: *The sun rises over the eastern horizon. Prices rise and fall.* ASCEND connotes rising step by step, literally or figuratively: *ascend a staircase; ascend through the ranks.* CLIMB suggests steady progress against gravity or some other resistance: *The rocket climbed rapidly. The actress eventually climbed to the top of her profession.* MOUNT often implies reaching a level or limit: *a death toll that mounted; mounting to the top of the hill.* SOAR suggests the effortless attainment of great height (*eagles soaring in the sky*); often it refers to what rises rapidly and suddenly, especially above what is normal (*The cost of living soared*).
Antonym: **fall.**

risible See **laughable.**

risk See **danger.**

ritual *n.* **ceremony, form, formality.**
Core meaning: A formal act or set of acts prescribed by convention or tradition (*the rituals of a religious service*).

rival See **opponent.**

romantic See **idealistic.**

root 1. See **origin.** 2. See **heart.**

rosy See **optimistic.**

rough 1. See **harsh.** 2. See **draft.**

roughly See **approximately.**

roundabout See **indirect.**

rouse See **provoke.**

rout See **defeat.**

rude See **impolite.**

rule 1. See **decide.** 2. See **law.**

run 1. See **administer.** 2. See **operate.**

rupture See **breach.**

sabotage *v.* **subvert, undermine.**
Core meaning: To damage, destroy, or defeat by underhand means (*tried to sabotage the contract negotiations*).

sad *adj.* **blue, dejected, depressed, desolate, melancholy, miserable, sorrowful, unhappy, wretched.**
All of these describe what shows, causes, feels, or expresses low spirits, gloom, etc. SAD and UNHAPPY are the most general: *a sad* (or *unhappy*) *smile; a sad message; an unhappy household.* BLUE implies gloom or depression: *He felt blue when he lost his job.* DEJECTED suggests a dark mood of rather short duration: *He was dejected when she turned him down but quickly found comfort in another.* DEPRESSED and MELANCHOLY refer to lingering periods of somber thoughts: *depressed for several days by the bad news; a melancholy disposition.* DESOLATE implies sadness due to loss or loneliness: *a desolate child whose mother had died.* MISERABLE and WRETCHED refer to any state of profound unhappiness: *made her life miserable; felt wretched when she finally left.* SORROWFUL describes extreme sadness: *a sorrowful voice.*
Antonym: **glad.**

---

sadistic See **cruel.**

safeguard See **defend.**

safety *n.* **security.**
Both SAFETY and SECURITY denote freedom from danger, accident, injury, or the threat of harm: *worked in safety while he was wearing his helmet; lived in the security of his home.*
Antonym: **danger.**

sagacious See **shrewd.**

sage See **wise.**

salary See **wage(s).**

sally See **joke.**

same *adj.* **equal, equivalent, identical.**
All of these adjectives refer to the absence of difference or disparity. SAME and IDENTICAL mean the very one, not another: *the same restaurant I went to yesterday; the identical words the President used.* They also apply to things that are exactly alike, as in kind, quality, amount, value, etc., but here *identical* is stronger in specifying strict agreement in every respect and detail: *books of the same size; identical machine parts.* EQUAL refers more generally to absence of difference between two or more things, as in extent, amount, value, etc.: *equal portions; equal rights for women.* What is EQUIVALENT to something else may not be identical but has the same worth, effect, force, or meaning: *francs equivalent to ten American dollars.*
Antonym: **different.**

sanction 1. See **approve. 2.** See **permission.**

sanguine See **optimistic.**

sarcastic *adj.* **caustic, ironic, sardonic, satirical.**
SARCASTIC and its synonyms apply to personal expression that is bitter, cutting, or derisive. *Sarcastic* suggests sharp and bitter mockery and ridicule. IRONIC implies a milder and subtler form of mockery; what is *ironic* suggests something different from what is expressed: *an ironic smile.* CAUSTIC can apply to any expression that is biting or cutting. SATIRICAL refers to expression that seeks to expose hypocrisy or

foolishness to ridicule, often by using humor or irony. Sardonic is associated with scorn, derision, mockery, and cyn-
icism.

sardonic See **sarcastic.**

satirical See **sarcastic.**

satisfactory See **sufficient.**

save *v.* **1. deliver, reclaim, redeem, rescue.**
In this sense all these verbs refer to the freeing of a person
or thing from danger, evil, confinement, or servitude. Save,
the most general, applies to any act of preserving from the
consequences of danger or evil: *saved her from drowning;
saving sinners.* Deliver applies chiefly to freeing persons
from confinement, restraint, or evil: *Deliver us from our
enemies.* Reclaim, when applied to persons, usually means
to restore to an earlier state of moral and physical soundness or to reform after a lapse (*reclaimed him from his
wicked life*); it can also mean to return or convert a thing to
usefulness or productivity (*reclaim eroded soil*). To redeem
is to free from captivity, pawn, or the consequences of sin,
error, or misuse, in every case by the expenditure of money
or effort (*redeemed hostages; redeemed his ring from the
pawnbroker*). Rescue usually implies saving from immediate harm or danger by direct action: *rescuing the victim of the fire.*
2. conserve, hoard, husband.
These all refer to the careful use of money, time, energy, or
any kind of supply. Save can apply to the prevention or
reduction of loss, expenditure, or waste (*save money at a
sale; save time*) or to the accumulation of something needed
for future use (*saved five dollars a week; saving on a
monthly basis*). Conserve is a more formal term; it usually
refers to the protection of something from loss or depletion
(*conserved his energy for the last push to win the race*) and
often to the taking of systematic measures to keep something in good condition (*Science and common sense tell us
we should conserve our forests*). To husband is to spend or
use economically or with care: *husbanded her strength;*

husbanding our resources. HOARD nearly always suggests secretiveness or greed: *hoarded food during a shortage; a miser hoarding gold.*
Antonym: **waste.**

savor See **flavor.**

say *v.* **articulate, communicate, convey, express, state, tell, utter, vent, voice.**
Core meaning: To put into words (*said what was on her mind and left*).

scare See **frighten.**

scatter *v.* **dispel, disperse, dissipate.**
These all denote separating and going in different directions. SCATTER refers to haphazard and often widespread distribution: *At the bell the class scattered into the hallways. The wind scattered the leaves.* DISPEL usually suggests scattering in a figurative sense: *dispel doubts and fears.* DISPERSE implies the breaking up of a mass or group: *The crowd dispersed at the command of the police.* DISSIPATE suggests a reduction to nothing: *A strong wind dissipated the clouds. His anger soon dissipated.*
Antonym: **gather.**

schedule See **program.**

schism See **breach.**

scholarship See **knowledge.**

scold *v.* **berate, nag, rail, revile, upbraid.**
All of these verbs express criticism or disfavor. SCOLD implies anger or irritation and often the tone and manner of one correcting a child at fault. UPBRAID is stronger and generally suggests rather formal criticism, such as that made by a superior. To BERATE is to scold severely and often at length. REVILE especially stresses the use of abusive language. NAG refers to complaining and faultfinding, usually prolonged and persistent. RAIL suggests persistent complaint but also implies bitterness and the use of strong or emphatic language.

scope See **ken.**

scorching See **hot.**

scorn See **despise.**

scourge See **afflict.**

scrumptious See **delicious.**

scruple See **qualm.**

scuffle See **conflict.**

scurrilous See **abusive.**

secluded *adj.* **cloistered, isolated, sequestered.**
Core meaning: Solitary and shut off from human contact (*led a secluded life in a convent*).

seclusion See **solitude.**

second See **moment.**

secondary 1. See **subordinate.** 2. See **minor.**

secret *adj.* **clandestine, covert, furtive, stealthy, surreptitious, underhand.**
SECRET and its synonyms apply to what is purposely concealed from view or knowledge. *Secret* is the most general and therefore weakest in suggesting anything beyond this basic sense. STEALTHY is most often applied to quiet action designed to avoid attracting notice. COVERT describes any act not taken openly. CLANDESTINE usually implies secrecy for the purpose of concealing some unlawful or improper purpose. FURTIVE suggests the slyness, shiftiness, and evasiveness of a thief. SURREPTITIOUS includes the meanings of *stealthy* and *furtive: a surreptitious glance at his watch.* UNDERHAND implies unfairness, deceit, fraud, or slyness as well as secrecy.

secrete See **hide.**

security See **safety.**

seduce *v.* **allure, entice, inveigle, lure, tempt.**
Core meaning: To draw into a wrong or foolish course of action (*seduced into gambling by the vision of easy money*).

---

see See **foresee.**

seem See **appear.**

seize See **catch.**

select See **choose.**

selection See **choice.**

self-centered See **selfish.**

self-confidence See **confidence.**

selfish *adj.* egotistic, self-centered.
SELFISH and SELF-CENTERED refer to persons who are concerned chiefly or only with themselves, without regard for the well-being of others. EGOTISTIC (or *egotistical*) implies an exaggerated sense of self-importance.
Antonym: **unselfish.**

selfless See **unselfish.**

sell *v.* market, merchandise, peddle, push, retail, vend.
These share the meaning of exchanging goods or services for money or its equivalent. However, only SELL and VEND, the more formal of the two, can be used interchangeably: *sells apples; vends caviar.* MARKET means both "to sell" and "to offer for sale": *markets cosmetics; marketing his new invention.* MERCHANDISE has the meanings "buy and sell" and "try to sell," the second meaning shared by one sense of PUSH (the slang sense implies illegal trafficking in narcotics: *pushes heroin*). PEDDLE suggests that the seller travels about rather than keeping a shop: *peddled his wares from a pushcart.* RETAIL specifically entails sale to consumers at full price: *retails blouses and skirts.*
Antonym: **buy.**

send *v.* address, dispatch, transmit.
These words mean "to cause to be conveyed from one place to another." SEND applies generally: *sent supplies by airlift; send a message; send a shipment.* ADDRESS in this sense implies directing something to a particular place or person: *address a letter.* To DISPATCH is to send to a specific

destination or on specific business: *The commander dispatched six battleships to the scene of the invasion.* TRANSMIT is used especially for signals and messages that travel by television or radio waves: *The astronauts transmitted reports from the moon.*
Antonym: **receive.**

sense See **meaning.**

sensible *adj.* **logical, reasonable.**
SENSIBLE and its synonyms describe what is in agreement with common sense. *Sensible* stresses good judgment (*a sensible hat for the occasion*); it shares the implications of REASONABLE, which suggests the ability to think, understand, and make decisions clearly and rationally (*a sensible—*or *reasonable—woman*). LOGICAL emphasizes correct and orderly thought: *a logical reason for going.*
Antonym: **absurd.**

sentiment See **opinion.**

separate *v.* **divide, part, sever.**
These verbs refer to setting or keeping apart. SEPARATE applies both to removing a portion or segment from a whole and to keeping apart by occupying a position between things: *He separated the wheat from the chaff. The Pyrenees separate France and Spain.* DIVIDE also has both of these senses. With respect to putting apart, it often implies separation into predetermined portions or groups: *divide a cake.* With respect to keeping apart, *divide* often implies separation into opposing or hostile groups: *Bad feelings have divided the team.* PART refers most often to separation of persons or of segments: *The travelers parted to go their separate ways. The curtains parted.* SEVER usually applies to cutting a part from a whole or cutting a whole into sections; figuratively it applies to ending a relationship: *The woodsman severed a limb from the tree. Diplomatic ties were severed at midnight.* See also **single.**
Antonym: **join.**

sequestered See **secluded.**

---

serene See **calm.**

serenity 1. See **equanimity. 2.** See **tranquillity.**

serious See **critical.**

serviceable See **practical.**

servitude See **bondage.**

set See **circle.**

settle See **decide.**

sever See **separate.**

severe 1. See **harsh. 2.** See **plain.**

severity *n.* **austerity, harshness, rigor, stringency.**
Core meaning: The fact or condition of being rigorous and unsparing (*an ordeal of extraordinary severity*).

shade See **trace.**

shadowy See **dark.**

shady See **dark.**

shake *v.* **quake, quiver, shiver, shudder, tremble, wobble.**
SHAKE, the most general of these terms, applies to any involuntary vibrating movement in a thing or a person: *The earthquake shook the ground. Jack shook with anger.* TREMBLE implies quick and rather slight movement, like that of a person affected by anger, cold, etc.: *leaves trembling in the breeze; a woman trembling with fear.* QUAKE refers to shaking or vibrating movement such as that caused by physical or emotional upheaval: *The ground quaked as the stampede passed. He had such stage fright that his legs quaked under him.* QUIVER suggests a slight and tremulous movement: *lips quivering with excitement.* SHIVER involves rapid and rather slight movement: *shivering in the cold.* SHUDDER chiefly applies to sudden strong, convulsive shaking, as that caused by fear, horror, or a revolting sight or thought. WOBBLE refers to pronounced and unsteady movement: *wobbled the table when he sat down; an old table that wobbles.*

---

shakiness See **instability.**

shallow *adj.* **superficial.**
SHALLOW literally describes what has little physical depth (*a shallow lake*); SUPERFICIAL, what pertains to a surface (*a superficial cut*). Figuratively *shallow* refers to what lacks depth of thought or feeling: *shallow ideas. Superficial* implies a concern only with what is apparent or obvious: *a superficial interest.*
Antonym: **deep.**

shame See **dishonor.**

shameless See **bold.**

shape See **make.**

sharp *adj.* **acute, keen.**
These adjectives describe edges or points that are not dull. SHARP applies to what can easily pierce or cut: *a sharp razor; a sharp knife.* KEEN usually specifies a long, sharp cutting edge: *a keen sword.* ACUTE applies to what has a pointed tip or end: *an acute mountain peak.* Figuratively *sharp* suggests cleverness (*a sharp mind*); *keen* implies astuteness and discernment (*a keen observer of men*); and *acute* even more strongly implies perceptiveness (*an acute awareness of one's surroundings*).
Antonym: **dull.**

shifty See **underhand.**

shirk See **neglect.**

shiver See **shake.**

shocking See **unspeakable.**

shoddy 1. See **careless.** 2. See **cheap.**

short *adj.* 1. **brief.**
SHORT describes what has little length (*a short skirt*), covers a small distance (*a short walk*), or takes a small amount of time (*a short trip*). BRIEF refers only to what is short in time or duration (*a brief period; a brief description*) or what is short in length (*a brief report; a brief letter*).
Antonym: **long.**

---

2. SHORT also applies to what has less than ordinary height: *a short, pudgy man.*
Antonym: **tall.**

shortage See **deficiency.**

shortcoming 1. See **disadvantage. 2.** See **weakness.**

show *v.* **display, exhibit, expose, reveal.**
All these verbs refer to presenting something to view. SHOW is the most general: *showed her the necklace; show goods in a store; a picture that shows a dinosaur.* DISPLAY usually suggests an attempt to present something to best advantage (*models displaying the latest fashion*), but it can imply ostentation (*displayed his wealth*) or even the making obvious of something better concealed (*ashamed to display his ignorance*). EXHIBIT suggests open, rather formal presentation that invites inspection: *an artist who exhibits his paintings at a gallery.* EXPOSE usually involves uncovering (*expose one's back to the sun*), bringing from concealment (*exposed the grain of the wood by cleaning*), or unmasking (*exposing a dishonest employee*). To REVEAL is often to disclose something that has hitherto been kept secret (*revealed her travel plans*).
Antonym: **hide.**

shrewd *adj.* **astute, quick-witted, sagacious.**
All of these adjectives refer to the possession of a keen, searching intelligence combined usually with sound judgment. SHREWD stresses perceptiveness, hardheadedness, cunning, and an intuitive knack in practical matters. SAGACIOUS emphasizes more profound wisdom and a gift for discernment and far-sightedness. ASTUTE suggests qualities associated with practical wisdom, such as acute understanding, insight, discernment, and immunity to being deceived. QUICK-WITTED, the narrowest term, refers to alertness and mental adroitness.

shrink See **contract.**

shudder See **shake.**

shun See **avoid.**

shy *adj.* **bashful, coy, diffident, modest.**
All of these describe persons who are fearful of intruding or being self-assertively brash. They can also apply to the behavior, actions, manner, etc., of such persons. SHY implies either a retiring or withdrawn nature (*a shy man who avoided parties*) or timidity resulting from lack of social experience (*a shy young girl*). BASHFUL suggests embarrassment or awkwardness in the presence of others: *They were too bashful to kiss good-by*. COY suggests false modesty or shyness designed to attract the interest of others: *a coy look*. DIFFIDENT implies lack of self-confidence: *diffident about making suggestions; a diffident greeting*. MODEST is associated with a retiring nature (*a modest and gentle woman*) and absence of vanity (*modest about his accomplishments*).
Antonym: **bold.**

shyness See **diffidence.**

sick *adj.* **ill, indisposed, unwell.**
These describe persons who are not in good physical or mental condition. SICK, ILL, and UNWELL are used interchangeably. INDISPOSED refers to minor sickness: *Although she was indisposed, the singer did not cancel her performance.*
Antonym: **healthy.**

sicken See **repel.**

sickening See **unspeakable.**

sidestep See **skirt.**

sign *n.* **badge, indication, mark, note, symptom, token.**
SIGN and its synonyms are compared as they denote outward evidence of something. SIGN, the most general, can refer to almost any such manifestation. A BADGE is usually something worn that shows rank, office, membership, condition, etc.: *Her mink coat was a badge of success*. MARK can refer to a personal characteristic or evidence of some quality or condition (*Intolerance is the mark of a bigot*); it can also denote evidence of an experience (*Poverty had left*

its mark on him). TOKEN usually refers to something that serves as a symbol, often of something intangible: *A white flag is a token of surrender.* INDICATION refers to evidence of a condition: *Dark clouds are often an indication of rain.* SYMPTOM frequently suggests visible evidence of an adverse condition: *Fever is a symptom of illness.* A NOTE is a characteristic or feature that reveals a certain quality: *a note of mysticism in his novels.*

significance See **meaning.**

significant See **important.**

signification See **meaning.**

silly See **foolish.**

simper See **smile.**

simple *adj.* **uncomplicated.**
SIMPLE and UNCOMPLICATED apply to what is not involved or complex. *Simple* can specifically describe what is not complicated in structure (*a simple microscope; a simple lens*) but also applies more generally (*a simple explanation; the simple truth*). *Uncomplicated* describes what is easy to understand or deal with: *an uncomplicated explanation; an uncomplicated jigsaw puzzle.* See also **easy; natural; plain; unintelligent.**
Antonym: **complex.**

simulate See **pretend.**

sincere See **true.**

single *adj.* **individual, separate, sole, solitary, unique.**
These adjectives refer in various ways to the condition of being one in number. SINGLE means "one only," that is, not in accompaniment or association or combination with another or others: *a single rose.* SOLE stresses the idea of "one and only," either in the sense of being the only one in existence or the only one involved in what is under consideration: *her sole purpose.* UNIQUE applies to what is the only one of its kind in existence: *Amassing a great fortune was his unique goal in life.* SOLITARY applies to what exists

alone (*a solitary traveler*) or to the condition of isolation (*solitary places*). INDIVIDUAL makes specific reference to one person or thing distinguished from the mass to which it belongs or from all others: *for each individual child; individual words.* SEPARATE, as compared here, implies the condition of being one and distinct by reason of being disunited from all others under consideration: *Libraries have a separate section for reference books.*

singular See **uncommon.**

size See **bulk.**

sizzling See **hot.**

skeleton See **draft.**

skepticism See **uncertainty.**

sketch See **draft.**

skid See **slide.**

skill See **ability.**

skinny See **thin.**

skirt *v.* **bypass, circumvent, hedge, sidestep.**
Core meaning: To evade, as a topic, by circumlocution (*skirted the serious questions*).

slack 1. See **loose.** 2. See **neglect.**

slacken See **relent.**

slam See **hit.**

slash See **lower.**

slavery See **bondage.**

sleek See **unctuous.**

slender See **thin.**

slice See **cut.**

slick See **glib.**

slide *v.* **coast, glide, skid, slip.**
SLIDE and its synonyms refer to moving smoothly and easily over or as if over a surface. *Slide* usually implies rapid and

easy movement without loss of contact with the surface: *slid the plate across the table.* SLIP more often is applied to accidental movement causing a fall, or threat of a fall, to the surface: *slipping on the ice.* GLIDE refers to smooth, free-flowing, and seemingly effortless movement: *glided his fingers along the strings of the instrument; a submarine gliding through the water.* COAST applies specifically to effortless movement due to gravity or inertia: *The car coasted to a stop.* SKID generally implies involuntary and uncontrolled movement with much friction: *The truck skidded on the slippery pavement.*

slim See **thin.**

slip See **slide.**

slipshod See **careless.**

sloppy 1. See **careless.** 2. See **disorderly.**

slow *adj.* **deliberate, dilatory, leisurely.**
All of these describe what acts, moves, happens, or is accomplished at a low speed. SLOW is the least specific: *slow traffic; a slow dance; slow motion.* DELIBERATE implies that lack of speed is related to careful consideration of every move or step: *a deliberate choice of words.* DILATORY implies such faults as delay and wasting time: *Your dilatory research has put us all behind schedule.* LEISURELY suggests lack of time pressure: *We took a leisurely tour of the islands.* See also **delay; dull.**
Antonym: **fast.**

slug See **hit.**

smack See **hit.**

small See **little.**

smart 1. See **clever.** 2. See **intelligent.**

smash See **hit.**

smile *n.* **grin, simper, smirk.**
SMILE and its synonyms denote facial expressions in which the mouth is curved upward slightly at the corners. *Smile* is the most general, since it can cover a wide range of feelings,

from affection to malice. A GRIN is a broad smile that exposes the teeth; usually it is a spontaneous expression of good humor, approval, or triumph. A SIMPER is a silly or self-conscious smile. A SMIRK is a knowing, simpering smile that often expresses derision or suggests smugness or conceit.

smirk See **smile.**

smooth See **level.**

snatch See **catch.**

sneaky See **underhand.**

soar See **rise.**

sober *adj.* **temperate.**
A person who is SOBER is not drunk. A TEMPERATE person exercises moderation and self-restraint and for that reason is unlikely to drink to excess.
Antonym: **drunk.**

sobriety See **abstinence.**

sociable See **social.**

social *adj.* **companionable, convivial, sociable.**
Core meaning: Characterized by or spent in the company of others (*a pleasant social afternoon*).

society 1. See **circle.** 2. See **union.**

sock See **hit.**

soften See **relent.**

soiled See **dirty.**

sole See **single.**

solid See **unanimous.**

solitary 1. See **alone.** 2. See **single.**

solitude *n.* **isolation, seclusion.**
SOLITUDE and its synonyms denote the state of being alone or of being withdrawn or remote from others. *Solitude* implies the absence of all other persons but is otherwise not

specific. ISOLATION can refer to the condition of one person, a group, or even a unit such as a country; in every case it emphasizes total separation from others. SECLUSION can apply to one person or a group and suggests being removed or apart from others though not necessarily completely inaccessible.

sophistic See **fallacious.**

sorrow *n.* **anguish, grief, heartache, regret, woe.**
These nouns relate to mental distress. SORROW connotes sadness caused by misfortune or loss; sometimes it suggests remorse for having done something: *sorrow at the illness of a friend; felt sorrow because she had treated her father with disrespect.* GRIEF is deep, acute personal sorrow resulting from irreplaceable loss: *Her death filled him with grief.* ANGUISH implies agonizing grief so painful as to be excruciating: *cries of anguish.* HEARTACHE is a feeling of sorrow that often implies longing for something out of reach: *heartache over his child's handicap.* REGRET ranges from suggesting mere disappointment (*a shrug of regret that their plans had not worked out*) to implying a painful sense of loss, bitterness, etc. (*deep regret over his failures*). WOE is intense, prolonged unhappiness or misery: *His isolation increased his woe.*
Antonym: **joy.**

sorrowful See **sad.**

sort See **type.**

sound 1. See **healthy. 2.** See **valid.**

source See **origin.**

spacious See **broad.**

species See **type.**

specific See **explicit.**

specious See **fallacious.**

spectral See **ghastly.**

speculation See **theory.**

---

speculative See **theoretical.**

speech *n.* **1. discourse, lecture, oration, talk.**
Core meaning: A formal oral communication to an audience (*a valedictory speech at graduation*).
2. See **language.**

speed See **expedite.**

speedy See **fast.**

spirit *n.* **brio, dash, élan, esprit, liveliness, pep** (*Informal*).
Core meaning: A lively, emphatic, eager quality or manner (*danced with great spirit*).

spiteful See **vindictive.**

splendid See **excellent.**

spoil See **pamper.**

spotless See **clean.**

spread *v.* **expand, extend, open, outstretch, unfold.**
Core meaning: To move or arrange so as to cover a larger area (*spread the blanket on the grass; a bird spreading its wings in flight*).

spur See **provoke.**

spurious See **fallacious.**

spurn See **reject.**

squabble See **argue.**

squander See **waste.**

square See **conventional.**

stale *adj.* **flat, tired.**
These describe what has lost its freshness or effectiveness through age or overuse. STALE has broad literal and figurative application: *stale crackers; stale ideas.* FLAT suggests a lack or loss of sparkle, either literal or metaphorical: *flat champagne; flat jokes.* TIRED refers to what is worn out (*tired outfits*) or hackneyed (*tired comments*).
Antonym: **fresh.**

stance See **posture.**

---

standard 1. See **ideal. 2.** See **normal.**

stare See **gaze.**

start See **begin.**

startle See **frighten.**

state 1. See **nation. 2.** See **say.**

stately See **grand.**

staunch See **faithful.**

stay See **stop.**

steadfast See **faithful.**

stealthy See **secret.**

step See **move.**

sterile See **barren.**

stern See **harsh.**

stick See **bond.**

stiff See **inflexible.**

still See **motionless.**

stimulant See **stimulus.**

stimulate See **provoke.**

stimulus *n.* **catalyst, impetus, impulse, incentive, motivation, stimulant.**
Core meaning: Something that causes and encourages a given response (*free enterprise as a stimulus to the economy*).

stingy *adj.* **close, miserly.**
These suggest reluctance to give or spend. STINGY is the most general; often it implies meanness of spirit as well as lack of generosity: *stingy with money and stingy with praise.* MISERLY suggests greed and hoarding: *too miserly to leave a tip.* CLOSE describes excessive and often annoying caution in money matters. See also **cheap.**
Antonym: **generous.**

stipend See **wage(s).**

stirring See **moving.**

stop *v.* **1. arrest, cease, check, discontinue, halt, stay.**
Core meaning: To prevent the occurrence or continuation of (*stopped the execution of the prisoner; told us to stop the noise*).
2. cease, desist, discontinue, halt, leave off, quit.
Core meaning: To come to a cessation (*snow that finally stopped; a guard who yelled for us to stop*).

story See **lie.**

stout See **fat.**

straight 1. See **direct. 2.** See **conventional.**

straightforward See **direct.**

strain See **effort.**

strange *adj.* **1. new, unaccustomed, unfamiliar.**
These describe what was previously unknown: *strange animals of the jungle; new information; unaccustomed difficulties; an unfamiliar face.*
Antonym: **familiar.**
2. bizarre, curious, eccentric, odd, peculiar, quaint, queer, unusual.
All of these describe persons or things that are notably out of the ordinary: *her strange appearance; a bizarre hat; a curious coincidence; an eccentric habit; an odd name; a peculiar point of view; a land full of sloths and other quaint animals; a queer expression on his face; an unusual dress.*
Antonym: **familiar.**

strength See **force.**

strike 1. See **affect. 2.** See **hit.**

strike out See **cancel.**

stringency See **severity.**

strip See **undress.**

stripe See **type.**

stubborn See **contrary.**

stuff See **matter.**

stupendous See **fabulous.**

stupid 1. See **dull. 2.** See **unintelligent.**

stupor See **daze.**

style See **fashion.**

subdued See **quiet.**

submissive *adj.* **compliant, obedient, passive.**
These adjectives describe what yields readily to the authority of another: *a submissive employee; a compliant pupil;
an obedient servant. Passive* implies offering no resistance
whatever: *a passive child who was attacked regularly by
the neighborhood bully.*
Antonym: **rebellious.**

submit See **yield.**

subordinate *adj.* **dependent, secondary.**
These describe what has less power or importance than
something else of its kind. SUBORDINATE, the most general,
applies to rank, authority, position, etc. DEPENDENT suggests a relationship based on need: *A child is dependent on
its parents for shelter.* SECONDARY refers to what is not primary: *an idea of secondary importance.*
Antonym: **dominant.**

subsequent See **later.**

subsidy See **bonus.**

subsistence See **living.**

substance 1. See **heart. 2.** See **matter.**

subvert See **sabotage.**

succeed *v.* **flourish, prosper, thrive.**
All of these denote success in a chosen activity or enterprise. SUCCEED focuses on accomplishing something desired
or attempted: *She succeeded in swimming the Channel.
Efforts to reach a cease-fire will succeed.* FLOURISH, PROS-
PER, and THRIVE suggest growth and progress: *Their marriage is flourishing. His business is prospering. She is thriv-
ing as a lawyer.*
Antonym: **fail.**

---

succinct See **concise.**

succumb See **yield.**

sufficient *adj.* **adequate, decent, enough, satisfactory.**
Core meaning: Being what is needed without being in excess (*sufficient fuel to complete the trip*).

suggest *v.* **hint, imply, insinuate, intimate.**
These verbs all refer to conveying thoughts or ideas indirectly. SUGGEST in this context usually refers to a process in which something is called to mind by an association of ideas or train of thought: *a cavern that suggests a cathedral.* IMPLY refers to something involved or suggested by logical necessity: *Life implies growth and death.* HINT refers to expression that is indirect but contains rather pointed clues: *Our hostess hinted that it was time to leave.* INTIMATE applies to veiled expression that may be the result of discretion or reserve: *He intimated that there was trouble ahead.* INSINUATE refers to conveying something, usually unpleasant, in a covert manner that suggests underhandedness: *Are you insinuating that I am dishonest?*

suggestion See **trace.**

suitable *adj.* **appropriate, apt, fit, fitting, proper.**
SUITABLE implies ability to meet requirements related to a particular need or to an occasion: *clothes suitable for everyday wear.* What is APPROPRIATE to a thing or for an occasion especially befits it, and what is APT is notably to the point: *appropriate remarks; an apt reply.* FIT in this sense refers to what is adapted to certain requirements or capable of measuring up to them: *tools fit for the job; fit for heavy duty.* FITTING suggests close agreement with a prevailing mood or spirit: *a fitting observance of the holiday.* PROPER describes what is harmonious, either by nature or because it observes reason, custom, propriety, etc.: *a proper setting for a monument; the proper way to hold a fork.*
Antonym: **unsuitable.**

suitableness See **qualification.**

sultry See **hot.**

summit See **climax.**

sum (up) See **add.**

super See **excellent.**

supercilious See **proud.**

supererogative See **gratuitous.**

supererogatory See **gratuitous.**

superficial See **shallow.**

superfluity See **excess.**

superintend See **administer.**

supple See **flexible.**

support See **living.**

supposition See **theory.**

surpass *v.* exceed, excel, outdo, outshine, outstrip, pass, top, transcend.
Core meaning: To be greater or better than (*a wheat crop that surpassed last year's by two million bushels*).

surplus See **excess.**

surprise See **ambush.**

surreptitious See **secret.**

surround *v.* circle, compass, encircle, enclose, gird, hem in, ring.
Core meaning: To shut in on all sides (*a city surrounded by suburbs*).

survey See **analysis.**

suspended See **hanging.**

suspension See **abeyance.**

suspicion 1. See **distrust.** 2. See **doubt.** 3. See **uncertainty.**

swaddle See **wrap.**

swat See **hit.**

swathe See **wrap.**

sway See **dispose.**

swear See **pledge.**

swell See **expand.**

sweltering See **hot.**

swift See **fast.**

symptom See **sign.**

synthetic See **artificial.**

system See **method.**

table *n.* **chart, tabulation.**
Core meaning: An orderly, columnar display of information (*a table of mortgage rates*).

tabulation See **table.**

tacit See **implicit.**

tactic See **move.**

tactless *adj.* **clumsy, impolitic, indelicate.**
Core meaning: Lacking sensitivity and skill in dealing with others (*tactless remarks*).

take in See **accept.**

take up See **accept.**

tale See **lie.**

talent See **ability.**

talk See **speech.**

tall See **high.**

tally See **add.**

tamper See **interfere.**

tardy See **late.**

taunt See **ridicule.**

tax See **charge.**

teach *v.* **drill, educate, instruct, train, tutor.**
All of these refer to imparting knowledge or skill. TEACH is the most widely applicable. INSTRUCT usually suggests

methodical direction in a specific subject or area: *instructing students in English literature*. EDUCATE is comprehensive and implies a wide area of learning, achieved either by experience or, more often, by formal instruction in many subjects: *It is the responsibility of a community to educate each child*. TUTOR usually refers to private instruction of one student or a small group: *tutors children in mathematics*. TRAIN generally implies concentration on particular skills intended to fit a person, or sometimes an animal, for a desired role: *training young men to be good citizens; a school that trains drivers*. DRILL implies instruction or training by continuous repetition: *drilled the girl in irregular verbs*.

tediousness See **monotony**.

tedium See **monotony**.

tell See **say**.

temperament See **disposition**.

temperamental See **capricious**.

temperance See **abstinence**.

temperate See **sober**.

temporary *adj*. **fleeting, momentary, provisional, transient, transitory**.
These refer to what lasts for a limited time only. TEMPORARY applies to what is meant to last either while regular conditions are interrupted or until definitive arrangements can be made: *a temporary secretary; a temporary state capital*. PROVISIONAL suggests a makeshift arrangement to meet an immediate need: *a provisional shelter*. FLEETING, MOMENTARY, and TRANSITORY describe what is of brief duration; *fleeting* adds a note of melancholy: *The joys of this earth are fleeting*. TRANSIENT usually refers to what remains only a short time: *the transient population of hotels*.
Antonym: **permanent**.

tempt See **seduce**.

tenable See **justifiable**.

tender See **offer.**

tentative See **conditional.**

terminal See **last.**

terminate See **end.**

terminology See **language.**

terrify See **frighten.**

terse See **concise.**

theorem See **law.**

theoretical *adj.* **abstract, academic, speculative.**
Core meaning: Concerned with or restricted to a theory (*a plan still in the theoretical stages*).

theory *n.* **1. hypothesis, supposition.**
Core meaning: A belief used as the basis for action (*the theory of progressive education*).
2. conjecture, speculation.
Core meaning: Abstract reasoning (*the theory that Bacon wrote the plays attributed to Shakespeare*).

thin *adj.* **bony, gaunt, lean, skinny, slender, slim.**
As they are compared, these adjectives share the meaning of having a lack of excess flesh. THIN is the most neutral: *a thin man.* GAUNT and BONY suggest an emaciated or haggard appearance: *a gaunt face; bony elbows.* LEAN suggests trimness and good muscle tone (*a lean and agile cat*); SLENDER and SLIM often suggest elegance: *a slender* (or *slim*) *model.* SKINNY describes what is very thin: *skinny legs.*
Antonym: **fat.**

thorough See **utter.**

threaten *v.* **intimidate, menace.**
THREATEN and its synonyms refer to foretelling danger, promising evil or injury, or inspiring fear. *Threaten,* the most widely applicable, can refer to verbal promise of harm (*threatening the prisoners with physical punishment*), to forewarning (*Dark skies threaten rain*), or to having a character that puts someone or something in danger (*Landslides*

threatened the mountain village). MENACE is limited principally to the last of the foregoing senses: *an oil slick that menaced the shoreline of California.* INTIMIDATE refers to inspiring fear in and often to inhibiting a person by a show or promise of force: *His pounding the table and shouting failed to intimidate the witness.*

thrifty See **economical.**

thrive See **succeed.**

tidy See **neat.**

tie *v.* **bind.**
TIE and BIND can often be used interchangeably when they literally mean to fasten or secure: *tie up a parcel; bind sheaves of grain together.* Figuratively *tie* sometimes implies confinement or restraint: *tied to his family because he was dependent on them; tied to his job because he was ambitious. Bind,* more strongly than *tie*, suggests bringing together positively or uniting: *Mutual interests often bind two people.*
Antonym: **untie.**

tight *adj.* **taut, tense.**
When they refer to what is literally drawn out to its fullest extent, TIGHT and TAUT can often be used interchangeably: *a tight* (or *taut*) *string. Tight* frequently suggests constriction or binding (*tight lips; tight shoes*). *Taut* implies strain (*a rope so taut it nearly broke; a taut and angry face*). TENSE describes what is stretched tight, often excessively tight (*tense muscles*), and to persons in a state of mental or nervous strain (*tense and anxious before the interview*).
Antonym: **loose.**

time(s) See **age.**

timid *adj.* **timorous.**
Both TIMID and TIMOROUS refer to persons who lack courage, boldness, or daring and therefore shrink from dangerous or difficult circumstances: *too timid to learn to swim; a timorous man who never asserted himself.* They can also apply to the behavior, actions, manner, etc., of those who are thus

easily frightened: *a timid expression on her face; a timorous attempt to explain why he did it.*
Antonym: **bold.**

timidity See **diffidence.**

timorous See **timid.**

tinker See **fiddle.**

tiny See **little.**

tipsy See **drunk.**

tirade *n.* **diatribe, harangue, jeremiad, obloquy.**
Core meaning: A long, violent, or blustering speech, usually of censure or denunciation (*went off on a tirade about the evils of big government*).

tire See **bore.**

tired See **stale.**

title See **name.**

toil See **work.**

token See **sign.**

tongue See **language.**

tool *n.* **implement, instrument, utensil.**
Core meaning: A device used to do work or perform a task (*carpentry tools*).

top See **surpass.**

topflight See **excellent.**

topnotch See **excellent.**

topple See **overthrow.**

torment See **afflict.**

torrid See **hot.**

torture See **afflict.**

total 1. See **utter.** 2. See **add.**

totalitarian See **absolute.**

touch 1. See **affect.** 2. See **trace.**

touching See **moving.**

towering See **high.**

toy See **fiddle.**

trace *n.* **dash, hint, shade, suggestion, touch.**
Core meaning: A barely perceivable indication of something (*not a trace of wrongdoing*).

trade See **business.**

traditional See **conventional.**

traffic See **business.**

train See **teach.**

trance See **daze.**

tranquil See **calm.**

tranquillity *n.* **calm, peace, serenity.**
In the sense in which they are compared, these nouns all indicate freedom from agitation, anxiety, or worry: *a feeling of tranquillity; sat down with deceptive calm; a little peace and quiet; the serenity that comes from solving a personal dilemma.*
Antonym: **anxiety.**

transcend See **surpass.**

transform See **change.**

transgression See **breach.**

transient See **temporary.**

transitory See **temporary.**

transmit See **send.**

transpose See **reverse.**

treacherous 1. See **faithless.** 2. See **false.**

treasure See **appreciate.**

tremble See **shake.**

trespass See **breach.**

trice See **moment.**

trifle See **fiddle.**

trim See **neat.**

triumph See **victory.**

troublesome See **difficult.**

true *adj.* **1. accurate, correct, right.**
These describe what is free from error or consistent with fact, reason, or reality: *a true statement; an accurate reading; correct calculations; the right answer.*
Antonym: **false.**
2. genuine, honest, sincere.
All of these refer to what is free from hypocrisy or not calculated to mislead: *true concern; genuine enthusiasm; an honest response; a sincere apology.*
Antonym: **false.**
3. constant, faithful, loyal.
These terms apply to persons who are firm and unchanging in attachment to a person, cause, etc.: *a true friend; a constant admirer; a faithful wife; loyal servants of the government.*
Antonym: **false.**
4. See **authentic.**

trust *n.* **confidence, faith.**

trustworthy See **reliable.**

truth See **veracity.**
These all denote a firm belief that something is true, reliable, etc.: *Put your trust in God. She won my confidence by keeping her word. He had faith in his own ability to drive.* See also **confidence.**
Antonym: **distrust.**

tumble See **overthrow.**

tutor See **teach.**

twit See **ridicule.**

twofold See **double.**

type *n.* breed, ilk, kind, sort, species, stripe, type, variety.
Core meaning: A class that is defined by the common attribute or attributes possessed by all its members (*the type of person who gets angry easily*).

typical 1. See **characteristic. 2.** See **normal.**

tyrannical See **absolute.**

ugly *adj.* hideous, unsightly.
These apply primarily to what is displeasing to the eye: *an ugly face; a hideous gash; an unsightly scar. Ugly* and *hideous,* the stronger term, can also describe what is emotionally, morally, or otherwise offensive: *the ugly details of the argument; a hideous murder; a hideous accident; a hideous miscarriage of justice.*
Antonym: **beautiful.**

ultimate See **last.**

umpire See **judge.**

unable *adj.* incapable, incompetent.
UNABLE and INCAPABLE, when they follow a verb like *be,* denote inability to serve in a given function or to do something but do not necessarily reflect a negative judgment: *She was unable to type. He was incapable of learning physics.* INCOMPETENT implies actual failure: *an incompetent dentist.*

unaccustomed See **strange.**

unaffected See **natural.**

unalterable See **irrevocable.**

unanimous *adj.* concurrent, solid.
Core meaning: Being in or characterized by complete agreement (*a unanimous decision*).

unattainable See **impossible.**

unaware *adj.* unconscious.
These share the meaning of being beyond knowledge or cognizance. UNAWARE often suggests that something is escaping one's notice: *unaware of her departure.* UNCONSCIOUS can describe anything from a suppressed emotion

(*unconscious rage*) to total lack of awareness (*so involved in the discussion that he was unconscious of the storm outside*).
Antonym: aware.

unbelievable 1. See **fabulous. 2.** See **implausible.**

uncalled-for See **gratuitous.**

uncertainty *n.* doubt, skepticism, suspicion.
These all involve the condition of being unsure about something or someone. UNCERTAINTY and DOUBT usually imply a questioning state of mind (*uncertainty about taking the trip; has doubts about the accuracy of the report*). SKEPTICISM suggests in addition a doubting state of mind that requires proof: *skepticism about his friend's motives.* SUSPICION implies resistance to belief or acceptance, more from lack of trust than from tentativeness of feelings: *a suspicion that the cashier was stealing.*
Antonyms: certainty; confidence.

uncivil See **disrespectful.**

unclean See **impure.**

uncommon *adj.* extraordinary, rare, singular, unique.
UNCOMMON and its synonyms describe what is not usual or ordinary. *Uncommon* applies to what is not customary, a daily occurrence, widely used, or generally known: *an uncommon problem; uncommon abilities.* What is EXTRAORDINARY is very unusual or remarkable: *an extraordinary event.* RARE indicates that something occurs infrequently (*a rare disease*) or is highly valued (*a rare jewel*). SINGULAR suggests that something is extremely uncommon (*a singular ability to predict the future*) or very strange (*a singular decision to eat only eggs*). UNIQUE implies that something is one of a kind: *Things are either unique or not unique—they do not have to be unique to be uncommon.*
Antonym: common.

uncomplicated See **simple.**

unconscious See **unaware.**

unconventional *adj.* **atypical, novel, offbeat, unusual.**
Core meaning: Not usual or ordinary (*unconventional business methods; unconventional dress*).

unctuous *adj.* **fulsome, oily, sleek.**
Core meaning: Affectedly and self-servingly earnest (*The candidate had an oozing, unctuous manner*).

undependable See **unreliable.**

underhand *adj.* **1. devious, disingenuous, duplicitous, guileful, shifty, sneaky, underhanded.**
Core meaning: Marked by treachery or deceit (*underhand business practices*).
2. See **secret.**

underhanded See **underhand.**

underlying See **radical.**

undermine See **sabotage.**

understand See **comprehend.**

undoubted See **authentic.**

undress *v.* **disrobe, strip.**
UNDRESS, DISROBE, and STRIP denote removing clothes. *Undress* is the most neutral: *I undressed the children for bed. She undressed and ran a bath. Disrobe* is a more formal term: *The doctor asked the patient to disrobe. Strip* involves the removal of all clothing: *The guards stripped the prisoners in a search for concealed drugs. The athlete stripped and showered.*
Antonym: **dress.**

uneducated See **ignorant.**

unethical See **immoral.**

unfair *adj.* **inequitable, unjust.**
These all describe persons, thoughts, or deeds that fail to show proper and due consideration for all parties or factors

concerned in a matter. UNFAIR applies most widely. INEQ-
UITABLE, a more formal term, implies partiality. What is
UNJUST violates principles of law and ethics.
Antonym: **fair.**

unfaithful See **false.**

unfamiliar See **strange.**

unfasten See **detach.**

unfavorable *adj.* **adverse.**
Both of these describe what is disadvantageous or exerts an
opposing influence and points to misfortune or an unsuccessful outcome. UNFAVORABLE has the wider application:
*unfavorable working conditions; an unfavorable progress
report; an unfavorable spot to grow roses.* ADVERSE sometimes implies hostility and opposition (*adverse criticism*)
and sometimes merely describes what works against one's
interest or welfare (*adverse circumstances*).
Antonym: **favorable.**

unfeasible See **impossible.**

unfit See **unsuitable.**

unfitting See **unsuitable.**

unfortunate *adj.* **unhappy, unlucky.**
UNFORTUNATE and the less formal UNLUCKY can be used
interchangeably to refer to what meets with or brings unde-
served misfortune: *an unfortunate* (or *unlucky*) *businessman; an unfortunate* (or *unlucky*) *investment.* UN-
HAPPY, which in this sense stresses that something is
unfavorable, is rarely used to describe persons: *made a
wrong decision in an unhappy moment; an unhappy outcome.*
Antonym: **fortunate.**

unfriendly *adj.* **antagonistic, hostile.**
UNFRIENDLY denotes the absence of friendliness; it often
describes what is merely unpleasant or disagreeable (*unfriendly replies*) but can also imply stronger feelings of hostility (*an unfriendly nation*). ANTAGONISTIC suggests active

unfriendliness (*an antagonistic attitude*) and often implies contention or opposition (*During the cross-examination the prosecutor and the witness grew openly antagonistic*). Hostile describes what shows unfriendliness (*a hostile colleague*), enmity (*hostile troops*), or opposition (*hostile to the suggestion*).
Antonym: **friendly.**

unfruitful See **barren.**

ungainly See **awkward.**

unhappy 1. See **sad.** 2. See **unfortunate.**

unification *n.* **coalition, consolidation, union, unity.**
Core meaning: A bringing together into a whole (*a large country resulting from the unification of many small city-states*).

unimportant *adj.* **inconsequential, insignificant.**
These describe what has little or no value or importance: *an unimportant message; an inconsequential decision; an insignificant writer.*
Antonym: **important.**

unintelligent *adj.* **simple, stupid.**
These three apply to what has or shows little intelligence. Unintelligent is the most general term: *an unintelligent boy; an unintelligent answer.* Simple can suggest not only lack of intelligence but also lack of sense: *a simple man who was easily cheated.* Stupid occasionally refers to a temporary state of mental dullness; it also applies to individual acts that are extremely foolish: *The class seemed a bit stupid today. Swallowing goldfish is a stupid way to spend your time.*
Antonym: **intelligent.**

uninterested *adj.* **incurious, indifferent.**
These are compared as they indicate a lack of interest or curiosity. Uninterested and indifferent simply denote such absence. Incurious is the most specific, implying a lack of both normal and intellectual curiosity.
Antonym: **curious.**

---

union *n.* **1.** association, club, confederation, congress, federation, fellowship, league, order, organization, society.
Core meaning: A group united in a common activity, interest, or purpose (*a trade union; a union of anti-war activists*).
2. See **unification.**

unique 1. See **single. 2.** See **uncommon.**

unite See **join.**

unity See **unification.**

universal See **law.**

universe *n.* cosmos, creation, macrocosm, nature, world.
Core meaning: The totality of all existing things (*man's continual quest to understand the universe*).

unjust See **unfair.**

unknown See **obscure.**

unlawful See **illegal.**

unlikely *adj.* improbable.
UNLIKELY and IMPROBABLE refer to what shows little or no likelihood of being true or of happening: *an unlikely story; an improbable alibi. Snow seems unlikely* (or *improbable*) *today.*
Antonym: likely.

unlucky See **unfortunate.**

unmannerly See **impolite.**

unmistakable See **clear.**

unmitigated See **utter.**

unnecessary *adj.* inessential, needless, nonessential, unneeded.
Core meaning: Not necessary (*used unnecessary force; unnecessary expenditures*).

unneeded See **unnecessary.**

unobtrusive See **quiet.**

unpleasant *adj.* **disagreeable, objectionable.**
UNPLEASANT and DISAGREEABLE describe what is offensive or fails to give pleasure or satisfaction: *an unpleasant, ill-tempered cab driver; an unpleasant confrontation between labor and management; a vain, disagreeable executive; a strong, disagreeable odor.* OBJECTIONABLE, a stronger term, implies that something is so offensive that it causes or is apt to cause protest: *objectionable language; a point of view that is objectionable to all parties in the dispute.*
Antonym: **pleasant.**

unpredictable See **capricious.**

unprincipled See **immoral.**

unprogressive See **reactionary.**

unqualified See **utter.**

unrealistic See **idealistic.**

unrealizable See **impossible.**

unreasonable *adj.* **illogical, irrational, unreasoned.**
Core meaning: Not governed by or predicated on reason (*unreasonable expectations; an unreasonable demand*).

unreasoned See **unreasonable.**

unreliable *adj.* **undependable, untrustworthy.**
These words describe persons and things that do not merit faith and confidence: *an unreliable acquaintance; an undependable old car; an untrustworthy opponent.*
Antonym: **reliable.**

unscrupulous See **immoral.**

unselfish *adj.* **selfless.**
UNSELFISH and SELFLESS can be used interchangeably to describe those who are without concern for themselves.
Antonym: **selfish.**

unsightly See **ugly.**

unspeakable *adj.* **1. indescribable, unutterable.**
Core meaning: That cannot be described (*unspeakable happiness*).

2. abominable, frightful, revolting, shocking, sickening.
Core meaning: Too awful to be described (*unspeakable acts of genocide*).

unsteadiness See **instability.**

unsuitable *adj.* improper, inappropriate, inapt, unfit, unfitting.
All of these can be used interchangeably to refer to what does not meet the requirements related to a particular need or occasion.
Antonym: **suitable.**

unthinkable See **impossible.**

untidy See **disorderly.**

untrustworthy See **unreliable.**

untruth See **lie.**

untruthfulness See **dishonesty.**

unusual 1. See **strange. 2.** See **unconventional.**

unutterable See **unspeakable.**

unwell See **sick.**

unworkable See **impossible.**

upbraid See **scold.**

update See **modernize.**

uprising See **rebellion.**

upset *adj.* desperate, distraught, frantic, nervous.
These apply to what shows mental or emotional disturbance. UPSET is the most general: *an upset man who had lost his briefcase.* DESPERATE has the additional sense of a feeling of despair and hopelessness: *a desperate appeal for help.* DISTRAUGHT suggests anxiety that makes concentration difficult: *distraught because of her son's death.* FRANTIC implies extreme agitation bordering on frenzy: *a frantic scream.* NERVOUS can describe moods ranging from mere unease to severe apprehension: *nervous about being late; so nervous he had to take a sedative.*
Antonym: **calm.**

urge *v.* **coax, exhort, plead, press.**
URGE and its synonyms refer to requesting or persuading a person to do something that one advocates. *Urge* suggests making an earnest appeal for such action: *urged her friend to accept the job; urging the passage of new laws to combat crime.* PRESS implies a more forceful and insistent attempt to persuade: *Joy pressed her aunt to stay for the weekend.* EXHORT suggests a strong or stirring appeal (*The preacher exhorted the congregation to repent*); PLEAD, a humble but fervent one (*His mother pled with him not to leave*); and COAX, an attempt to persuade through persistent use of courtesy, flattery, etc. (*coaxing the child to take her medicine*). See also **encourage.**

used See **old.**

useful See **practical.**

usual See **familiar.**

utensil See **tool.**

utopian See **idealistic.**

utter 1. *adj.* **all-out, complete, consummate, outright, thorough, total, unmitigated, unqualified.**
Core meaning: Completely such, without qualification or exception (*an utter fool; utter chaos; had utter confidence in them*).
2. See **say.**

vacant See **empty.**

vacillate See **hesitate.**

vague *adj.* **hazy, indefinite, indistinct.**
These all apply to what is unclear to the eye, ear, or mind. VAGUE, the most general, basically indicates a lack of definite form: *a vague outline of a tree; vague sounds; a vague statement of goals.* HAZY applies to what is indistinctly felt, understood, or recalled: *a hazy recollection of the incident.* INDEFINITE refers to what lacks clarity or is unclearly expressed: *an indefinite statement of purpose.* INDISTINCT suggests what is ill defined and lacks shape,

form, or character: *an indistinct footprint.* See also **ambiguous.**
Antonym: **clear.**

valiant See **brave.**

valid *adj.* **conclusive, convincing, sound.**
These apply to statements, arguments, and reasoning; they greatly heighten the effectiveness or force of what they describe. VALID and SOUND apply to what can be shown to be in accord with fact, truth, right, common sense, or legal force, and therefore is able to resist challenge or attack: *a valid objection; a valid passport; a sound case; sound title to the property.* CONVINCING applies to what is persuasive, even though it may not in fact be true: *His presentation is very convincing, but his evidence is suspicious.* What is CONCLUSIVE is decisive and thus capable of putting an end to doubt or debate: *a conclusive argument.*
Antonym: **invalid.**

valuable *adj.* **inestimable, invaluable, precious, priceless.**
Core meaning: Of great value (*valuable Elizabethan manuscripts*).

value See **appreciate.**

vanished *adj.* **dead, defunct, extinct, lost.**
Core meaning: No longer in use, force, or operation (*vanished languages of ancient peoples*).

variety *n.* **1. diversity, heterogeneity, multifariousness, multiformity, multiplicity, variousness.**
Core meaning: The quality of being made of many different forms, kinds, or individuals (*lives a life of great variety; the incredible variety of cultural expression in New York*).
2. See **type.**

variousness See **variety.**

vary See **change.**

vaunt See **boast.**

vend See **sell.**

venerable See **old.**

---

veneration See **honor.**

vengeful See **vindictive.**

venomous See **malevolent.**

vent See **say.**

veracity *n.* **1.** accuracy, correctness, exactitude, fidelity, truth.
Core meaning: Correspondence with facts or truth (*trusted in the veracity of her report*).
2. See **honesty.**

verbosity See **wordiness.**

vernacular See **language.**

vertical *adj.* perpendicular.
VERTICAL and PERPENDICULAR refer to what is at right angles—or approximately so—to the plane of the horizon or of a supporting surface: *a vertical takeoff; the vertical walls of an apartment; the perpendicular side of a building.*
Antonym: horizontal.

vex See **annoy.**

vice *n.* corruption, depravity, immorality, wickedness.
These all denote serious moral failings. VICE is the most general; it can refer to a moral flaw or weakness that inclines a person to evil or, in a weaker sense, to any defect of character: *Vice is not hereditary. Some people consider smoking a vice.* CORRUPTION connotes lack of moral restraint (*corruption in the court of the aging emperor*) or dishonesty or improper behavior, often by persons in positions of authority (*corruption at city hall*). DEPRAVITY suggests moral debasement: *a molester of children whose depravity was obvious to his fellow prisoners.* IMMORALITY in this sense often suggests extreme indulgence in sensual pleasures. WICKEDNESS implies viciousness.
Antonym: virtue.

vicious See **cruel.**

victory *n.* conquest, triumph.
These refer to the fact of winning, in war or in a competition. VICTORY, the general term, is broadly interchangeable

with the others but lacks their overtones. CONQUEST connotes physically forcing an enemy nation to submit; it can also refer to overcoming barriers of other sorts, as to understanding or control: *the conquest of yellow fever.* TRIUMPH refers to a victory or success that is noteworthy because it is decisive, significant, or spectacular: *Caesar's triumph in Gaul; a role that was the triumph of the actor's career.* *Antonym:* **defeat.**

view *n.* **1. outlook, perspective, prospect.**
Core meaning: An evaluation or prediction about something (*curious about her views on the upcoming contract negotiations*).
2. See **opinion.**

vigilant See **alert.**

vigorous See **active.**

vindicate *v.* **absolve, acquit, exonerate.**
This group shares the common meaning of demonstrating innocence of guilt or blame. To VINDICATE is to clear with supporting proof. To ABSOLVE is to clear of blame or guilt. To ACQUIT suggests a judicial decision in answer to a specific formal charge. To EXONERATE is to declare blameless.
Antonym: **accuse.**

vindictive *adj.* **revengeful, spiteful, vengeful.**
Core meaning: Disposed to seek revenge (*a bitter, vindictive person*).

violation See **breach.**

violence See **force.**

virile See **male.**

virtue *n.* **goodness, morality, righteousness.**
All of these denote moral excellence. VIRTUE, MORALITY, and RIGHTEOUSNESS suggest conformity to standards of what is right and just or to approved codes of behavior; all imply uprightness: *Virtue is its own reward. The newspaper ques-*

---

tioned the morality of supplying weapons to both sides in the foreign uprising. They were convinced of the righteousness of their cause. GOODNESS often connotes inherent qualities of kindness, benevolence, or generosity: *Goodness and honesty showed in his every action.*
Antonym: **vice.**

virtuous See **moral.**

visionary See **idealistic.**

vital See **necessary.**

vituperative See **abusive.**

vivid See **graphic.**

vogue See **fashion.**

voice See **say.**

void See **invalid.**

volatile See **capricious.**

volume See **bulk.**

voluntary *adj.* **deliberate, intentional, willful.**
These four describe actions that are subject to control by the will of an individual. VOLUNTARY is the most general; it implies the exercise of free will (*a voluntary contribution to the pension fund*) or of choice (*living in voluntary exile*). DELIBERATE suggests what is done or said on purpose: *a deliberate theft.* INTENTIONAL further implies action that is undertaken for a specific purpose: *intentional insolence.* What is WILLFUL is said or done in accordance with one's own will and often suggests obstinacy: *a willful waste of time; willful disobedience.* See also **intentional; optional.**
Antonym: **involuntary.**

voracious *adj.* **avid, omnivorous, rapacious, ravenous.**
Core meaning: Having an insatiable appetite for an activity or pursuit (*a voracious reader*).

vow See **pledge.**

vulgar See **coarse.**

---

wage(s) *n.* earnings, emolument, fee, pay, salary, stipend.
Core meaning: Payment for work done (*an hourly wage of $8.50*).

wallop See **hit.**

wanton See **gratuitous.**

wares See **goods.**

warning *n.* admonishment, admonition, caution, caveat, forewarning.
Core meaning: Advice to beware of a person or thing (*disregarded his friend's warnings*).

wary See **alert.**

waste *v.* consume, deplete, dissipate, drain, exhaust, expend, fritter, squander.
These refer to the unwise or needless use of money, time, energy, or any kind of supply. WASTE is the least specific: *wasted $100 on a new gadget that he didn't need; wastes hours watching television when he should be studying; wasting space.* CONSUME, DRAIN, EXHAUST, and EXPEND often suggest that something has been used up completely: *Haggling over the details consumed precious hours. The hectic life he led began to drain his resources. The diver exhausted his air supply. The rocket's fuel was expended rapidly when the auxiliary tank began to leak.* To DEPLETE is to reduce the amount of something until little or none remains: *Our oil supplies have been seriously depleted.* FRITTER (always used with *away*) also implies gradual reduction: *kept the boys from frittering away their time.* SQUANDER nearly always suggests extravagance: *squander money.* To DISSIPATE is to use up in an intemperate manner: *He dissipated his life's savings by gambling.*
Antonym: save.

wasted See **haggard.**

watchful See **alert.**

waver See **hesitate.**

way See **method.**

---

waylay See **ambush.**

weak See **implausible.**

weaken See **relent.**

weakness *n.* failing, foible, frailty, infirmity, shortcoming.
Core meaning: A liking or personal preference (*a weakness for chocolate*).

wealthy See **rich.**

weary See **bore.**

wedding See **marriage.**

wedlock See **marriage.**

weight See **charge.**

weighty 1. See **heavy.** 2. See **important.**

welcome 1. See **pleasant.** 2. See **accept.**

well See **healthy.**

whack See **hit.**

wicked See **malevolent.**

wickedness See **vice.**

wide See **broad.**

wield See **handle.**

will *n.* decision, determination, resolution, resolve.
Core meaning: The power to make choices and act upon them in spite of difficulty or opposition (*lacked the will to gamble on his plan*).

willful 1. See **contrary.** 2. See **voluntary.**

win See **earn.**

windiness See **wordiness.**

wise *adj.* judicious, prudent, sage.
These terms describe persons, ideas, deeds, etc., that have or show understanding of what is true, right, or lasting. WISE and SAGE both suggest sound judgment, knowledge,

---

and experience; *sage,* the stronger of the two terms, sometimes has connotations of veneration and is often applied to intellectuals: *a wise statesman; a wise decision; a sage philosopher; a sage remark.* JUDICIOUS suggests forethought and caution: *a more judicious use of natural resources; a judicious man who chose his career with his limitations in mind.* PRUDENT stresses good judgment and common sense: *a prudent woman; a prudent approach to budgeting.*
Antonym: **unwise.**

wisecrack See **joke.**

wish *n.* **craving, desire, longing.**
WISH and DESIRE apply to any strong inclination for a particular thing: *a wish to go to Paris; a desire to see the Eiffel Tower.* CRAVING implies an eager or intense desire: *a craving for strawberries.* LONGING suggests a persistent yearning, often for something unattainable: *a longing to go home.*

wistful See **pensive.**

withdraw See **recede.**

withhold See **refrain.**

withstand *v.* **combat, fight, oppose, resist.**
These verbs all imply a struggle or effort to overcome, defeat, or destroy. RESIST suggests an active attempt to work against something (*People resist change; they resist with all their might*); it often implies a successful effort (*resisted temptation*). WITHSTAND always stresses successful resistance: *They withstood every attack.* COMBAT, FIGHT, and OPPOSE do not necessarily connote a favorable outcome: *drugs to combat infection; combat an enemy; fighting crime; guerrilla groups fighting in the mountains; oppose an enemy; oppose new legislation.*
Antonym: **yield.**

witticism See **joke.**

wobble See **shake.**

woe See **sorrow.**

womanly See **female.**

wonderful See **fabulous.**

wondrous See **fabulous.**

wordiness *n.* prolixity, verbosity, windiness.
Core meaning: Words or the use of words in excess of those needed for clarity or precision (*obscured her meaning with wordiness*).

wording *n.* diction, parlance, phraseology, phrasing.
Core meaning: Choice of words and the way in which they are used (*the complex wording in a contract*).

work 1. *n.* business, employment, job, occupation.
These nouns apply specifically to what one does to earn a living. WORK is the most general; it can refer to the mere fact of employment (*looking for work*) or to a specified activity (*Her work was nursing*). A BUSINESS is the work or trade in which a person engages: *went into the detective business.* EMPLOYMENT and JOB both suggest activity in which a person is engaged and paid by another: *got regular employment at an airport; had a job in a bookstore.* An OCCUPATION as a means of making a living does not necessarily imply being employed by others: *Madame Curie was by occupation a chemist.*
2. *n.* drudgery, labor, toil.
These denote physical or mental effort to make or do something. WORK and LABOR are least specific: *at work in the field; put in hard work on writing his new book; the labor involved in planting a garden; the labor of correcting and grading papers.* DRUDGERY implies tedious or menial work: *household drudgery.* TOIL is strenuous and exhausting work.
3. *v.* See **operate.**

world See **universe.**

worn 1. See **haggard. 2.** See **old.**

worry See **anxiety.**

wrangle See **argue.**

---

wrap *v.* **enfold, envelop, invest, swaddle, swathe.**
Core meaning: To cover completely and closely, as with clothing (*wrapped the baby in a blanket*).

wrath See **anger.**

wretched See **sad.**

wrong 1. See **false.** 2. See **awry.**

yield 1. *v.* **bow, capitulate, defer, submit, succumb.**
These share the sense of giving in to what one can no longer oppose or resist. YIELD has the widest application: *yield to an enemy; yield to a superior argument; yielded when she saw it was hopeless.* Bow suggests giving in out of sheer necessity or out of respect for another: *bow to defeat; bow to greater expertise.* To CAPITULATE is to surrender under specified and stated conditions (*The Axis powers capitulated*); the word can also suggest surrender more generally (*capitulated to her demand for additional help*). DEFER implies giving way to superior authority or for reasons of courtesy: *I defer to your better judgment.* SUBMIT applies when one gives way out of necessity after offering resistance unsuccessfully: *They withstood the siege for months but submitted when their supplies gave out.* SUCCUMB strongly suggests submission to something overpowering or overwhelming: *succumbed to the pressures of society; succumbed to her desire for a candy bar.*
Antonym: **withstand.**
2. *n.* See **production.**
3. *v.* See **relent.**

yoke See **couple.**

young *adj.* **adolescent, juvenile, youthful.**
All of these apply to persons in the age group between childhood and adulthood. YOUNG and YOUTHFUL are the most general (*the young—or youthful—hero*); both can also suggest the freshness, vigor, appearance, etc., associated with youth (*young for her age; a youthful face*). ADOLES-

CENT and JUVENILE usually stress immaturity: *adolescent attitudes; juvenile behavior.*
Antonym: old.

youthful See **young.**

zeal See **passion.**

zenith See **climax.**

zone See **area.**

appendix
to the
thesaurus

COLLECTIVE NOUNS

The words in the following list are collective, or group, terms—that is, names given to companies of animals, birds, or fish of the same kind. Each word is followed by an indication of the things that make up the group. When the word is also applied to human beings, that fact is noted and explained. The first seven words are basic ones, important to an understanding of the more special terms, which are arranged alphabetically and complete the listing.

brood	Young offspring under the care of the same mother; especially, birds (fowl) or fish having a common birth. Or the word can be applied to the children of a single family.
drove	Animals (most often cattle, sheep, swine, or geese) being driven as a body from one location to another. Less often, a large body of people moving or acting as one.
flight	A group of birds or aircraft in flight together.
flock	Sheep, goats, or other animals or birds (especially when on the ground) that live, feed, or travel together. Said of persons, the word usually means the congregation of a church or the followers of a single clergyman or leader in another sphere. Less formally, any large number of things, such as difficulties.
gang	A company of wolves or wild dogs, or of buffalo or elk when herded. Applied to people, a company of young persons associating on a social basis; a band engaged in criminal or other unlawful pursuits; or a group of laborers on one job such as a construction project. Also, a set of matched tools.

herd	Cattle when tended by persons, or other animals such as antelope, elephants, zebras, and aquatic mammals such as whales and seals. The expression *the herd* refers to the multitude of common people regarded, unfavorably, as a mass of cattle.
pack	A band of wolves or dogs that run and hunt as a unit; less often birds, especially grouse. Or a band of persons, often engaged in criminal pursuits but sometimes associated as followers of a celebrity.
bevy	Animals, especially roe deer, or birds, particularly larks or quail. Or a group or assemblage of persons, often attractive girls or young women.
cast	Falcons or hawks, usually a pair, released by a falconer at one time.
cete	A company of badgers.
covert	A flock of coots.
covey	A family of partridges, grouse, or other game birds.
drift	A drove or herd, usually of pigs, hogs, or boars.
exaltation	A flight of larks.
fall	A group of animals born at one birth; also a covey of woodcock.
gaggle	A flock of geese.
gam	A herd of whales or a social gathering of whalers at sea.
kennel	A pack of dogs, especially hounds, usually housed in one place or under the same ownership.
kindle	A brood or litter, especially of kittens.
litter	Offspring produced at one birth by a mammal that bears more than one offspring at one time.

muster	A flock of peacocks.
nide	A nest or brood of pheasants.
pod	A large group of seals or whales.
pride	A company of lions.
rout	In much earlier usage, a company of people or animals, especially of knights or wolves.
school, shoal	A large group of aquatic animals, particularly fish, swimming together.
shrewdness	A company of apes.
skein	A flight of geese or other wildfowl.
skulk	In earlier usage, a band of stealthily moving creatures, especially of foxes.
sloth	A company of bears.
sord	A flight of mallards.
sounder	A herd of wild boar.
spring	A flock of teal.
stable	Horses (including racehorses) lodged in one place or under one ownership. Less often, a group of boxers under a single manager.
swarm	A large number of insects or other small organisms, especially when in motion; or a group of bees, with a queen bee, migrating to establish a new colony. Less often, a large number of persons or animals when moving in mass or in a disorderly fashion.
troop	Animals or birds, especially when on the move. Or a body of soldiers or other military personnel, or a unit of Boy Scouts or Girl Scouts.
warren	A colony of rabbits.
watch	A flock of nightingales.
wisp	A flock of birds, especially of snipe.

COLLATERAL ADJECTIVES

A collateral adjective is one that corresponds to a certain noun in meaning but not in form (appearance). The words are descended from different linguistic lines. For example, *cardiac* is the collateral adjective of *heart,* and *feline* of *cat.* The phrase *cardiac deficiency* indicates a heart ailment; *feline quickness* expresses a characteristic of cats. Collateral adjectives are especially useful to one who writes, but often are not readily accessible to the average writer. This is so because, in many cases, the adjectives are not everyday words and because their identity is not suggested by a corresponding noun.

The following list of collateral adjectives is not exhaustive but includes many of the more common ones. On each line the noun (the word known to the writer) appears first; following it is the corresponding adjective (the word sought). The list is arranged so that related pairs of terms are grouped together—those, for example, that apply to animals, those that name or describe parts of the body, and so on. The concluding portion of the list contains words that are unrelated.

Zoology

ant	formic; formican; myrmecoid
ape; monkey	simian
bat	chiropteran; chiropterous
bear	ursine
bee	apian
bird	avian
bird of prey	raptorial
bull	taurine
butterfly, moth, etc.	lepidopteral; lepidopteran; lepidopterous
cat	feline
cattle	bovine
chicken	gallinaceous; galline
cockroach	blattid
crab	cancrid; cancroid

crow; raven; rook	corvine
deer	cervine
dog	canine; cynoid
dragon	draconic
duck	anatine
eagle	aquiline
fish	piscine
flamingo	phoenicopteroid; phoenicop-terous
flea	siphonapterous
fly, mosquito, etc.	dipteran; dipterous
fox	vulpine
frog	ranine; raninian
goat	capric; caprid; caprine; hir-cine
goose	anserine
hare; rabbit	leporid; leporine
hawk; falcon	accipitral; accipitrine
horse	equine; hippic
kangaroo; opposum	marsupial
lion	leonine
lizard	saurian
louse	pedicular
mite; tick	acarid
mole	talpid; talpoid
mouse; rat	muriform; murine
ostrich	struthionine; struthious
otter	lutrine
peacock	pavonian; pavonine
pig	porcine
pigeon	columbaceous; columbine
porpoise	phocaenid
sea horse	hippocampal; hippocampine
seal	phocacean; phocaceous; phocal; phocid; phocine
shark; ray	squalid; squaloid; selachian
sheep	ovine
skunk	mephitine

snake	ophidian
spider	arachnoid
squirrel	sciurid; sciuroid
swallow	hirundine; hirundinous
thrush	turdine; turdoid
tiger	tigrine
turtle, tortoise, etc.	chelonian; testudinal; testudinarious; testudinate
weasel, mink, etc.	mustelid; musteline
whale	cetacean; cetaceous
wolf	lupine
worm	annelid; annelidan; vermicular

Points of the Compass

east	oriental
north	boreal
south	austral
west	occidental

Parts of the Body

ankle	talar
arm	brachial
back	dorsal
belly	ventral
bladder	vesical
blood	hemal; hematic; hematoid
blood vessel	vascular
bone	osseous; osteal; osteoid
brain	cerebral
breast	mammary
buttocks	pygal
calf	sural
cheek	buccal
chest	pectoral; thoracic
chin	mental
ear	aural; otic

elbow	cubital
eye	ocular
eyebrow	superciliary
eyelash	ciliary
finger	digital
foot	pedal
forearm	cubital
forehead	frontal
gall bladder	cholecystic
gums	gingival
hair	capillary; pilar; pilary
hand	manual
head; skull	cephalic
heart	cardiac
heel	calcaneal; calcanean
hoof; nail; claw	ungual; ungular
joint	articular
kidney	nephric; nephritic; renal
knee	genual
leg	crural
lip	labial
liver	hepatic
loin	lumbar
lung	pulmonary
mouth	oral
neck	cervical; jugular; nuchal
nerve	neural
nose	nasal; rhinal
rib	costal
shoulder	scapular
side	sagittal
skin	cutaneous; dermal; dermic
skull	cranial
sole	plantar
spleen	lienal
stomach	gastric
tail	caudal
thigh	femoral

throat	faucial; jugular; pharyngeal
toe	digital
tongue	glossal; lingual
tooth	dental
vein	venous
wrist	carpal

Time

dawn	auroral
day	diurnal; quotidian
evening	vesperal; vespertinal; vespertine
hour	horal
month	mensal
morning	matutinal
night	nocturnal
week	hebdomadal; hebdomadary
year	annual

Seasons

fall	autumnal
spring	vernal
summer	aestival; estival
winter	brumal; hibernal; hiemal

Celestial Bodies

moon	lunar
star	astral; sidereal; stellar
sun	heliacal; solar

Family

brother	fraternal
daughter	filial
father	paternal
husband	marital
mother	maternal
nephew	nepotal; nepotic

sister	sororal
son	filial
uncle	avuncular
wife	uxorial

General

answer	respondent; responsive
apple	pomaceous
ashes	cinereous
atonement; expiation	piacular
author	auctorial
baldness	alopecic; glabrous
bank of a river or lake	riparian
barber	tonsorial
basis; foundation	fundamental
beard	barbate
beast	bestial
beauty	pulchritudinous
beginning	inchoate; incipient; initial
bell	tintinnabular; tintinnabulary; tintinnabulous
bishop	episcopal
blood; bloodshed	sanguineous
body	corporal; corporeal
boredom	tedious
brass	brazen
bristle	setaceous
bundle	fascicular; fasciculate
cave	spelean
chance	fortuitous
childhood; immaturity	puerile
church	ecclesiastical
circle; sphere	orbicular; orbiculate
city	metropolitan; urban
clay	argillaceous
commotion; disturbance	tumultuous
complaint	querulous
confusion; agitation	turbulent

contemplation	pensive
copper	cupreous; cupric; cupriferous; cuprous
cough	tussal; tussive
country	rustic
curve	sinuous
custom; habit	consuetudinary
dance	terpsichoreal; terpsichorean
danger	perilous
darkness	tenebrious; tenebrous
death	lethal; mortal; thanatoid
delay	cunctative
devil	diabolic; diabolical
diamond	adamantine
diligence	sedulous
drinking	bibulous
eagerness; sprightliness	alacritous
earthquake	seismic
egg	ovoid; ovoidal; ovular; ovulary
enemy; enmity	hostile
evil; infamy	nefarious
fear	pavid
feather	plumate; plumose
fever	febrile
field	campestral
fire	incendiary; igneous
flood	diluvial; diluvian
foam; froth	spumous; spumy
fold; crease; wrinkle	rugate; rugose
forest; tree	silvan; sylvan
form; shape; structure	morphic; morphologic; morphological
friendliness	amicable
fringe	fimbriate; fimbriated
frost	gelid
gambling	aleatory
gardening	horticultural

gardening, decorative	topiary
glass	vitreous; vitrescent
glue	glutinous
god	deific
gold	auric; auriferous; aurous
grain, especially wheat	frumentaceous
green	virid; viridescent
healthfulness	salubrious; salutary
heat	caloric; calorific; thermal; thermic
hiss	sibilant
honey	melliferous; mellific; melliflu-ous
hood; cowl	cucullate; cucullated
horn	corneous
hump; swelling	gibbous
hunger; starvation	famished
ice	glacial
impulsiveness	impetuous
indecency	obscene
indiscriminateness; im-morality	promiscuous
indolence; futility	otiose
introduction; preliminary	prefatory
iron	ferric; ferriferous; ferrous; ferruginous
irritability; peevishness	petulant
island	insular
ivory	eburnean; eburneous
jumping; dancing	saltant; saltatorial; saltatory
kettle drum	tympanic
king; queen; monarch; ruler	regal; royal
kiss	osculatory
lake	lacustrine
land; earth	terrene; terrestrial
laugh	risible

law	jural; juridic; juridical; juristic; legal
laxity; negligence	remiss
leaf	foliaceous; foliar; foliate; foliose; frondescent, frondose
learning; knowledge	erudite
left	sinistral
legal proceedings; argumentation; debate	forensic
letter	epistolary
library	bibliothecal
life	vital
light	luminous; photic
love	amatory; amorous
marble	marmoreal; marmorean
marriage	hymeneal; marital; matrimonial
master; teacher, authority	magisterial
melancholy; gloom	morose
menace	minatorial; minatory
milk	lactary; lacteal; lactescent; lactic; lactiferous
model; specimen	exemplary
moisture	humid
money	financial; pecuniary
mother-of-pearl	nacreous
need	indigent
net; netting	reticular
notoriety	infamous
number	numeric; numerical
oak	quercine
oath	jurant; juratory
oceans or seas, open	pelagic
oil	oleaginous; unctuous
old age	senescent; senile

parish	parochial
pearl	margaric; margaritic
pleasure	hedonic; hedonistic
plunder	predaceous; predacious; predatory
pregnancy	gravid
priest	sacerdotal
probability; likelihood	verisimilar
prophesy	vaticinal
punishment	penal
rain	pluvial; pluvian; pluviose; pluvious
reason	rational
relentlessness	inexorable
resistance; disobedience	contumacious
resistance to motion, action, etc.	inert
right	dextral
ring	annular; annulate; annulated
river	fluvial
rudeness	contumelious
salt	saline
scale, as of fish	squamose; squamous; squamulose
school	academic
sea	marine; maritime
sewer	cloacal
shore; coast	littoral
shrub	frutescent; fruticose
silence	taciturn
silver	argent; argentine
sin; guilt	peccable; peccant
skin; film	pellicular
sky; heavens	celestial
slave; slavishness	servile
sleep	somnifacient; somniferous; somnific; somnolent
smell	olfactory

snow	nival
spontaneity	extemporaneous; extempo- rary; extempore
spot; stain	maculate
stone	lithic; petrous
stone, precious	lapidary
strap	ligulate
stubbornness	obstinate
stupidity; silliness	asinine; fatuous
sugar	saccharine
swamp	paludal
sweat	sudatory; sudorific
swimming	natant; natatorial; natatory
tailor; tailoring	sartorial
talkativeness	loquacious
taste	gustatory
tear	lachrymal
tenacity	pertinacious
tendency	prone
thorn	spinose; spinous
thrift	frugal
throat	guttural
tickle; agreeable excite- ment	titillative
time	chronological; temporal
touch	tactile
tree	arboreal; arboreous
trust	fiducial; fiduciary
twilight	crepuscular
universe	cosmic
walk	ambulant; ambulatory
wall	mural
wastefulness; extrava- gance	prodigal
water	aquatic
wax	ceraceous; cerated
wedge	cuneal; cuneate; cuneated; cuneiform

widow	vidual
wildness	feral
window	fenestrated
wing	alar; alate; alated
wink	nictitant; nictitating
whisper	susurrant; susurrous
whistle	sibilant
worthlessness; invalidity	nugatory
yawn	oscitant

SCIENCES AND TECHNOLOGY

Following are the names of some of the major sciences or branches of technology. Each name is preceded by a brief indication of its particular field of study and activity.

aircraft navigation	**aeronautics**
ancient life forms and fossils	**paleontology**
animals as an area of biological study	**zoology**
atmosphere, phenomena of the	**meteorology**
atomic and molecular systems, the composition, strucuture, properties, and reactions of	**chemistry**
bacteria, especially in relation to medicine and agriculture	**bacteriology**
biological substances and processes, chemistry of	**biochemistry**
birds, observation of as a branch of zoological study	**ornithology**
caves, the physical, geologic, and biological aspects of	**speleology**
celestial bodies	**astronomy**
cells, the formation, structure, and function of, considered as a branch of biology	**cytology**
charts and maps, the making of	**cartography**
drugs	
the composition, uses, and effects of	**pharmacology**
the preparation and dispensing of	**pharmacy**
earth, the	
and its features	**geography**
the mechanical properties of	**seismology**
the origin, history, and structure of	**geology**

earthquakes	**seismology**
electronic phenomena	**electronics**
energy and matter and the interaction be-tween them	**physics**
environment, the relationship between or-ganisms and their	**ecology**
fossils and ancient life forms	**paleontology**
heredity, the biology of	**genetics**
human beings, emergence of from earlier forms of life	**evolution**
insects, the world of	**entomology**
life and life processes	**biology**
life processes, activities, and functions, essential and characteristic, consid-ered as a biological science	**physiology**
light and vision, the properties of	**optics**
living organisms	
the function, early growth, and devel-opment of	**embryology**
the structure, functioning, growth, ori-gin, evolution, and distribution of	**biology**
existing outside the earth or its atmo-sphere, the biology of	**exobiology or astrobiology**
maps and charts, the making of	**cartography**
material systems, the action of forces on	**mechanics**
matter	
the composition, structure, properties, and reactions of	**chemistry**
the action of forces on	**mechanics**
and energy and the interactions between them	**physics**

mental processes and behavior	**psychology**
metals, the extraction of from their ores, the purification of, and the creation of useful objects from	**metallurgy**
minerals, the distribution, identification, and properties of	**mineralogy**
molecular and atomic systems, the composition, structure, properties, and reactions of	**chemistry**
mountains, including their physical geography	**orology**
nature, the constitution of	**cosmography**
nervous system, the, the structure and disorders of, considered as part of medical science	**neurology**
ocean, the, and its phenomena as an area of exploration and scientific study	**oceanography**
organisms	
and their environment, the relationship between	**ecology**
and their parts, the shape and structure of	**anatomy**
plant life, considered as a branch of biology	**botany**
radiation, the use of as a means of medical diagnosis and therapy and in the scientific examination of material structures	**radiology**
related groups of organisms, the historical development of	**evolution**
sound, the nature and properties of	**acoustics**
space flight	**astronautics**
tissue, animal and plant, anatomical study of the microscopic structure of	**histology**

universe, the	
evolution of	**cosmogony**
the origin, processes, and structure of	**cosmology**
beyond the earth	**astronomy**
upper atmosphere, the	**aeronomy**
vision and light, the properties of	**optics**
water, the properties, distribution, and effects of	**hydrology**
weather and weather conditions	**meteorology**

PREFIXES AND SUFFIXES

The list below gives some common prefixes and suffixes with their meanings and example words.

Prefixes

a-, an- Without; not: *amoral; anaerobic.*

ante- 1. Earlier; prior to: *antepenult.* **2.** Before; in front of: *anteroom.*

anti- 1. Against; opposing: *antismoking.* **2.** Counteracting: *antihistamine.*

auto- 1. Self; same: *autobiography.* **2.** Automatic: *autopilot; autoloading.*

bi-, bin- Two: *bimonthly; binocular.*

bio- 1. Life; living organism: *biohazard.* **2.** Biology: *bioengineering.*

centi- 1. One hundred: *centipede.* **2.** One-hundredth: *centimeter.*

chemo- Chemicals; chemical: *chemotherapy.*

chromat-, chromo- Color: *chromatic; chromolithograph.*

chrono- Time: *chronology.*

circum- Around; about: *circumsolar.*

co-, col-, com-, con- Together; with: *cooperate; commingle.*

contra- Against; opposite: *contradiction.*

counter- Opposite; opposing: *counterclaim.*

de- 1. Reverse; undo: *decriminalize.* **2.** Remove; remove from: *declaw.* **3.** Reduce: *degrade.*

deca-, deka- Ten: *decade; decaliter.*

deci- One-tenth: *decigram.*

dis- 1. Not: *dissatisfied.* **2.** Undo: *disarrange.* **3.** Used as an intensive: *dissever.*

dys- Bad; impaired; abnormal: *dysfunction.*

electro- Electric; electricity: *electromotive.*

en-[1], em- 1. To put or go into or on: *emplane; enlist.* **2.** To cause to be: *enable; encamp.* **3.** Thoroughly: *encompass; entwine.*

en-[2], em- In; into: *enzootic.*

equi- Equal; equally: *equilateral.*
eu- Good: *eulogy; euphony.*
extra- Outside; beyond: *extracurricular.*
fore- **1.** Before; earlier: *foretell.* **2.** In front of: *forefront.*
geo- Earth; geography: *geothermal.*
hemat-, hemo- Blood: *hemocyte.*
hepta- Seven: *heptagon.*
hetero- Other: *heterodox.*
hexa- Six: *hexagon; hexadecimal.*
homo- Same: *homophone.*
hydro- **1.** Water: *hydroelectric.* **2.** Hydrogen: *hydrocarbon.*
hyper- **1.** Over; beyond: *hypertext.* **2.** Excessive; exceedingly: *hyperactive.*
hypo- Below; under: *hypodermal.*
in-¹, il-, im-, ir- Not: *incapable; illiterate; irrelevant.*
in-², il-, im-, ir- In; into: *inbreed; illuminate; irradiate.*
inter- Among; between: *interplanetary.*
intra- Within: *intraocular.*
kilo- Thousand: *kilogram.*
macro- Large; long; inclusive: *macrobiotics.*
mal- Bad; abnormal: *maladapted.*
mega- **1.** One million: *megabyte.* **2.** Very large: *megavitamin.*
micro- **1.** Very small: *microfilm.* **2.** One-millionth: *micrometer.*
mid- Middle: *midweek.*
milli- **1.** One-thousandth: *milligram.* **2.** One thousand: *millipede.*
mis- Bad; wrong: *misdiagnose.*
mono- One; single; alone: *monocellular.*
neo- New; recent: *neoclassic.*
non- Not: *nondenominational.*
octo-, octa- Eight: *octopus.*
omni- All: *omnipresent.*
ortho- Straight; correct: *orthopedics.*
paleo- Ancient; early: *paleozoology.*
pan- All; whole: *panoptic.*
penta- Five: *pentagon.*
phono- Sound; speech: *phonograph.*
photo- Light; radiant energy: *photoreception.*

---

poly- Many: *polytheism.*

post- 1. After; later: *postcolonial.* 2. Behind: *postcranial.*

pre- 1. Earlier; before: *prehistoric.* 2. In front of: *preposition.*

pro-[1] Earlier: *proactive.*

pro-[2] Supporting; in favor: *promilitary.*

pseudo- False; deceptive: *pseudonym.*

quadr- Four: *quadrilateral.*

re- 1. Again: *reenact.* 2. Back; backward: *rewind.* 3. Used as an intensive: *refine.*

semi- 1. Half: *semicircle.* 2. Partial; partially: *semisolid.* 3. Resembling: *semiofficial.*

sub- 1. Below: *subzero.* 2. Secondary: *subplot.*

super- 1. Over; above: *superscript.* 2. Exceedingly: *superfine.* 3. Larger; more inclusive: *supermarket.*

sur- 1. Above; beyond: *surpass.* 2. In addition: *surcharge.*

syn-, sym-, syl- Together: *synchronize; symphony.*

tri- Three: *tricycle.*

un-[1] 1. Not: *uncertain.* 2. Opposite: *untruth.*

un-[2] 1. To reverse: *untie.* 2. Used as an intensive: *unloose.*

xeno- Stranger; foreign: *xenophobia.*

Suffixes

-able, -ible Capable of: *readable.*

-cide 1. Killer: *pesticide.* 2. Act of killing: *fratricide.*

-cracy Government: *autocracy.*

-er, -or 1. One that does an action: *lover; editor.* 2. Native or resident of: *New Yorker.*

-ese From or relating to: *Chinese.*

-ess Female: *princess.*

-ful Full of: *joyful.*

-gram Something written: *telegram.*

-graph 1. An instrument that writes: *seismograph.* 2. Something written: *autograph.*

-ic Relating to: *echoic.*

-ish 1. Of; like: *Scottish.* 2. To some degree: *bluish.*

-ism 1. Action or process: *terrorism.* 2. Characteristic behavior:

heroism. **3.** Doctrine; theory: *communism.*
-less Without: *homeless.*
-oid Resembling: *spheroid.*
-philia Liking; attraction: *bibliophilia.*
-phobia Intense fear: *xenophobia.*
-some Characterized by: *bothersome.*
-ule Small: *globule.*
-ward In a direction: *northward.*
-wise **1.** In a manner or direction: *clockwise.* **2.** In regard to: *dollarwise.*